STUDENT WORKBOOK

THIRD EDITION

HUMAN PHYSIOLOGY

AN INTEGRATED APPROACH

Dee Unglaub Silverthorn

Dee Unglaub Silverthorn
University of Texas

Richard Damian Hill

PEARSON

Benjamin
Cummings

San Francisco   Boston   New York
Capetown   Hong Kong   London   Madrid   Mexico City
Montreal   Munich   Paris   Singapore   Sydney   Tokyo   Toronto

Publisher: Daryl Fox
Executive Editor: Leslie Berriman
Associate Project Editor: Ziki Dekel
Editorial Assistant: Michael Roney
Managing Editor: Deborah Cogan
Manufacturing Buyer: Stacey Weinberger
Executive Marketing Manager: Lauren Harp

ISBN: 0-13-140176-9

OWNER'S MANUAL

Welcome! Please take a moment to look through this material to familiarize yourself with the features contained in your workbook. The workbook is divided into the following sections to help you effectively study the chapters in the text.

Summary
For each chapter in the textbook, you will find a brief list that points out the key learning tasks for the chapter, along with a short narrative summary.

Teach Yourself the Basics
This section is organized using the section headers from the chapter. *Teach Yourself the Basics* has a series of questions about each section, with figure numbers and cross-references so that you can refer back to the book for pertinent material.

There are two ways to use *Teach Yourself the Basics:*

Answer questions as you read, using the workbook to actively direct your reading and notetaking. This is an excellent method for making sure that you are getting the important information out of each section of the chapter.

Use the questions to test yourself. Wait until you have studied the chapter, then see if you can answer the questions without referring to the textbook.

Look for these helpful symbols throughout the workbook:

∫   This symbol marks cross-referenced information that can be integrated into the current chapter.

◎   These bullets give you interesting facts or helpful ways to remember information.

Talk the Talk is a vocabulary list of the important terms from the chapter. Use this list to quiz yourself.

Quantitative Thinking includes quantitative problems and shows how to go about solving them.

Practice Makes Perfect is a set of questions that deal with material in the chapter. They range from simple "memorization" questions to difficult "application" questions. The answers to these questions are contained in an appendix at the back of the workbook.

Beyond the Pages contains additional material that is related to the chapter.
> **Running Problem** sections provide additional information about the Running Problem in the text chapter.
> **Try It** sections include activities that you may want to try, such as mini-experiments and demonstrations or interesting web sites
> **Further Explorations** in the workbook are similar to Explorations in the text. They provide additional Web exercises, readings, and ethic questions to ponder.

A Note on Conventions Used in the Workbook
Ions in the workbook are written in the following format: Na^+, Ca^{2+}, Cl^-, K^+, P_i, and PO_4^{3-}. If you are not familiar with the concept of ions, read pg. 30 in Chapter 2.
Body fluid compartments are abbreviated as follows:
> ICF = intracellular fluid
> ECF = extracellular fluid
> IF = interstitial fluid

Study Hints for Physiology Students

There are several differences you will notice when studying and learning science:

✓   There is a large volume of unfamiliar and frequently intimidating vocabulary.

✓   Science textbooks have a different writing style and need to be read differently than textbooks in the humanities.

✓   The thought process for science requires linear thinking and the ability to trace a process in some detail from beginning to end. Humanities students are used to analyzing interrelationships and tend to think too broadly.

Here are some suggestions to use in class and when studying physiology.

◆ Notetaking

Do not try to write down every word the instructor says. Listen particularly for vocabulary, concepts, points the instructor emphasizes. Develop your own shorthand so that you can get down more information. *Example*: Use up and down arrows for "increase" and "decrease."

Stop the instructor when a major point is unclear, or if the instructor has gone too fast.

If you can't ask a question about something or if you get behind in your notetaking, put a ? in the margin so that you know that your notes in that section are lacking. Check with a friend or the instructor to clear up what you missed.

Develop one or two "study buddies" with whom you can compare your notes. If you have to miss class, try to get notes from more than one person. Notes are a memory aid rather than a verbatim copy of the lecture, so two different sets of notes are more likely to give you a complete overview of the lecture.

◆ Vocabulary

Most scientific words sound terribly complicated and difficult to remember. However, you can learn some common prefixes, suffixes, and roots that will help you to remember the words. In the textbook after some vocabulary words, there will be a note in [ ] that shows the roots and their meanings. In this workbook, there is a list of some of the most common roots you will encounter in physiology. You can also use a dictionary to find out the origin of a word. Start a list in your own notebook of other suffixes, prefixes, and roots.

◆ Reading the Textbook

Find out from your instructor if you are responsible for material that is in the text but has not been covered in lecture. If you are, you will need to add the extra information from the text to the information in your class notes. If you are not, then you need to be familiar with your notes so that you can pay less attention to material in the text that is not relevant.

Science texts are written with important facts in every sentence. You cannot speed-read a science text. Go slowly and analyze each sentence as you read it. Ask yourself if you understand the concepts in that sentence, and how that sentence relates to the facts presented in previous sentences.

Use the charts and diagrams in the book. Read the captions to the figures as they will frequently explain what is in the diagram. Sometimes the figures in a physiology text provide a summary of material in a section.

♦ Organizing Your Studying

As soon as possible after class, you should glance over your notes and mark the points that are unclear or where your notes may be lacking.

Some students sit down and spend a lot of time rewriting their notes. Usually there are other, more profitable ways of spending your study time. You will still be writing down the information in your notes, but you will also be reorganizing it into study notes of a form that you can remember. The following are some possible ways to do this. You probably won't have time to do all of them, so experiment until you find the method that works best for the way you learn.

1. **Mark up your original notes with colored pens.**

   Use colored pens to see if you can divide the notes into levels and sublevels for an outline. Assign a different color to each level of organization. Underline or draw a box around the word(s) that fits into that heading. For example:
   SUBJECT HEADING: Purple
   I. Major topic = red
         A. Secondary topic = green
              1. Facts under that topic = turquoise

   Give vocabulary words and concepts their own color, such as yellow.

   Once you have marked your notes this way, go back and make a skeleton outline using the words you marked. It probably won't be a perfect outline (Topic I may have A but not B), but don't let that worry you. Use this outline to give yourself an overview of the material covered and the progression of the ideas or concepts covered.

2. **Make a working vocabulary list.**

   ➤ Take a sheet of lined notebook paper and fold it in half lengthwise.
   ➤ Down the left-hand side, list all the words and concepts you have marked in yellow in your notes.
   ➤ Down the right-hand side (on the other side of the fold), list an abbreviated definition.
   ➤ Study with the paper open so that you can see both sides. When you think you have learned the material, fold the paper in half so that you see only the list of words. Test yourself by going down the list and saying the definitions to yourself. If you don't know a definition, keep going. When you reach the end of the list, go back and look at the definitions of the words you missed.
   ➤ Now turn the paper over so that you are looking at the definitions. Read the definitions and see if you can say and spell the word that fits each definition.

3. Get the big picture as well as the details.

In physiology, for each system studied, you should make an outline, study sheet, or chart that answers the following questions:

➢ What is the anatomical structure of the system? Can you trace a molecule involved in the system through all the parts? Example: trace a drop of blood from the aorta to various parts and back through the heart. What kinds of tissues or cells make up this system? What kind of muscle? Is there some structural entity that we can call the "functional unit?"

➢ What is the function(s) of the system? Which parts carry out which function? How are the functions carried out?

➢ How is the system regulated? Consider control by the nervous system and the endocrine system. Are there any reflexes? Know where any pertinent hormones are secreted and what controls their release.

➢ How is the circulatory system involved with this system?

➢ Certain themes will keep popping up throughout the chapters. Make note of them. They include:
> Movement of molecules across membranes
> Pressure and flow
> Biomolecules: carbohydrates, fats, proteins. Their roles, transport, and metabolism.
> Ions: Na^+, K^+, H^+, HCO_3-
> Gases: oxygen and carbon dioxide
> Energy use and storage

4. Make charts, diagrams, flow charts, and concept maps

One advantage of a chart is that it also allows you to compare and contrast different concepts that at first glance may not seem to have much relationship.

To make a chart:

Divide your paper into columns and rows. Across the top, write the topics you want to compare (Example: male and female reproduction). Down the left side, label the rows or blocks with the points you want to compare (Example: name of gamete, name of gonad, hormones). Go back and fill in the chart.

One technique some students have used is to try to condense everything they have learned about a system onto a piece of poster paper. One effective way to do this is to make a giant drawing of the structure (anatomy) of the system and then add in all the physiological processes at or near the appropriate structure.

Example: Make a poster of the respiratory system.
On the board you might draw a large upper body with the upper and lower respiratory systems drawn in and labeled. In the head you would also include the neurological control of ventilation. Add an enlarged cluster of alveoli just below the lung, and draw in the circulatory system going to a single cell.

5. Practice higher level thinking

One objective of many physiology courses is to teach students how to use what are called higher level thinking skills. How many levels do you usually use when you study?

Experts* recognize four types of knowledge:

1. **Factual knowledge**   facts, terms, vocabulary, details
2. **Conceptual knowledge**   principles, theories, models, generalizations, categories: the big picture
3. **Procedural knowledge**   how to do things: skills, research methods, algorithms
4. **Metacognitive knowledge**   Understanding how you (and people in general) learn

Each type of knowledge has a range of cognitive levels associated with it. These levels of knowing and understanding are given below, ranked from lowest to highest:

1. **Remember**   Ability to recognize or recall information. ("I knew this material...")

2. **Understand**   A deeper understanding of the information than simple memorization. Examples include the ability to classify items into similar groups, summarize information, explain a process, give examples.

3. **Apply**   Ability to solve or explain a problem by applying what the person has learned to the problem.

4. **Analyze**   Ability to solve a problem by systematically examining facts and looking for patterns and relationships.

5. **Evaluate**   Ability to make a judgment based on some standard or criteria

6. **Create**   Ability to use original, creative thinking to create something

If you want to use the higher levels of thinking skills, you must master the first two levels. In other words, you must have a memorized database of information upon which to act and you must really *understand* it, not just *know* it.

* <u>A Taxonomy for Learning, Teaching, and Assessing</u>. L.W. Anderson, D.R. Krathwohl *et al.*, editors. Longman, New York, 2001.

Ten Tasks for Students in Classes That Use Active Learning

Written by Marilla Svinicki, Ph.D.
Director, University of Texas Center for Teaching Effectiveness

1. Make the switch from an "authority-based" conception of learning to a "self-regulated" conception of learning. Recognize and accept your own responsibility for learning.

2. Be willing to take risks and go beyond what is presented in class or the text.

3. Be able to tolerate ambiguity and frustration in the interest of understanding.

4. See errors as opportunities to learn rather than failures. Be willing to make mistakes in class or in study groups so that you can learn from them.

5. Engage in **active** listening to what's happening in class.

6. Trust the instructor's experience in designing class activities and participate willingly, if not enthusiastically.

7. Be willing to express an opinion or hazard a guess.

8. Accept feedback in the spirit of learning rather than as a reflection of you as a person.

9. Prepare for class physically, mentally, and materially (do the reading, work the problems, etc.).

10. Provide support for your classmate's attempts to learn. The best way to learn something well is to teach it to someone who doesn't understand.

Dr. Dee's Eleventh Rule

DON'T PANIC! Pushing yourself beyond the comfort zone is scary but you have to do it in order to improve.

Word Roots for Physiology

a- or **an-**	without; absence		**patho-, -pathy**	related to disease
anti-	against		**para-**	near, close
-ase	signifies an enzyme		**peri-**	around
auto-	self		**poly-**	many
bi-	two		**post-**	after
brady-	slow		**pre-**	before
cardio-	heart		**pro-**	before
cephalo-	head		**pseudo-**	false
cerebro-	brain		**re-**	again
contra-	against		**retro-**	backward or behind
-crine	a secretion		**semi-**	half
crypt-	hidden		**sub-**	below
cutan-	skin		**super-**	above, beyond
-cyte or **cyto-**	cell		**supra-**	above, on top of
de-	without, lacking		**tachy-**	rapid
di-	two		**trans-**	across, through
dys-	difficult, faulty			
-elle	small			
endo-	inside or within		Add your own here:	
exo-	outside			
extra-	outside			
-emia	blood			
epi-	over			
erythro-	red			
gastro-	stomach			
-gen, -genic	produce			
gluco-, glyco-	sugar or sweet			
hemo-	blood			
hemi-	half			
hepato-	liver			
homo-	same			
hydro-	water			
hyper-	above or excess			
hypo-	beneath or deficient			
inter-	between			
intra-	within			
-itis	inflammation of			
kali-	potassium			
leuko-	white			
lipo-	fat			
lumen	inside of a hollow tube			
-lysis	split apart or rupture			
macro-	large			
micro-	small			
mono-	one			
multi-	many			
myo-	muscle			
oligo-	little, few			

LITERATURE RESEARCH

Everyone uses the Internet now to look up information. But how valid is it? For scientific work such as physiology research, you will want to be sure that you are using authoritative sources. This section tells you a little about valid ways that research results are disseminated to other scientists and to the public at large.

JOURNALS: Scientific journals are usually sponsored by a scientific organization and consist of contributed papers that describe the **original scientific research** of an individual or group. When a scientist speaks of writing "a paper," he/she is usually referring to the scientific paper published in a journal. Many journals will publish **review articles,** a synopsis of recent research on a particular topic. Reviews are an excellent place to begin a search for information.

Most articles published in scientific journals have gone through a screening process known as **peer review**, in which the article is read and critiqued by other specialists in a particular field. The purpose of peer-review is to ensure good quality. In some cases, submitted articles are rejected by the journal editor, and in many cases the authors must make revisions to the article before it can be published. This process acts as a safeguard against the publication of poorly done research.

☞ Most articles on the Web are <u>not</u> peer-reviewed unless they are in an online journal!

Anyone can create a web page and publish information on the Web. There is no screening process, and the reader must decide how valid the information is. Web sites that are published by recognized universities (URLs that end in *.edu*) and not-for-profit organizations (*name.org*) are likely to have good information. But an article in vitamins on the web page of a health food store (*name.com*) should be viewed with a skeptical eye unless the article cites published research.

CITATION FORMAT: Citation formats for published papers will vary but will usually include the following elements somewhere:

Title. [Brackets around the title indicate an English translation of a foreign language paper.]
Year the paper was published.
Name of author(s). Within a body of work, a multiauthor paper is usually cited as **first author, et al**. Et al. is the abbreviation for the Latin *et alii* meaning "and others," and indicates that there are additional authors.
Journal abbreviation, **volume (issue)**: inclusive **pages**. A **volume** number is usually given to all issues published in one calendar year (six months for weekly journals). **Issue** 1 would be the first issue published in a volume, Issue 2 would be the second, etc.

Example: Horiuchi M., Nishiyama H., and Katori R. Aldosterone-specific membrane receptors and related rapid non-genomic effects. [Review] Trends Pharmacol Sci 14(1):1-4, 1993.

In many citations, the name of a journal is abbreviated. Here is a list of commonly used abbreviations.

Adv	advances	**Am**	American
Ann	annals	**Annu**	annual
Appl	applied	**Arch**	archives
Assoc	association	**Behav**	behavior
Biochem	biochemistry	**Biol***	biology or biological
Biophys	biophysics	**Br**	British
Can	Canadian	**Chem**	chemistry or chemical
Clin	clinical	**Commun**	communications
Curr	current	**Dev**	developmental
Dis	disease	**Eur**	European
Exp	experimental	**Gen**	general
Hum	human	**Int**	internal
Intl	international	**J**	journal
Med	medicine or medical	**Monogr**	monograph
Nat	natural	**Natl**	national
Pharm	pharmacy	**Physiol***	physiology or physiological
Proc	proceedings	**Q**	quarterly
Res	research	**Rev**	review
Sci	science	**Soc**	society or social
Surg	surgery or surgical	**Symp**	symposium
Ther	therapy		

* Most words ending with -ology or -ological will be abbreviated by stopping after the "l".
  Titles of one word such as "Nature" are never abbreviated.

Citing Sources Published on the World Wide Web

Citing sources from the Web requires a different format. Here is one suggested format:

Author. Title. Web page sponsor. URL. Date accessed.

Example:

English, Peter. Birds of the Ecuadorian Rainforest. University of Texas..
http://www.utexas.edu/depts/grg/gstudent/grg394k/spring97/english/english.html (1997 Nov 10)

MAPPING STRATEGIES FOR PHYSIOLOGY

Introduction

Mapping is a technique to improve a student's understanding and retention of subject material. It is based on the theory that each person has a memory bank of knowledge organized in a unique way based on prior experience. Learning occurs when you attach new ideas to your preexisting framework. By actively interacting with the information and by organizing it in your own way before you load it into memory, you will find that you remember the information longer and can recall it more easily.

Mapping is a non-linear way of organizing material, closely related to the flow charts used to explain many physiological processes. A map can take a variety of forms but usually consists of terms or concepts linked by explanatory arrows. The map may include diagrams or figures. The connecting arrows can be labeled to explain the type of linkage between the terms (structure/function, cause/effect) or may be labeled with explanatory phrases ("is composed of").

You will find a number of maps in the text that you can simply memorize, but the real benefit from using maps occurs when you create the maps yourselves. By organizing the material yourself, you question the relationships between terms, organize concepts into a hierarchial structure, and look for similarities and differences between items. Such interaction with the material ensures that you process it into long-term memory instead of simply memorizing it for a test. Teaching you how to map is an important part of the process, as you may not know where to begin.

Key Elements of Maps

A map has only two parts: the concepts and the linkages between them. A concept is an idea, event or object. Concepts do not exist in isolation; they have associations to other relevant concepts. An example is the sentence "The heart pumps blood." Heart and blood are two concepts related by the verb pumps. A map consists of a group of related terms that are hierarchically ranked and linked by explanatory arrows. In this Student Workbook, we have provided some groups of words to be mapped. You will probably want to develop your own groups of words to fit the material you are studying.

How to make a map

1. Choose the concepts to map. Begin at either the top or the center with the most general, important, or overriding concept from which all the others naturally stem. If this is a reflex pathway, you would start with the stimulus. Next, use the other concepts to break down this one idea into progressively more specific parts or to follow the reflex pathway. Use horizontal cross-links to tie branches together. The downward development of the map may reflect the passage of time if the map represents a process or increasing levels of complexity if the map represents something like a cell.

If you are trying to map a large number of terms, you might try writing each term on a small piece of paper. You can then lay out the papers on a table and rearrange them until you are satisfied with your map. Even an experienced physiologist may draw a map several times before being satisfied that it is the best representation of the information.

2. Think about the type of association between two concepts. Arrows will point the direction of the linkage, but you should also label the kind of linkage. You may label the line with linking words or by the type of link, such as CE (cause or effect). Color is very effective on maps. You can use colors for different types of links or for different sections.

3. Once you have your map, sit back and think about it. Are all the items in the right place? You may want to move them around once you see the big picture. Revise your map to expand the picture with new concepts or to correct wrong linkages. Review the information in the map by beginning with recall of the main concept and then moving to the more specific details. Ask yourself questions like, "What is the cause? effect? parts involved? main characteristics?" to jog your memory.

4. The best way to study with a map is to trade maps with your study partner and see if you can understand each other's maps. You may want to find an empty classroom, put your maps on the blackboards, then step back and compare them. Did one of you put in something the other forgot? Did one of you have an incorrect relationship between two items?

Practice making maps. The study questions in each chapter of your textbook will give you some ideas of what you should be mapping. Your instructor can help you if you do not know how to get started.

1

INTRODUCTION TO PHYSIOLOGY

SUMMARY

What should you take away from this chapter?

✓ **An understanding of the different levels of organization for living organisms.**
✓ **Ability to name the physiological systems of the human body.**
✓ **Understanding of the difference between a teleological and a mechanistic approach to science.**
✓ **Ability to list seven key themes in physiology.**
✓ **Ability to describe how scientists design and execute experiments.**

Physiology is the study of how organisms function and adapt to a constantly changing environment. The human body is comprised of ten organ systems. However, these organ systems do not act as isolated units. Instead they communicate and cooperate to maintain homeostasis, a relatively stable internal environment composed of the extracellular fluid that bathes the cells.

Physiologists use a wide variety of techniques to study how the human body operates. Some of these techniques examine the activities of molecules and cells, while others focus on the response of entire organ systems. Physiology is usually approached from a functional, or mechanistic, viewpoint. Physiological events can also be explained in terms of their significance, which is considered a teleological approach to physiology.

Scientific experimentation includes formulation of a hypothesis, observation and experimentation, and data collection and analysis. Experiments using human subjects are difficult to perform and analyze because of tremendous variability within human populations and because of ethical problems.

TEACH YOURSELF THE BASICS

LEVELS OF ORGANIZATION

1. List the ten levels of organization, starting with atoms and ending with the biosphere. (Fig. 1-1)

2. List the ten human organ systems. (Table 1-1)

PHYSIOLOGY IS AN INTEGRATIVE SCIENCE

3. What do we mean when we say that physiology is an integrative science?

FUNCTION AND PROCESS

4. Use possible answers to the question "Why do we breathe?" to explain the difference between a teleological approach to physiology and a mechanistic approach.

THE EVOLUTION OF PHYSIOLOGICAL SYSTEMS

5. Humans are animals adapted to a terrestrial environment. What is the primary challenge of life on land?

6. Name some mechanisms terrestrial animals have evolved to cope with their environment.

HOMEOSTASIS

7. What is the "external environment" for the individual cells of the body?

8. Define homeostasis.

9. What happens when the body is unable to maintain homeostasis? What are some factors that might contribute to a failure of homeostasis? (Fig. 1-5, 1-6)

THEMES IN PHYSIOLOGY
∕IP Fluids & Electrolytes: Water Homeostasis

10. In addition to homeostasis, list and briefly define 7 key themes of physiology. How many physiological examples can you think of for each theme?

THE SCIENCE OF PHYSIOLOGY

11. List the key steps a scientist goes through in a scientific inquiry.

12. In an experiment, which are independent variables and which are dependent variables?

13. Why should every experiment have a control?

14. How does a scientific theory differ from a hypothesis?

15. Why is a crossover study better than a study in which the experimental and control groups are composed of different organisms from a population?

16. What advantage is gained by having a blind study? A double-blind study? A double-blind crossover study?

17. Briefly define and contrast the following types of studies:

Longitudinal study:

Prospective study:

Cross-sectional study:

Retrospective study:

18. What is accomplished by a meta-analysis?

TALK THE TALK: (important vocabulary in this chapter)

Aristotle	blind study	cell-to-cell communication
cell	circulatory system	concept map
control	cross-sectional study	crossover study
data	dependent variable	digestive system
double-blind crossover study	double-blind study	effectors
elastance	emergent property	endocrine system
energy	external environment	extracellular fluid
fertilization	fetal development	Hippocrates
homeostasis	gradient	histogram
hypothesis	immune system	independent variable
integration of body systems	integrating centers	integumentary system
internal environment	law of mass balance	longitudinal study
lumen	mass flow	mechanistic approach
meta-analysis	musculoskeletal system	nervous system
nocebo	organ system	pH
pathophysiology	physiology	placebo
placebo effect	prospective study	regulated variables
reproductive system	respiratory system	retrospective study
salinity	scientific method	signal transduction
skin	teleological approach	compliance
temperature regulation	tissue	urinary system

PRACTICE MAKES PERFECT

1. How does physiology differ from anatomy?

2. A scientist wants to study the effects of the cholesterol-lowering drug pravastatin in rats.

    a)   What might be the hypothesis in this experiment?

    b)   The scientist decides to use four different doses of pravastatin. What would be an
         appropriate control for this experiment?

3. Write one or two sentences that summarize the graph below.

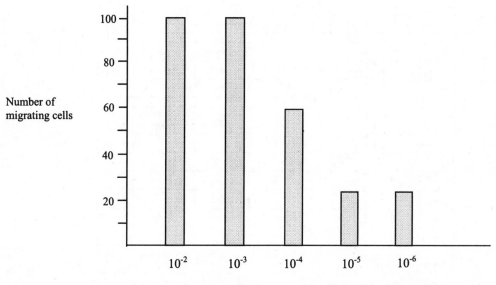

Number of
migrating cells

Concentration of nerve growth factor (moles/liter)

4. Glucose is transported into cells from the extracellular fluid. Construct a graph using the following data and label the axes. Summarize these results in the legend. Identify and distinguish between the independent and dependent variables.

Extracellular concentration of glucose (mM)	Intracellular concentration of glucose (mM)
150	100
140	101
130	100
120	91
110	83
100	75
90	61
80	52

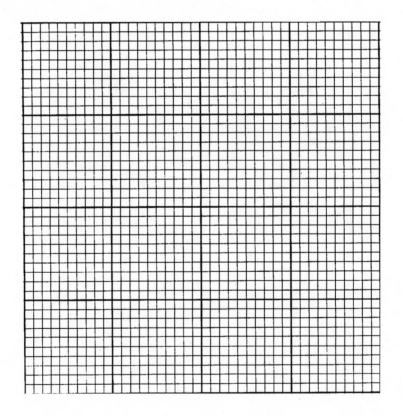

5. What kind of graph would be most appropriate for the following data sets? What labels go on the x-axis and y-axis?

(a) oxygen consumption in summer-collected fish and winter-collected fish acclimated to 10℃, 25℃, and 30℃

(b) Growth in boys and girls from ages 1 to 15 as indicated by measurements of height and weight

(c) The effect of food intake on body weight, measured in a population of people selected at random.

BEYOND THE PAGES

GRAPHS
Find examples of good and bad graphs in your textbooks or in newspapers and magazines. *USA Today* is an excellent source of misleading graphs.

FURTHER EXPLORATIONS

The biological basis of the placebo effect. The Scientist 16(24): 30-31, 2002 Dec 9. Available online at www.the-scientist.com. This site requires free registration for access.

Is science logical? Craig M. Pease and J.J. Bull. 1992. Bioscience 42 (4): 293-298. April.

How important is the placebo effect in medicine? Some topics to consider are:
• alternative medicine (see the National Center for Complementary and Alternative Medicine at http://nccam.nih.gov/)
• intercessory prayer, where one person prays for another person's healing
• therapeutic touch

How would you design a double-blind controlled experiment to test for the efficacy of these treatments?

CHAPTER 2

ATOMS, IONS, AND MOLECULES

SUMMARY

What should you take away from this chapter?

✓ Ability to describe the general structure of atoms.
✓ Ability to discuss the different subatomic particles and how they affect the nature of atoms.
✓ A general knowledge of the four types of bonds.
✓ The difference between polar and nonpolar molecules.
✓ A solid foundation about the nature of solutions and solutes.
✓ The quantitative basics of molarity and osmolarity, equivalents, and percent solutions.
✓ The basic differences between the biomolecules.

Atoms are composed of protons, neutrons and electrons, but it is the number of protons that distinguishes one element from another element. Atoms of a particular element that have a differing numbers of neutrons are called isotopes. Electrons are located in shells that circle the nucleus. Covalent, ionic and hydrogen bonds are formed by specific types of interactions between electrons of different atoms. Van der Waals forces are very weak bonds formed by nonspecific attractions and repulsions between atoms.

Water is known as the universal solvent. Molecules that easily dissolve in water are called hydrophilic, and molecules that do not dissolve are called hydrophobic. The concentration of a solution can be expressed in molar, equivalent, and percent solutions. Concentration is important to many body functions. Understanding concentration allows you to predict water movement and cell volume changes. The body has many homeostatic mechanisms, to be discussed later in the book, that are specifically designed to maintain concentration and water balance.

The concentration of hydrogen ions (H^+) determines body pH. Acids are molecules that contribute H^+; bases bind H^+. The body contains specific buffers that act to maintain a normal body pH of 7.4.

There are four basic groups of biomolecules: carbohydrates, lipids, proteins, and nucleotides. Carbohydrates are structurally divided into monosaccharides, disaccharides and polysaccharides. The most common lipid, the triglyceride, is composed of three fatty acids linked to a glycerol. Other lipid-related molecules include phospholipids, steroids and eicosanoids. Proteins are composed of hundreds of amino acids that are arranged into chains, spirals, sheets and complex globular configurations. These molecules have a wide variety of functions, ranging from structural components to carriers and enzymes. Lipoproteins, glycoproteins and glycolipids are frequently associated with cell membranes. Nucleotides consist of one or more phosphate groups, a five-carbon sugar and a nitrogenous base. Examples of nucleotides include ATP, ADP, cAMP, NAD, FAD, DNA, and RNA.

TEACH YOURSELF THE BASICS

ELEMENTS AND ATOMS

Atoms Are Composed of Protons, Neutrons, and Electrons

1. List the subatomic particles and describe their characteristics.

2. What is found in the nucleus of an atom? (Fig. 2-1)

An Element Is Distinguished by the Unique Number of Protons in Its Nucleus

3. Know how to read a periodic table. (Fig. 2-2)

4. What is the significance of essential elements?

5. What determines the atomic number of an element?

6. What determines the atomic mass of an element?

Isotopes of An Element Are Atoms with Different Numbers of Neutrons

7. Describe isotope characteristics. Use hydrogen as an example (Figs. 2-3, 2-4).

8. What are some of the uses of isotopes?

Electrons Form Bonds Between Atoms and Capture Energy

9. Describe how electrons are arranged in an atom. (Fig. 2-5)

10. What is a high-energy electron?

11. What role do high-energy bonds play in the cell?

MOLECULES AND BONDS

12. What is a molecule?

What does the Chemical Formula of a Molecule Tell Us?

13. Know how to calculate the molecular weight of a molecule.

14. What does a chemical formula tell you about the atoms in a compound? What does it not tell you?

15. List the four common bond types.

Covalent Bonds Are Formed When Adjacent Atoms Share Electrons

16. Explain how covalent bonds are formed.

17. How can you determine the number of covalent bonds that an atom can form? (Fig. 2-6)

Functional groups

18. Know the most common functional groups in biological molecules. (Table 2-1)

19. What are the characteristics of a functional group?

Molecular shape

20. Describe some of the shapes found in biological molecules (Figs. 2-7, 2-16, 2-18).

Polar and nonpolar molecules

21. What are the properties of a polar molecule? Give at least one example. (Fig. 2-8)

22. What are the properties of a nonpolar molecule? Give at least one example.

Ionic Bonds Form When Atoms Gain or Lose Electrons

23. What is an ion?

24. What is a cation? What is an anion? Give an example of each.

25. How is an ionic bond different from a covalent bond? (Fig. 2-9)

Hydrogen Bonds Are Weak Bonds Between Molecules or Regions of a Molecule

26. How are hydrogen bonds formed and what elements form hydrogen bonds? (Fig. 2-10)

27. What property of water is associated with hydrogen bonds between water molecules?

Van der Waals Forces Are Weak Attractions Between All Molecules

28. Define van der Waals forces.

29. Name a function of van der Waals forces.

SOLUTIONS AND SOLUTES
✓ **IP Fluids & Electrolytes: Acid-Base Homeostasis**

30. What is a solute? A solvent? A solution?

Not All Molecules Dissolve in Aqueous Solution

31. What is the difference between a hydrophilic and a hydrophobic molecule? (Fig. 2-11)

32. What property of a molecule determines its solubility?

There Are Several Ways to Express the Concentration of a Solution

33. Concentration is defined as:

34. When describing the concentration of a solution,

   a. Weight is usually expressed in what units?

   b. Number of solute molecules is usually expressed in what units?

   c. Solute ions can also be expressed in what units?

   d. Volume is usually expressed in what units?

Moles and molarity

35. 1 mole = _____ atoms

36. Define a molar solution.

37. Sodium chloride (NaCl) has a molecular weight of 58.5. How would you make a 1 molar solution of NaCl? (p. 26-27; answer in workbook appendix)

Equivalents

38. Define an equivalent.

39. One mole of magnesium ions (Mg^{2+}) contains _____ equivalents. (answer in workbook appendix)

Weight/volume and percent solutions

40. How would you make 250 mL of a 10% solution of NaCl? (answer in workbook appendix)

41. If a solution contains 200 mg NaCl/dL, what is its concentration in g/L? (answer in workbook appendix)

The Concentration of Hydrogen Ions in the Body Is Expressed in pH Units

42. Molecules that ionize and release an H^+ are called _____.

43. Molecules that combine with H^+ or produce OH^- are called _____.

44. Define pH in words. (Fig. 2-12)

45. Define pH mathematically: ($\int$ Appendix A)

46. How do buffers in the body help maintain normal pH?

BIOMOLECULES

47. What is an organic molecule and what elements are most commonly found in these molecules?

48. Name the four basic classes of biomolecules.

Carbohydrates Are the Most Abundant Type of Biomolecule (Fig. 2-13)

49. What is the basic formula of a carbohydrate?

50. What are monosaccharides? Give some examples.

51. What are disaccharides? Give some examples.

52. What are polysaccharides? What are some of their functions? Give examples.

53. In what form do animals store complex sugars?

Lipids Are the Most Diverse Biomolecules (Fig. 2-14)

54. What elements are lipids made of? How do lipids differ from carbohydrates?

55. Name three types of lipid-related molecules. Give at least one function for each type.

56. What is the difference between glycerol and a fatty acid?

57. What is the difference between a saturated, a mono-unsaturated and a polyunsaturated fatty acid?

Proteins Are the Most Versatile of the Biomolecules

58. What biomolecules are the building blocks of proteins? (Fig. 2-15; Table 2-3)

59. What is an essential amino acid?

60. Name some amino acids that do not occur in proteins.

61. Describe the organization of proteins, starting with amino acids and ending with the quaternary structure. (Fig. 2-16)

62. What functions do proteins serve in the body?

Some Molecules Combine Carbohydrates, Proteins, and Lipids

63. What is a conjugated protein?

64. Name three different types of conjugated proteins and tell where in the body they are found.

Nucleotides Are Responsible for the Transmission and Storage of Energy and Information

65. List the components of a nucleotide. (Fig. 2-17)

66. List as many examples of nucleotides as you can.

67. Name the bases that make up the DNA molecule. How does DNA differ from RNA? (Fig. 2-18; ∫ Appendix B)

TALK THE TALK

acid	adenine	ADP
alkaline	alpha-helix	amino acid
amino group	anion	antioxidant
atom	atomic mass	atomic mass unit
atomic number	ATP	base
bicarbonate ion	biomolecule	buffer
carbohydrate	carbonic acid	carboxyl group
cation	cellulose	chemical formula
compound	concentration	conjugated protein
covalent bond	Crick, F.H.C.	cyclic AMP
cytosine	dalton	deciliter (dL)
deoxyribose	dextrose	disaccharide
DNA	eicosanoid	electron
element	equivalent	essential amino acid
essential element	essential element	fat
fatty acid	fibrous protein	free radical
fructose	galactose	globular protein
glucose	glycerol	glycogen
glycolipid	glycoprotein	guanine
hydrogen bond	hydrophilic	hydrophobic
hydroxyl group	ion	ionic bond
isotope	lactose	lipid
lipoprotein	maltose	molarity
mole	molecular weight	molecule
monosaccharide	neutron	nonpolar molecule
nucleotide	orbital	organic compound
peptide	peptide bond	per cent solution
pH	phosphate group	phospholipid
pleated sheet	polar molecule	polarity
polymer	polypeptide	polysaccharide
primary structure of a protein	protein	proton
purine	pyrimidine	quaternary structure of a protein
radiation	radioisotope	ribose
RNA	saturated fatty acid	secondary structure of a protein
solute	solution	solvent
starch	steroid	sucrose
superoxide	surface tension	tertiary structure of a protein
thymine	trace element	triglyceride

QUANTITATIVE THINKING

In the laboratory, you may be asked to make up or mix solutions. The first example below shows you how to make up a molar solution. The second example shows how to calculate concentration when you mix two different solutions.

Task 1: Make 500 mL of a 150 millimolar (mM) NaCl solution.

Step 1: Calculate the molecular weight of NaCl. One mole of a substance contains its molecular weight in grams; this is known as its gram molecular weight.

Atomic weight of Na is 23 x 1 atom of Na =	23
Atomic weight of Cl is 35.5 x 1 atom of Cl =	35.5
Sum	58.5

* One mole of NaCl therefore weighs 58.5 grams.

Step 2: Molar solutions are expressed in moles per liter of solution. You want to make a solution with 0.150 moles per liter (= 150 mM). However, you cannot weigh out moles of a compound. So you must calculate how many grams of NaCl are equal to 0.150 moles. You know that one mole weighs 58.5 grams.

Set up a ratio as shown:

(a) $\dfrac{58.5 \text{ g NaCl}}{1 \text{ mole}}$ = $\dfrac{? \text{ g NaCl}}{0.15 \text{ moles}}$

(b) $\dfrac{58.5 \text{ g NaCl} \bullet 0.15 \text{ moles}}{1 \text{ mole}}$ = $? \text{ g NaCl}$

(c) $? = 8.8 \text{ g NaCl}$

* Therefore 0.15 moles of NaCl weighs 8.8 grams, and a 0.15 M solution has 8.8 g/liter of solution.

Step 3: You know from step 2 how much NaCl to use to make one liter of 0.15 M NaCl. But you have been asked to make up 500 mL, not one liter. Again, set up a ratio:

$\dfrac{8.8 \text{ g NaCl}}{1000 \text{ mL}}$ = $\dfrac{? \text{ g}}{500 \text{ mL}}$

* The answer is 4.4 grams of NaCl needed to make up 500 mL of a 150 mM solution.

The next example shows you how to calculate concentration when you mix two different solutions.

Task 2: Mix 2 liters of 3 M NaCl with 1 liter of 6 M glucose. What is the concentration of glucose in the mixed solution? What is the concentration of NaCl?

Step 1: Figure out the amount of solute that you have in the two starting solutions:

3 moles NaCl/L x 2 L	=	6 moles NaCl
6 moles glucose/L x 1 L	=	6 moles glucose

Step 2: Now put those amounts in the total volume formed when the solutions are added to each other:

$$\frac{6 \text{ moles NaCl} + 6 \text{ moles glucose}}{3 \text{ L total volume}}$$

6 moles/3 liters = 2 moles/liter for NaCl and 2 moles/liter for glucose

* Therefore the NaCl concentration is 2 M and the glucose concentration is 2 M.

What is the total concentration of the mixed NaCl/glucose solution? Show your work.

Task 3: Make 600 mL of a 300 mM glucose solution. (Mol. wt. of glucose = 180)

PRACTICE MAKES PERFECT

1. Draw a carbon atom and an oxygen atom with the appropriate number of protons, neutrons and electrons.

2. A carbon dioxide molecule consists of covalent bonds between one carbon and two oxygen atoms. Draw how their valence (outer shell) electrons are arranged using an electron-dot model.

3. Matching:

_____ atomic mass   A. atoms with different numbers of neutrons
_____ atomic number   B. protons plus neutrons
_____ isotopes   C. capture and transfer energy
_____ electrons   D. number of protons
_____ radioisotopes   E. atoms with different numbers of protons
_____ radiation   F. unstable isotopes
_____ atomic mass unit   G. energy emitted by radioisotope
                                      H. dalton

4. Using what you know about atomic number, atomic weight, protons, neutrons, and electrons in atoms, fill in the table below. There is no way to predict the number of neutrons in the different isotopes of an element, but you can guess the number of neutrons in the most common isotope by using the atomic weight. Check your answers against the periodic table on p. 15 of the text.

ELEMENT	SYMBOL	ATOMIC NUMBER	PROTONS	ELECTRONS	NEUTRONS*	ATOMIC WEIGHT
Calcium		20			20	40.1
Carbon			6	6		12.0
Chlorine			17		18	35.5
	Co		27	27		58.9
Hydrogen				1	0	
Iodine	I	53			74	
Magnesium			12	12	12	
	N	7		7		14
Oxygen	O		8			16.0
Sodium			11			23
Zinc			30		35	
Copper				29	35	
	Fe	26				55.8
Potassium		19	19		20	

* Number of neutrons in the most common isotope.

5. What is the molecular weight of water? Indicate the proper units.

6. Matching:

_____ anion
_____ cation
_____ covalent bond
_____ ion
_____ molecule
_____ compound

A. two or more atoms that share electrons
B. a pair of electrons shared by two atoms
C. molecule that contains more than one element
D. bond that shares protons or neutrons
E. positively charged ion
F. negatively charged ion

A.

B.

C.

D.

7. Which of the above structural formulas for the amino acid leucine ($C_6H_{13}O_2N$) is (are) correct? Be able to explain your reasoning.

8. Answer the following questions about the properties of water.

      a. What type of bond holds a single water molecule together?

      b. What type of bond holds many individual water molecules together?

      c. Why is water called the universal solvent?

      d. When a salt crystal of sodium chloride is dropped into water, how do the molecular properties of water and the ionic properties of the salt interact?

9. What happens to an oxygen atom if it gains a proton?

10. When potassium and chloride form an ionic bond, which ion gains an electron and which ion loses an electron? Which ion(s) becomes stable? Explain your reasoning.

11. Why are polar molecules hydrophilic and nonpolar molecules hydrophobic?

12. What is the weight of a half mole of sodium chloride?

13. How would you make a 500 mL NaCl solution that has a molarity of 0.5 M?

14. A 0.1 M solution is equal to how many millimoles per liter? _____

15. How many grams of glucose are in 100 mL of a 50 mM glucose solution? _____

16. How would you make 100 mL of a 3% glucose solution? What would be the molarity of this solution? (The molecular weight of glucose is 180.)

17. If you mix 1 liter of 0.4 M glucose with 1 liter of 0.8 M NaCl:

   a) What is the total concentration of the mixed solution? _____

   b) What is the NaCl concentration in the mixed solution? _____

   c) What is the glucose concentration in the mixed solution? _____

18. The plasma concentration of Na^+ is 142 mEq/L. What is the concentration of Na^+ in millimoles per liter?

19. The plasma concentration of Ca^{2+} is 5 mEq/L. What is the concentration of Ca^{2+} in millimoles per liter?

20. Matching. (Blanks may have more than one correct answer.)
   _____ acid
   _____ base
   _____ pH
   _____ alkaline
   _____ buffer

   A. concentration of hydrogen ions
   B. prevents pH changes
   C. molecule that ionizes and donates H+
   D. molecule that combines free H+
   E. molecule that produces hydroxide ions (OH⁻)
   F. solution with a low concentration of H+

21. Amines are organic compounds that act as acids and bases. Identify the acids and bases in the reaction below.

$$CH_3 - \overset{\overset{\displaystyle CH_3}{|}}{N} - H \quad + \quad H - OH \quad \longrightarrow \quad CH_3 - \overset{\overset{\displaystyle CH_3}{|}}{\underset{\underset{\displaystyle H}{|}}{N^+}} - H \quad + \quad OH^-$$

22. The reaction below occurs in red blood cells. Identify the acids and bases in this reaction.

$$CO_2 \ + \ H_2O \ \longleftrightarrow \ H_2CO_3 \ \longleftrightarrow \ H^+ \ + \ HCO_3^-$$

23. Which HCl solution is more acidic, a 50 mM or a 0.5 M? _____

24. Matching:

_____ triglycerides	A. large molecules with repeating units
_____ fatty acids	B. long carbon chains with terminal carboxyl groups
_____ carbohydrates	C. fatty acid chains linked to a glycerol
_____ polymers	D. polar, hydrophilic molecules
_____ steroids	E. $(CH_2O)_n$
	F. lipid-related molecules with four carbon rings

25. Matching. (Blanks may have more than one answer, and answers may be used more than once.)

_____ essential amino acid	A. made from amino acids
_____ protein	B. a molecule that has proteins plus lipids
_____ conjugated protein	C. a molecule that has proteins plus carbohydrates
_____ glycoprotein	D. amino acid not made by the body
_____ phospholipid	E. may act as a membrane receptor
	F. major component of membranes

26. Use the following terms to create a map of biomolecules. Be sure to put labels on your linking arrows. The term "biomolecule" is the most general term and should appear at the top of your map.

amino acids	carbohydrates	cellulose
disaccharides	fats	fatty acids
glucose	glycogen	glycolipids
Lipids	lipoproteins	maltose
monosaccharides	peptide	phospholipids
polymer	polypeptide	polysaccharides
proteins	proteins	saturated fatty acids
Starch	steroids	sucrose
triglycerides	unsaturated fatty acids	

BEYOND THE PAGES

FURTHER EXPLORATION

The discovery of X-rays. Scientific American, November, 1993.

Breast cancer imaging. Science & Medicine, January/February 1996.

The photon radiosurgery system. Science & Medicine, November/December 1995.

Electromagnetic fields and power lines. Science & Medicine, July/August 1995.

Health effects of ozone. Science & Medicine, May/June 1997.

Xenon-enhanced CT of cerebral blood flow. Science & Medicine, September/October 1995.

3

SUMMARY

What should you take away from this chapter?

✓ General knowledge of cellular organization. Learn the organelles and their functions.
✓ Ability to describe differences between the tissue types and subtypes: epithelia, connective tissue, neural tissue, and muscle.
✓ An understanding of the importance of the extracellular matrix.

The study of cytology has greatly benefited from the use of sophisticated light and electron microscopes. These instruments, combined with other techniques, have illuminated the structure and function of cellular organelles. This chapter discusses the basic components of a cell, how cells are held together, and the different types of tissues formed by highly differentiated cells.

An extracelluar matrix, composed mostly of glycoproteins and protein fibers, helps hold cells together and provides a structural base for cell growth and migration during development. Various types of cell junctions, formed by proteins and glycoproteins, also hold cells together and participate in cell-to-cell communication. Adhesive junctions, such as desmosomes, resist physical stresses, while tight junctions prevent the leakage of material between cells. Gap junctions are pores or channels between cells that allow substances, such as ions, to pass directly between cells.

The four basic tissue types are: epithelial, connective, muscle and neural. Epithelia can be functionally divided into five types: exchange, transporting, ciliated, protective, and secretory. The seven types of connective tissue are: loose connective tissue, dense regular and dense irregular connective tissue, adipose, blood, cartilage and bone. These connective tissues consist of an extracellular matrix that contains one or more of the following protein fibers: collagen, elastin, fibrillin and fibronectin. There are three types of muscle tissue: skeletal, cardiac and smooth. Neural tissue and muscle are considered to be excitable tissues. Organs are composed of collections of tissues that perform certain functions.

TEACH YOURSELF THE BASICS

STUDYING CELLS AND TISSUES

1. What is the difference between cytology and histology?

2. What can light microscopes do that electron microscopes cannot? What can a scanning electron microscope do that a transmission electron microscope cannot?

CELLULAR ANATOMY

3.   What happens to a cell when it differentiates?

4.   What is extracelluar fluid?

The Cell Membrane Separates the Cell from Its Environment
5.   Describe cell membrane structure. (Fig. 3-5)

6.   What are the two primary functions of the cell membrane?

The Cytoplasm Includes Cytosol and Organelles
7.   What is the difference between cytosol and cytoplasm?

8.   Based on their structure, organelles are divided into what two groups?

Nonmembranous Organelles Are in Direct Contact with the Cytosol
9.   Name the 2 groups of nonmembranous organelles.

Ribosomes Participate in Protein Synthesis
10. Ribosomes are made of _____ (Fig. 3-6).

11. What do ribosomes do in the cell?

12. Distinguish between free ribosomes, fixed ribosomes, and polyribosomes.

Vaults Are Newly Discovered Organelles
13. Describe the structure of a vault.

There are Three Sizes of Protein Fibers in the Cytoplasm
14. List the three sizes of cytoplasmic protein fibers.

15. List four types of proteins that make up these fibers.

The Cytoskeleton Is a Changeable Organelle
16. Describe the structure of the cytoskeleton. (Fig. 3-7)

17. List five functions of the cytoskeleton.

18. What are microvilli?

Centrosomes and Centrioles Are Associated with Microtubules
19. What are centrosomes?

20. Describe the structure and function of centrioles. (Fig. 3-8a,b)

Cilia and Flagella Are Movable Hairlike Structures
21. Compare the structure of cilia and flagella. (Fig 3-8c,d)

22. Compare the functions of cilia and flagella and the cell types on which they are found.

Membranous Organelles Create Compartments for Specialized Functions
23. What functional advantage do membranous organelles have?

24. List five membranous organelles.

25. Define the term lumen.

Mitochondria Are the Powerhouse of the Cell
26. Describe the structure of a mitochondrion. Be sure to include the following words: matrix, cristae, intermembrane space. (Fig. 3-9)

27. What is the primary function of the mitochondria?

28. What two unusual characteristics do mitochondria possess?

The Endoplasmic Reticulum Is the Site of Protein and Lipid Synthesis
29. What are the anatomical and functional differences between rough and smooth ER? (Fig. 3-10)

The Golgi Apparatus Packages Proteins into Membrane-Bound Vesicles
30. Describe the structure of the Golgi apparatus. (Fig. 3-11)

31. Describe the relationship between the Golgi apparatus and the RER.

32. Distinguish between secretory vesicles, transport vesicles, storage vesicles, and lysosomes.

Lysosomes Are the Intracellular Digestive System (Fig. 3-12)
33. Give examples of lysosome function.

34. How is lysosomal enzyme activity regulated?

35. What happens to cells if lysosomes fail to function? If they leak enzymes into the cytosol?

Peroxisomes Contain Enzymes That Neutralize Toxins (Fig. 3-12)
36. How do peroxisomes differ from lysosomes?

The Nucleus Is the Cell's Control Center
37. Describe the organization and components of the nucleus. (Fig. 3-13)

38. How does communication take place between the nucleus and other cellular components?

39. What is the difference between the nucleus and a nucleolus?

TISSUES OF THE BODY
✓ IP Muscular: Anatomy Review – Skeletal Muscle Tissue

40. What is a tissue?

41. List four physical features that histologists use to describe tissues.

42. Name the four primary tissue types and give some distinguishing characteristics of each type. (Table 3-5)

Extracellular Matrix Has Many Functions

43. Describe the composition of extracellular matrix.

44. How do cells interact with the matrix?

45. Give examples of and describe how matrix differs between tissue types.

Cell Junctions Hold Cells Together to Form Tissues

46. How are individual cells within tissues connected to each other? (Fig. 3-14 and 15)

47. Describe the structure and function of gap junctions. Where in the body would you likely find gap junctions?

48. Describe the structure and function of tight junctions. Where in the body might you find tight junctions?

49. Describe the structure and function of anchoring junctions.

Cell Adhesion Molecules

50. Describe the generalized structure of CAMs. (Fig. 3-14)

51. What are some specific examples of CAMs, and how do the CAMs function in these examples? (Table 3-2)

Anchoring Junctions

52. Which CAMs are responsible for creating anchoring cell-cell junctions in vertebrates?

53. Describe two cell-cell junctions, including the proteins involved.

54. Which CAMs are used in cell-matrix junctions?

55. Describe two cell-matrix junctions, including the proteins involved.

Epithelia Provide Protection and Regulate Exchange

56. List three general functions of epithelial tissues.

Structure of Epithelia

57. What is the basal lamina and what is its function? (Fig. 3-16)

58. Describe or draw the general structural composition of epithelia.

59. Physiologists characterize epithelia as either _____ or _____. Upon what do they base this characterization?

60. Give some examples of epithelia that fit these two structural characterizations:

61. The tightness of an epithelium is directly related to:

Types of Epithelia

62. Name two general types of epithelia.

63. Name the two types of layering and the three cell shapes found in sheet epithelia.

64. Name the five functional types of epithelia and give examples of where each type can be found in the body. (Table 3-3; Fig. 3-17)

65. Explain how the function of each type of epithelium (exchange, transporting, etc.) is reflected by its structure.

66. Draw a diagram and then explain the significance of these terms as they relate to a transporting epithelium: lumen, apical membrane, microvilli, basolateral membrane, tight junction, extracellular fluid. (Fig. 3-18)

67. Define secretion.

68. Distinguish between an endocrine gland and an exocrine gland. (Fig. 3-21)

69. What is the difference between a serous secretion and a mucous secretion?

Connective Tissues Provide Support and Barriers (Table 3-4; Fig. 3-22 thru 25)
70. What is the distinguishing characteristic of connective tissues?

Structure of Connective Tissue
71. Describe the basic components of connective tissue matrix.

72. Where do the actual cells of connective tissue reside? Describe the different types of cells. (Fig. 3-22)

73. What is implied by the following suffixes?
        -blast:
        -clast:

74. Name the four main protein fibers of matrix and describe their key properties.

Types of Connective Tissue

75. Name and give examples for the seven types of connective tissue and tell where they are found. (Table 3-4)

Muscle and Neural Tissues Are Excitable

76. What is meant by the term "excitable tissue?"

77. What is the primary characteristic of muscle?

78. List the three types of muscle tissues and give examples for each.

79. What are the two types of neural tissue and what are their primary functions?

TISSUE REMODELING

Apoptosis Is a Tidy Form of Cell Death

80. Briefly describe the two forms of cell death.

Stem Cells Can Create New Specialized Cells

81. If cells in the adult body are constantly dying, where do their replacements come from?

82. Distinguish between the following terms:
    Totipotent:
    Pluripotent:
    Multipotent:

83. What are stem cells? Why are they important?

ORGANS

84. What is an organ?

TALK THE TALK

actin	adherens junction
anchoring junction	Antonie van Leeuwenhoek
basal body	basal lamina
basolateral membrane	blood
cadherin	cartilage
centriole	ciliated epithelium
claudin	collagen
crista ‡	cytology
cytoskeleton	cytosol
desmosome	differentiation
elastin	endocrine gland
exchange epithelium	exocrine gland
extracellular matrix	fibrillin
fixed ribosome	flagellum ‡
gap junction	goblet cell
hemidesmosome	histology
inclusion	intermediate filament
keratin	kinesin
loose connective tissue	lysosome
matrix metalloproteinase	membranous organelle
microfilament	microtubule
mitochondria *	mucous
myosin	nerve-cell adhesion molecule (N-CAM)
nonmembranous organelle	nuclear envelope
nucleus ‡	occluding junction
organ	organelle
plaque	plasticity
polyribosome	pore
proteoglycans	ribosome
rough endoplasmic reticulum	secretion
secretory vesicle	selectin
smooth endoplasmic reticulum	spot desmosome
thick filament	tight junction
transport epithelium	transport vesicle
actin	adherens junction
anchoring junction	Antonie van Leeuwenhoek
basal body	basal lamina
basolateral membrane	blood
cadherin	cartilage
centriole	ciliated epithelium
claudin	collagen

* These words are in the plural form. What are their singular forms?
‡ These words are in the singular form. What are their plural forms?

PRACTICE MAKES PERFECT

1. Which organelle, if separated from its cell, would have the highest probability of existing and evolving into a functional life form? Explain your reasoning.

2. What is the advantage of having the nucleus partially separated from the cytoplasm?

3. If intestinal cells lacked a cytoskeleton, how would their structure and function be affected?

4. Why are epithelia more susceptible to developing cancer than most other tissues?

5. A histological examination of a tissue shows that it has tight junctions. Would you expect the solutions normally found on either side of the epithelium to be the same or different? Explain.

6. What anatomical and functional qualities of the epidermis (skin) help regulate body temperature and prevent dehydration?

7. Matching:

_____ ground substance   A. exceptionally strong, inelastic protein fiber
_____ fibroblast   B. cell that breaks down extracellular matrix
_____ collagen   C. matrix of glycoproteins, water, protein fibers
_____ elastin   D. cell that secretes extracellular matrix
_____ fibrillin   E. a coiled protein fiber with elasticity
_____ fibronectin   F. protein fiber that connects cells to extracellular matrix
                       G. a very thin fiber that combines with elastin

8. Choose the type of protein fiber(s), if any, that is associated with a particular type of connective tissue.

a) collagen   b) elastin   c) fibrillin   d) fibronectin   e) none

_____ under the skin   _____ tendons and ligaments
_____ sheaths that surround nerves and muscles   _____ blood
_____ cartilage   _____ lungs and blood vessels
_____ adipose   _____ bones

9. Put the letter of the correct answer in front of the phrase below:

a) rough endoplasmic reticulum   b) Golgi apparatus   c) both   d) neither

_____ packages proteins into vesicles
_____ modifies proteins by adding or subtracting fragments
_____ a series of interconnected hollow tubes or sacs
_____ proteins are synthesized in this location

10. Be sure you can distinguish between the following pairs or groups. Give examples when appropriate.

a) desmosome, intermediate junction, gap junction, tight junction, junctional complex

b) cilia and flagella

c) microfilaments, microtubules, microvilli, and intermediate filaments

d) exchange and transporting epithelia

e) intracellular, extracellular, and intercellular compartments

f) cristae and matrix of mitochondria

g) lysosomes and peroxisomes

h) rough and smooth endoplasmic reticulum

i) epithelium and endothelium

j) apical and basolateral sides of an epithelium

k) movement of substances across a tight epithelium and a leaky epithelium

l) endocrine and exocrine glands

m) serous and mucous secretions

n) fibroblasts, melanocytes, adipocytes, macrophages, and mast cells

o) collagen and elastin

p) tendons and ligaments

BEYOND THE PAGES

FURTHER EXPLORATIONS

Artificial organs. Scientific American, September 1995. Engineering artificial tissue.

Sunlight and skin cancer. Scientific American, July 1996.

Bioengineered skin substitutes. Science & Medicine, July/August 1997.

Tissue culture in microgravity. Science & Medicine, May/June 1997.

Tissue Engineering: repairing wounded knees. Science & Medicine 6(2), 1999 Mar/Apr.

Tissue Engineering: The science of tissue engineering. Science & Medicine 5(6), 1998 Nov/Dec.

Tissue Engineering: Biodegradable polymers. Science & Medicine 6(1), 1999 Jan/Feb.

+ Rent the movie ***Lorenzo's Oil***, about a family whose child has an inherited peroxisomal disorder.

+ **The Visible Human** project. The Visible Man was a 39 year old prisoner who was executed and donated his body to science. It was embedded in gelatin, frozen, and sliced crosswise into 1878 slices 1 mm thick. The slices were photographed, digitized, and colored. The entire set occupies about 14 GIGABYTES, so don't even think about downloading it! To view it, go to: http://www.nlm.nih.gov and look under Research Programs.

+ The **WWW Virtual Library of Cell Biology** (http://vlib.org/Science/Cell_Biology/index.shtml) has a wonderful collection of links to resources on many aspects of cell biology. Check it out!

4

SUMMARY

Key concepts to take from this chapter:

✓ Energy is required to do work. There are two types of energy: kinetic and potential.
✓ There are many different types of work. [See Appendix A for more discussion.]
✓ Chemical reactions transfer energy. You should take away a general understanding of activation energy, free energy, endergonic/exergonic reactions, reversible reactions, and coupled reactions.
✓ Enzymes exhibit specificity, competition, and saturation. These three characteristics are observed in all protein-substrate interactions. [∫ Ch 5 and membrane transporters]
✓ Cells use a series of chemical reactions to release the energy stored in the bonds of biomolecules. Energy from these bonds is transferred to the bonds of ATP and other high-energy compounds. The high-energy compounds are used by the body to do work. Ask your instructor which details you should learn about cellular metabolism at this point.
✓ Take some time to become very familiar with protein synthesis. This concept is key to understanding many aspects of physiology, and the time you spend learning it will be well spent.

This chapter discusses how cells obtain and store energy in the form of chemical bonds. The potential energy stored in chemical bonds is later used as kinetic energy to perform work. In biological systems, this work can be chemical, transport or mechanical work. The types of work performed by chemical bond energy include protein synthesis, transport of substances across membranes, and muscle contraction.

Chemical reactions are of two general types, exergonic or endergonic. During exergonic reactions, the free energy of the products is less than that of the reactants. In endergonic reactions, the opposite occurs. Many exergonic and endergonic biological reactions are coupled and use nucleotides (e.g., ATP) to capture, store and transfer energy. Some of these reactions are irreversible, but many are reversible. Most reversible reactions require the aid of an enzyme to overcome their activation energy.

Enzymes are involved in many biological reactions. Enzymatic activity depends in part upon the ability of a substrate to bind to the active site of the enzyme. Numerous other factors affect enzyme activity including proteolytic activation, cofactors or coenzymes, modulation, and the concentration of enzyme, substrate or product. The reaction rate of enzymes is measured by how fast products are synthesized. This rate is determined by modulators, enzyme and substrate concentrations, and the ratio of substrates to products (law of mass action). Types of biological reactions catalyzed by enzymes include oxidation-reduction, hydrolysis and dehydration, and addition-subtraction-exchange reactions.

Metabolic reactions are either catabolic (net breakdown) or anabolic (net synthesis). The activity of metabolic pathways can be altered in a variety of ways, including mechanisms that regulate enzyme activity and ATP concentrations.

Glucose, fatty acids, glycerol and amino acids are used as energy sources to produce ATP. During glycolysis (an anaerobic pathway), one glucose molecule yields 2 pyruvate molecules, 2 ATP, 2 NADH, 2 H^+ and 2 H_2O molecules. In the absence of sufficient oxygen, pyruvate is converted to lactate. However, during aerobic metabolism pyruvate is converted to acetyl CoA, which enters the citric acid cycle. The yield from the citric acid cycle metabolism of two pyruvate molecules is 8 NADH, 2 $FADH_2$, 2 ATP and 2 CO_2 molecules. NADH and $FADH_2$ enter the electron transport system, and donate their electrons and H^+ to produce up to 38 ATP, H_2O and heat.

Glucose is not the only fuel source for making ATP during anaerobic and aerobic respiration. Glycogen can be converted to glucose-6-phosphate. Amino acids can be converted (via deamination) to pyruvate, acetyl CoA or other intermediates of the citric acid cycle. Glycerol can enter glycolysis, and fatty acids can be converted to acetyl CoA to enter the citric acid cycle.

Many fuel sources can be synthesized by the body. For example, glucose can be synthesized from glycogen, glycerol or amino acids whenever there is not enough glucose for ATP production. Most glucose is synthesized in the liver and released into the bloodstream for transport to other cells. Nerve cells normally only use glucose for fuel, so the body always tries to maintain adequate glucose concentrations in the blood. Lipids can be synthesized from glucose, acetyl CoA, glycerol and fatty acids.

Proteins are synthesized by an elaborate processes that includes transcription and translation. Genes are selected for transcription by initiation factors that bind to specific promoter regions on DNA. DNA is transcribed into mRNA, and mRNA is translated into a protein. These proteins are sorted, modified, packaged, and directed to a specific destination.

TEACH YOURSELF THE BASICS

ENERGY IN BIOLOGICAL SYSTEMS

1. Where do plants get energy and in what form(s) do they store excess energy? (Fig. 4-1)

2. Where do animals get energy and in what form(s) do they store excess energy?

Energy Is Used to Perform Work

3. Define energy.

4. List three kinds of work in biological systems and give an example of each.

Energy Comes in Two Forms: Kinetic and Potential

5. What is the difference between kinetic energy and potential energy? (Fig. 4-2)

Energy Can Be Converted from One Form to Another
6. When potential energy is converted to kinetic energy, what happens to the energy released?

7. How is potential energy stored in biological systems?

Thermodynamics Is the Study of Energy Use
8. State the first law of thermodynamics.

9. State the second law of thermodynamics.

10. What is entropy?

CHEMICAL REACTIONS
11. Define bioenergetics?

Energy Is Transferred Between Molecules During Reactions
12. Combine these words into a sentence that explains their relationship: reaction, product, molecule(s), substrate, reactant.

13. How do we measure the rate of a chemical reaction?

Energy Transfer in Reactions
14. Define and give an example of free energy.

15. What is the relationship between free energy and chemical bonds?

Activation Energy
16. Define and give an example of activation energy. (Fig. 4-3)

17. If a reaction proceeds spontaneously, what does that tell you about its activation energy?

Endergonic and Exergonic Reactions
18. What is the difference between exergonic reactions and endergonic reactions?

19. Compare the free energy of the products in an exergonic reaction to the free energy of the products in an endergonic reaction. (Fig. 4-4)

Coupled Reactions

20. What is the advantage of coupling exergonic and endergonic reactions?

21. What is a common way that our cells couple reactions?

Reversible and Irreversible Reactions

22. What is the difference between reversible and irreversible reactions?

ENZYMES

Enzymes Lower the Activation Energy of Reactions

23. What is the function of an enzyme? What are substrates? (Fig. 4-7)

24. How does an enzyme increase the rate of reaction?

Enzymes Bind to Their Substrates

25. How do enzymes and substrates interact?

26. What is a binding site on an enzyme? an active site?

27. What is the difference between the lock-and-key model of enzyme activity and the induced-fit model?
    (Fig. 4-8)

Enzyme Specificity

28. What do we mean by the specificity of an enzyme?

29. Give an example of an enzyme, state the reaction it catalyzes, and explain its specificity. (Table 4-4)

An Enzyme's Name Gives Information About Its Function

30. What suffix is often found on enzyme names?

31. The first part of an enzyme name usually refers to:

32. What are isozymes?

33. How are enzymes important to medical diagnosis?

Some Enzymes Must Be Activated

34. Why are some enzymes manufactured as inactive precursors?

35. What are these inactive enzyme precursors called, collectively?

36. How are inactive precursor enzymes activated? (Fig. 4-9) What is this activation process called?

37. What suffix is used to indicate an inactive enzyme?

Some Enzymes Require Cofactors or Coenzymes

38. What is the difference between a cofactor and a coenzyme? Give examples.

Modulators Alter Enzyme Activity

39. What are the two basic mechanisms by which modulators can influence enzyme activity?

Acidity and Temperature

40. How do acidity and temperature modulate enzyme activity? (Fig. 4-12)

41. What does it mean when a molecule is "denatured?"

Chemical Modulators

42. What is the difference between a competitive inhibitor and an allosteric inhibitor of an enzyme? (Fig. 4-13 and 4-14)

43. How do covalent modulators work? Give an example of one.

Enzyme and Substrate Concentration Affect Reaction Rate

44. List four possible factors that can affect the rate of an enzymatic reaction.

Reaction Rate is Directly Related to the Amount of Enzyme Present

45. What happens to the rate of a reaction if the amount of enzyme present is increased? (Fig. 4-15)

Reaction Rate Can Reach a Maximum

46. What happens to the rate of a reaction as the amount of substrate decreases? (Fig. 4-16)

47. Define enzyme saturation. (Fig. 4-16)

Reversible Reactions Obey the Law of Mass Action

48. Explain the concept of equilibrium as it applies to a reversible reaction $(A + B \leftrightarrow C + D)$.

49. If the previous reaction is at equilibrium, what happens as you add more substrate? (Fig. 4-17b)

50. Define the law of mass action.

Enzymatic Reactions Can Be Categorized (Table 4-4)

Oxidation-Reduction Reactions

       MNEMONIC: OIL RIG = Oxidation Is (electron) Loss, Reduction Is Gain

Hydrolysis-Dehydration Reactions

51. Briefly describe what happens in a dehydration reaction. Now describe a hydrolysis reaction.

Addition-Subtraction-Exchange Reactions

52. Briefly describe addition reactions, subtraction reactions, and exchange reactions. Give an example of each. (Fig. 4-27)

Ligation Reactions

53. What happens in a ligation reaction? Give an example.

54. Fill in the blanks in the following table (Table 4-4)

REACTION TYPE	WHAT HAPPENS	TYPE OF ENZYME
Hydrolysis of lipids		
	add a phosphate	
	gain electrons	
		dehydrogenase
Hydrolysis		
Exchange	phosphate	
		deaminase
Oxidation		
	subtract a phosphate	
Exchange	amino group	
Add	amino group	

METABOLISM
55. Define metabolism.

56. Distinguish between catabolic and anabolic reactions.

57. Define a kilocalorie (kcal).

58. What is a metabolic pathway? What are intermediates? (Fig. 4-18)

Cells Regulate Their Metabolic Pathways
59. List five basic ways that cells regulate metabolism.

Enzyme Modulation
60. Explain feedback inhibition, using the pathway L → M → N → P as an example. (Fig. 4-19)

Enzymes and Reversible Reactions
61. What is the advantage of having a reaction that is regulated by two enzymes (one for the forward direction, the other for the reverse direction)? (Fig 4-20)

Isolation of Enzymes within the Cell
62. What advantage does a cell gain by isolating some enzymes within specific intracellular compartments (organelles)? [∫ p. 59-62]

Ratio of ATP to ADP
63. If the ATP:ADP ratio decreases (i.e., ATP levels drop), what do you expect to see happen to the metabolic pathways that synthesize ATP?

ATP Transfers Energy Between Reactions
64. What is the biological significance of ATP?

65. What is the difference between aerobic and anaerobic pathways?

66. Compare ATP production by aerobic and anaerobic pathways.

ATP PRODUCTION
⁄ IP Muscular: Muscle Metabolism

67. Name two major pathways that produce compounds carrying high-energy electrons.

68. What biomolecules can be used in these pathways?

69. What pathways transfer energy from high-energy electrons to ATP?

Glycolysis Converts Glucose and Glycogen into Pyruvate

70. Where in the cell does glycolysis take place? (Fig. 4-21 and 4-22)

71. What are the possible end products of glycolysis and what is their fate? (Fig. 4-21 and 4-22)

Anaerobic Metabolism Converts Pyruvate into Lactate

72. Under what conditions is pyruvate converted into lactate?

73. What is the net energy yield from the conversion of one glucose to two lactate? (Fig. 4-23)

_____ ATP _____ NADH _____ FADH$_2$

Pyruvate Enters the Citric Acid Cycle in Aerobic Metabolism

74. In aerobic metabolism, pyruvate is converted into _____.

75. Where in the cell does this reaction take place? (Fig. 4-23)

76. What are the end products of the citric acid cycle and what is their fate? (Fig. 4-24)

77. The net energy for two pyruvate molecules completing the citric acid cycle is:

_____ ATP _____ NADH _____ FADH$_2$

The Electron Transport System Transfers Energy from NADH and FADH$_2$ to ATP

78. Relate the terms chemiosmotic theory, electron transport system, cytochromes, and oxidative phosphorylation. (Fig 4-25)

79. How do NADH and FADH$_2$ participate in the electron transport system?

ATP Production Is Coupled to Movement of Hydrogen Ions across the Inner Mitochondrial Membrane

80. How is potential energy created across the inner mitochondrial membrane?

81. Draw and label a diagram or explain how the electron transport system makes ATP and water. (Fig. 4-25)

The Maximum Energy Yield of One Glucose Molecule Is 30-32 ATP

82. Total energy production from 1 glucose in aerobic metabolism = _____ ATP. (Table 4-5)

83. Explain how the net energy yield can vary.

Large Biomolecules Can Be Used to Make ATP

Glycogen Converts to Glucose

84. When glycogen is broken down for energy, it is converted to _____ or _____.

85. What is the name of the process by which glycogen is broken down for metabolism?

Proteins Can Be Catabolized to Produce ATP (Fig. 4-27)

86. The first step in protein catabolism is:

87. Organic acids derived from catabolized amino acids can enter which of the metabolic pathways?

Lipids Yield More Energy per Unit Weight than Glucose or Proteins

88. In lipolysis, lipids are converted into _____ and _____.

89. What happens to fatty acids that undergo beta oxidation?

90. Liver cells convert some fatty acids into _____ rather than into acetyl CoA.

SYNTHETIC PATHWAYS

Glycogen Can Be Made from Glucose

91. What two locations have the largest glycogen stores?

92. Through which pathway(s) can glycogen be made? (Fig. 4-26)

Glucose Can Be Made from Glycerol or Amino Acids

93. What is gluconeogenesis? (Fig. 4-29)

94. What organ is the primary site of gluconeogenesis during periods of fasting?

Acetyl CoA Is an Important Precursor for Lipid Synthesis

95. What two-carbon precursor can be used to synthesizer fatty acids? (Fig. 4-30)

96. In which organelle does triglyceride formation take place?

97. Can the body make cholesterol or must it come from the diet?

Proteins Are the Key to Cell Function

98. Why are proteins considered to be more variable and also more specific than any other biomolecule?

The Protein "Alphabet" Begins with DNA

99. What is a codon? (Fig. 4-31)

100. What relationship do codons of DNA have to the codons of mRNA?

101. What is the difference between transcription and translation?

During Transcription, DNA Guides the Synthesis of a Complementary mRNA Molecule

102. Describe the process by which transcription is initiated. (Fig. 4-32)

103. What is the role of RNA polymerase?

104. Explain the relationship between introns, exons, mRNA processing, and alternative splicing. (Fig. 4-33)

Translation of mRNA Produces a String of Amino Acids
105. What is the difference between mRNA, rRNA, and tRNA? (Fig. 4-34)

106. What do ribonucleases do?

Protein Sorting Directs Proteins to Their Final Destination
107. What is a signal sequence/targeting sequence?

108. What happens to proteins as they come off the ribosome?

Final Protein Structure Is Determined by Post-Translational Modification
109. List five possible post-translational modifications that a newly formed protein could experience.

Protein Folding
110. How does a protein accomplish its folded structure?

111. What are molecular chaperones?

112. How does the cell deal with misfolded proteins?

Cross-linkage
113. What are disulfide bonds? (Fig. 4-9)

Cleavage
114. What is accomplished by post-translational protein cleavage?

Addition of other molecules or groups
115. List examples of molecules that might be added to a protein.

Assembly into multimeric proteins
116. What is meant by "multimeric?"

Proteins Made on the Endoplasmic Reticulum Enter the Secretory Pathway
117. Trace the path of a newly synthesized protein from the ribosome to a secretory vesicle. (Fig. 4-35)

TALK THE TALK

acetyl coenzyme A	activation energy	active site
aerobic metabolism	aerobic respiration	allosteric modulator
alternative splicing	amination	anabolism
anaerobic metabolism	anticodon	antisense strand
ATP synthase	beta-oxidation	catabolism
catalyst	chemical reaction	chemical work
chemiosmotic theory	citric acid cycle	codon
co-enzyme	co-factor	compartmentation
competitive inhibitor	concentration gradient	coupled reaction
covalent modulator	deamination	dehydration
denatured	DNA	electron transport system
endergonic reaction	energy	entropy
enzyme	exergonic reaction	exon
FADH$_2$	feedback inhibition	free energy
gene	gluconeogenesis	glucose 6-phosphate
glycogen metabolism	glycogenolysis	glycolysis
high-energy phosphate bond	Human Genome Project	Human Proteomics Initiative
hydrolysis	induced fit model	initiation factor
intermediate	intron	irreversible reaction
isozyme	ketone bodies	key intermediate
kilocalorie	kinase	kinetic energy
Krebs cycle	lactate	lactate dehydrogenase
Law of Mass Action	laws of thermodynamics	lipolysis
lock-and-key model	matrix (of mitochondria)	mechanical work
metabolism	methylation	modulator
molecular chaperone	mRNA	mRNA processing
multimeric protein	NADH	oxidation
oxidative pathway	oxidative phosphorylation	pathway
peptidase	phosphorylation	post-translational modification
potential energy	product	promoter
protease	proteasome	protein sorting
proteolytic activation	proteome	pyruvate
reactant	reaction rate	reduction
reversible reaction	ribonuclease	ribosomal RNA (rRNA)
RNA polymerase	saturation	sense strand
signal sequence	specificity	substrate
targeting sequence	tetramer	transamination
transcription	transition vesicle	translation
transport work	ubiquitin	work

FOCUS ON PHYSIOLOGY: The Law of Mass Action

The Law of Mass Action is a simple relationship that holds for chemical reactions ranging from those in a test tube to those in the blood. This law says that the ratio of the concentrations of the molecules is a constant number, known as the *equilibrium constant*, K.*

$$K = \frac{[\text{substrates}]}{[\text{products}]}$$

*Mathematically:

$$K = \frac{[A]^m \cdot [B]^n}{[C]^p \cdot [D]^q}$$

where m, n, p, and r represent the number of molecules of A, B, C, and D respectively in the balanced equation.

In very general terms, the Law of Mass Action says that when a reaction is at equilibrium, the ratio of the substrates to the products is always the same. If the concentration of a substrate (A or B) increases, the equilibrium will be disturbed. To restore the proper substrate/product ratio, some of the added substrates will convert into product. Conversely, if the amount of product (C or D) decreases, such as would occur when they are used up in a different reaction, some substrate will convert into product to replace that which was lost. This has the effect of decreasing the amount of A and B but keeping the ratio at the value needed for K.

The equilibrium constant is important in physiology because as the concentrations of substrates change, the change will be reflected in the concentrations of the products. This is most easily illustrated by equating the chemical reaction to a scale, with the number of blocks on each side representing the concentrations of the substrates and products. The reaction is reversible. The equilibrium constant, K, is indicated by the position of the triangular base of the scale. For simplicity, our example has an equilibrium constant of 1, so that the reaction is in equilibrium when there are equal numbers of blocks on each side,: 1 = [S]/[P]. The figure below shows the reaction at equilibrium, with substrate and product concentrations balanced at the equilibrium constant (K) for the reaction.

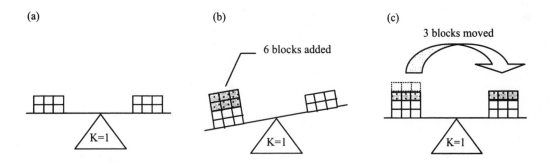

(a)

(b)

6 blocks added

(c)

3 blocks moved

K=1   K=1   K=1

In part (b) of the figure, some outside force has added substrate to the left side of the reaction, sending the reaction out of equilibrium. Now, without removing any blocks from the scale, how can you get the reaction back to equilibrium? Easy...move some of the added blocks over to the product side. Then each side still has an equal number of blocks (the 1:1 ratio that we set up as our equilibrium constant) and the reaction is at equilibrium. Notice that BOTH product and substrate have increased, but by an equal amount. You cannot change the K since this is a constant for any given reaction.

The next figure shows a different reaction that is at equilibrium when the product is twice the substrate (d). That means the K for this reaction is ½. Notice that the balance point has moved to compensate for the K value: 1/2 = [S]/[P]. In part (e) of this figure, 9 units have been added to the substrate side. How can you rearrange the blocks so that you balance the scale at the 1/2 ratio? Try this on your own, using part (f).

(d)   (e)   (f)

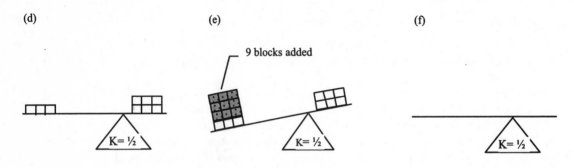

In the figures below, you again have the reaction with a K value of 1/2 (g). In part (h), 3 units of product are removed by another metabolic reaction. Without adding or subtracting any new units to the scales, move the units between the scales until the reaction is at equilibrium again (i).

(g)   (h)   (i)

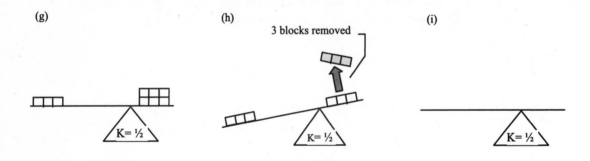

Now, instead of blocks on a scale, assume that the reaction is: $A \rightarrow C + D \rightarrow E$

If more substrate A is added to the reaction, what happens to the amounts of the following when the reaction reaches equilibrium?

    A _____   C _____   D _____

If C and D are converted into E, when the system again reaches equilibrium, what has happened to the

amount of A in the system? _____

PRACTICE MAKES PERFECT

1. Matching. More than one letter may apply to each blank.

_____ entropy	A. ATP
_____ potential energy	B. a muscle contracting
_____ kinetic energy	C. reaction that converts glucose to ATP
_____ exergonic	D. second law of thermodynamics
_____ endergonic	E. free energy
	F. reaction that releases a lot of energy
	G. reaction that requires a lot of energy

2. Most breakfast cereals would not be very nutritious unless they were supplemented with vitamins and ions such as Mg^{2+}. How do some of these ions and vitamins affect enzyme activity?

3. In the human body, carbonic anhydrase (CA) has maximum activity at pH 7.4. Some other animals have an isozyme that has maximum activity at about 6.4. Draw a curve of the activity of human carbonic anhydrase and its isozyme as a function of pH, using the graph below.

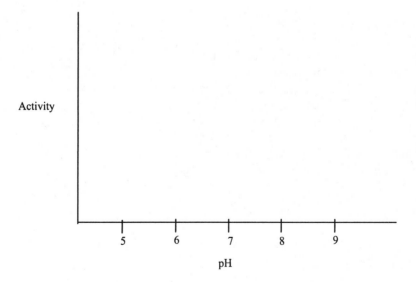

Activity

5   6   7   8   9

pH

4. Answer the questions using the two graphs below.

    a. Which graph represents an exergonic and which graph represents an endergonic reaction?

    b. Which reaction is more likely to proceed in the forward direction? Why?

    c. Which reaction products yield more free net energy?

    d. Which reactions below belong with graph A and which belong with graph B?
       (Reactions 2, 3, and 4 are from the glycolysis pathway.)

1. ___ $6\ CO_2 + 6\ H_2O + \text{sunlight} \rightarrow C_6H_{12}O_6 + 6\ O_2$
2. ___ glucose + ATP $\rightarrow$ glucose-6-phosphate + ADP
3. ___ 3-phosphoglyceraldehyde + P_i + NAD^+ $\rightarrow$ 1,3 diphosphoglycerate + NADH
4. ___ 1,3 diphosphoglycerate + ADP $\rightarrow$ 3-phosphoglycerate + ATP

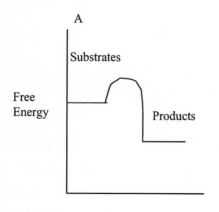

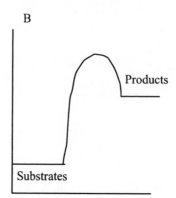

5. Matching:
    _____ hydrolysis   A. lose electron or gain H^+
    _____ dehydration   B. removal of water
    _____ oxidation   C. –OH is added to one molecule and –H to another
    _____ reduction   D. gain electron or lose H^+
    _____ kinase   E. loss of activity
    _____ deamination   F. transfer of an amino group
    _____ transamination G. enzyme that transfers a phosphate group
                            H. removal of an amino group

6. Ribonuclease is a digestive enzyme secreted by the pancreas. This enzyme catalyzes the hydrolysis of RNA.

> a. A 100 mM solution of ribonuclease is added to a series of test tubes with RNA concentrations ranging from 10% to 70%. Plot the reaction rate as a function of substrate concentration on the graph below. Assume that the reaction rate is maximal at a 50% substrate concentration.
>
> b. What is the relationship between the substrate and the enzyme when the reaction rate is maximal?
>
> c. If the enzyme concentration was only 50 mM, indicate on the graph below how the reaction rate would change as a function of substrate concentration.

Reaction
Rate

| | | | | | | |
| 10 | 20 | 30 | 40 | 50 | 60 | 70 |

RNA Concentration (%)

7. During anaerobic metabolism, the reaction shown below occurs. Which molecules have been reduced and which have been oxidized?

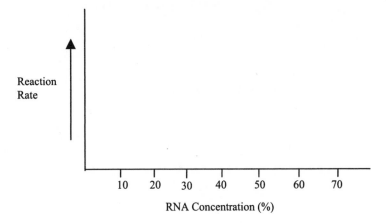

$$CH_3 - C - COO^- \xrightarrow[\text{lactate dehydrogenase}]{\text{NADH} + H^+ \quad \text{NAD}^+} CH_3 - CH - COO^-$$

pyruvate   lactate

8. During glycolysis, the reaction shown below occurs. What type of reaction is this?

$$
\begin{array}{l}
\text{OH} \\
| \\
\text{CH}_2 \quad\quad \text{O} \\
|\quad\quad\quad | \\
\text{CH}-\text{O}-\text{P}-\text{O}^- \\
|\quad\quad\quad | \\
\text{COO}^- \quad \text{O}^-
\end{array}
\qquad
\xrightarrow{\text{H}_2\text{O}}
\qquad
\begin{array}{l}
\text{CH}_2 \quad\quad \text{O} \\
|\quad\quad\quad | \\
\text{C}-\text{O}-\text{P}-\text{O}^- \\
|\quad\quad\quad | \\
\text{COO}^- \quad \text{O}^-
\end{array}
$$

2-phosphoglycerate   phosphoenolpyruvate

9. Matching:

_____ chemiosmotic theory	A. described citric acid cycle
_____ Sir Hans A. Krebs	B. conversion of proteins or fats to glucose
_____ NADH and FADH$_2$	C. converted to glucose-6-phosphate
_____ glycolysis	D. using H$^+$ gradient to make ATP
_____ beta-oxidation	E. derived from pyruvate and the vitamin pantothenic acid
_____ glycogen	F. pathway that converts glucose to pyruvate
_____ gluconeogenesis	G. donates electrons and H$^+$
_____ glycogenolysis	H. glycogen breakdown
_____ acetyl coenzyme A	I. removes NH$_3$ from amino acid to make organic acid that enters aerobic metabolic pathway
_____ deamination	J. converts fatty acid or glycerol into pyruvate
	K. converts fatty acids into acetyl CoA

10. Explain the function of the following in the electron transport system:

    a. NADH -

    b. FADH$_2$ -

    c. oxygen -

    d. ATP synthase -

    e. H$^+$ -

    f. complex inner membrane proteins -

MAPS

1. The three major food groups, proteins, carbohydrates and fats, are used as fuel sources to produce ATP. Create a map using the list of terms (and any terms you wish to add) to show:

      a) the important or key intermediates
      b) where the breakdown products of these food groups enter the pathway
      c) the major products for each part of the pathway. What are the fates of these products?
      d) both aerobic and anaerobic pathways
      e) where these reactions occur in the cell

acetyl CoA	$ADP + P_i$	aerobic
anaerobic	ATP	carbohydrates
citric acid cycle	cytoplasm	electron transport system
electrons	fats	fatty acids
gluconeogenesis	glucose	glycerol
glycogen	glycogenesis	glycolysis
H^+	H_2O	lactic acid
liver	mitochondria	NADH
oxygen	proteins	pyruvate

2. Design a map that outlines the events of translation and protein sorting. Include in your answer the following terms (plus any terms you wish to add):

amino acid	anticodon
codon	Golgi complex
mRNA	peptide bond
polypeptide	ribosomes
rough endoplasmic reticulum	signal sequence
transition vesicles	tRNA

BEYOND THE PAGES

ETHICS IN MEDICINE

Suppose that both Sarah and David were carriers of the Tay Sachs gene. What parenting options are available for such a couple?

A couple where both partners are carriers has a one-in-four chance of conceiving a child who will be born with the disease. These are the basic options that the genetic counselor presents to them:

1. The couple can decide not to have children.
2. They can decide to adopt children.
3. They can elect to use an egg or sperm donor who does not carry the gene.
4. If they decide to have their own children, they can take the 1-in-4 chance that their child will be born with the disease. Screening techniques are available to test the genetic makeup of a fetus as early as 6 weeks after conception to determine whether it will be born with Tay Sachs disease. If the couple's personal convictions allow, they can screen for the disease in the fetus and elect to abort a fetus that would be born with the disease.

FURTHER EXPLORATIONS

"Why introns?" *News in Physiological Sciences* 10:98-99 1995 Apr.

"About benefits and costs: Genetic testing for Huntington's disease," *Science & Medicine* 1995 , March/April.

SUMMARY

This chapter discusses some key themes that recur throughout the remainder of the book. Learn them well now to make your life easier as the class progresses!

✓ Cell membranes are fluid-mosaics consisting of a phospholipid bilayer with proteins and carbohydrates.
✓ What are the differences between integral proteins and peripheral proteins?
✓ Membrane proteins have various functions. Learn the different groups of membrane proteins (enzymes, receptors, transporters, etc.) and understand how they participate in cellular activities.
✓ The body fluids are compartmentalized. Learn the compartments and what keeps them separate.
✓ Several factors affect diffusion. You should be familiar enough with these factors to explain them verbally and express them mathematically.
✓ There are two types of active transport: primary and secondary. You should be able to compare and contrast these processes.
✓ Large particles use different forms of vesicular transport to enter or leave the cell. Learn the distinctions between phagocytosis, endocytosis, and exocytosis.
✓ Cells can be polarized. This is an important concept for transepithelial transport. Understand how polarization creates directional transport.
✓ Osmolarity and tonicity are very important concepts! It's important that you understand the difference between them and learn the terminology for comparing solutions.
✓ Cell membranes create a selectively permeable barrier that allows cells to maintain electrochemical disequilibrium across the membrane. Learn how this disequilibrium is maintained so that you can understand its roles in physiological processes to be discussed in later chapters.
✓ Learn how controlled changes in membrane potential can serve as a means of cellular communication. What is the difference between depolarization, repolarization, and hyperpolarization?

Cell membranes act as a selectively permeable barrier between the cells and their external environment, mediating transport and communication between the two compartments. In addition, membranes provide structural support. A cell membrane consists of a phospholipid bilayer with proteins that are inserted partially or entirely through the membrane. Many of these proteins are mobile, while others have restricted movement. Membrane proteins can play a structural role; they can form channels, carriers, receptors, or enzymes; or, they might have multiple duties. Carbohydrates attach to some membrane proteins and lipids, serving as cellular markers for recognition by other cells (like cells of the immune system) and giving the membrane a "sugar coating."

The ability of a substance to cross a cell membrane depends upon the properties of the membrane and upon the size and lipid solubility of the substance. Small, lipid soluble substances can cross a membrane by passive diffusion. Channels formed by transmembrane proteins allow the passage of water and smaller ions. Larger molecules and ions are transported by protein carriers. One form of carrier-mediated transport, primary active transport, uses ATP while other forms of carrier-mediated transport use the energy stored in concentration gradients. Large molecules and particles move into and out of cells by vesicles that fuse with the membrane. Epithelial cells are polarized, with the apical and basolateral membranes containing different types of protein-mediated transporters. This allows the one-way transport of certain molecules.

Water is able to move freely across most membranes, moving primarily through open water channels. The movement of water from a region of lower solute concentration to one of higher solute concentration is called osmosis. Osmolarity describes the number of particles in a solution; tonicity is a comparative term that describes how the volume of a cell changes by osmosis when exposed to a solution.

Ions and most solutes do not diffuse freely across cell membranes, and therefore, a state of chemical disequilibrium exists between the cell and its environment. All cells have a resting membrane potential resulting from chemical and electrical gradients of ions. Depending upon the type of cell, resting membrane potentials are usually between -50 to -90 mV, relative to the extracellular fluid. The resting potential in human cells is established by a membrane that is more permeable to K^+ than to Na^+ or other ions. Active transport maintains this potential by transporting Na^+ and K^+ ions across the membrane. Controlled changes in membrane potential, by means of ion movement, provide a means for intracellular and intercellular communication.

TEACH YOURSELF THE BASICS

MEMBRANES IN THE BODY (Fig. 5-1)
1. Describe the different types of membranes in the body.

CELL MEMBRANES (Fig. 5-10)
2. List the four general functions of membranes.

Membranes Are Mostly Lipid and Protein
3. What biomolecules form the three main components of biological membranes?

4. Diagram a typical membrane based on the fluid mosaic membrane model. (Fig. 5-2)

5. Why is the membrane described by the word "fluid"?

Membrane Lipids Form a Barrier Between the Cytoplasm and Extracellular Fluid

6. Describe the structure and polarity of a phospholipid molecule. (Fig. 5-3)

7. Distinguish between a micelle, liposome, and phospholipid bilayer. (Fig. 5-3)

Membrane Proteins May Be Loosely or Tightly Bound to the Membrane (Fig. 5-12)

8. Name and distinguish between the two anatomical classifications of membrane proteins (Fig. 5-4)

Membrane-Spanning Proteins

9. Describe the characteristics and regions of membrane-spanning proteins. You could also draw a diagram. (Fig. 5-5)

Membrane Proteins Function as Structural Proteins, Enzymes, Receptors, and Transporters (Fig. 5-12)

10. List four functions of membrane proteins.

Structural Proteins

11. What are the three major roles of structural membrane proteins?

Enzymes

12. Give one example each of an intracellular and an extracellular membrane enzyme.

Receptors

13. What role do receptor proteins play?

14. What is a ligand? (Fig. 5-6)

Transporters
15. How does the role of a membrane receptor differ from the role of a membrane transporter?

Channel Proteins (Fig. 5-7)
16. What types of molecules pass through channel proteins?

17. What factors determine a channel protein's specificity?

18. What is the difference between an open channel and a gated channel? (Fig 5-8)

19. List the three types of gated channels and tell what opens each type.

Carrier Proteins (Fig. 5-9)
20. What kinds of molecules can cross a membrane by using a carrier protein? What kinds cannot cross with a carrier?

21. Describe or diagram the molecular mechanism by which carrier proteins move molecules.

22. How do carrier proteins differ from channel proteins?

Membrane Carbohydrates Attach to Both Lipids and Proteins
23. What is the glycocalyx and where in the cell is it found?

24. Name one important function of membrane glycoproteins.

BODY FLUID COMPARTMENTS (Fig. 5-13)
⟋ IP Fluids & Electrolytes: Introduction to Body Fluids

25. What makes up the external environment of a cell?

26. What separates extracellular fluid from intracellular fluid?

27. What separates interstitial fluid from the plasma?

MOVEMENT ACROSS MEMBRANES
28. What two properties of a molecule determine whether it can diffuse across a membrane?

29. If a molecule cannot move into a cell, we say that the cell is _____ to the molecule.

30. What is the difference between active transport and passive transport?

Diffusion Uses Only the Energy of Molecular Movement
31. Define diffusion. (Fig. 5-15)

32. List seven properties of diffusion.

Lipophilic Molecules Can Diffuse Through the Phospholipid Bilayer
33. List the factors that influence the rate of simple diffusion of molecules across the phospholipid bilayer. For each factor, if it were to increases in magnitude, would the rate of diffusion increase or decrease? (Fig. 5-16)

34. Fick's Law describes simple diffusion. (Fig. 5-16) Write the mathematical expression for Fick's Law in words:

        diffusion rate $\propto$

35. Do ions obey the rules for simple diffusion? Explain.

Carrier-Mediated Transport Exhibits Saturation, Specificity, and Competition
36. What is the relationship between mediated transport, facilitated diffusion, and active transport?

37. Distinguish between a cotransporter, a symport protein, and an antiport protein. (Fig. 5-17)

Specificity
38. Describe specificity as it relates to carrier-mediated transport.

Competition
39. Describe competition as it relates to carrier-mediated transport. (Fig. 5-18)

40. What is the difference between a competitor for a transport protein and a competitive inhibitor? (Fig. 5-19)

Saturation
41. Describe saturation as it relates to carrier-mediated transport. (Fig. 5-20)

42. What is transport maximum?

Facilitated Diffusion Is Diffusion That Uses Membrane Proteins
43. How is facilitated diffusion similar to simple diffusion? (Fig. 5-21)

44. How is facilitated diffusion different from simple diffusion?

45. How does the cell manage equilibrium? (Fig. 5-22)

Active Transport Requires the Input of Energy from ATP
46. How does active transport differ from facilitated diffusion?

47. How is active transport similar to facilitated diffusion?

Primary Active Transport
48. Describe and give an example of primary active transport (Fig. 5-23, 5-24; Table 5-3).

Secondary Active Transport
49. Describe and give an example of secondary active transport. (Fig. 5-25; Table 5-4)

50. How does secondary active transport differ from primary active transport? (Fig. 5-26)

51. How does secondary active transport differ from facilitated diffusion?

Vesicles Move Large Molecules Across Membranes
52. What distinguishes molecules that move by vesicular transport from molecules that move by mediated transport?

Phagocytosis, Endocytosis, (Receptor-mediated endocytosis, Potocytosis and caveolae), Exocytosis
53. Compare phagocytosis to endocytosis. (Fig. 5-27)

54. What is the difference between pinocytosis and receptor-mediated endocytosis? (Fig. 5-28)

55. What role do clathrin-coated pits play in receptor-mediated endocytosis?

56. Explain the process of membrane recycling.

57. What is potocytosis, and how is it different from receptor-mediated endocytosis?

58. Describe or diagram the steps of exocytosis and give some examples of molecules released by this method. (Fig. 5-26)

Molecules Entering or Leaving the Body Must Cross an Epithelium

59. What distinguishes the apical membrane from basolateral membrane of a transporting epithelium? (Fig. 5-29)

60. Why are transporting epithelial cells said to be *polarized*?

61. Contrast absorption and secretion.

Transepithelial Transport Using Membrane Proteins

62. Name the three transport systems involved in transepithelial transport of glucose. (Fig. 5-30)

63. Where does the Na^+-glucose symporter get the energy to move glucose against its concentration gradient?

64. Why must ion concentrations be so tightly regulated in these cells?

Transcytosis and Vesicular Transport

65. Describe or diagram transcytosis and vesicular transport. (Fig. 5-31)

66. What kinds of molecules are likely to move by transcytosis?

DISTRIBUTION OF WATER AND SOLUTES IN THE BODY
✓ IP Nervous I: The Membrane Potential

67. What is meant by the terminology *selectively permeable*?

The Body Is Mostly Water

68. Name the three body compartments.

69. Which compartment contains the most water?

70. What relative percentage of the total body water can be found in each body compartment?

Living Cells Use Energy to Maintain a State of Chemical and Electrical Disequilibrium

71. Explain what is meant by *a state of chemical disequilibrium in the body*. Include relative ion concentrations. (Fig. 5-33)

72. Is chemical disequilibrium maintained passively or actively?

The Body Is in Osmotic Equilibrium
73. Is water in a state of disequilibrium in the body?

74. Distinguish between osmosis, osmotic pressure, osmotic equilibrium, osmolarity, and osmolality.

Osmolarity Describes the Number of Particles in Solution
75. Sulfuric acid, H_2SO_4, dissociates into three ions when placed in water. What is the osmolarity of a 1 mM solution of sulfuric acid?

76. Contrast osmolarity and osmolality.

Comparing Osmolarities of Two Solutions
77. If solution A has more particles per liter than solution B, then A is said to be _____ osmotic to solution B, and solution B is said to be _____ osmotic to solution A.

78. How does this apply to water movement? Can you predict water movement based on relative osmolarities? Why or why not?

The Tonicity of a Solution Describes How the Size of a Cell Would Change If It Were Placed in the Solution
79. Compare osmolarity and tonicity.

80. Compare penetrating solutes to nonpenetrating solutes.

81. Solution C has 100 mosmoles/L and solution D has 200 mosmoles/L. Can we describe the tonicities of these two solutions relative to each other? Explain your reasoning.

82. What determines the tonicity of a solution relative to a cell? (Fig. 5-35)

83. How can a solution isosmotic to a cell be hypotonic?

⊙ *HELPFUL HINT: To remember what happens to a cell in hypotonic solutions versus hypertonic solutions, look at the letter directly preceding the "t" in each word. For hypotonic, the "o" can be a visual reminder that cells swell in hypotonic solutions. The "r" in hypertonic can be a visual reminder that cells shrink in hypertonic solutions.* (Table 5-8)

The Body Is in a State of Electrical Disequilibrium

84. List the major intracellular ions and the major extracellular ions. (Fig. 5-33)

85. Define electrical disequilbrium.

Electrical Signals are Generated in Many Types of Cells

86. Describe the law of conservation of electric charges.

87. What distinguishes a conductor from an insulator? Which of these terms describes the cell membrane?

The Cell Membrane Allows Separation of Electrical Charge in the Body

88. What forces create the electrical disequilibrium that exists between the intracellular and extracellular compartments? (Fig. 5-36)

89. What is an electrochemical gradient?

90. Define the resting membrane potential difference (or just membrane potential) of a cell. (Fig. 5-36)

91. If the membrane potential of a cell is -70 mV and the extracellular fluid is assumed to have a charge of zero millivolts, what happened to the "extra" positive charges that must exist according to the law of conservation of electric charges?

92. If a cell were freely permeable to all charged molecules, would it have a resting membrane potential? Explain.

The Resting Membrane Potential Is Due Mostly to Potassium

93. What is the equilibrium potential for an ion? (Figs. 5-38, 5-39, 5-40)

94. Which ion contributes most to the resting potential of most cells? Why?

95. Why is the Na^+-K^+-ATPase considered to be an electrogenic pump?

Changes in Ion Permeability Change the Membrane Potential

96. What two factors influence the cell's membrane potential?

Terminology for Changes in Membrane Potential

97. Explain the difference between the terms depolarized, hyperpolarized, and repolarized. (Fig. 5-41)

Changes in Ion Permeability Change Membrane Potential

98. Which four ions contribute the most to changes in membrane potential?

99. To change the membrane potential by 100 mV, how many K^+ must enter or leave the cell?

INTEGRATED MEMBRANE PROCESSES: INSULIN SECRETION

100. Do only nerve and muscle cells exhibit communication via electrical changes?

101. Describe why insulin secretion from pancreatic beta cells is a good example of integrated membrane processes, including membrane potential. Give an overview of the cellular mechanism for insulin secretion and discuss the roles played by the membrane potential and the various membrane components. (Fig. 5-42)

TALK THE TALK

active transport	antiport	apical
atherosclerosis	basolateral	cell (plasma) membrane
chemical disequilibrium	chemical equilibrium	chemical gradient
chemically gated channel	cholesterol	clathrin-coated pit
competitive inhibitor	constitutive process	co-transporter
diffusion	electrical gradient	electrochemical gradient
electrogenic pump	endocytosis	endosome
equilibrium	equilibrium potential	exocytosis
extracellular fluid	facilitated diffusion	fluid mosaic model
freezing point depression	gated channels	glycocalyx
hyperosmotic	hypertonic	hyposmotic
hypotonic	impermeable	integral proteins
interstitial fluid	isosmotic	isotonic
liposome	low-density lipoprotein	mechanically gated channel
mediated transport	membrane recycling	membrane-spanning protein
micelle	nonpenetrating solute	osmolarity
osmosis	osmotic equilibrium	osmotic pressure
passive transport	penetrating solute	peripheral proteins
permeable	phagocytosis	phagosome
phospholipid bilayer	pinocytosis	plasma
polarized	primary active transport	receptor-mediated endocytosis
resting membrane potential	restricted diffusion	saturation
secondary active transport	selectively permeable	sodium-potassium ATPase
specificity	symport	tonicity
transcytosis	transepithelial transport	vesicular transport
voltage-gated channel		

QUANTITATIVE PHYSIOLOGY

Volumes of distribution

The techniques by which the volumes of the body compartments are determined provides us with interesting insight into experimental design. The determination of a volume of liquid can be estimated using a **dilution technique**. There are several requirements for this experiment. (1) The volume to be measured must be well-mixed, so that any marker that is given will distribute evenly throughout the compartment. (2) The marker must be able to be measured. If the system is a living organism, the marker must also be non-toxic, not metabolized or excreted, and must distribute only into the compartment being measured.

To carry out a dilution experiment, a known amount of marker in a known volume is administered. It is allowed to distribute, then a sample of the compartment liquid is removed and analyzed for its marker content. Because the concentration of marker in the sample is the same as the concentration throughout the compartment, the following ratio is used to calculate the compartment volume:

$$\frac{\text{amount marker in sample (known)}}{\text{volume of sample (known)}} \quad = \quad \frac{\text{total amount of marker (known)}}{\text{total volume of compartment (unknown)}}$$

For example, 1 gram of dye is put into a giant vat of water. The dye is stirred until it is evenly distributed throughout the vat. A 1 mL sample of water is taken out, analyzed, and found to contain 0.02 mg of dye. What is the volume of the vat?

0.02 mg dye/1 mL = 1000 mg dye/ χ mL

χ = 1000 mg dye • 1 mL/0.02 mg dye

χ = 50,000 mL or 50 L

The dye distributed into a volume of 50 L. For this reason, the volumes calculated by this method are known as *volumes of distribution*.

The determination of body compartment volumes in humans has been done using a variety of markers. The marker must be restricted to the compartment being measured in order to give accurate results. **Total body water** has been estimated using water with radioactive isotopes of hydrogen. Both deuterium oxide (D_2O or heavy water) and tritium oxide can be used. Calculating the volume of distribution for the **extracellular fluid (ECF) volume** requires a molecule that can move freely between the plasma and the interstitial fluid but that cannot enter the cells. Sucrose, the disaccharide commonly known as table sugar, fits this requirement as does a molecule called *inulin*. Inulin is a plant polysaccharide extracted from the roots of dahlias. It is not metabolized by humans but is excreted in the urine, so this must be taken into account when estimating ECF volume. The final compartment that can be directly measured is the **plasma volume**. This measurement requires a large molecule that distributes in the plasma but cannot cross the leaky epithelium to the interstitial fluid. Since endogenous plasma proteins meet this requirement, researchers found a dye, Evans blue, that binds to plasma proteins and therefore distributes only in the plasma.

There are no markers for the interstitial fluid and the intracellular compartment, but we have been able to accurately estimate those volumes as well. Using the information in the paragraph above, can you explain how to calculate interstitial fluid and the intracellular volumes? (Answer in appendix)

Volumes of distribution: interstitial volume = ECF - plasma;
ICF volume = total body water - ECF volume.

PRACTICE MAKES PERFECT

1. According to Einstein, the time required for a molecule to diffuse from point A to point B is proportional to the square of the distance. Fill in the table below and graph the relationship:

Distance	Time
1 mm	
2 mm	
3 mm	
4 mm	

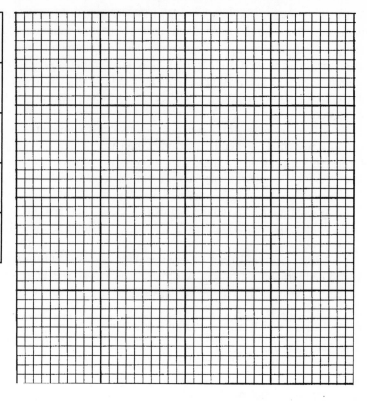

2. A person with pneumonia has an accumulation of fluid in her lungs. This has an effect similar to that of increasing membrane thickness by a factor of 2. How does this affect the rate of diffusion? Give a quantitative and qualitative answer. Assume that all other parameters do not change.

3. Complete the table below.

METHOD	MOVEMENT RELATIVE TO CONCENTRATION GRADIENT	ENERGY SOURCE	WHAT AFFECTS RATE?	THROUGH MEMBRANE BILAYER OR THROUGH PROTEIN TRANSPORTER?	EXHIBITS SPECIFICITY ?	EXHIBITS COMPETITION ?	EXHIBITS SATURATION ?	EXAMPLES
SIMPLE DIFFUSION								
FACILITATED DIFFUSION								
PRIMARY ACTIVE TRANSPORT								
SECONDARY ACTIVE TRANSPORT								

4. Match the transporter with all the descriptions that apply.

_____ Na^+-K^+-ATPase   A. symport

_____ Na^+-glucose transporter   B. antiport

_____ Ca^{2+}-ATPase   C. active transport

_____ Na^+-K^+-2 Cl^- -transporter   D. cotransport

_____ Na^+-H^+ -transporter   E. secondary active transport

5. After completing physiology, you become so fascinated by biology that you go on to become a world-famous zoologist. In the year 2045 you are part of a scientific expedition to investigate newly discovered life forms on the planet Zwxik in another solar system. You are assigned to study a single-cell organism found in the aqueous swamps of Zwxik. In one of your first studies using a radioisotope of calcium, you observe that calcium moves freely in and out of the cell during daylight hours but is unable to get into or out of the cell in the dark. What is your hypothesis about how calcium is crossing the cell membrane in this organism? Be as specific and as scientific as possible.

6. In the compartments below, diagram the osmotic, chemical, and electrical equilibrium/disequilibrium that exists in the living body. For ions, use large symbols where concentrations are high and small symbols where concentrations are low.

Key: Na^+, K^+, Ca^{2+}, Cl^-, proteins, osmolarity (mOsm), plasma, interstitial fluid, cells

impermeable Na^+/K^+ -ATPase

8. The addition of solute to water disrupts the hydrogen bonds of water and interferes with the crystalline lattice formation of ice. As a result, the water will not freeze until cooled below the freezing point for pure water, a phenomenon known as freezing point depression. For an ideal solution, its freezing point will drop 1.86° Celsius for each osmole of solute/liter of water. A plasma sample from a patient shows a freezing point depression of 0.55° C. What is the osmolarity of this patient's plasma? What is the intracellular osmolarity in this patient?

9. You put 5 grams of glucose into a giant beaker of water and stir. You then take a 1 mL sample and analyze it for glucose. If the 1 mL sample contains 1 mg of glucose, how much liquid is in the beaker?

10. You are monitoring the absorption of a new drug, Curesall, across the intestine of a rat *in vitro*. After numerous experiments, you get data that give you the graph below. The only difference between experiments A and B is that in experiment A, the apical solution contains 150 mM Na^+ and in experiment B the apical solution contains 50 mM Na^+. What conclusion(s) can you draw about Curesall absorption based on the graph? Based on what you have learned about different kinds of transport, hypothesize about the type of transporter that carries Curesall.

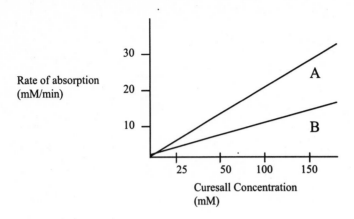

11. What is the osmolarity of a 0.9% NaCl solution? Assume complete dissociation of NaCl. (To review molar solutions, and percent solutions, see p. 26-27 of the text. For atomic weights, see pg. 16-18 of text.)

12. What is the osmolarity of a 5% dextrose (= glucose, $C_6H_{12}O_6$) solution?

13. An artificial cell with zero glucose inside is placed in a solution of glucose. The amount of glucose inside the cell is measured at different times. The two graphs below show the results of the experiments.

GRAPH #1:

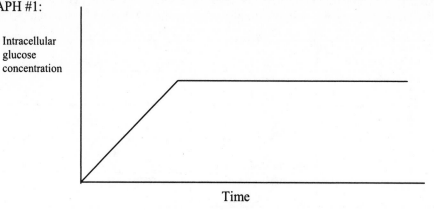

Graph #2

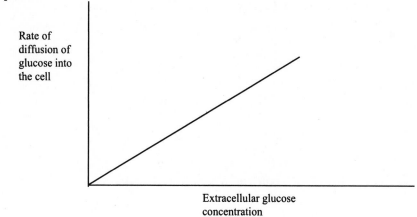

a. In what units might the rate of diffusion be measured? _____

b. Is glucose moving into the artificial cell by diffusion or by protein-mediated transport, or can you tell from these graphs? If it is mediated transport, is it active or passive?

c. Why does the line in graph #1 level off?

14. For each row in the table below, assume that the row represents two compartments separated by a membrane that is freely permeable to water but impermeable to solutes. Show which way water will move by osmosis for each row by drawing in an arrow in the direction of water movement in the column labeled "MEMBRANE." In the last column, tell the osmolarity of solution A relative to solution B.

SOLUTION A	MEMBRANE	SOLUTION B	OSMOLARITY OF A RELATIVE TO B
100 mM glucose		100 mM urea	
200 mM glucose		100 mM NaCl	
300 mOsM NaCl		300 mOsM glucose	
300 mM glucose		200 mM CaCl₂	

15. A one liter intravenous infusion of 300 mOsM NaCl is administered during a 15 minute period to a person whose starting osmolarity was 300 mOsM. What effect will this infusion have on the volume and osmolarity of the extracellular and intracellular fluid compartments? Explain your answer.

16. A red blood cell whose internal osmolarity is 300 osmol/L is placed into a solution that has a composition of 200 osmol/L NaCl and 100 osmol/L of urea.

This solution is _____ osmotic to the cell. This solution is _____ tonic to the cell.

Draw a fully labeled graph showing the volume change of the cell from the time it is placed into the solution (at the arrow) until it reaches equilibrium.

17. A person comes into the emergency room dehydrated after working out in the summer sun. His ECF volume is 13 liters and his ECF osmolarity is 340 MOsM. (Ignore ICF in this problem)

   a. How many milliosmoles of solute are in his ECF when he comes in? _____

   b. An intravenous (IV) infusion of 1 liter of 160 mOsM NaCl is given. How many millimoles of solute are in the IV?

   c. Assuming that no water or solute move out of the ECF, calculate the new ECF volume and osmolarity after the man has been given the IV.

18. Assume that a membrane which is permeable to Na^+ but not to Cl^- separates two compartments. Two different sodium chloride solutions are placed in the compartments. The concentration of NaCl on side 1 is 0.3 M, while the NaCl solution on side 2 is 2 M. In which direction will ion movement occur? Explain. Will a membrane potential difference develop across the membrane? Explain.

19. If you are told that the extracellular K^+ concentration has increased from 2 mEq/L to 3 mEq/L, does this also mean that the extracellular fluid has become more positive? What happens to the resting membrane potential of a liver cell when the extracellular K^+ concentration increases? Explain.

20. You are doing an experiment and have an intracellular recording electrode stuck into a liver cell. The resting membrane potential is -70 mV relative to the outside of the cell. At the arrowhead you add ouabain to the extracellular fluid bathing the cell. On the graph below draw what will happen to the resting membrane potential of the cell over time. Write an explanation of the forces at work in this situation.

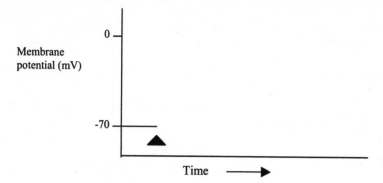

BEYOND THE PAGES

FURTHER EXPLORATIONS

✯ Interactive animations of osmosis, diffusion, and the Nernst equation can be found at
http://cweb.middlebury.edu/cr/labbook/

✯ Try Google searches (www.google.com) for the following topics:

Nernst – This will bring up pages with the biography of Walther Nernst as well as pages with problems, simulators, and other interactive Nernst equation goodies.

IV fluids – This will bring up pages with clinical information about the use of IV fluids.

 Articles and books

Cellular secretion: It's in the pits. American Scientist 85: 123-124, Mar-Apr, 1997.

Potocytosis: Sequestration and transport of small molecules by caveolae. Science 255: 410-411, 24 Jan 1992.

Caveolae caveat (secrets of cell caveolae explored). Discover 16:91, Jan 1995.

A is for ...: Caveolae. Science & Medicine, May/June 1995.

Caveolae and caveolins. Current Opinion in Cell Biology 8:542-548, Aug. 1996.

And still they are moving.... dynamic properties of caveolae. FEBS Letters 389: 52-52, 24 Jun 1996.

Cellular mechanisms of phagocytosis (a series of six articles). Trends in Cell Biology 5:89-119, 5 Mar. 1995.

Liposomes revisited. Science 267: 1275-1276, 3 Mar 1995.

The Mammalian Facultative Glucose Transporter Family. News in Physiological Sciences 10: 67-70, Apr. 1995.

Epithelial sodium channels: Their role in disease. News in Physiological Sciences 11: 102-103, April 1996.

Patch-clamp recording of ion channels. News in Physiological Sciences 5: 155-158, August 1990.

Steps to the Na^+-K^+ pump and Na^+-K^+-ATPase (1939-1962). News in Physiological Sciences 10: 184-188, August 1995.

Epithelial secretion driven by anions other than chloride. News in Physiological Sciences 8: 91-93, April 1993.

Channelopathies: Their contribution to our knowledge about voltage-gated ion channels. News in Physiological Sciences 12: 105-112, June 1997.

What is new about the structure of the epithelial Na^+ channel? News in Physiological Sciences 11: 195-201, Oct. 1996.

Ion channels and human genetic diseases. News in Physiological Sciences 11: 36-42, Feb. 1996.

Signal transduction pathways in caveolae. Science & Medicine 7(1), 2000 Jan/Feb.

6

COMMUNICATION, INTEGRATION, AND HOMEOSTASIS

SUMMARY

The key questions whose answers you should be able to discuss after reading this chapter:

✓ What are the forms of communication in the body, and when are they used?
✓ What important role do receptors play?
✓ What are the different signal transduction pathways?
✓ What is homeostasis and how is it maintained?
✓ What are the patterns in communication/response loops?

For a society of distinct individuals to exist, its members must learn to communicate effectively. The cells in a multi-cellular organism comprise such a society, and they have evolved effective and efficient means of communication so that each component can do its job correctly and respond to changes in the environment. This chapter introduces the concepts of cellular communication and homeostasis, and provides patterns by which you can organize more detailed information that will be presented later for each specific physiological system. In other words, learn the patterns presented in this chapter, and use them to make files in your mental filing cabinet under which you can store specific information later.

Communication in the body is either electrical or chemical. Electrical communication is limited to nerves and muscles, while chemical communication is an activity in which all cells participate to some extent. Local communication is accomplished by paracrines, autocrines, and cytokines that work close to the cells that secrete them. Long-distance communication is accomplished by any combination of the following: hormones, neurohormones, cytokines, or electrical impulses. Chemical communication is limited by diffusion, as increasing distance increases the time required for action. Hormones (and sometimes cytokines) are secreted into the blood and carried to all parts of the body, but ultimately have to diffuse to their target cells. Therefore, electrical impulses are a faster form of long-distance communication (milliseconds-minutes) than hormones (minutes-hours). However, electrical communication is short-lived, while chemical communication can have long lasting effects.

A cellular response to a signal depends more on the receptor than on the signal. For instance, different cells can have different responses to the same signal depending on the receptor type (isoform) present. There are four major categories of membrane receptors: ligand-gated ion channels, integrins linked to the cytoskeleton, receptor-enzymes, G protein-coupled receptors. In the latter three categories, ligand binding causes receptors to turn on enzymatic machinery that ultimately directs the cellular response. If the receptor is on the cell membrane, it turns on signal transduction machinery to amplify the signal and relay it to the appropriate organelles via second messengers. Signal ligands are called first messengers, and products of the transduction machinery are called second messengers.

If the receptor is in the cytoplasm, then no signal transduction machinery is employed, but enzymes are still activated to direct the cellular response—often transcription of new gene products. In addition, receptors can be down-regulated or up-regulated depending on a given situation.

Homeostasis means maintaining a "similar condition" despite changes in physiological parameters. Walter B. Cannon outlined four postulates regarding the properties of homeostasis. The body uses a system of local control and reflex control pathways to maintain homeostasis. Local control depends on paracrines, autocrines, and cytokines. Reflex control pathways handle widespread or systemic challenges, and these reflex pathways are composed of nervous, endocrine and cytokine components (starting to look familiar?).

Reflex pathways are further broken down into response loops and feedback loops. Response loops contain the following steps: stimulus, receptor, afferent pathway, integrating center, efferent pathway, effector, response (cellular and systemic). This is an important pattern to learn, and the various endocrine and/or nervous system combinations involved serve as good file headings for future information (Fig. 6-30, p. 199). Feedback loops can be either negative feedback loops or positive feedback loops. Negative feedback loops turn off the response that created them, and are therefore homeostatic. Positive feedback loops continue the response that created them, are therefore not homeostatic, and must be controlled from outside the response loop. Feedforward control responses can anticipate changes.

TEACH YOURSELF THE BASICS

CELL-TO-CELL COMMUNICATION

1. List the three basic methods of cell-to-cell communication.

Gap Junctions Transfer Chemical and Electrical Signals Directly Between Cells

2. What kinds of signals pass through gap junctions? (Fig. 6-1a) [∫ p. 64]

3. What proteins create gap junctions?

4. Where do you find gap junctions?

Contact-Dependent Signals Require Cell-to-Cell Contact

5. Give examples of contact-dependent signals.

Paracrines and Autocrines Are Chemical Signals Distributed by Diffusion

6. How do chemical signals secreted by cells spread to adjacent cells?

7. Paracrine and autocrine communication is limited to (long or short?) distances [∫ p. 124-137]

8. Distinguish between paracrines and autocrines. (Fig. 6-1c)

Electrical Signals, Hormones, and Neurohormones Carry Out Long-Distance Communication
9. What are hormones?

10. How do hormones reach their target cells?

11. Why don't all cells react to all hormones? (Fig. 6-2a)

12. In the nervous system, what kinds of signals are used to transmit information?

13. What is the difference between a neuromodulator, a neurotransmitter and a neurohormone? (Fig. 6-2b,c)

Cytokines Act as Both Local and Long-Distance Signals
14. How are cytokines different from hormones?

15. What kinds of cell functions do cytokines control?

SIGNAL PATHWAYS (Fig. 6-3)
16. Why do some cells respond to a chemical signal while other cells ignore it? (Fig. 6-4)

17. What four steps do all signal pathways share in common?

Receptors Are Located Inside the Cell or on the Cell Membrane
18. How do chemical signals interact with receptors?

19. In what part(s) of a cell are receptors found? (Fig. 6-4)

20. List some differences between lipophilic signal molecules and lipophobic signal molecules.

21. List the four major groups of membrane receptors. (Fig. 6-5)

Membrane Proteins Facilitate Signal Transduction
22. What is signal transduction? (Fig. 6-6)

Describe signal amplification. (Fig. 6-7)

23. Briefly recount or diagram the basic steps in signal transduction. (Fig. 6-8)

24. What is a second messenger?

25. How are signal transduction pathways a cascade? (Fig. 6-9)

26. Take some time to familiarize yourself with the common signal transduction pathways presented in Table 6-1 and common second messengers in Table 6-2.

Receptor-Enzymes Have Protein Kinase or Guanylyl Cyclase Activity
27. How do receptor-enzymes work? (Fig. 6-5)

28. What are two types of enzymes typically found in receptor-enzymes? (Fig. 6-10)

Most Signal Transduction Uses G Proteins
29. Briefly describe the G protein-coupled receptors.

30. What types of ligands bind to G protein-coupled receptors?

31. How are G proteins activated, and what are two possible cellular actions that activated G proteins might bring about?

Adenylyl Cyclase-cAMP Is the Signal Transduction System for Many Lipophobic Hormones
32. Outline or diagram the G protein-coupled adenylyl cyclase-cAMP system. (Fig. 6-11) Identify the amplifier enzyme and the second messenger.

G Protein-Linked Receptors Also Use Lipid-Derived Second Messengers
33. Outline or diagram the G protein-linked phospholipase C (PL-C) signal pathway. (Fig. 6-12) Identify the amplifier enzyme and second messengers.

34. What cellular actions do the lipid-derived second messengers initiate?

Integrin Receptors Transfer Information from the Extracellular Matrix

35. What are integrins and what do they do? (Fig. 6-3)

36. How do they participate in signal transduction?

The Most Rapid Signal Pathways Change Ion Flow Through Channels

37. What are the simplest receptors?

38. Describe how this type of receptor produces a cellular response. (Fig. 6-13)

NOVEL SIGNAL PATHWAYS

Calcium Is an Important Intracellular Signal

39. How does extracellular calcium enter the cell?

40. Where is intracellular calcium stored?

41. Outline or diagram a Ca^{2+}-based signal pathway. How do calcium ions exert their effect, and what are some of those calcium-related cellular effects? (Fig. 6-15)

Gases Are Ephemeral Signal Molecules

42. What is nitric oxide, and how does it bring about a cellular response?

43. How is NO synthesized in tissues?

44. What are some of the effects brought about by NO?

45. How does CO exert signal effects?

Some Lipids Are Important Paracrines

46. What are orphan receptors?

47. What are eicosanoids, and why are they important?

48. How are eicosanoid signal molecules made? (Fig. 6-16)

49. Name two major groups of paracrines derived from arachadonic acid. Give examples of their actions.

50. How are NSAIDs related to lipid-derived paracrines?

MODULATION OF SIGNAL PATHWAYS

51. For most signal molecules, the target cell response is determined by _____
rather than _____.

Receptors Exhibit Saturation, Specificity, and Competition

52. Why do receptors exhibit characteristics of specificity, competition, and saturation? [Review these phenomena in enzymes (Ch 4) and in transporters (Ch 5).]

Specificity and Competition: Multiple Ligands For One Receptor

53. Use the given example of norepinephrine and epinephrine to describe specificity and competition for membrane receptors.

Agonists and Antagonists (Fig. 6-14)

54. (Agonists/Antagonists?) are:
   • Molecules or drugs that mimic normal ligand
   • Bind to and activate receptors

55. (Agonists/Antagonists?) are:
   • Molecules or drugs that mimic normal ligand
   • Bind and block ligand from binding so that the receptor never gets turned on

Multiple Receptors for One Ligand

56. What are isoforms? What is their significance?

57. Give one example of isoforms found in the body. (Fig. 6-18)

Up- and Down-Regulation of Receptors Enables Cells to Modulate Cellular Response

58. What is saturation, and what causes it?

59. What causes down-regulation of a cell's receptors?

60. In down-regulation, the number of receptors (increases/decreases?) or their binding affinity (increases/decreases?).

61. When a cell down-regulates its receptors, what happens to its responsiveness to the ligand that binds to that receptor?

62. Up-regulation of receptors (increases/decreases?) the number of receptors and (enhances/lessens?) the cell's response.

Cells Must Be Able to Terminate Signal Pathways
63. What are some ways in which a cell is able to terminate signal pathways? Give examples.

Many Diseases and Drugs Target the Proteins of Signal Transduction
64. Give an example of a disease involving abnormal receptors. Identify the abnormal receptor. (Table 6-3)

HOMEOSTASIS
65. Define homeostasis. [∫ p. 6]

The Development of the Concept of Homeostasis
66. What role did Claude Bernard play in the development of the concept of homeostasis?

67. What are some parameters under physiological control?

Cannon's Postulates Describe Regulated Variables and Physiological Control Systems
68. List Walter B. Cannon's four postulates.

CONTROL PATHWAYS: RESPONSE AND FEEDBACK LOOPS
69. Name the three components common to homeostasis.

Homeostasis May Be Maintained by Local or Long-Distance Pathways (Fig. 6-21)
70. What is a reflex control pathway?

71. What role do cytokines play in long-distance reflex pathways?

72. What are two other control systems involved with long-distance pathways?

Local Control
- Involves paracrines or autocrines
- Response is restricted to where change took place

73. Give an example of local control:

Reflex control
74. A reflex pathway can be broken into two parts. Name them:

75. List the three main components of a response loop.

76. Fill in the missing terms: Stimulus $\rightarrow$ _____ $\rightarrow$ _____ pathway $\rightarrow$ _____ center $\rightarrow$ _____ pathway $\rightarrow$ _____ $\rightarrow$ response

Sensory receptors
77. Give two different meanings for the word receptor. (Fig. 6-23)

78. What is the threshold of a receptor?

Afferent pathway
79. An afferent pathway carries information away from a/an _____ to a/an _____.

Integrating center
80. What is the role of an integrating center?

81. Where are the integrating centers for nervous reflexes?

82. Where are the integrating centers for endocrine reflexes?

Efferent pathway
83. An efferent pathway carries information away from a/an _____ to a/an _____.

84. In the nervous system, the efferent pathway is a/an _____ signal.

85. In endocrine reflexes, the efferent pathway is a/an _____ signal.

86. How are efferent signals named or described in nervous and endocrine pathways?

Effectors
87. Define and give some examples of effectors.

Responses
88. Distinguish between and give examples of cellular and systemic responses.

Response Loops Begin with a Stimulus and End with a Response
89. Reiterate the seven steps of a response loop. (Fig. 6-24)

90. Compare tonic control to antagonistic control. (Fig. 6-19, 6-20)

Setpoints Can Be Varied
91. Distinguish between acclimatization and acclimation.

Feedback Loops Modulate the Response Loop
92. What is the purpose of a feedback loop?

93. When is a reflex completed, becoming a feedback loop?

Negative Feedback Loops Are Homeostatic
94. Negative feedback (opposes/reinforces?) the original stimulus. Most feedback loops are negative. (Fig. 6-26a)

95. Negative feedback loops _____ the physiological parameter being regulated.

Positive Feedback Loops Are Not Homeostatic
96. Positive feedback loops (oppose/reinforce?) the original stimulus (Fig. 6-26b).

97. Give an example of a positive feedback loop. (Fig. 6-27)

98. What shuts off a positive feedback loop?

Feedforward Control Allows the Body to Anticipate Change and Maintain Stability
99. Give an example of feedforward control.

100. Feedforward control (opposes/enhances?) homeostasis.

Biological Rhythms Result from Changes in the Setpoint
101. What is a circadian rhythm? (Fig. 6-28)

102. What is the adaptive significance of functions that vary with a circadian rhythm?

103. Name some body functions that exhibit circadian rhythms.

Control Systems Vary in Their Speed and Specificity
104. What is a neuroendocrine reflex? (Fig. 6-29, 6-30; Table 6-4)

Specificity
105. Compare the specificity of nervous and endocrine control. How is the specificity of the reflex determined in each type of reflex?

Nature of the Signal
106. The nervous system uses (chemical / electrical / both chemical and electrical?) signals.

107. Electrical signals travel _____ distances; chemical signals travel _____ distances.

108. The endocrine system uses (chemical / electrical / both chemical and electrical?) signals. (Fig. 6-30, pattern 6)

Speed
109. Nervous reflexes are much (faster / slower?) than endocrine reflexes.
[◎ Review: diffusion principles, p. 134-137]

Duration of Action
110. Nervous control is of much (shorter/longer?) duration than endocrine control.

111. Short-term functions tend to be under (nervous/endocrine?) control, while long-term functions tend to be under (nervous/endocrine?) control.

Coding for Stimulus Intensity
112. Compare how stimulus intensity is coded in the nervous and endocrine systems.

113. Complex Reflexes Have Several Integrating Centers (Fig. 6-30; Table 6-5)
114. In endocrine reflexes (pattern 6), the integrating center is _____ and the efferent pathway is the _____.

115. In nervous reflexes (pattern 1), the integrating center is _____ and the efferent pathway is the _____.

116. In neuroendocrine reflexes (patterns 2, 3, 4, 5), the afferent neuron leads to a/an _____.
The efferent pathway(s) is/are _____.

117. Take some time to draw out the different reflexes for yourself. Color-code the components and learn the distinctions between the reflex types.

TALK THE TALK

acclimation	acclimatization	adenosine 3', 5'-cyclic monophosphate (cAMP)
adenylate cyclase	afferent pathway	agonist
alpha (α) adrenergic receptor	amplifier enzyme	arachidonic acid
autocrine	beta (β) adrenergic receptor	biorhythm
cascade	central receptor	circadian rhythm
Claude Bernard	connexin	contact-dependent signals
cyclic AMP (cAMP)	cyclic GMP(cGMP)	cycloxygenase (COX)
cytokine	diacylglycerol (DAG)	down-regulation
drug tolerance	effector	efferent pathway
epinephrine (adrenaline)	feedback loop	feedforward control
first messenger	G protein	gap junction
guanosine 3', 5'-cyclic monophosphate (cGMP)	guanosine diphosphate (GDP)	guanosine triphosphate (GTP)
guanylate cyclase	histamine	homeostasis
hormone	inositol triphosphate (IP$_3$)	integrating center
leukotriene	lipoxygenase	local control
negative feedback	neurocrine	neuroendocrine reflex
neurohormone	neuromodulator	neuron
neurotransmitter	nitric oxide (NO)	nitric oxide synthase (NOS)
orphan receptor	paracrine	parameter
pathophysiology	pepsin	peripheral receptor
phospholipase A$_2$ (PLA2)	phospholipase C	positive feedback loop
prostaglandin	prostanoid	protein kinase
receptor	reflex control pathway	response loop
second messenger	sensitivity	signal amplification
signal transduction	stimulus	syncytium
target cell	threshold	tonic control
tyrosine kinase	up-regulation	Walter B. Cannon

PRACTICE MAKES PERFECT

1. Describe the basic ways cells communicate with each other. Which modes are faster?

2. Why are there different isoforms and subtypes of receptors? Is the number of receptors on a cell constant?

3. What is the advantage of having a cascade of events as opposed to having just a single event drive a response?

4. Would you expect the secretion of growth hormone to be regulated through negative feedback? Explain.

MAPS

1. Use the following terms to design a map or flow chart describing the events that are associated with signal transduction and the activation of second messenger systems. You may add any terms that you deem necessary. You may draw a cell and associate the terms with different components of the cell (a structure/function map).

adenylate cyclase	amplifier enzyme
cAMP	cGMP
DAG	first messenger
GDP	GTP
guanylate cyclase	hormone
IP$_3$	membrane receptor
phospholipase C	protein kinase
second messenger	target cell
tyrosine kinase	integrin receptors
receptor-enzymes	G protein-coupled receptors
calcium	calmodulin
nitric oxide (NO)	

2. Use the following terms to design a map or flow chart describing the events that are associated with reflex control pathways. You may add any terms you feel are necessary to complete the map.

afferent pathway   effector
efferent pathway   integrating center
negative feedback   receptor
response   sensory receptor
stimulus   threshold
tonic control   antagonistic control

BEYOND THE PAGES

FURTHER EXPLORATIONS

Diseases caused by impaired communication among cells. Scientific American, March 1980.

Drugs by design. Scientific American, December 1993.

G proteins. Scientific American, July 1992.

Internal timekeeping. Science & Medicine, May/June 1996.

New clues found in circadian clocks. Science 276: 1030-1031. May 16, 1997.

Perspectives in imaging of second messengers. News in Physiological Sciences 11: 281-287, December 1996. Use of fluorescent indicator dyes to track second messenger activity. (http://nips.physiology.org)

Venom peptides as human pharmaceuticals. Science & Medicine, September/October 1997.

Cellular communication via gap junctions. Science & Medicine 7(2):18-27, 2000 Mar/Apr.

CHAPTER 7

INTRODUCTION TO THE ENDOCRINE SYSTEM

SUMMARY

Themes to look for in this chapter:

✓ Compare peptide, steroid, and amine hormones with regard to synthesis, storage, release, transport, and cellular mechanism of action.
✓ How are the anterior and posterior pituitary lobes different? What hormones does each lobe secrete?
✓ How are endocrine control pathways organized? What role does negative feedback play?
✓ What are the different types of hormone interactions?
✓ What factors are important for diagnosing endocrine pathologies?

This chapter focuses on the basic physiology of the endocrine system and its hormones. A hormone is defined here as a chemical, secreted by a cell or group of cells into the blood, that acts on a distant target and is effective at very low concentrations. Chemically, hormones fall into one of three classes: peptide, steroid, or amine. Generally, the three groups can be distinguished by how they are synthesized, stored and released; how they are transported in the blood; and the mechanisms by which they cause a cellular response. Hormones can interact with other hormones, and in doing so, alter cellular response. Three types of hormone interaction are discussed in this chapter: synergism, permissiveness, and antagonism. You should familiarize yourself with these distinctions and, as you did with the information in Chapter 6, use them to make mental file folders under which you will store more specific information later.

The release of hormones can be under multiple levels of control: classic hormones are under direct control of the parameter they regulate, but other hormones can have a multi-level control pathway. Those hormones that fall into the latter category represent the more complex response loops (those mental file folders from Chapter 6 are already coming in handy; review Figure 6-30.)

If a hormone causes the release of another hormone, that first hormone is called a trophic hormone. Most of the six hormones of the anterior pituitary are trophic hormones, and they are in turn controlled by trophic neurosecretory hormones of the hypothalamus. The hypothalamus and the pituitary communicate via the hypothalamic-hypophyseal portal system. Conversely, the posterior pituitary, which is derived of neural tissue, only releases two hormones – that are actually neurohormones synthesized in the hypothalamus. There are clear distinctions between the anterior and posterior pituitary; become well-acquainted with these differences.

You should also familiarize yourself with the concepts of control pathways (more mental file folders). Specifically, learn how negative feedback affects hormone release in a control pathway and how feedback factors into diagnosing and understanding an endocrine pathology (primary or secondary?). While studying pathologies, you will also need to grasp the concepts of hypersecretion, hyposecretion, up- and down-regulation, and abnormal tissue responsiveness.

TEACH YOURSELF THE BASICS

HORMONES

✓ IP Endocrine System: Endocrine System Review

1. Hormones control:

2. By doing what to their target cells?

Hormones Have Been Known Since Ancient Times
3. List the four classic steps for identifying an endocrine gland.

What Makes a Chemical a Hormone?
4. Define a hormone.

Hormones Are Secreted by a Cell or Group of Cells
5. What types of cells and tissues secrete hormones?

Hormones Are Secreted into the Blood
6. Define secretion.

7. What is an ectohormone?

8. What are pheromones? What do they do?

Hormones Are Transported to a Distant Target
9. When is the term "factor" used?

Hormones Exert Their Effect at Very Low Concentrations
10. Define nanomolar and picomolar.

11. Distinguish between the terms hormone, factor, and cytokine. Give examples of when the distinction becomes blurry.

Hormones Act by Binding to Receptors
12. What is meant by "cellular mechanism of action?"

Hormone Action Must Be Terminated
13. What happens to hormones in the bloodstream?

14. What is the half-life of a hormone?

15. How are hormones that have bound to target cells terminated?

THE CLASSIFICATION OF HORMONES

✓ **IP Endocrine System: Biochemistry, Secretion and Transport of Hormones**
✓ **IP Endocrine System: The Actions of Hormones on Target Cells**

16. REVIEW organelle function. Can you describe all the steps of protein synthesis, starting with transcription? [∫ pp. 53; 111-117]

17. List the three chemical classes of hormones (Table 7-1).

Most Hormones in the Body Are Peptides or Proteins

18. Peptide hormones are composed of _____.

19. Exclusion rule: If a hormone isn't a steroid or an amine, then it must be a peptide.

Peptide Hormone Synthesis, Storage, and Release (Fig. 7-3, 7-4)

20. Peptide hormones are synthesized where in the cell? _____

21. Explain the difference between the preprohormone, the prohormone, and the hormone. Where is each made? [∫ p. 117]

22. How are peptide hormones released from endocrine cells?

Post-Translational Modification of Prohormones

23. Name some of the post-translational modification scenarios that a hormone can undergo. (Fig. 7-4)

Transport in the Blood and Half-Life of Peptide Hormones

24. Peptide hormones are (lipophobic/lipophilic?) and therefore (will/ will not?) dissolve in plasma.

25. Describe the half-life of most peptide hormones.

Cellular Mechanism of Action of Peptide Hormones

26. Peptide hormones are (lipophobic/lipophilic?), so they have (intracellular/membrane?) receptors.

27. What is the target cell's response to hormone-receptor binding? (Fig. 7-5)

28. The target response time is (quick/slow?). Explain.

Steroid Hormones Are Derived from Cholesterol

29. List the tissues/organs from which steroid hormones are secreted.

Steroid Hormone Synthesis and Release

30. Steroid hormones are synthesized where in the cell?

31. Can steroid hormones be stored? Explain.

32. How are steroid hormones released from endocrine cells?

Transport in the Blood and Half-Life of Steroid Hormones

33. Steroid hormones are (lipophobic/lipophilic?) and therefore (will/ will not?) dissolve in plasma.

34. Describe the half-life of steroid hormones. What factor can affect half-life?

Cellular Mechanism of Action of Steroid Hormones

35. Steroid hormones are (lipophobic/lipophilic?), so they have (intracellular/membrane?) receptors.

36. What is the target cell's response to hormone-receptor binding? (Fig. 7-7)

37. The target response time is (quick/slow?). Explain.

38. Explain nongenomic responses to steroid hormones. How do these differ from traditional steroid responses?

Amine Hormones Are Derived from a Single Type of Amino Acid (Fig. 7-8)

39. List three different groups of amine hormones and the amino acids from which each group is derived.

◎ Be sure you can list the tissues/glands that secrete steroid and amine hormones. If a hormone doesn't come from these tissues, then it must be a peptide!

CONTROL OF HORMONE RELEASE
✗ IP Endocrine System: The Hypothalamic-Pituitary Axis

◎ Review local and reflex control [∫ p. 191] and reflex pathways: input → integration → output. [∫ p. 199]

Hormones Can Be Classified by Their Reflex Pathways

◎ Classify hormones and control pathways by type of endocrine reflex pathway. [∫ p. 191-199]

The Endocrine Cell Is the Sensor in the Simplest Endocrine Reflexes (Fig. 7-10)

40. In the simplest endocrine pathways, what is the receptor that senses the stimulus?

41. In this type of pathway, what acts as the integrating center?

Many Endocrine Reflexes Involve the Nervous System

42. Name two different ways that insulin release may be stimulated. (Fig. 7-9)

Neurohormones Are Secreted into the Blood by Neurons

43. Name three types of neurohormones and the specific tissues that synthesize and secrete them.

44. What is the signal for release of neurohormones? [∫ Fig. 6-30, pattern 2]

The Pituitary Gland Is Actually Two Fused Glands (Fig. 7-11)

45. Compare the tissue types that make up the anterior and posterior pituitary.

46. The anterior pituitary is also called:
47. The posterior pituitary is also called:

The Posterior Pituitary Stores and Releases Two Neurohormones

48. What two neurohormones are stored and released by the posterior pituitary?

49. Where are these neurohormones made and how do they get to the posterior pituitary? (Fig. 7-12)
    [∫ Ch 8 axonal transport]

The Anterior Pituitary Secretes Six Hormones (Fig. 7-13)

50. List (spell out!) the six hormones synthesized by endocrine cells of the anterior pituitary.

51. In the answer above, put a star next to the hormone(s) that is/are not trophic hormones.

Feedback Loops in the Hypothalamic-Pituitary Pathway

52. Explain how negative feedback works in the hypothalamic-pituitary system.
[∫ negative feedback, p. 194]

53. Distinguish between long-loop negative feedback and short-loop negative feedback. (Fig. 7-14, 7-15)

The Hypothalamic-Hypophyseal Portal System Directs Trophic Hormone Delivery

54. How do hypothalamic hormones reach the anterior pituitary? (Fig. 7-16)

55. Describe a portal system. Where are the three portal systems found in the body?

56. What is the primary advantage of a portal system?

Anterior Pituitary Hormones Control Growth, Metabolism, and Reproduction
57. You listed the six anterior pituitary hormones earlier. Now, list them again, but include their target tissues.

HORMONE INTERACTIONS
58. Name three types of hormone interactions.

In Synergism, the Effect of Interacting Hormones Is More Than Additive (Fig. 7-18)
59. Explain a synergistic relationship between hormones A and B.

60. Give an example of a synergistic hormone interaction.

A Permissive Hormone Allows Another Hormone to Exert Its Full Effect
61. Explain the relationship if hormone A is permissive for hormone B.

62. Give an example of a permissive hormone interaction.

Antagonistic Hormones Have Opposing Effects
63. Explain the relationship if hormone A is antagonistic to hormone B. [∫ p. 188]

64. Give an example of an antagonistic hormone interaction.

ENDOCRINE PATHOLOGIES
65. Cortisol secretion by adrenal cortex is used as an example. (Fig. 7-15) Fill in the hormones of this pathway:
Hypothalamus secretes _____ →
anterior pituitary secretes _____ →
adrenal cortex secretes _____

Hypersecretion Exaggerates a Hormone's Effects
◎ Excess hormone secretion may be due to benign (adenomas) or malignant tumors; iatrogenic causes. (Fig. 7-19)

66. Define atrophy.

67. Why is it important to taper steroid doses?

Hyposecretion Diminishes or Eliminates a Hormone's Effects

◎ Hyposecretion of a hormone may be due to atrophy of the endocrine gland, lack of vitamin, mineral, etc.

68. Describe or diagram the effects hyposecretion will have on other components in the control pathway.

Receptor or Second Messenger Problems Cause Abnormal Tissue Responsiveness

69. In abnormal tissue responsiveness, hormone levels are (normal/abnormal?).

70. What are some reasons for abnormal tissue responsiveness? [∫ p. 174]

Down-Regulation

71. (High/Low?) hormone levels will cause down-regulation of receptors. [∫ p. 174]

Receptor and Signal Transduction Abnormalities

72. Mutations cause defects in receptor structure or signal transduction. [∫ p. 176]
    Receptor abnormalities: Lack of or abnormal receptors
        Example: Testicular feminizing syndrome
    Signal transduction abnormalities: Missing or abnormal transduction
        Example: Pseudohypoparathyroidism: Inherited defect in _____ protein

Diagnosis of Endocrine Pathologies Depends on the Complexity of the Reflex

73. What is the difference between a primary endocrine pathology and a secondary endocrine pathology?

74. Explain why the concentrations of trophic hormones change with primary and secondary pathologies.

75. The questions below apply to hypersecretion of cortisol (Fig. 7-20, 7-21):
    High cortisol, high ACTH, low CRH: (primary /secondary?) pathology as a result of a defect in the (anterior pituitary / adrenal cortex?).

    High cortisol, low ACTH, low CRH: (primary /secondary?) pathology as a result of a defect in the (anterior pituitary / adrenal cortex?).

HORMONE EVOLUTION

76. Why does insulin from cows, pigs, or sheep work in humans? Where do we get exogenous insulin now?

77. Speculate as to why growth hormone from cows, pigs, or sheep doesn't work in humans?

78. What is a vestigial structure?

79. How has the evolutionary conservation of hormone activity aided in the study of human endocrine function?

FOCUS ON...The Pineal Gland

80. Once thought to have no function, the pineal gland is now known to secrete _____.

81. What are the functions of melatonin in humans?

TALK THE TALK

abnormal tissue responsiveness
adenoma
amine hormone
anterior pituitary
atrophy
cAMP second messenger system
castration
cellular mechanism of action
cortisol
cytokine
diffuse endocrine system
ectohormone
endocrinology
erythropoietin
exogenous
goiter
growth factor
half-life
hormone deficiency
hyperinsulinemia
hyposecretion
hypothalamus
immunocytochemistry
long-loop negative feedback
melanocyte-stimulating hormone (MSH)
metabolite
neurohypophysis
oxytocin
permissiveness
pituitary gland
portal system
preprohormone
prohormone
pseudohypoparathyroidism
short-loop negative feedback
somatotropin
steroid hormone
tamoxifen
testicular feminizing syndrome
thyroid-stimulating hormone (TSH)
transcription factor
vasopressin

adenohypophysis
adrenocorticotrophic hormone (ACTH)
antagonism
antidiuretic hormone
calcitonin
candidate hormone
catecholamine
corticotropin
co-secretion
diabetes mellitus
down-regulation
endocrine gland
endogenous
etiology
follicle-stimulating hormone
gonadotropin
growth hormone
hormone
hormone replacement therapy
hypersecretion
hypothalamic-hypophyseal axis
iatrogenic
insulin
luteinizing hormone (LH)
melatonin
negative feedback
organotherapy
peptide hormone
pineal gland
placebo effect
posterior pituitary gland
primary endocrine pathology
prolactin
secondary endocrine pathology
somatostatin
specificity
synergism
testes
thyroid hormone
thyrotropin
trophic hormone
vestigial

PRACTICE MAKES PERFECT

1. Fill in the chart below for the two primary types of hormones.

	Peptide	Steroid
Transport in plasma		
Synthesis site in endocrine cell		
Method of release from endocrine cell		
General response of endocrine cell to hormone stimulation (i.e. mechanism of action)		

2. Write "A" next to the statements that apply to the anterior pituitary, and "P" next to the statements that apply to the posterior pituitary.

_____ Connected to hypothalamus by nerve fibers

_____ Connected to hypothalamus by blood vessels

_____ Secretes hormones produced by hypothalamus

_____ Controlled by releasing hormones from hypothalamus

_____ Secretes peptide hormones

3. Which of the following seems to be a major function of the pineal gland?
   a) sense of appetite
   b) sense of thirst
   c) regulation of behavioral responses
   d) regulation of temperature responses
   e) acts as a biological clock

4. Match the items below to the questions. Answers may be used once, more than once, or not at all.

a) cortisol   b) aldosterone   c) growth hormone   d) adrenaline
e) vasopressin   f) prolactin   d) parathyroid hormone   h) thyroxine

   1) Hormone(s) produced by the adrenal cortex _____

   2) Hormone(s) produced by the anterior pituitary _____

   3) Name the two hormones most important for normal growth and development. _____

   4) Name a hormone whose target is the kidney. _____

5. True or false? Defend your answer.

   a) Endocrine gland cells that synthesize steroid hormones have lots of hormone stored in vesicles in the cytoplasm.

   b) These same endocrine cells have lots of smooth endoplasmic reticulum and Golgi body.

6. Hormone XTC causes decreased neural transmission of pain, inducing a pleasant but misleading lack of pain. Another hormone, Y-ME, acts on XTC-producing cells to inhibit transcription of XTC-mRNA. The ultimate result of combining XTC and Y-ME is normal pain sensation.

(a) Would the interaction between XTC and Y-ME be best described as:

    1. synergism   2. antagonism   3. permissiveness   4. none of the above

(b) From the information given, would you say that hormone XTC is probably:

    1. a peptide hormone   2. a steroid hormone   3. insufficient information to decide

7. You have been doing research on the pancreatic endocrine cells that secrete insulin and the adrenal cortex cells that secrete corticosteroids. You prepared tissue for examination under the electron microscope, but the labels fell off the jars when the fixative dissolved the glue. You sent the tissue off anyway and got back the following description for one of the tissues. Which tissue is being described? Defend your answer.

"...cells are close to blood capillaries. Numerous dense, membrane-bounded granules throughout the cytoplasm with reduced rough endoplasmic reticulum and free ribosomes Cells with fewer secretory granules show an increase in rough ER and ribosomes."

8. A woman has secondary hypocortisolism due to a pituitary problem. If you give her ACTH, what happens to her cortisol secretion? Draw the complete control pathway with hormones and the glands as part of your answer.

9. Graves' disease is caused by the production of auto-antibodies to the TSH receptor. These antibodies interact with the TSH receptor to stimulate the thyroid gland in a manner similar to TSH. The antibodies are not subject to negative feedback. Which of the sets of lab values below would indicate Grave's disease? BRIEFLY defend your choice. (HINT: On which tissue would you find TSH receptors?)

	Serum thyroxine	Serum TSH
Patient A	6 μg/100 mL	1.5 μIU*/mL
Patient B	16 μg/100 mL	0.75 μIU/mL
Patient C	2.5 μg/100 mL	20 μIU/mL
Patient D	12 μg/100 mL	10 μIU/mL
Normal	4-11 μg/100 mL	1.5-6 μIU/mL

*IU = international units, a standard way of quantifying TSH amounts.

(Please see the GRAPHING question for these data on the following page.)

BEYOND THE PAGES

FURTHER EXPLORATIONS

A bright future for the sunshine hormone. (melatonin) Science & Medicine, March/April 1995.

Human exposure to putative pheromones and changes in aspects of social behavior. Journal of Steroid Biochemistry & Molecular Biology 39 (4B): 647-659, 1991.

In search of human skin pheromones. Archives of Dermatology 130 (8): 1048-1051, 1994.

Menstrual synchrony pheromones: cause for doubt. Human Reproduction 14(3):579-80, 1999 Mar.

On the nature of mammalian and human pheromones. Annals of the New York Academy of Sciences 855:390-2, 1998 Nov 30.

GRAPHS

Graph the data for the Graves' disease patients in problem #10 above. What kind of graph is most appropriate: a scatter plot? a bar graph? a line graph?

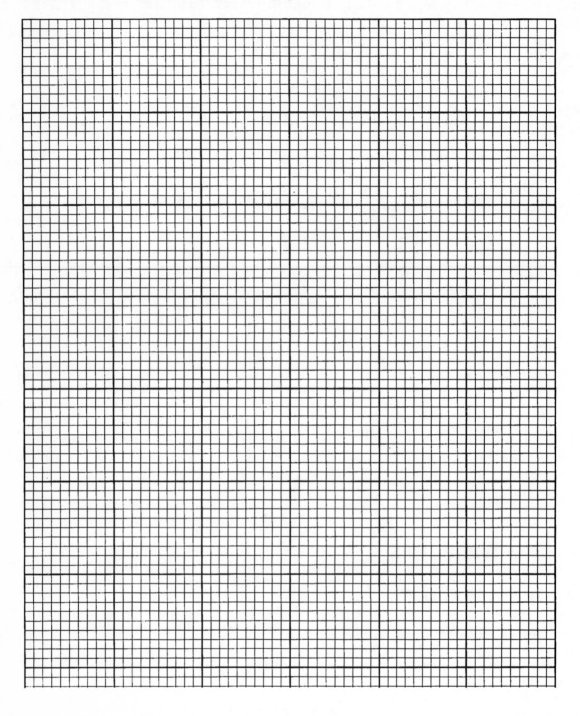

8

SUMMARY

This chapter contains information that forms the foundation of our understanding of cell excitability and nerve cell function. Be warned! It is very heavy with terminology and contains some of the most difficult information you will need to master in physiology. If you did not understand the concept of electrochemical gradients and the movement of ions along those gradients, go back and learn this <u>before</u> you begin this chapter [∫ pp. 150-162].

So what do you need to take from this chapter? Here are some key points:

✓ Be able to map the divisions of the nervous system.

✓ Know the different types of neural tissue and their functions.

✓ How does electrical signaling work? (Spend most of your time on this!) Include in your study: What roles do voltage-gated ion channels play? What are the differences between graded potentials and action potentials? How are action potentials conducted and what factors affect conduction of action potentials?

✓ Understand the details of the synaptic events.

The nervous system is a complex arrangement of branching divisions, each with specific functions. Take some time to map out the divisions of the nervous system and become familiar with their duties. The nervous system is composed of two basic cell types: neurons and glial cells. The neurons are the functional units of the system, producing electrical and chemical signals to communicate with other cells. The glial cells are the supporting cells, providing support or insulation for the neurons.

A neuron has three parts: the cell body, the dendrites, and the axon. Axons lack organelles for protein synthesis, so the cell body ships materials to the axon terminals via axonal transport. Neurons synapse on their target cells. Information passes from the presynaptic cell, across the synapse, to receptors on the postsynaptic target cell(s).

Electrical signaling in neurons is a result of ion movement across the membrane. Compare creation of membrane potential with electrical signaling. What specific cellular components make electrical excitability possible? It is very important that you take the time to learn the specifics of how ion movement creates graded potentials and action potentials (APs). Graded potentials are summed, and if they surpass the threshold, an AP is created. APs cannot be summed: they are all or none. Conduction mechanisms allow APs to travel the axon at high speeds and at full strength. Conduction is affected by axon diameter and resistance. Saltatory conduction takes advantage of myelin sheaths and nodes of Ranvier to give high-speed conduction at biologically reasonable axon diameters. Take time to learn how conduction works and how it is altered.

Cells still communicate by electrical or chemical means (memories of Chapter 6...). At electrical synapses, electrical signals pass directly from cell to cell. At chemical synapses, neurotransmitters are released onto the postsynaptic cell, where they bind specific receptors to elicit a specific response. Neurotransmitters are made in the cell body or axon terminal and stored in synaptic vesicles until signaled for release. When signaled, synaptic vesicles are released by calcium-dependent exocytosis. If these details are fuzzy, go back through this chapter and Chapter 6 to review. Chemical signals can work directly on ion channels or by second messenger systems.

TEACH YOURSELF THE BASICS

ORGANIZATION OF THE NERVOUS SYSTEM

(Try putting this section into a concept map or flow chart)

1. Information flow in nervous system follows a reflex pathway. List all six parts of a reflex. [∫ p. 199]

2. The nervous system divides into what two major divisions? (Fig. 8-1)

3. The peripheral nervous system (PNS) can be divided into what two divisions?

4. Afferent neurons link sensory receptors to _____. (See also Ch. 10)

5. Efferent neurons carry information (to/from?) the CNS. Efferent neurons can be classified into two groups:

        Somatic motor neurons control (Ch. 12):

        Autonomic neurons control (Ch. 11):

6. Autonomic neurons can be divided into these groups:

7. What is the enteric nervous system?

CELLS OF THE NERVOUS SYSTEM

✔ IP Nervous System I: Anatomy Review

8. Name the two primary cell types found in the nervous system.

Neurons Are Excitable Cells That Generate and Carry Electrical Signals

9. Name the three main parts of a typical neuron. (Fig. 8-2)

10. How do interneurons, (afferent) sensory neurons, and efferent neurons differ in their function? (Fig. 8-3)

The Cell Body Is the Control Center of the Neuron

11. List the organelles typically found in the neuron cell body. [∫ p. 53]

Dendrites Receive Incoming Signals

12. Describe the structure and function of dendrites. (Fig. 8-3)

13. What takes place at the integrating region of a neuron?

Axons Carry Outgoing Signals to the Target
14. Describe the structure and function of an axon. (Fig. 8-2) From what structure does it originate?

15. Axons may divide, forming branches known as _____.

16. What is the purpose of axonal transport?

17. Describe the mechanism by which vesicles move during fast axonal transport. (Fig. 8-4)

18. Forward or _____ axonal transport moves _____
   from the _____ to the _____.

19. Backward or _____ axonal transport moves _____
   from the _____ to the _____.

Glial Cells Are the Support Cells of the Nervous System (Fig. 8-5)
20. Are there more neurons or glial cells in the nervous system?

21. Do glial cells communicate with other cells? How?

22. What is the function of glial cells?

23. Describe the extracellular matrix of neural tissue.

24. What is the function of Schwann cells, oligodendrocytes, satellite cells, astrocytes, and microglia? Where are they found?

25. Describe the structure and function of myelin. (Fig. 8-6)

26. One (Schwann cell/oligodendrocyte?) forms myelin around portions of several axons in the (CNS/PNS?), but in the (CNS/PNS?), each (Schwann cell/oligodendrocyte?) associates with only one axon. (Fig. 8-6b)

27. What are the nodes of Ranvier?

ELECTRICAL SIGNALS IN NEURONS

✔ **IP Nervous System I: The Membrane Potential**   ✔ **IP Nervous System I: Ion Channels**

✔ **IP Nervous System I: The Action Potential**

28. Neurons and muscle cells are considered excitable tissues because they do what?

The Nernst Equation Predicts Membrane Potential for a Single Ion; The GHK Equation Predicts Membrane Potential Using Multiple Ions

29. What two factors influence membrane potential?

30. How do cells create electrical signals?

31. Write out the Nernst equation and define all the components of the equation. What does the Nernst equation predict?

32. Write out the GHK equation and define all the components of the equation. What does the GHK equation predict?

Ion Movement Across the Cell Membrane Creates Electrical Signals

33. Which ions are most important in the electrical signaling of excitable tissues?

34. A sudden (increase/decrease?) in Na^+ permeability allows Na^+ to (enter/leave?) the cell. When Na^+ moves, it is moving (down/against?) its concentration gradient and (down/against?) its electrical gradient.

35. The (influx/efflux?) of Na^+ ions (depolarizes/hyperpolarizes/repolarizes?) the membrane potential, creating an electrical signal.

36. Describe two examples of how ion movement can hyperpolarize a cell.

Gated Ion Channels Control the Ion Permeability of the Neuron

37. How do cells alter their permeability to ions?

38. How are ion channels classified?

39. Name four types of selective ion channels in the neuron:

40. Mechanically gated ion channels open in response to _____.

41. Chemically gated ion channels open in response to _____.

42. Voltage-gated ion channels open in response to _____.

43. Electrical signals can be classified into two basic types (Table 8-3)

Graded Potentials Reflect the Strength of the Stimulus That Initiates Them
44. What is a graded potential? (Fig. 8-7)

45. What is local current flow?

46. What determines the strength of the initial depolarization?

47. Opening K^+ or $Cl^{\ominus}$ channels will cause (depolarizing/hyperpolarizing?) graded potentials.

48. Why do graded potentials lose strength as they move through the cytoplasm?

49. Graded potentials travel through neurons until reaching the _____ _____.

50. Where are the trigger zones in sensory neurons?
    In efferent neurons?

51. If a graded potential reaches threshold at the trigger zone, what happens? (Fig. 8-8b)

52. If a graded potential does not reach threshold at the trigger zone, what happens? (Fig. 8-8a)

53. Depolarizing graded potentials are also called _____.
 (EPSP)

54. Hyperpolarizing graded potentials are also called _____
 (IPSP)

55. What is an average threshold for a mammalian neuron? (include units!)

Action Potentials Travel Long Distances without Losing Strength
56. Define an action potential (AP).

57. How do APs differ from graded potentials?

58. Because APs either don't occur or occur at maximal depolarization, they are sometimes called
_____-_____-_____ phenomena.

Action Potentials Represent Movement of Na⁺ and K⁺ across the Membrane

59. In one sentence, explain how action potentials are generated. (Fig. 8-9)

60. Diagram or outline the phases of an action potential (Fig. 8-9). Be sure to include details about
electrochemical gradients, voltage-gated ion channels, ion movement, ion permeability, and membrane
potential changes.

    The rising phase:

    The falling phase

Na⁺ Channels in the Axon Have Two Gates

61. In the resting neuron, the activation gate is (open/closed?) and the inactivation gate is (open/closed?).
(Fig. 8-10a)

62. In this configuration, what can you say about Na⁺ movement through the channel?

63. Depolarization opens the _____ gate. (Fig. 8-10b)

64. Na⁺ moving into the ICF down its electrochemical gradient (Fig. 8-10c) causes (more /less?)
depolarization and creates a (negative / positive / feedforward?) feedback loop. (Fig. 8-11)

65. The inactivation gate closes in delayed response to _____ and
this closure stops Na⁺ _____. (Fig. 8-10d)

66. What must happen to the gates before the next action potential can take place? (Fig. 8-10e)

Action Potentials Will Not Fire During the Refractory Period

67. Define refractory period.

68. How do the absolute and relative refractory periods differ? (Fig. 8-12)

69. Why can a greater-than-normal stimulus trigger an AP during the relative refractory period but not during the absolute refractory period?

70. Refractory periods limit the _____ of AP transmission.

Stimulus Intensity Is Coded by the Frequency of Action Potentials
71. Explain how stimulus intensity can be coded by action potentials if all action potentials are identical. (Fig. 8-13)

72. How does one neuron transmit information about stimulus intensity to the next neuron?

One Action Potential Does Not Alter Ion Concentration
73. (True / false?) Following an action potential, the Na^+ concentration gradient reverses.

74. (True / false?) If the Na^+-K^+-ATPase is poisoned, the neuron will immediately become unable to fire action potentials.

Action Potentials Are Conducted from the Trigger Zone to the Axon Terminal
75. Explain what is meant by the conduction of action potentials. (Fig. 8-14, 8-15)

76. Conduction ensures that electrical energy is replenished so that the electrical signal does not lose _____ over distance like _____ potentials.

77. Cellular mechanisms of conduction are (similar to / different from?) those initiating the AP.

◎ There is no one action potential. An AP is simply a representation of membrane potential in a membrane segment at given period in time. A series of recording electrodes along an axon will measure a series of identical APs in different stages, just like falling dominos frozen in different positions. (Fig. 8-15)

78. When Na^+ channels in the middle of an axon open, depolarizing local current flow will spread in both directions along the axon. What happens to the current that flows backward from the trigger zone into the cell body?

Larger Neurons Conduct Action Potentials Faster
79. List two factors that affect the speed of AP conduction. (These are called cable properties).

80. The larger the diameter of the axon, the (faster / slower?) an action potential will move through it. Why don't all animals have giant axons? (Fig. 8-16)

Conduction Is Faster in Myelinated Axons
81. What do we mean when we say "the resistance of a membrane?"

82. What mechanism allows some animals to have high-resistance, small diameter axons that rapidly transmit signals?

83. The nodes of Ranvier are small sections of bare membrane in axons between Schwann cells that have (high / low?) concentrations of voltage-gated Na^+ and K^+ channels in nodes.

84. Explain saltatory conduction. (Fig. 8-17)

85. What happens to conduction through axons that have lost their myelin?

Electrical Activity Can Be Altered by a Variety of Chemical Factors
86. What happens to AP conduction in a neuron whose Na^+ channels have been blocked?

87. What happens to the likelihood of firing an action potential when the extracellular K^+ increases? (Fig. 8-18)

88. Explain how hypokalemia decreases neuronal excitability. What happens to the membrane potential difference in this instance? (Fig. 8-18d)

◎ *Because of the importance of K^+ in nervous system function, the body regulates K^+ levels tightly.*

CELL-TO-CELL COMMUNICATION IN THE NERVOUS SYSTEM
✔ **IP Nervous System II: Anatomy Review**   ✔ **IP Nervous System II: Synaptic Transmission**
✔ **IP Nervous System II: Ion Channels**

Information Passes from Cell to Cell at the Synapse
89. Define a synapse and give its three components. (Fig. 8-19)

90. Name two kinds of synapses.

Electrical Synapses

91. Explain how information is transmitted at electrical synapses.

92. What is the main advantage of an electrical synapse?

Chemical Synapses

93. Explain how information is transmitted at chemical synapses. (Fig. 8-19)

94. Where are polypeptide neurotransmitters and protein enzymes for axon metabolism made, and how do they get to the axon?

Calcium Is the Signal for Neurotransmitter Release at the Synapse

95. The release of neurotransmitters into the synapse takes place by _____. Describe the process of neurotransmitter release. (Fig. 8-20)

Neurocrines Convey Information from Neurons to Other Cells

96. Name and describe the activity of the general types of neurocrines.

The Nervous System Secretes a Variety of Neurotransmitters

97. Name the seven structural classes of neurotransmitters. (Table 8-4)

98. Where is the largest variety of neurotransmitters found?

Acetylcholine

99. Acetylcholine (ACh) is made from _____, found in membrane phospholipids, and _____, a metabolic intermediate linking glycolysis and the citric acid cycle. [ʃ p. 103]

100. Where is ACh synthesized (Fig. 8-21)?

101. Neurons that secrete ACh and receptors that bind ACh are described as _____.

Amines

102. From where are amine neurotransmitters derived?

103. List some examples of amine neurocrines and their functions?

104. Adrenergic refers to:

Amino Acids

105. Give examples of four amino acids that behave as neurotransmitters in the CNS. What are their functions?

Polypeptides

106. List examples and include the function of some polypeptides that act as neurocrines.

Purines

107. Name some purine neurotransmitters.

108. What is the descriptive name for purine receptors? _____.

Gases

109. Nitric oxide (NO) is an unstable gas synthesized from _____ and _____.

110. What similar gas might also be produced in small amounts to serve as a neurotransmitter?

Multiple Receptor Types Amplify the Effects of Neurotransmitters

111. All neurotransmitters except nitric oxide have one or more receptor types with which they bind. Each receptor type might also have multiple subtypes. (Table 8-4)

112. What are the two categories of membrane receptors into which neurotransmitters fall? What are the descriptive terms given to the function of these receptor types?

Cholinergic Receptors

113. What are the two main subtypes of cholinergic receptors? By which mechanism does each exert its effect?

114. Where in the body are each of the subtypes commonly found?

Adrenergic Receptors

115. Name the isoforms of adrenergic receptors are found in our bodies? How do they initiate cellular response?

Glutaminergic Receptors

116. What is significant about glutamate in the CNS? What are the two receptor types?

117. What is the mechanism of action for AMPA receptors?

118. What is unusual about NMDA receptors? (Fig. 8-29)

Not All Postsynaptic Responses Are Rapid and of Short Duration (Fig. 8-22)

119. In fast postsynaptic responses, what does the neurotransmitter do to the postsynaptic cell?

120. How do slow postsynaptic responses differ from fast responses?

Neurotransmitter Activity Is Rapidly Terminated

121. How is the short duration of nervous signaling achieved? (Fig. 8-23)

Acetylcholine

122. Where and how is ACh degraded? (Fig. 8-21)

Norepinephrine

123. How is norepinephrine action terminated?

CNS Neurotransmitters

124. How is the activity of the various CNS neurotransmitters terminated?

INTEGRATION OF NEURAL INFORMATION TRANSFER
✔ IP Nervous System II: Synaptic Potentials and Cellular Integration

Neural Pathways May Involve Many Neurons Simultaneously
125. What is the difference between divergence and convergence? (Fig. 8-24)

126. Name one advantage of convergence. (Fig. 8-25)

127. What is spatial summation? (Fig. 8-26)

128. Describe postsynaptic inhibition. (Fig. 8-26b)

129. Describe temporal summation. (Fig. 8-27)

Synaptic Activity Can Be Modulated at the Axon Terminal
130. How is presynaptic modulation accomplished? (Fig. 8-28)

131. Why is presynaptic modulation a more precise means of control than postsynaptic modulation? (Fig. 8-28)

132. Name some of the ways modulators are able to alter synaptic activity.

Long-Term Potentiation Alters Synaptic Communication
133. Define long-term potentiation.

134. Outline the role of glutamate and its receptors in the process of long-term potentiation. (Fig. 8-29)

Disorders of Synaptic Transmission Are Responsible for Many Diseases
135. Some nervous system disorders are caused by synaptic transmission abnormalities. Give some examples of these disorders.

136. List some pharmacological agents that can alter synaptic transmission.

Development of the Nervous System Depends on Chemical Signals

137. How do embryonic nerve cells find their target cells? (Fig. 8-30)

138. Synapse formation and maintenance require that what take place?

139. What is plasticity?

When Neurons Are Injured, Segments Separated from the Cell Body Die

140. If a neuron is damaged at the cell body, what happens to the neuron?

141. Describe what happens to a neuron if the cell body survives but the axon is severed. (Fig. 8-31)

TALK THE TALK

absolute refractory period
action potential
after-hyperpolarization
astrocyte
axon hillock
axoplasmic flow
cell body (soma)
channelopathy
choline
demyelinating diseases
depolarization
electrical synapse
enkephalin
excitable tissue

fast synaptic potential
glia

growth cone
hypokalemia
initial segment
ion channel
local anesthetic
microglia
myelin

nerve growth factor
Neuroepithelium
neuromuscular junction
neurotransmitter
nodes of Ranvier
opioid peptides
Parkinson's disease
positive feedback loop
potassium channel
receptor potential
resting membrane potential
difference
Schwann cell
slow synaptic potential

acetylcholine, ACh
activation gate
all-or-none
autonomic neuron
axon terminal
brain
cell processes
chemical synapse
collateral
dendrite
depression
end plate potential
enteric nervous system
excitatory post-synaptic potential
(EPSP)

fusion pore
Goldman-Hodgkin-Katz (GHK)
equation
hyperkalemia
inactivation gate
innervated
kinesin
local current flow
multiple sclerosis
Na^+/K^+-ATPase, role in action
potentials

nervous system
neuroglia
neuron
neurotrophic factor
norepinephrine
overshoot
peripheral nervous system
postsynaptic cell
presynaptic cell
relative refractory period
saltatory conduction

sensory neuron
sodium channel

acetylcholinesterase
afferent neuron
anaxonic neuron
axon
axonal transport
calcium channel
central nervous system, CNS
chloride channel
conduction
dendritic spine
efferent neuron
endorphin
epinephrine
fast axonal transport

generator potential
graded potential

hyperpolarization
inhibitory post-synaptic potential (IPSP)
interneuron
kiss-and-run pathway
membrane resistance
myasthenia gravis
nerve

neural stem cell
neuromodulator
neurotoxin
nitric oxide
oligodendrocyte
parasympathetic neuron
plasticity of synapses
post-synaptic response
purinergic receptor
repolarization
schizophrenia

slow axonal transport
sodium permeability

PRACTICE MAKES PERFECT

1. What is probably the biggest advantage of using the nervous system for a homeostatic response rather than the endocrine system?

2. On the figure below, label the boxes with either K^+ or Na^+ to show the ion concentration in the two body compartments.

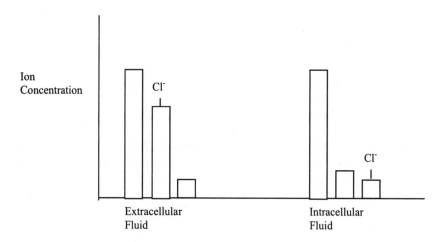

3. Anatomically trace a signal from one end of a neuron to the other, using the correct sequence. Assuming that there is a chemical synapse, describe how a signal passes from one neuron to the next.

4. In the year 2045 you are part of a scientific expedition to investigate newly discovered life forms on the planet Zwxik in another solar system. You are assigned to study a single-cell organism found in the aqueous swamps of Zwxik. In one of your first studies (see Chapter 5), using a radioisotope of calcium, you observe that calcium moves freely in and out of the cell during daylight hours but is unable to get into or out of the cell in the dark.

You follow up this study with an electrophysiology study. You use an intracellular electrode to measure the electrical charge inside the cell and find that it has a resting membrane potential of +60 mV when the outside fluid is arbitrarily set at 0 mV. From additional studies you find that the ion concentrations in the cell and the surrounding swamp water are as follows:

	Cell	Swamp
K^+	50	50
Na^+	175	15
Cl^-	200	90

All concentrations in millimoles per liter.

You now use contemporary molecular biology techniques to insert some protein channels into the cell membrane. These channels will allow both Na^+ and K^+ to pass; no other molecules can go through them.

a) Predict which ion(s) will move. Tell what direction it/they will move and what force(s) is acting on it/them.

b) The Nernst potential for an ion describes two things: 1) the resting membrane potential if it were determined by only one permeable ion, and 2) the point at which ion movement across a membrane ceases because electrical and osmotic work directly oppose each other. Using the Nernst equation [see text p. 246], determine the Nernst potential for Na^+ in the above situation. You have measured the temperature in the swamp to be 37° C.

_____ 5. During repolarization of a nerve fiber:
     a. potassium ion leaves the cell
     b. potassium ion enters the cell
     c. neither occurs, as the fiber is in its refractory period

_____ 6. Treatment of a nerve cell with cyanide, an inhibitor of ATP synthesis, will:
(choose all that are correct)
     a. immediately reduce the resting membrane potential to zero
     b. cause a slow increase in the intracellular sodium concentration
     c. immediately prevent the cell from propagating action potentials
     d. inhibit the movement of potassium ions across the membrane

_____ 7. The conduction of an action potential along a nerve axon: (circle all that are correct)
     a. is faster for a strong stimulus than a weak one
     b. occurs at a constant velocity
     c. is faster in unmyelinated nerve fibers than in myelinated nerve fibers
     d. decreases in magnitude as it is propagated along the axon
     e. is slower in a long nerve than in a short nerve of the same diameter

8. Fill in the following table that asks you to list different types of voltage- and chemically-gated ion channels in neurons. Tell which ion(s) moves through the channel. For all channels, fill in the blocks showing the type of gating (chemical or electrical) and the physiological process that is linked to the ion movement. For action potentials, state to which phase the ion movement is linked.

	Location of channel	Ion(s) that moves	Chem or volt gating?	Physiological process in which ion participates
NEURON				
	dendrite			
	axon			
	axon			
	axon terminal			

9. What is the function of the ground electrode when recording an action potential in a nerve? (See also chapter 5, p. 159, Fig. 5-37)

10. What would you guess is the reason(s) that stretching the nerve disrupts its functions?

11. Explain to your parents or your unscientific roommate what an action potential graph looks like, what it represents, and how it is generated.

MAPS

1. Draw a map showing the relationship of the central and peripheral nervous system, in as much detail as you can. Label the parts with the corresponding parts of a nervous reflex: AP for afferent pathway, IC for integrating center, and EP for efferent path. (Or use the colors and symbols of the prototype reflex pathway shown in Fig. 6-22, p. 191 of the text.)

BEYOND THE PAGES

FURTHER EXPLORATIONS

How does an ion channel sense voltage? News in Physiological Sciences 12: 203-210, October 1997.

Action potentials in dendrites: Do they convey a message? News in Physiological Sciences 11:101-102, April 1996.

SUMMER RESEARCH OPPORTUNITY

The Jackson Laboratory in Bar Harbor, Maine is a non-profit research institution that emphasizes genetic research. They develop and keep track of the mutant mouse and rat strains that are being developed and that have yielded so much valuable information for medical research. Each summer they have outstanding undergraduate students come to the lab to conduct biomedical research under the guidance of staff scientists. To learn more about the Jackson Laboratory and its programs, check out its web site at www.jax.org

CHAPTER 9

THE CENTRAL NERVOUS SYSTEM

SUMMARY

This entire chapter should fit into your mental file folder for the central nervous system division of the nervous system.

Goals for this chapter include:

✓ Be able to describe the gross anatomy and cellular anatomy of the CNS.
✓ Know how information is transmitted through the spinal cord to the brain.
✓ Know the major divisions of the brain and their functions.
✓ Learn the organization of the cerebral cortex.
✓ Understand how we learn information and store it into memory.

The central nervous system (CNS) is made of the brain and spinal cord. Both are encased in membrane and protected by bone. Cerebrospinal fluid (CSF), secreted by the choroid plexus, cushions the CNS and provides a chemically controlled environment. Impermeable brain capillaries create a blood-brain barrier to protect the brain from a possibly toxic blood chemical. Gray matter consists of nerve cell bodies, dendrites, and axon terminals. Cell bodies form layers or cluster into nuclei. White matter, on the other hand, is made primarily of myelinated axons.

The spinal cord is the main pathway between the brain and effectors of the body. The cord is protected by the vertebrae. Severing the spinal cord leads to loss of sensation or paralysis. In the spinal cord, each spinal nerve has a dorsal and ventral root. Dorsal roots carry incoming sensory information while ventral roots carry information from the CNS to effectors.

The brain is divided into the brain stem, the cerebellum, and the cerebrum. The brain stem plays a major role in the unconscious functions of the body, and it is where many neurons cross sides. The cerebellum processes sensory information and coordinates body movements. The cerebrum, consisting of two hemispheres connected by the corpus callosum, accomplishes the higher order brain functions like memory and perception.

The diencephalon has the thalamus and hypothalamus. The thalamus is an integration and relay center for sensory information; the hypothalamus plays a key role in homeostasis, autonomic function, and endocrine function. The cerebrum houses the basal ganglia, participating in movement control; and the limbic system, linking higher brain function and emotion.

The cerebral cortex houses our reasoning ability. Neurons here are highly ordered into vertical columns and horizontal layers. The cortex has sensory areas, motor areas, and association areas. The sensory areas are specialized for specific sensory information: visual cortex, auditory cortex, olfactory cortex. Motor areas direct skeletal movement. Association areas integrate sensory information and create our perception of the sensory world. For example, spoken language is processed in Wernicke's area and Broca's area. Each cerebral hemisphere has become lateralized, not sharing certain functions with the other hemisphere. CNS neurons exhibit plasticity.

The CNS has a variety of neurotransmitters and neuromodulators that create complex pathways for information storage and transmission. Diffuse modulatory systems influence a wide range of body functions. Sleep is a reversible state of inactivity. Sleep consists of REM and slow-wave (non-REM) sleep.

Learning is our acquisition of knowledge. Associative learning occurs when we learn to associate two stimuli. Nonassociative learning includes imitative behaviors like language. Habituation is showing a decreased response to a repeated stimulus, and sensitization is just the opposite. Memory has multiple storage levels: short-term and long-term. Short-term memories can be consolidated into long-term memories.

This chapter presents many details with which you are simply going to have to get familiar. HINT: Break this information up in a way that makes the most sense to you, and then memorize the details. For example, if it makes more sense for you to divide by function, go that way. If you prefer to move around by anatomy, do that. You'll probably have to change game plans later in the chapter, but do what works best for you. If you memorize things quickly, then this chapter won't seem that hard. If you have trouble memorizing, then start making flash cards, maps, charts or whatever best helps you learn this type of material.

TEACH YOURSELF THE BASICS

EMERGENT PROPERTIES OF NEURAL NETWORKS

1. What property of neural networks is the most difficult to duplicate in an artificial intelligence system?

2. Distinguish between affective and cognitive behaviors.

EVOLUTION OF NERVOUS SYSTEMS

3. What is a ganglion?

4. What is a spinal reflex?

5. Which division of the brain is most developed in sophisticated animals?

ANATOMY OF THE CENTRAL NERVOUS SYSTEM
The Central Nervous System Develops from a Hollow Tube
6. Outline the development of the CNS. (Fig. 9-2)

7. Which three regions of the brain are obvious by four weeks of human development? By six weeks? (Fig. 9-3)

The Central Nervous System Is Divided into Gray and White Matter

8. Describe the composition of the CNS.

9. Describe gray matter. What are nuclei? (Fig. 9-4)

10. Describe white matter. What are tracts?

11. Describe the consistency of the brain and spinal cord.

Bone and Connective Tissue Support the Central Nervous System

12. Why do the brain and spinal cord require protection?

13. Name the bones that protect the brain and spinal cord.

14. The stacked vertebrae are separated by tissue disks. What type of tissue makes up these disks? What is the function of these disks?

15. What are meninges?

16. List the three layers of meninges, moving from bone to tissue. (Fig. 9-4)

17. Fluid within the skull is divided into what two distinct extracellular compartments?

The Brain Floats in Cerebrospinal Fluid

18. What is the choroid plexus and what is its function? (Fig. 9-5)

19. How do choroid plexus cells secrete fluid into the ventricles?

20. Describe or diagram the anatomical route followed by cerebrospinal fluid from its point of secretion to its point of reabsorption back into the blood. (Fig. 9-5)

21. Name the two functions of the cerebrospinal fluid.

22. Describe the composition of the cerebrospinal fluid. How does CSF compare with other extracellular fluids?

23. When physicians need a sample of CSF, how do they acquire it?

The Blood-Brain Barrier Protects the Brain from Harmful Substances in the Blood
24. What is the blood-brain barrier and what is its function? (Fig. 9-6)

25. What kinds of molecules can cross the blood-brain barrier?

26. Why are brain capillaries less leaky than other capillaries?

27. What cells induce formation of tight junctions in brain capillaries and how do they do this?

28. Name two brain areas that lack a blood-brain barrier. What are the functions of these areas that require their contact with blood?

Nervous Tissue Has Special Metabolic Requirements
29. Neurons have a high rate of oxygen consumption so that they can produce ATP for what purpose? [∫ p. 140]

30. Why is a large percentage of the blood pumped by the heart directed to the brain?

31. What is the only fuel source for neurons under normal metabolic circumstances?

32. Define hypoglycemia.

THE SPINAL CORD
33. The spinal cord is divided into four regions. Name these regions. (Fig. 9-4)

34. How are the bilateral pairs of nerves that exit the spinal cord named?

35. Draw a diagram, map, or outline to explain the relationships between the following terms: axons, brain, cell bodies, columns, dorsal horns, dorsal roots, dorsal root ganglia, efferent signals, gray matter, nuclei, sensory information, spinal reflexes, tracts (ascending, descending, propriospinal), ventral horns, ventral roots, white matter. (Fig. 9-7, 9-8)

THE BRAIN
The Brain Has Six Major Divisions
36. List the six major divisions of the brain. (Fig. 9-9)

The Brain Stem Is the Transition Between Spinal Cord and Midbrain
37. What are cranial nerves? How many pairs are there, and in general terms, what are their functions? (Table 9-2)

38. What is the reticular formation and what are its best-known functions?

◎ Nuclei in the brain stem are involved in many basic processes.

The Brain Stem Consists of Medulla, Pons, and Midbrain

39. List the three sections of the brain stem. (Fig. 9-9d)

40. Differentiate between corticospinal tracts and somatosensory tracts. Between which regions do they convey information?

41. Corticospinal tracts cross to the other side of the body in the region called the

    _____.

42. Where is the pons located and what is its primary function?

43. Where is the midbrain located and what is its primary function?

The Cerebellum Coordinates Movement

44. The cerebellum receives sensory input from which sensory receptors?

The Diencephalon Contains the Centers for Homeostasis

45. Name the two main sections of the diencephalon.

46. What is the primary function of the thalamus?

47. Sensory information destined for which part of the brain travels through the thalamus?

48. Can the thalamus integrate information? _____

49. Where is the hypothalamus located?

50. Describe the relationship between the pituitary and the hypothalamus. [∫ p. 221]

51. Name eight major functions of the hypothalamus. (Table 9-2)

◎ *REVIEW: Hypothalamic control of anterior pituitary hormone release [∫ p. 197-198]*

52. The hypothalamus receives input from _____.

53. What is the pineal gland? [∫ p. 232]

The Cerebrum Is the Site of Higher Brain Functions (Figure 9-8)

54. The two hemispheres of the cerebrum are connected at the _____ _____.
(Fig. 9-9)

55. Name the four lobes found in each hemisphere. (Fig. 9-8)

56. What is the adaptive significance of the intricate folding of the surface of the cerebrum?

57. Name the three major clusters of nuclei in the interior of the cerebrum and give their functions.
(Fig. 9-9)

The Cerebrum Has Distinct Regions of Gray and White Matter

58. Describe the anatomical arrangement of cortical neurons. (Fig. 9-12)

59. The basal nuclei are involved with:

60. The limbic system is involved with:

61. Name the major components of the limbic system.

62. Where do nerve fibers cross hemispheres?

Chemical Communication Influences Neural Pathways

63. The meanings of signals in the nervous system depends on two factors:

64. What are the two components of chemical signaling?

65. Chemical signals in the nervous system have three roles:

BRAIN FUNCTION

66. Identify three systems that influence output by motor systems of the body:

The Cerebral Cortex Is Organized into Functional Areas

67. Name the following functionally specialized areas of the cerebral cortex. (Fig. 9-15)

68. _____ direct perception

69. _____ direct movement

70. _____ integrate information, direct voluntary behaviors

71. Describe cerebral lateralization. (Fig. 9-12)

72. The right side of the brain is associated with which functional skills?

73. The left side of the brain is associated with which functional skills?

Sensory Information Is Integrated in the Spinal Cord and Brain
74. The primary somatic sensory cortex in the _____ lobe receives information from
   _____.

75. Damage to this region results in:

76. The visual cortex in the _____ lobe receives information from
   _____.

77. The auditory cortex in the _____ lobe receives information from
   _____.

78. The olfactory cortex, a small region in the _____ lobe, receives information from
   _____.

79. The gustatory cortex in the _____ lobe receives information from the _____.

Sensory Information Is Processed into Perception
80. Define perception. (Fig. 9-11)

81. What brain areas integrate sensory information into perception?

The Motor system Governs Output from the Central Nervous System
82. Identify and characterize the three major types of motor output.

83. Voluntary movements are initiated by the cognitive system and originate here (Fig. 9-15):

84. Damage to a motor area will be exhibited as paralysis or loss of function on the _____ side of
   the body.

85. Where are visceral and neuroendocrine responses coordinated?

The Behavioral State System Modulates Motor Output
86. Describe diffuse modulatory systems and list some actions they influence. (Fig. 9-19; Table 9-4)

The Reticular Activation System Influences States of Arousal
87. Define consciousness.

88. Describe the reticular activation system. How does it influence the "conscious brain?"

89. What distinguishes being awake from being sleep? sleep from coma? coma from death?

90. How do brain wave patterns differ with different states of arousal? (Fig. 9-20)

Physiological Functions Exhibit Circadian Rhythms
91. What are circadian rhythms?

92. Why is the suprachiasmatic nucleus important to circadian rhythms? Where is it located?

93. How does our circadian "clock" work?

Why Do We Sleep?
94. Name the two major phases of sleep and describe them.

95. Why do we sleep? Describe one hypothesis and cite the chemical evidence that tends to support it.

96. List some common sleep disorders.

Emotion and Motivation Are Complex Neural Pathways (Fig. 9-21)
97. What is the amygdala a center for?

98. Name the brain regions involved in emotional neural pathways. (Fig. 9-15)

99. What is motivation?

100. What are three properties shared by motivational drives?

101. Give examples of some motivational behaviors.

Moods Are Long-Lasting Emotional States
102. Define moods.

103. Describe depression. What are some current therapies for depression?

Learning and Memory Change Synaptic Connections in the Brain
Learning Is the Acquisition of Knowledge

104. What is learning?

105. Distinguish between associative and nonassociative learning.

106. Distinguish between habituation and sensitization.

Memory Is The Ability to Retain and Recall Inforamtion

107. What brain region is important for learning and memory?

108. Explain anterograde amnesia. Which brain area is likely involved?

109. Distinguish between short-term and long-term memory.

110. What is working memory?

111. Describe the process of memory consolidation.

112. Distinguish between reflexive and declarative memory.

Language Is the Most Elaborate Cognitive Behavior

113. Why is language considered a complex behavior? (Fig. 9-23)

114. Language ability is found primarily in the _____ cerebral hemisphere, even in most left-handed or ambidextrous people.

115. Damage to Wernicke's area results in _____ aphasia, which is

116. Damage to Broca's area results in _____ aphasia, characterized by:

Personality Is a Combination of Experience and Inheritance

117. If we all have similar brain structure, what makes us different?

TALK THE TALK

affective behavior	alpha wave	amygdala
anterograde amnesia	arachnoid membrane	artificial intelligence
association areas	associative learning	auditory cortex
basal ganglion	blood-brain barrier	brainstem
Broca's area	central nervous system	cerebellum
cerebral cortex	cerebral lateralization	cerebrospinal fluid
choroid plexus	circadian rhythm	cognitive behavior
column	consciousness	consolidation
cranium	declarative (explicit) memory	deep wave sleep
delta wave	diencephalon	diffuse modulatory system
dopamine	dorsal horn	dorsal root
dorsal root ganglion	dura mater	electroencephalography
emotion	ependyma	expressive aphasia
propriospinal tracts	glycine	ganglia
glutamate	hippocampus	gray matter
habituation	learning	hypothalamus
L-DOPA	long term potentiation	limbic system
long term memory	meninges	medulla oblongata
memory trace	motivation	mesencephalon
midbrain	nonassociative learning	nerve fiber
NMDA receptor	parallel processing	Parkinson's disease
olfactory cortex	pia mater	plasticity
perception	motor cortex	somatic sensory cortex
	pons	pyramids
receptive aphasia	gamma-aminobutyric acid (GABA)	
REM (rapid eye movement)	sleep	reticular activation system
reflexive (implicit) memory	sensitization	short-term memory
satiety	sleep	sleepwalking
skull	suprachiasmatic nucleus	thalamus
spinal reflex	ventral horn	ventral root
tract	vertebral column	visual cortex
ventricle	Wernicke's area	white matter
visual imaging	working memory	

PRACTICE MAKES PERFECT

1. You are walking to class, pondering the intricacies of physiology, when you suddenly trip over an uneven place in the sidewalk. Unhurt but embarrassed and angry, you jump up and glance around to see if anyone is watching. From your knowledge of neuroanatomy and function, BRIEFLY explain how the following areas of the brain might be involved in this scenario.
   a) cerebrum
   b) cerebellum

2. What does an electroencephalogram tell us?

3. Give the function of the following parts of the brain:

   a. cerebrum   _____
   b. hypothalamus   _____
   c. brain stem   _____
   d. cerebellum   _____

_____ 4. Meninges are:
   a. bacterial infections of the brain or spinal cord
   b. connective tissue coverings around the central nervous system
   c. synapses between the meningeal nerve fibers and the post-synaptic membranes of other neurons
   d. non-neuronal cells in the brain and spinal cord that help regulate the ionic concentrations of the extracellular space

_____ 5. The cerebellum:
   a. if destroyed would result in the loss of all voluntary skeletal muscle activity
   b. initiates voluntary muscle movement
   c. is essential for the performance of smoothly coordinated muscular activity
   d. contains the center responsible for the regulation of body temperature
   e. is of no importance in the control of posture and balance

_____ 6. Which of the following is true of REM sleep?
   a. The average level of activity of brain cells decreases
   b. Students sleeping peacefully through a physiology lecture are awakened and report that they had no dreams
   c. This type of sleep occurs periodically through the night and accounts for 25% of total sleeping time
   d. The blood flow to the brain decreases markedly
   e. REM sleep develops immediately after a person has fallen asleep

MAPS

Create a map of the central nervous system using the following terms:

amygdala	arachnoid membrane	association areas
auditory cortex	axons	basal ganglion
blood-brain barrier	brain	brainstem
cell bodies	central nervous system	cerebellum
cerebral cortex	cerebrospinal fluid	choroid plexus
columns	cranium	diencephalon
dorsal horns	dorsal root ganglia	dorsal roots
dura mater	efferent signals	ependyma
ganglia	gray matter	hippocampus
hypothalamus	limbic system	medulla oblongata
meninges	mesencephalon	midbrain
nuclei	nuclei	olfactory cortex
pia mater	pons	primary motor cortex
reticular activation system	sensory information	skull
spinal reflex	suprachiasmatic nucleus	thalamus
tract	ventral horn	ventral root
ventricle	vertebral column	visual cortex
white matter	propriospinal tracts	pyramids
primary somatic sensory cortex		

BEYOND THE PAGES

FURTHER EXPLORATIONS

A window on the sleeping brain. Scientific American, April 1983.

Adult cortical plasticity and reorganization. Science & Medicine, January/February 1997

Amyloid protein and Alzheimer's disease. Scientific American, November 1991.

Anesthesiologists wake up to the biochemical mechanisms of their tools. Journal of NIH Research 9: 37-41. December 1997.

Anesthesiology. Scientific American, April 1985.

Apolipoprotein E and Alzheimer's disease. Science & Medicine, September/October 1995.

Artificial intelligence: a debate. Scientific American, January 1990.

Astrocytes. Scientific American, April 1989.

Barriers in the developing brain. News in Physiological Sciences 12: 21-31, February 1997.

Brain damage caused by prenatal alcohol exposure. Science & Medicine, July/August 1996.

Breaching the blood-brain barrier. Scientific American, February 1993.

Can science explain consciousness? Scientific American, August 1994.

Chemical signaling in the brain. Scientific American, November 1993.

Dopamine receptors and psychosis. Science & Medicine, September/October 1995.

Dyslexia. Scientific American, November 1996.

Emotion, memory, and the brain. Scientific American, June 1994.

GABAergic neurons. Scientific American, February 1988.

Memory storage and neural systems. Scientific American, July 1989.

Molecular basis for functional differences on AMPA-subtype glutamate receptors. News in Physiological Sciences 11: 77-82, April 1996.

Molecular mechanisms of antiepileptic drugs. Science & Medicine, July/August 1997.

Neural transplants work. News in Physiological Sciences 11: 255-261, December 1996. Dopaminergic neurons transplanted to treat Parkinson's disease.

Neurological effects of serotonin. Science & Medicine, July/August 1995.

Obsessive-compulsive disorder. Science & Medicine, March/April 1997.

Pathophysiology of the migraine aura. Science & Medicine, July/August 1996.

Perceiving shape from shading. Scientific American, August 1988.

Plasticity in brain development. Scientific American, December 1988.

Polymer-based drug delivery to the brain. Science & Medicine, July/August 1996.

Prostanoids: Intrinsic modulators of cerebral circulation. News in Physiological Sciences 12: 72-77. April 1997.

Rx for addiction. Scientific American, March 1991.

Scaling of the mammalian brain: The maternal energy hypothesis. News in Physiological Sciences 11: 149-156, August 1996.

Sleep and energy conservation. News in Physiological Sciences 8: 276-281, December 1993.

The puzzle of conscious experience. Scientific American, December 1995.

The brain's immune system. Scientific American, November 1995.

The biology of sleep apnea. Science & Medicine, September/October 1996.

The gene that rewards alcoholism. Science & Medicine, March/April 1996.

The neurobiology of fear. Scientific American, May 1993.

The physiology of perception. Scientific American, February 1991.

The blood-brain barrier. Scientific American, September 1986.

The machinery of thought. Scientific American, August 1997.

The mammalian choroid plexus. Scientific American, November, 1989.

Understanding Parkinson's disease. Scientific American, January 1997.

Visualizing the mind. Scientific American, April 1994.

Vomiting: Its ins and outs. News in Physiological Sciences 9: 142-147, June 1994

Neural stem cells for brain repair. Science & Medicine 6(5):18-27, 1999 Sep/Oct.

Gene therapy: Diseases of the central nervous system. Science & Medicine 6(6):4-5, 1999 Nov/Dec.

Molecular mechanisms of general anesthetic action. Science & Medicine 5(3), 1998 May/Jun.

Glutamate and schizophrenia. Science & Medicine 6(2), 1999 Mar/Apr.

Experimental models of Alzheimer's disease. Science & Medicine 5(2), 1998 Mar/Apr.

Gene therapy: Learning and memory. Science & Medicine 7(1), 2000 Jan/Feb.

10

SUMMARY

This chapter deals with the following reflex pattern:

stimulus → sensory receptor → sensory neurons → CNS → integration, perception, response.

It should look familiar – it's an application of the same reflex pattern you first learned in Chapter 6 [∫ p. 191]. The sensory neurons work like the typical neurons you studied in Chapter 8. The CNS integrates sensory information as you learned in Chapter 9. This chapter presents you with more details, but you already know the basic patterns—retrieve them from the mental file folders you've been making and insert these new details.

Key points to learn in this chapter:

- ✓ Know the similarities and differences of somatic senses and special senses: where the receptors are, how the receptors work, where those senses are integrated.
- ✓ Learn how lateral inhibition and receptive fields influence our perception of stimuli.
- ✓ Understand how the nervous system can localize a stimulus and determine its strength.
- ✓ Know the difference between tonic and phasic receptors.

The somatic senses are touch, temperature, pain, and proprioception. The five special senses are vision, hearing, taste, smell, and equilibrium. Sensory stimuli are converted into electrical potentials by specialized receptors. Receptors have an adequate stimulus, a particular form of energy to which they are most responsive. There are four types of sensory receptors: chemoreceptors, mechanoreceptors, thermoreceptors, and photoreceptors. If the stimulus depolarizes the receptor membrane potential past threshold, then an action potential results and sensory information is sent to the CNS (If this is unfamiliar, go back to Chapter 8 and review neuron function). The CNS integrates the information and creates our perception of the stimulus.

Receptive fields are created when primary neurons converge on secondary neurons. Lateral inhibition enhances contrast within the receptive field so that sensation is more easily located (except in hearing and smell). Auditory localization is accomplished by interpreting the timing of stimuli. Stimulus intensity is coded by the number of activated receptors and by frequency of the action potentials transmitted. Tonic receptors send information for the duration of a stimulus; phasic receptors respond only to changes in stimulus intensity.

The facts above summarize the themes in sensory physiology. The rest of the chapter provides details about the special senses and somatic senses. Study the chapter one sense at a time and become comfortable with how each sensory organ/receptor transduces energy, how that information is sent to the CNS, where the information is integrated in the CNS, and how the information becomes perception. Then, think about what responses the body might exhibit upon perceiving specific sensory information.

TEACH YOURSELF THE BASICS

GENERAL PROPERTIES OF SENSORY SYSTEMS

1. Distinguish between the special senses and the somatic senses.

Receptors Are Sensitive to Particular Stimuli

2. Name and describe the simplest sensory receptors.

3. Sensory receptors are (circle all that are correct) specialized neurons / specialized nonneural cells.

4. Name the four major types of receptors and describe the stimuli that activate each receptor type. (Table 10-2)

5. Explain the law of specific nerve energies.

Sensory Transduction Converts Stimuli into Graded Potentials

6. How is sensory transduction similar to signal transduction you studied in Chapter 6? [∫ p. 176]

7. Explain the concept of adequate stimulus for a receptor.

8. Define threshold. What happens in a sensory neuron if a stimulus is above threshold?

9. How do stimuli create electrical signals in sensory receptors?

◎ *Review: electrical signals in neurons and the role of ions, beginning on pp. 156 (Ch 5) and 246 (Ch 8).*

10. Define receptor (or generator) potential. Are receptor potentials more like action potentials or graded potentials? [∫ p. 222]

Each Sensory Neuron Has a Receptive Field

11. What is the receptive field of a sensory neuron? (Fig. 10-2)

12. Explain how receptive fields and convergence create some areas of the body that can sense two pins separated by only a few millimeters, while in other areas two pins 30 mm apart are sensed as separate stimuli. (Fig. 10-3)

The Central Nervous System Integrates Sensory Information

13. Name the parts of the brain that process the following types of sensory information. (Fig. 10-4)

Visual information = _____   Sound = _____

Somatic senses = _____   Smell = _____

Equilibrium = _____   Taste = _____

14. Which part of the brain processes all sensory information except smell?

15. What happens to the perceptual threshold for a stimulus when we "tune it out?" Explain the mechanism that allows us to do this.

Coding and Processing Distinguish Stimulus Modality, Location, Intensity, and Duration

16. Name four attributes of stimuli that must be preserved during nervous system processing.

Sensory Modality

17. What do we mean by modality? What indicates the modality of a signal?

18. Explain what is meant by labeled line coding. _____

Location of the Stimulus

19. How can the brain tell which part of the body is sending sensory information?

20. Give an example of the topographical organization of the cerebral cortex.

21. How does the brain determine where sound stimuli originate? (Fig. 10-5)

22. Explain how lateral inhibition enhances contrast, allowing better localization of stimuli. (Fig. 10-6)

Intensity and Duration of the Stimulus

23. Name two ways that stimulus intensity is coded. (Fig. 10-7)

24. The amplitude of a receptor potential increases in proportion to stimulus intensity, but any action potentials that result are identical in amplitude. How then can the primary sensory neuron send information about the strength of a stimulus?

25. Compare the response of tonic receptors and phasic receptors to a constant stimulus. (Fig. 10-8)

26. What is the advantage of phasic receptors? Give some examples.

27. What happens during adaptation of a receptor?

SOMATIC SENSES
28. Name the four somatosensory modalities.

Pathways for Somatic Perception Project to the Somatosensory Cortex and Cerebellum
29. Distinguish between primary, secondary, and tertiary sensory neurons.

30. Sensations from the left side of the body are processed in the (left / right?) hemisphere of the brain because (Fig. 10-9):

31. How does the somatosensory cortex recognize where ascending sensory tracts originate? (Fig. 10-10)

Touch Receptors Respond to Many Different Stimuli (Fig. 10-11; Table 10-4)
32. Where are touch-pressure receptors found?

33. Describe the structure and function of the Pacinian corpuscle. (Fig. 10-1b)

34. Are Pacinian corpuscles tonic or phasic?

Temperature Receptors Are Free Nerve Endings
35. Describe the anatomy of temperature receptors.

36. Do temperature receptors adapt? Explain.

Nociceptors Initiate Protective Responses
37. What stimuli activate nociceptors?

38. Describe the anatomy of nociceptors.

39. Why is it inaccurate to call nociceptors "pain receptors?"

40. What are the differences between slow pain and fast pain fibers? (Table 10-5)

◉ REVIEW: How do axon diameter and myelination affect conduction? See Ch. 8, p. 258.

41. List some chemicals released by injured tissues that activate or sensitize nociceptors.

42. What are the two pathways that nociceptors might activate?

43. Draw the complete reflex pathway for the withdrawal reflex when a frog's leg is placed in hot water. (Stimulus, receptor, afferent path, etc.)

Pain and Itching Are Mediated by Nociceptors
44. Distinguish between fast pain, slow pain, and itch.

45. Where do ascending pain pathways terminate in the brain?

46. Explain how pain perception can be modulated by the brain.

47. Explain or diagram the gating theory of pain modulation. (Fig. 10-12)

48. What is referred pain and why does it occur? (Fig. 10-13)

49. Briefly describe some analgesics and their mechanisms of action.

CHEMORECEPTION: SMELL AND TASTE
50. List the five special senses.

51. What are the technical terms for smell and taste?

Olfaction Is One of the Oldest Senses
52. Where do primary olfactory neurons terminate? (Fig. 10-14)

53. What is the VNO, and what it its function?

Olfactory Cells Are Neurons
54. Describe the olfactory epithelium. (Fig. 10-14)

55. By what mechanism do odorant receptors transduce sensory information?

Taste Is a Combination of Five Basic Sensations
56. List and briefly describe the five taste sensations.

57. What is the adaptive significance of our taste sensations?

58. Where are taste cells located? (Fig. 10-14a)

59. Describe or diagram our taste buds and their associated structures.

60. Which taste sensations activate the taste cells using receptors and second messenger systems? Name the receptors and second messenger systems for each sensation. (Fig. 10-16) [∫ p. 176]

61. Which taste sensations activate taste cells by altering ion channels? Explain what happens to the ion channels and to membrane potentials when the taste ligands bind.

62. What is specific hunger? Give an example.

THE EAR: HEARING

63. The ear contains sensory receptors for what two functions?

64. Outline or diagram the anatomy of the ear. (Fig. 10-17)

Hearing Is Our Perception of Sound

65. Define hearing.

66. Name two ways sound waves can be characterized. (Fig. 10-18)

67. What do these two attributes represent, and in what units do we measure them?

Sound Transduction Is a Multistep Process

68. Trace the anatomical path followed by sound wave energy as it moves from air through the inner ear.
   (Fig. 10-19)

69. List or diagram the steps by which the energy of sound waves in air is converted into action potentials
   in the sensory neuron.

The Cochlea of the Inner Ear Is Filled with Fluid

70. Describe or diagram the structure of the cochlea, naming all fluids, windows, and ducts. (Fig. 10-20)

71. Compare the composition of perilymph and endolymph.

72. Describe the location and structure of the organ of Corti.

73. Explain how hair cells convert fluid waves into action potentials. Include a description of stereocilia,
   ion channels, protein bridges, and neurotransmitter. (Fig. 10-20, 10-21)

Sounds Are Processed First in the Cochlea

74. List the four properties of sound waves used for sound discrimination. In what part(s) of the auditory system are these properties processed?

75. What role does the basilar membrane play in sound processing? (Fig. 10-22)

76. How is loudness coded by the auditory system?

Auditory Pathways Project to the Auditory Cortex

77. Trace the anatomical path that action potentials follow from the auditory sensory neurons to their final destination in the brain.

78. How does the brain localize sound? _____

Hearing Loss May Result from Mechanical or Neural Damage

79. List and explain the three different forms of hearing loss.

THE EAR: EQUILIBRIUM

80. Define equilibrium.

81. What receptors in the body provide sensory information about body position?

82. How are hair cells of the inner ear similar to hair cells of the cochlea?

The Vestibular Apparatus Is Filled with Endolymph

83. Diagram the anatomy of the vestibular apparatus. (Fig. 10-23)

84. What fluid fills the vestibular apparatus?

The Vestibular Apparatus Provides Information About Movement and Position in Space

85. Name the two components of equilibrium.

86. What are kinocilia? What is their function?

87. Compare the functions of the semicircular canals and otolith organs.

The Semicircular Canals Sense Rotational Acceleration
88. Why is the presence of endolymph in the inner ear key to the body's ability to sense rotation? (Fig. 10-24)

The Otolith Organs Sense Linear Acceleration and Head Position
89. What force acts on the otolith organs to alert them to changes in head position? (Fig. 10-25)

90. How is this information transduced to alert the brain to changes in head position?

Equilibrium Pathways Project Primarily to the Cerebellum
91. Trace the anatomical pathway that action potentials follow from the hair cells of the inner ear to their final destination in the brain. (Fig. 10-26)

92. Describe the descending (efferent) pathways from the brain to effectors in an equilibrium reflex.

THE EYE AND VISION
93. Define vision.

The Eye Is Protected by the Skull
94. Outline or diagram the anatomy of the eye and its associated structures. (Fig. 10-27, 10-28)

Light Enters the Eye Through the Pupil
95. How does the eye control the amount of light hitting the retina?

96. How does the eye focus light onto the retina?

97. Explain the pupillary reflex.

98. Explain "shallow depth of field" and tell what change in the pupil would lengthen the depth of field.

The Lens Focuses Light on the Retina

99. What happens to a beam of light when it passes from air into a medium of different density such as the cornea?

100. Compare concave and convex lenses.

101. Compare the focal point and the focal distance. (Fig. 10-30)

102. How do you change the focal distance for a lens?

103. Define accommodation. (Fig. 10-31)

104. Ciliary muscles are attached to the lens by _____. (Fig. 10-32)

105. To make the lens more round, the ciliary muscles (contract / relax?) which (increases / decreases?) tension on the zonulas.

106. When the lens is more rounded, the focal distance becomes (shorter / longer?) (Fig. 10-32)

107. Explain the following vision problems and tell what shape lens would correct for each. (Fig. 10-33)
Presbyopia: _____
Myopia: _____
Hyperopia: _____

108. What is astigmatism?

Phototransduction Occurs at the Retina

109. What is the frequency range of the EM spectrum that contains visible light?

110. Describe or diagram the layers of the retinal neurons. (Fig. 10-34)

111. What is phototransduction?

112. What is the function of melanin in the pigment epithelium?

113. How are the photoreceptors in the fovea different? (Fig. 10-36)

114. The image projected onto the retina is upside down. Why then do we see things in the correct orientation? (Fig. 10-37)

115. What is the optic disk and why is it also called the blind spot?

116. One hallmark of signal processing in the retina is:

The Optic Tract Extends from the Eye to the Visual Cortex

117. Describe the function(s) of each of the following components of the eye: (Fig. 10-27)

Lens: _____

Retina: _____

Cornea: _____

Pupil: _____

Aqueous and vitreous
humors: _____

Photoreceptors: _____

Optic disk: _____

118. Trace the anatomical route action potentials follow from the photoreceptors to their final destination in the brain.

119. What do the extrinsic eye muscles, eyelids, lacrimal apparatus do?

Photoreceptors Transduce Light into Electrical Signals

120. Distinguish between rods and cones. Describe their sensitivities.

121. Describe the three-segment structure of rods and cones and tell what process(es) occurs in each segment. (Fig. 10-38,10-39)

122. What are visual pigments? How many are there?

123. The perceived color of an object depends on the color(s) of light that the object (reflects / absorbs?).

Phototransduction

124. Describe the rhodopsin molecule and explain how it changes when activated by light.

125. Describe the state of each of the following for a rod in the dark. (Fig. 10-40)

Rhodopsin molecule: _____

Transducin: _____   cGMP levels: _____

Na$^+$ channels: _____   K$^+$ channels: _____

Membrane potential: _____   Neurotransmitter release: _____

126. Describe the state of each of the following for a rod exposed to light. (Fig. 10-40)

Rhodopsin molecule: _____

Transducin: _____   cGMP levels: _____

Na$^+$ channels: _____   K$^+$ channels: _____

Membrane potential: _____   Neurotransmitter release: _____

127. Why do our eyes require some time to adjust to changes in light intensity?

Signal Processing Begins in the Retina

128. What is the neurotransmitter released from photoreceptors?

129. This neurotransmitter excites some bipolar neurons but inhibits others. Explain how one signal molecule can have opposing effects.

130. What is the relationship between photoreceptors, bipolar neurons, ganglion cells and visual fields? (Fig. 10-42)

131. What are two properties of visual fields?

132. Visual acuity is greatest when a ganglion cell has (many / few?) photoreceptors in its visual field.

133. Vision is better when light entering the eye (is high intensity / is high contrast?)

134. Describe the two ganglion cell types in the retina.

135. Optic nerves enter the brain at the optic _____. (Fig. 10-42)

136. In this region, (all / some?) fibers from the right field of vision cross to the left side of the brain.

137. Explain how we see things in three dimensions with binocular vision. (Fig. 10-42)

138. Fibers from the optic chiasm to the midbrain serve what purpose?

139. Fibers from the optic chiasm to the lateral geniculate body of thalamus serve what purpose? (Fig. 10-42)

TALK THE TALK

accommodation	acuity	adaptation of receptors
adequate stimulus	amplification	ampulla
analgesic drug	aqueous humour	astigmatism
auditory cortex	basilar membrane	bipolar neurons
bitter	bleaching	blind spot
central hearing loss	cerumen	chemoreceptor
ciliary muscle	cochlea	cochlear duct (scala media)
cochlear implant	coding sound for pitch	cold receptor
color-blindness	conductive hearing loss	cone
convergence	cornea	crista
cupula	decibel (dB)	depth of field
electromagnetic wave	endolymph	equilibrium
eustachian tube	fast pain	focal distance
focal point	fovea	ganglion cells
Gate control theory	G_{olf}	gustation
hair cell	helicotrema	hertz (Hz)
hyperopia	incus	ischemia
kinocilium	labeled line coding	labyrinth
lacrimal apparatus	lateral geniculate nucleus	lateral inhibition
law of specific nerve energies	lens	M cell
macula	malleus	mechanoreceptor
melanin	Meniere's disease	modality
myopia	nociceptor	olfaction
olfactory binding protein	olfactory bulb	olfactory neuron
ophthalmoscope	opsin	optic chiasm
optic disk	optic nerve	optics
organ of Corti	otitis media	otolith membrane
otolith organ	otolith	oval window
P cell	Pacinian corpuscle	perception
perceptual threshold	perilymph	phantom limb pain
phasic receptor	pheromone	photoreceptor
phototransduction	pinna	pitch
presbyopia	primary sensory neuron	proprioception
pupillary reflex	receptive field	receptor (generator) potential
referred pain	refraction	retina
retinal	rhodopsin	rods
round window	saccule	salt appetite
salty	secondary sensory neuron	semicircular canal
sense organ	sensorineural hearing loss	slow pain
somatic senses	somatosensory cortex	somatosensory receptor
sound wave	sour	special senses
specific hunger	stapes	stereocilia
substance P	sweet	taste bud
tectorial membrane	thermoreceptor	threshold
tonic receptor	zonule	transducin
transduction	two-point discrimination test	tympanic duct (scala tympani)
tympanic membrane	umami	utricle
vestibular apparatus	vestibular duct (scala vestibuli)	visible light
visual field	visual pigment	vitreous chamber
vomeronasal organ	warm receptor	Endogenous opiates
opioid receptors	olfactory cell	taste cell
melanopsin	ipsilateral:	contralateral
presbycusis	glaucoma	orbit
consensual reflex		

PRACTICE MAKES PERFECT

1. Why aren't you constantly aware of your clothing touching your body?

2. If a salty solution is placed at the rear of the tongue, it cannot be tasted. Why not?

3. TRUE / FALSE? Explain your reasoning:
Light travels through nerves and blood vessels before striking the rods and cones.

___4. Chemoreceptors
        a. are involved in the perception of taste
        b. are found in the olfactory mucosa
        c. cover the retina except at the optic discs
        d. are found in the cochlea
        e. can be described by both a. and b.

5. How does astigmatism differ from nearsightedness?

6. A sensory nerve is termed (circle the best one):
   a. efferent
   b. afferent
   c. monoefferent
   d. none of the above

7. If a person with hearing impairment has good bone conduction and no air conduction, where would you predict the problem to be?

8. Stare hard at a bright light, then shift your gaze to a white sheet of paper. What do you see on the paper? Can you explain this in terms of what you know about rhodopsin and bleaching?

9. You are sitting up straight on a stool and are spinning to your left. Suddenly, you are stopped and you remain sitting up straight. Which one of the three semicircular canals is involved in this sensation?

10. You would expect to find more of which type of visual receptor cell if you dissected the retina of a nocturnal (i.e., active at night) animal? Why?

11. The organ of Corti sends electrical information about sound to the brain. The pitch of sound is determined by (circle the best answer):
    a. the location of the activated hair cells on the basilar membrane
    b. the frequency of the action potentials received by the brain
    c. the amplitude of the action potentials received by the brain
    d. a & b

MAPS

1. Create a map of the inner ear using the following terms and any functions/actions that you wish to add.

ampulla   crista
cupula   endolymph
hair cells   inner ear
macula   otolith membrane
otolith organs   otoliths
saccule   semicircular canals
utricle   vestibular apparatus
vestibular nerve

2. Using the vocabulary list from Talk the Talk as a starting point, select related terms and create similar maps for vision, hearing, taste and smell.

BEYOND THE PAGES

TRY IT - Here are some fun demonstrations of sensory physiology.

✎ Taste and Smell
The relationship between taste and smell can be shown with the following experiment. Cut a small slice of potato and a small slice of apple. Remove the skin or peel. Close your eyes and pinch your nose shut. Have a friend put either a piece of apple or potato in your mouth. Chew it with your nose pinched shut. Can you tell whether it is apple or potato? Repeat the experiment with your nose open so that you can smell what you are eating.

✎ Mapping Taste Receptors
Can you map the location of taste receptors on the tongue? Old textbooks said you could…but do the areas for different tastes overlap? Try this experiment.

Assemble the following materials: cotton swabs, 1 tsp. sugar dissolved in 1 T. water, 1 tsp. salt dissolved in 1T. water, vinegar diluted 1:1 with water, monosodium glutamate (Accent®) dissolved in a little water. Dry the tongue with a tissue. Dip a cotton swab in one of the solutions. Touch the swab to the tip, sides, and back of the tongue, and notice where you taste the dissolved solute. On the drawing of the tongue below, record the area where you noticed the taste. Rinse your mouth with water, dry the tongue with a tissue, and repeat using each of the different solutions.

✎ The Blind Spot
In each field of vision we have a **blind spot** at the **optic disc**, the point on the retina where the fibers from the rods and cones converge to form the **optic nerve**. Normally we are not aware of this blind spot, but the following test will allow you to find it. Hold the X in the figure below directly in front of your right eye and about 20 inches from your face. Close your left eye and focus your right eye on the X. You should see both the X and the black dot. Keeping your left eye closed and focusing on the X, bring the page closer to your face until the dot disappears from your field of vision. With a ruler, have a friend measure the distance from the page to your eye at which the dot disappears.

X   ●

Focal distance for the blind spot: _____ cm = _____ mm

You can now calculate the distance from the blind spot to the fovea in the eye, using the following formula:

$A/B = a/b$ where

A= distance between the center of the X and the center of the dot above (in mm)
B = the focal distance for the blind spot (in mm)
a = distance between the optic disk and the fovea (unknown)
b = distance from the lens of the eye to the retina (assume 20 mm)

What was the distance between the optic disk and the fovea? _____

Negative after-images
Stare at a bright light like a penlight for about 30 seconds. Rapidly shift your gaze to a plain white surface. You should see a dark reverse image of the light. This after-image occurs because the cones have become fatigued (adapted) to the bright light.

Complementary after-images
You can also get color after-images. Place a red or green cardboard square under a bright light and stare at it intently for about 30 seconds. Then transfer your gaze to a piece of white paper. The colors will change and you will see the **complement** of the color at which you were staring. The complement of a color is the color that appears opposite the color on a traditional color wheel. The three main pairs of complimentary colors are red-green, purple-yellow, and blue-orange. When you stare at one color, certain cones become fatigued, leaving the other cones to react to the light. If you looked at a red square, you'll see green on the paper, and vice versa.

Eye dominance
With both eyes open, hold a cardboard cone or tube with both hands at arm's length directly in front of your nose. Center an object in the opening. Without moving the tube, close your right eye. Does the object move out of the opening? Now repeat with your left eye. If the object stayed in the opening when your right eye was open, then you are right-eye dominant. If it stayed in the opening with your left eye open, then you are left-eye dominant. Eye dominance usually matches hand dominance, that is, if you are right-handed, you will be "right-eyed."

Depth perception
Because the images seen with each eye are not identical, the brain can interpret the two views into a three-dimensional representation of the image. With one eye closed, the field of vision becomes two-dimensional, and the relative distances between near and far objects become much harder to gauge. Try the following to demonstrate depth perception.

1. Extend your arms to the side, palms facing front and index fingers extended. Close one eye. Now try to touch the tips of the index fingers to each other about one foot in front of your face. Without input from both eyes, this can be more difficult than it would seem.

2. Close one eye and pick up a very large needle and thread. Keeping one eye closed, try to thread the needle. Repeat with both eyes open. Which was easier?

✎ Binaural localization of sound

Our ability to pinpoint the location of the source of sounds depends on the reception of sound waves by both ears. Our brain uses two parameters in processing the information received: the difference in loudness between the two ears and the difference in the time the sound reaches each ear.

Have the subject close his or her eyes. The tester should move around the subject with a "cricket clicker," metronome, or other noisemaker, turning it on periodically and asking the subject to identify the location of the sound source. You should experiment with the distance the noisemaker should be placed from the subject's head, as this will vary with the loudness of other masking noises in the room.

Repeat at the same distances, but this time have the subject block one ear with a finger. With one ear blocked, was the subject as accurate in pinpointing the location of the sound source?

✎ Two-point discrimination

Two pins touched to the skin close together will sometimes be perceived as a single point if only a single secondary receptive field is stimulated (see Fig. 10-4, p. 286). In order for two points to be perceived, two different receptive fields must be stimulated. The distance by which the points must be separated in order for them to be felt as distinct points is known as the **two-point threshold**.

You need a small ruler and a compass with two points or two <u>dull</u> pins.

1. Have the subject close his or her eyes. Use a single point of the compass or set the points 5, 15, 25, and 50 mm apart. In random order, touch the compass to the skin. Try to keep the pressure equal each time. **Do not push so hard that you break the skin!**

2. Note the distance between pins when the subject first feels two distinct points. Vary the distance between the points randomly. Repeat several times for accuracy. Record the results below.

Site	Minimum distance for two-point discrimination (mm)
fingertip	
back of neck	
cheek	
back of calf	
lateral surface of forearm	

How do these distances relate to the functions of these body parts?

THERMORECEPTORS

Our perception of temperature is related to stimulation of cold receptors, warmth receptors, and pain receptors. Most parts of the body have many more cold receptors than warmth receptors. All of the thermoreceptors **adapt** very rapidly, i.e., the intensity of the signal decreases with time so that the perception of the stimulus decreases. This means that our temperature receptors are much more sensitive to *changes in temperature* than to constant temperatures. (Are thermoreceptors tonic or phasic?) The following experiment shows adaptation of temperature receptors.

✎ Adaptation of receptors

1. Place one hand in 40° C. water and the other hand simultaneously into the large tub of ice water. Leave them there for one minute.

2. Now place both hands into a tub of room temperature water. Do they feel the same? Can you explain what you feel based on the past thermal history for each hand?

✎ Referred pain

In certain cases when a pain receptor fires, it will stimulate other neurons that run in the same nerve. This can lead to sensations of pain far from the actual site of the stimulus. One example of referred pain is irritation of the abdominal side of the diaphragm that is sensed as a pain in the shoulder. Another example can be demonstrated by placing your bent elbow into ice water. Leave it there for a minute or until you cannot stand the feeling any more. Was the sensation in your elbow or elsewhere?

VISUAL REFLEXES

✎ Pupil dilation reflex.

This reflex helps regulate the amount of light that enters the eye and strikes the retina.

With a penlight, shine light into one eye of the subject. What happens to the pupil? Repeat, this time watching both pupils. Do they respond simultaneously?

Have the subject sit facing the window or a lighted area of the room. Note the pupil size. Keep watching while the subject places a hand over one eye. What happens to the pupil of the uncovered eye? This is known as the **consensual reflex**.

✎ Accommodation reflex

The ability of the eye to focus at different distances depends on the accommodation reflex. Smooth muscle fibers (**ciliary muscle**) attach to ligaments around the edge of the lens of the eye. In normal distance vision, the ciliary muscle is relaxed and objects that are about twenty feet away are in focus. Because light rays from objects that are closer than twenty feet are not parallel, these rays are refracted to a principal focus point that is behind the retina. As a result, objects closer than twenty feet will be blurred.

In the accommodation reflex, as the ciliary muscles contact, the lens becomes more spherical. The **focal distance** shortens so that it strikes the retina and the close objects come into focus. As we age, the lens loses its elasticity and we lose our ability to accommodate for near and far vision. This is the reason people starting around age 40 may need to use reading glasses or bifocals.

1. Have subject look at a distant object. Note the size of the pupils.

2. As you continue to watch, ask the subject shift focus to a nearer object on the same line of sight. What happens to the pupils? The nervous pathways that cause the lens to accommodate also cause a change in pupillary size at the same time.

✐ Near point of accommodation

1. Lay a meter or yard stick flat on the table, perpendicular to the edge. In one hand take a 3x5 card with a letter "e" from the newspaper pasted on it. Close your right eye. Place your nose at the end of the meter stick.

2. Starting at arm's length, move the card in toward your face. Note the distance at which you can no longer see the "e" clearly. This distance is known as the **near point of accommodation**.

As discussed previously, this distance increases with age as the lens loses elasticity. Average distances for near point of accommodation are 10 cm at age 20 and 13 cm at age 30. By age 70, the near point averages 100 cm.

Find the near point of accommodation for each eye. Left _____ cm   Right _____ cm

✐ Ciliospinal reflex

While watching the subject's pupils, suddenly pinch the skin on at the nape of his or her neck. Watch the pupil of the eye on the side you pinched. (This is called the ipsilateral side). What happens? Sudden pain stimulates the sympathetic nerves and causes a pupillary response.

FURTHER EXPLORATIONS

Acupuncture:
Acupuncture is moving out of the realm of "alternative medicine" and into traditional medicine. It is now approved by the Federal Drug Administration as a legitimate form of therapy. Here is some of the research that helped validate this form of therapy.

Alterations in electrical pain thresholds by use of acupuncture-like transcutaneous electrical nerve stimulation in pain-free subjects. *Physical Therapy* 72(9):658-67, 1992 Sep.

Electroacupuncture suppresses a nociceptive reflex: naltrexone prevents but does not reverse this effect. *Brain Research* 452(1-2):227-31, 1988 Jun 14.

Nod to an ancient art; the FDA has OK'd acupuncture needles - and they could help you. *U.S. News & World Report* 120(19): 78(2). May 13, 1996.

Olfaction:

How we smell: The molecular and cellular bases of olfaction. *News in Physiological Sciences* 13, February 1998.

Hearing:
The middle ear muscles. *Scientific American*, August 1989.

Listening with two ears. *Scientific American*, April 1993.

Vision:

The excimer laser in ophthalmology. *Science & Medicine*, January/February 1997.

Retinal transplantation. *Science & Medicine* January/February 2000

11

EFFERENT DIVISION: AUTONOMIC AND SOMATIC MOTOR CONTROL

SUMMARY

So, what should you take from this chapter?

✓ Be able to compare and contrast the autonomic and somatic motor divisions.
✓ Be able to do the same for the sympathetic and parasympathetic divisions. Where are the ganglia? The preganglionic, postganglionic neurons? What neurotransmitters are secreted from each?
✓ Learn the autonomic receptor types and their affinities. When and where are they used?
✓ Be familiar with how things work at neuroeffector and neuromuscular junctions.

This chapter starts filling in the details of the peripheral nervous system — mainly the autonomic nervous system. Learn the details so that you can apply them later as you're exposed to specific examples of efferent function. Break out the colored pens and the paper! Design color-coded pictures and diagrams to help organize the material in this chapter. Recreate figures in the book and, if necessary, change them to fit your learning style.

Remember from Chapter 8 that the peripheral nervous system is divided into the somatic motor division and the autonomic division. The autonomic division is further divided into the sympathetic and parasympathetic divisions. Sympathetic and parasympathetic divisions are often antagonistic, allowing tight control over homeostasis. Review Cannon's postulates on homeostasis [∫ Ch. 6, p. 188] and see how the two autonomic divisions fulfill all four postulates. Somatic motor neurons always innervate skeletal muscle; autonomic neurons innervate smooth muscle, cardiac muscle, glands and some adipose tissue.

An autonomic pathway consists of a preganglionic neuron from the CNS to an autonomic ganglion, and a postganglionic neuron from the ganglion to a target. Preganglionic divergence onto multiple synapses allows rapid control over many targets. Sympathetic pathways have ganglia near the spinal cord, while parasympathetic pathways have ganglia near their target. The synapse between a postganglionic neuron and its target is called a neuroeffector junction. Autonomic axons have varicosities from which neurotransmitter is released. CNS control over the autonomic division is linked to centers in the hypothalamus, pons, and medulla. Autonomic responses can be spinal reflexes, and the cerebral cortex and limbic system can also influence autonomic output.

Here are some points to remember: All preganglionic neurons secrete acetylcholine (ACh). Sympathetic postganglionic neurons secrete norepinephrine; parasympathetic postganglionic neurons secrete ACh. The type and concentration of neurotransmitter plus the receptor type at the target determine autonomic response. Cholinergic receptors respond to ACh and come in two isoforms: nicotinic at the ganglia and muscarinic at parasympathetic neuroeffector junctions. Adrenergic receptors respond to epinephrine and norepinephrine and come in three isoforms: α on most sympathetic tissue, β1 on heart muscle and kidney, β2 on tissues not innervated by sympathetic neurons.

Somatic motor pathways have only one neuron that originates in the CNS and projects to a skeletal muscle. Somatic motor neurons always excite muscles to contract, and muscle contraction can only be inhibited by inhibiting the somatic motor neuron. One motor neuron may branch to control many muscle fibers. The synapse between the neuron and the skeletal muscle is called the neuromuscular junction. ACh is the neurotransmitter at the neuromuscular junction, and the motor end plates of the muscle cell have a high concentration of nicotinic ACh receptors.

TEACH YOURSELF THE BASICS

THE AUTONOMIC DIVISION

1. What is a mixed nerve?

2. What are the two efferent divisions of the peripheral nervous system?

3. Why is the autonomic division also called the visceral nervous system?

4. Characterize and compare the parasympathetic and sympathetic divisions.

Autonomic Reflexes Are Important for Homeostasis

5. What regions of the brain contain most of the control centers for autonomically regulated functions? (Fig. 11-2, 11-3)

6. List some autonomic functions that do not require any input from the brain.

Antagonistic Control Is a Hallmark of the Autonomic Division

7. Use the example of heart beat regulation by the autonomic divisions to explain Cannon's postulates of tonic control and antagonistic control. (Fig. 11-4)

8. Explain how epinephrine (a catecholamine) will cause some blood vessels to constrict but other vessels to dilate.

Autonomic Pathways Have Two Efferent Neurons in Series

9. In the space below, draw and label an autonomic pathway. (Fig. 11-4) Include the following terms: autonomic ganglion, CNS, preganglionic neuron, postganglionic neuron

10. What comprises an autonomic ganglion? What happens within the ganglion?

11. What is the significance of divergence?

Sympathetic and Parasympathetic Branches Exit the Spinal Cord in Different Regions

12. Describe the anatomical differences between sympathetic and parasympathetic pathways. (Fig. 11-5)

13. Which nerve makes up the primary parasympathetic tract? (Fig. 11-5)

The Autonomic Nervous System Uses a Variety of Neurotransmitters and Modulators

14. List the rules for distinguishing the sympathetic and parasympathetic branches of the autonomic nervous system. (Fig. 11-7)

15. Match the following:
    1. Adrenergic neurons   _____ autonomic preganglionic neurons
    2. Cholinergic neurons   _____ sympathetic postganglionic neurons
                                   _____ parasympathetic postganglionic neurons
                                   _____ sympathetic neurons innervating sweat glands

16. What are non-adrenergic, non-cholinergic neurons, and what are some of the communication chemicals they employ?

Autonomic Pathways Control Smooth Muscle, Cardiac Muscle, and Glands

17. The synapse between a postganglionic autonomic neuron and its target cell is called the
    _____ junction. [∫ p. 263]

18. List the targets of autonomic neurons:

19. Describe or diagram the components of the neuroeffector junction. (Fig. 11-8)

20. Cite examples of modulation in autonomic neurotransmitter release.

Neurotransmitter Activity at Target Tissues Is Limited

21. Where does neurotransmitter synthesis take place in neurons of the autonomic nervous system? What are the main neurotransmitters?

22. Outline the steps of neurotransmitter release, beginning with the arrival of an action potential. (Fig. 11-9)

23. Give examples of ways in which the various neurotransmitters are removed from the synapse.

24. Why is neurotransmitter concentration an important factor in autonomic function?

25. What is the name of the main enzyme responsible for degradation of catecholamines?

The Adrenal Medulla Also Secretes Catecholamines

26. Describe the anatomy and embryological origin of the adrenal glands. (Fig. 11-10)

27. Discuss the neuroendocrine nature of the adrenal medulla.

Most Sympathetic Pathways Secrete Norepinephrine onto Adrenergic Receptors

28. Give the locations and the neurocrine-binding affinities of the α, β_1, and β_2 adrenergic receptors.

29. Describe the second messenger mechanisms for the various adrenergic receptor types. (Table 11-1)

Parasympathetic Pathways Secrete Acetylcholine onto Muscarinic Receptors

30. As a rule, parasympathetic neurons release _____ onto _____ muscarinic receptors at their targets. (Fig. 11-10)

31. What are the signal tranduction pathways used by all muscarinic receptors?

Autonomic Agonists and Antagonists Are Important Tools in Research and Medicine

32. Why has the discovery and synthesis of autonomic agonists and antagonists led to better understanding of the function of the autonomic nervous system? (Table 11-3)

33. Give an example of one important pharmaceutical breakthrough related to autonomic agonists/antagonists. (Is it an agonist/antagonist? to which receptor? clinical significance?)

Primary Disorders of the Autonomic Nervous System Are Relatively Uncommon

34. Give two examples of autonomic nervous system disorders.

35. What is the result of continued diminished sympathetic output?

Summary of Sympathetic and Parasympathetic Divisions

36. Refer to Figure 11-11 and Table 11-4. Create a map, an outline, a diagram, or table to compare the two branches of the autonomic nervous system. Use specific details.

THE SOMATIC MOTOR DIVISION

37. Anatomically and functionally, how do somatic motor pathways differ from autonomic pathways? (Table 11-5)

A Somatic Motor Pathway Consists of One Neuron

38. Describe the anatomy of the somatic motor pathways. (Fig. 11-11)

39. Describe or diagram the components of the neuromuscular junction (Fig. 11-12)

The Neuromuscular Junction Contains Nicotinic Receptors

40. Outline the events that result in neurotransmitter release, beginning with the arrival of an AP at the axon terminal.

41. Which neurotransmitter is used, and how does it get to its receptors?

42. Give an overview of the signal pathway used by nicotinic receptors on the skeletal muscle membrane. (Fig. 11-13)

43. _____ (neurotransmitter) acting on the motor end plate is always _____ (excitatory/inhibitory?) and creates muscle contraction.

44. How is skeletal muscle relaxation achieved?

TALK THE TALK

acetylcholinesterase	adrenal medulla	adrenalin
adrenergic neuron	adrenergic receptor	alpha receptor
anticholinesterase	autonomic ganglion	autonomic neuron
$beta_1$ receptor	$beta_2$ receptor	bouton
bungarotoxin	catecholamine	cholinergic neuron
chromaffin cell	denervation hypersensitivity	monoamine oxidase (MAO)
motor end plate	muscarine	muscarinic receptor
myasthenia gravis	neuroeffector junction	neuromuscular junction
neuron	nicotinic receptor	non-adrenergic, non-cholinergic
parasympathetic branch	post-ganglionic neuron	pre-ganglionic neuron
somatic motor neuron	sympathetic branch	sympathetic cholinergic neuron
vagus nerve	varicosity	

PRACTICE MAKES PERFECT

_____ 1. The parasympathetic nervous system is characterized by:
   a. long pre-ganglionic and short post-ganglionic nerve fibers
   b. short pre-ganglionic and long post-ganglionic nerve fibers
   c. direct connections (no synapses) between the central nervous system and the innervated
      organs
   d. mediation by adrenaline (epinephrine)
   e. the axons coming into immediate contact with the effector organs lying inside the central
      nervous system

2. Review agonists and antagonists. In the following scenarios, would the experimental drug be an
agonist or antagonist?

   a) You have just discovered a new vertebrate species while doing field work in the rain forest.
   After obtaining proper permission, you begin studying the effects of different known
   neurotransmitters on the heart rate of this organism. You inject ACh alone and observe that it
   decreases heart rate. After letting the heart rate return to resting values, you inject GABA. You see
   that GABA increases the heart rate. After letting the creature rest again, you inject ACh + GABA
   and notice that the heart rate does not change. Without further experiments you can't be certain,
   but at this point, do you think that GABA is an agonist or antagonist to ACh? Explain your
   reasoning.

b) You're having a very successful expedition, and the next day you find another new vertebrate species that has some very interesting properties. The creature has bright red skin early in the morning, but by midday, the creature has dull brown skin. From other observations, you suspect that this process is under the control of the autonomic nervous system. Therefore, you decide to test this idea by injecting the animal with various chemicals. The results of your experiments are in the table.

	Initial skin color	Inject	Resulting skin color
1	fading from red to brown	Norepinephrine	color returns to bright red
2	dull brown, beginning to change to red	Ach	skin returns to the dull brown
3	beginning to turn from red to brown	chemical that binds ACh and prevents it from acting for several hours	skin stays red
4	red	chemical named Compactine	skin changes to dull brown

From these experiments, do you think Compactine is acting as an agonist or antagonist to ACh?

3. In what way(s) is autonomic neurotransmitter action different from that of somatic motor neuron neurotransmitter action?

4. Certain drugs inhibit the activity of monoamine oxidase. In general terms, predict what these drugs would do to autonomic activity.

5. True/False? Defend your answer.
The adrenocorticosteroid hormones, such as cortisol, are useful in fight-or-flight situations.

MAPS

1. Create a map that shows all efferent divisions of the nervous system. Show all neurons, all receptor types on their respective tissues, and all neurotransmitters.

12

SUMMARY

Here's what you should know after reading this chapter:

✓ What are the structural components of skeletal muscle fibers? Know your sarcomere.
✓ What causes skeletal muscle contraction? Describe the molecular events.
✓ Discuss the differences in skeletal muscle fibers. Where do you find them?
✓ How do muscles meet their energy requirements?
✓ Now answer those same questions for smooth muscle.
✓ Be able to compare the three muscle types.

Lots of good details here. Draw pictures and make maps to help you really grasp this material.

There are three types of muscles: skeletal, smooth, and cardiac. Remember from the last chapter that skeletal muscle contracts in response to somatic motor neurons. Our skeletal muscles move us around. Smooth and cardiac muscles respond to nervous and chemical signals. They move things through us and help maintain homeostasis.

Take some time to learn the basic anatomy of skeletal muscle — both macro and micro. Be able to recount information about all the components of a sarcomere. According to the sliding filament theory, contraction boils down to stationary myosin fibers (thick filaments) pushing along mobile actin fibers (thin filaments), driven by the power of ATP consumption. Here are the molecular events in a nutshell (you should be able to elaborate on these): an action potential created by opening an acetylcholine-gated ion channel depolarizes the muscle fiber. Depolarization spreads across the muscle membrane and t-tubule system, opening Ca^{2+} channels in the sarcoplasmic reticulum. Ca^{2+} flows into the cytoplasm, where it binds to troponin. Ca^{2+}-binding moves tropomyosin, which uncovers actin-binding sites on myosin. Myosin can now bind fully to actin and complete the power stroke. For relaxation, Ca^{2+} is pumped back into the sarcoplasmic reticulum, decreasing intracellular Ca^{2+} concentrations. Ca^{2+} unbinds from troponin, actin-myosin binding is partially blocked again, and the muscle fiber relaxes.

Skeletal muscle fibers are classified by their speed of contraction and their resistance to fatigue. Learn the difference between fast-twitch glycolytic fibers, fast-twitch oxidative fibers, and slow-twitch oxidative fibers. Where would you expect to find each? Fatigue is the condition of not being able to generate or sustain muscle power. It is affected by a variety of factors.

The tension possible in a single muscle fiber is determined primarily by the length of its sarcomeres before contraction. Force in a muscle can be increased by increasing the stimulus, up to a point of maximal contraction, or tetanus. Isotonic contraction creates force and moves loads, while isometric contraction creates force without movement. A motor unit is a group of muscle fibers and the somatic motor neuron that controls them. Recruitment is a means of creating more force within a skeletal muscle. When done asynchronously, recruitment helps prevent fatigue.

Smooth muscle is more complex than other muscle types because the different varieties have differing properties. In general, it is much more fatigue-resistant due to its design. Many of the same intracellular fibers create contraction in both skeletal and smooth muscle, but the organization of the contractile unit and the molecular events are different for the two muscle types. In contrast to skeletal muscle, smooth muscle contraction is dependent on extracellular Ca^{2+} influx, and contraction may be graded according to this influx. Smooth muscle molecular events in a nutshell: Ca^{2+} binds to calmodulin, and the Ca^{2+}-calmodulin complex activates myosin light chain kinase (MLCK). Active MLCK phosphorylates myosin, which in turn activates myosin ATPase. This results in a power stroke and contraction as actin and myosin slide past each other. For relaxation, Ca^{2+} is pumped out of the cytoplasm, and phosphatase dephosphorylates myosin. Smooth muscle can have unstable membrane potentials that create action potentials if threshold is met; otherwise only slow wave potentials are generated. Smooth muscle contraction can also be influenced by a number of other factors, like chemical modulation and muscle stretch, making it a difficult tissue to study.

Cardiac muscle has qualities of both skeletal and smooth muscle. It is striated like skeletal muscle, but is under autonomic and endocrine control like smooth muscle. Cardiac muscle has intercalated disks, gap junctions that allow action potentials to spread throughout the tissue.

TEACH YOURSELF THE BASICS

1. List the three types of muscles. (Fig. 12-1)

SKELETAL MUSCLE

✔ IP Muscular System: Anatomy Review   ✔ IP Muscular System: Muscle Metabolism
✔ IP Muscular System: Neuromuscular Junction   ✔ IP Muscular System: Contraction of Motor Units
✔ IP Muscular System: Sliding Filament Theory   ✔ IP Muscular System: Contraction of Whole Muscle

2. How do skeletal muscles attach to bones?

3. Define the following terms:
   Origin   _____
   Insertion   _____
   Joint   _____
   Flexor   _____
   Extensor   _____
   Antagonistic muscle groups   _____

Skeletal Muscles Are Composed of Muscle Fibers
4. What is the difference between a muscle and a muscle fiber? (Fig. 12-3)

5. What do you find in skeletal muscle besides muscle fibers?

Muscle Fiber Anatomy
6. Explain the following terms: (Table 12-1)
Sarcolemma _____
Sarcoplasm _____
Myofibril _____
Sarcoplasmic reticulum (SR) _____
(Fig. 12-4)
Transverse tubules _____
(t-tubules)

7. Why does muscle tissue have many glycogen granules in the cytoplasm?

Myofibrils Are the Contractile Structures of a Muscle Fiber
8. Name the two contractile proteins of the myofibril.

9. Name the two regulatory proteins.

10. Describe or diagram the structure of myosin. (Fig. 12-3e)

11. Describe the structure of actin. (Fig. 12-3f)

12. What is the difference between G-actin and F-actin?

13. Describe the relationship between actin and myosin in a myofibril.

14. What is a crossbridge?

15. What is a sarcomere? (Fig. 12-3c, 12-5)

16. Explain what creates the following bands of a sarcomere. How many of each are in one sarcomere?
A band _____
H zone _____
I band _____
M line _____
Z disk _____

17. What is the function of titin?

18. What is the function of nebulin?

Muscle Contraction Creates Force
19. What is muscle tension?

20. What is meant by the term "load?"

21. What are the major steps leading to a muscle contraction? (Fig. 12-7)

Muscles Shorten When They Contract
22. Briefly explain the sliding filament theory of contraction.

23. According to this theory, the amount of tension developed by a muscle fiber depends on:

Sliding Filament Theory of Contraction
24. In the sliding filament theory, which filaments move and which remain stationary? (Fig. 12-8)

25. Explain why the A bands of the sarcomere do not shorten during contraction.

26. Explain why the I band and H zone almost disappear during contraction.

27. What is a motor protein?

28. Describe or diagram the power stroke in terms of actin and myosin.

29. Outline or diagram the molecular events of contraction, beginning with the rigor state. (Fig. 12-9)

30. Why do muscles freeze in the state known as rigor mortis after death?

Contraction Is Regulated by Troponin and Tropomyosin
31. Describe or diagram the regulatory role of troponin, tropomyosin, and calcium in muscle contraction and relaxation. (Fig. 12-10)

Acetylcholine from Somatic Motor Neurons Initiates Excitation-Contraction Coupling
32. What is excitation-contraction coupling? (Table 12-2, Fig. 12-11)

33. To initiate contraction, (nicotinic / muscarinic?) (adrenergic / cholinergic?) receptors on the motor end plate combine with (norepinephrine / ACh?) and open (Na+ / K+ / nonspecific monovalent cation?) channels. Net (Na^+ entry / Na^+ efflux / K^+ entry / K^+ efflux?) depolarizes the cell, creating an end-plate potential (EPP). The EPP results in a/an (graded potential / action potential?) that spreads across the (cytoplasm / sarcolemma?). The electrical signal then spreads into the _____, where _____ receptors open (Na^+ / K^+ / Ca^{2+} ?) channels in the _____. (Fig. 12-11) [∫ p. 382]

34. What is the immediate signal for contraction: ACh, an action potential, Na^+, or Ca^{2+}?

35. A single contraction-relaxation cycle is called a(n) _____.

36. What is the latent period and what creates it? (Fig. 12-11)

Skeletal Muscle Contraction Requires a Steady Supply of ATP
37. Where does the ATP needed for muscle contraction come from?

38. What is the role of phosphocreatine in muscle? (Fig. 12-13)

39. Compare the ATP yield for aerobic and anaerobic metabolism of one glucose. [∫ p. 103]

40. Muscles can only use glucose for energy. True or false? Explain your answer.

Muscle Fatigue Has Multiple Causes
41. What is muscle fatigue?

42. What factors are believed to contribute to muscle fatigue?

43. What is central fatigue and why is it considered to be a protective mechanism?

44. Why do H$^+$ and inorganic phosphate accumulate during exercise?

45. K$^+$ (enters / leaves?) the muscle fiber with each action potential. With repeated APs, what effect will this have on the fiber's membrane potential?

46. What effect would this change in membrane potential have on Ca^{2+} release from the sarcoplasmic reticulum?

Skeletal Muscle Fibers Are Classified by Contraction Speed and Resistance to Fatigue

47. List the three classifications of muscle fibers and describe their speed of contraction and resistance to fatigue. (Table 12-2; Fig. 12-15)

48. What factor determines speed of tension development?

49. What factor determines duration of contraction?

50. Which fiber type has the longer duration of contraction?

51. Compare the types of movements for which the three fiber types are best suited.

52. What contributes to fatigue in fast twitch fibers?

53. What is the role of myoglobin in skeletal muscle? Which fiber type has the most myoglobin?

54. What are the differences in the two types of fast-twitch muscle?

Tension Developed by Individual Muscle Fibers Is a Function of Fiber Length

55. What determines muscle tension at the molecular level? (Fig. 12-16)

56. For a single muscle fiber, explain why long and short sarcomeres develop less tension than sarcomeres at optimal length. (Fig. 12-16)

Force of Contraction Increases with Summation of Muscle Twitches
57. Explain the process of summation in a muscle fiber. [∫ neuronal summation, p. 270] (Fig. 12-17)

58. Would you consider summation in a muscle to be an example of spatial or temporal summation?

59. Describe the difference between unfused tetanus and fused (complete) tetanus. (Fig. 12-17)

A Motor Unit Is One Somatic Motor Neuron and the Muscle Fibers It Innervates
60. What is a motor unit? (Fig. 12-16)

61. A muscle responsible for fine muscle movements will have (more /fewer?) muscle fibers in its motor units than a muscle responsible for gross motor actions.

62. Fibers in a motor unit are of the (same / different?) fiber type.

63. During development, what determines the type of muscle fibers that will be in each motor unit?

64. Do muscle fibers exhibit plasticity, the ability to alter metabolic characteristics with use? _____

Contraction in Intact Muscles Depends on the Types and Numbers of Motor Units in the Muscle
65. Explain the two ways that the body can vary force of contraction in a muscle. (Fig. 12-18)

66. What is recruitment and how does it take place?

67. What is asynchronous recruitment? Why is it helpful for avoiding fatigue during a sustained contraction?

MECHANICS OF BODY MOVEMENT
68. What does the term mechanics mean when applied to muscle physiology?

Isotonic Contractions Move Loads but Isometric Contractions Create Force Without Movement
69. Compare and contrast isotonic and isometric contractions. (Fig. 12-19)

70. What is an eccentric contraction? a concentric contraction?

71. What are the series elastic elements (Fig. 12-18a) and what role do they play in isometric contractions?

Bones and Muscles Around Joints Form Levers and Fulcrums

72. The body uses lever and fulcrum systems to move loads. What are the levers of the body and what are the fulcrums? (Fig. 12-21)

73. What advantage does the body gain by using lever and fulcrum systems?

74. The work done by muscle = Force x _____ (Fig. 12-21)

75. For a given muscle, what is the relationship between the speed of contraction and the load being moved by the muscle? (Fig. 12-22)

Muscle Disorders Have Multiple Causes

76. List three major causes of skeletal muscle pathologies.

SMOOTH MUSCLE

77. Where in the body are smooth muscles found? _____

78. Compare the speed and duration of smooth and skeletal muscle contraction. (Fig. 12-24)

79. Why are some smooth muscles in the body tonically contracted? Give an example.

80. Why is smooth muscle more difficult to study than skeletal muscle?

Smooth Muscle Fibers Are Much Smaller Than Skeletal Muscle Fibers

81. Compare the neuromuscular junction in neurally controlled smooth muscle to that of skeletal muscle.

82. Contrast single-unit smooth muscle and multi-unit smooth muscle. Give examples of where each can be found.

Smooth Muscle Has Longer Actin and Myosin

83. The isoform of myosin found in smooth muscle has (faster / slower ?) ATPase activity. This (increases / decreases ?) the rate of crossbridge cycling and (lengthens / shortens ?) the contraction phase.

84. Myosin light chains are:

85. Compare the amounts of actin, tropomyosin and troponin in smooth muscle with the amounts of these elements in skeletal muscle.

86. Smooth muscle has (less / more ?) sarcoplasmic reticulum than skeletal muscle.

87. What is the primary Ca^{2+} release channel in smooth muscle sarcoplasmic reticulum?

88. What role do caveolae play in smooth muscle? (Fig. 12-26)

Smooth Muscle Contractile Filaments Are Not Arranged in Sarcomeres

89. Describe or diagram the arrangement of contractile fibers in smooth muscle. (Fig. 12-27) How does this compare to the organization of contractile fibers in skeletal muscle?

Phosphorylation of Proteins Plays a Key Role in Smooth Muscle Contraction

90. Where does the Ca^{2+} for contraction in smooth muscle come from? (Fig. 12-28, Table 12-3)

91. In skeletal muscle, Ca^{2+} entering the cytoplasm binds to _____. In smooth muscle, Ca^{2+} entering the cytoplasm binds to _____.

92. In skeletal muscle, Ca^{2+} binding to troponin does what?

93. In smooth muscle, Ca^{2+} binding to calmodulin does what?

94. Looking at its name, can you tell what myosin light chain kinase (MLCK) does? Explain.

95. Phosphorylation of myosin light chains (inhibits / enhances ?) the ATPase activity of myosin and (stimulates / inhibits?) crossbridge formation and (contraction / relaxation ?). (Fig. 12-28)

Relaxation in Smooth Muscle Has Several Steps

96. What events are necessary for relaxation in smooth muscle? (Fig. 12-29)

97. What is a latch state and what are its advantages?

98. In some smooth muscle, actin can be regulated by a protein called _____.

99. Actin regulation also requires phosphorylation of a protein. Explain or diagram the steps for activation of actin.

Calcium Entry Is the Signal for Smooth Muscle Contraction
100. What are the ways in which Ca^{2+} enters smooth muscle?

Muscle Stretch Opens Ca^{2+} Channels
101. Explain how stretching a smooth muscle could cause it to contract. What is the term used to describe this type of contraction?

102. A smooth muscle is stretched and initiates a myogenic contraction in response. Yet over time, the muscle begins to relax even though it remains stretched. Explain how this occurs.

Some Smooth Muscles Have Unstable Membrane Potentials
103. What are the differences between a resting membrane potential, slow wave potentials, and pacemaker potentials? (Fig. 12-31)

104. What is pharmacological coupling?

Smooth Muscle Activity Is Regulated by Chemical Signals
105. Hyperpolarization of a smooth muscle cell will usually (enhance / inhibit ?) contraction.

Autonomic Neurotransmitters
106. List some of the neurotransmitters that can alter smooth muscle activity.

107. How does neurotransmitter control of smooth muscle contraction increase the complexity of the process?

Hormones and Paracrines
108. What do each of the following chemicals do to smooth muscle contraction?
        nitric oxide   _____
        histamine   _____
        epinephrine   _____

CARDIAC MUSCLE

109. How is a cardiac muscle fiber similar to a skeletal muscle fiber?

110. How is a cardiac muscle fiber different from a skeletal muscle fiber?

111. How is a cardiac muscle fiber similar to a smooth muscle fiber?

112. How is a cardiac muscle fiber different from a smooth muscle fiber? (see Table 12-3)

113. What are intercalated disks?

TALK THE TALK

A band	acidosis	actin
aerobic metabolism in muscle	anaerobic metabolism in muscle	antagonistic muscle groups
asynchronous recruitment	atherosclerosis	atrophy
beta-oxidation in muscle	botulinum toxin	Ca^{2+}-induced Ca^{2+} release
Ca^{2+}-release channels	calmodulin	caveolae
central fatigue	contraction	creatine kinase (CK)
crossbridge	crossbridge tilting	dense bodies
dihydropyridine (DHP) receptor	eccentric action	endothelium-derived relaxing factor (EDRF)
end-plate potential (EPP)	excitation-contraction coupling	extensor
fast twitch fiber	fast-glycolytic muscle fiber	fast-intermediate muscle fiber
fatigue, muscle	flexor	H zone
Huxley, Sir Andrew	I band	in vitro motility assay
insertion of a muscle	intercalated disk	IP_3 receptor-channels
isometric contraction	isotonic contraction	isozyme
joint	knockout mice	lactic acid, muscle
latch state	latent period	length-tension relationships, muscle
lever and fulcrum system	load	M line
motor unit	multi-unit smooth muscle	muscle
muscle cramp	muscle fiber	muscular dystrophy
myofibril	myogenic contraction	myoglobin
myosin	myosin light chain kinase (MLCK)	myosin light chain phosphatase
nebulin	Niedeigerke, Rolf	origin of a muscle
pacemaker potentials	pharmacomechanical coupling	phosphocreatine
power stroke	protein kinase	recruitment
relaxation	rigor mortis	rigor state
Ryanodine receptor-channels (RyR)	sarcolemma	sarcomere
sarcoplasm	sarcoplasmic reticulum	series elastic element
single-unit smooth muscle	skeletal muscle	sliding filament theory of contraction
slow wave potential	slow-twitch fiber	sphincter
store-operated Ca^{2+} channels	striated muscle	summation in muscle fibers
tendon	tension	tetanus
thick filament	thin filament	titin
tone	transverse tubule (t-tubule)	tropomyosin
troponin	twitch	unfused tetanus
unfused tetanus	visceral smooth muscle	Z disk

PRACTICE MAKES PERFECT

1. What ion is required for muscle contraction? What form(s) of cellular energy are used?

2. Which neurotransmitter is secreted by somatic motor neurons? _____

3. TRUE or FALSE? (Defend your answer.) A single motor neuron can have synapses on more than one muscle fiber.

4. Why does Na^+ entry exceed K^+ efflux when ACh-gated channels open at the motor end plate?

5. Which of the following characteristics are typical of vertebrate skeletal muscle fibers? (circle all that apply):
   a. When stimulated, they produce Ca^{2+}-dependent action potentials.
   b. Depolarization of the muscle fiber results in an influx of Ca^{2+} from ECF, which causes contraction.
   c. They twitch spontaneously.
   d. Each muscle fiber is a multi-nucleated single cell.
   e. None of the above

6. Why is muscle contraction faster than relaxation?

7. Describe and explain the difference between temporal summation in muscle and temporal summation in nerves.

8. Why does a fatigued muscle take longer to relax than a "fresh" muscle?

9. What would be the disadvantage of having gap junctions between skeletal muscle cells like there are between cardiac muscle cells?

10. TRUE or FALSE? (Defend your answer.) Muscle length changes during an isotonic muscle contraction.

11. Which of the following statements applies to isometric muscle contraction? (circle all that apply)
    a. Thick and thin filaments slide past each other.
    b. An isometric twitch lasts longer than an isotonic twitch.
    c. Thick and thin filaments do not slide past each other.
    d. Maximum tension is always generated, irrespective of initial fiber length.

12. In order to move a load, isotonic muscle tension should be:
    a. greater than the load
    b. equal to the load
    c. less than the load
    d. equal to the square root of the load

13. Can you give some examples of motor proteins that you studied in the nervous system? in the chapter on cell organelles?

14. In the muscular disorder myasthenia gravis, an autoimmune response causes a reduction in the number of ACh receptor sites at the motor end plate. Predict the symptoms of this disease and explain them based on your knowledge of the neuromuscular junction.

15. You have isolated the leg muscle of a frog and the nerve that innervates the muscle. To obtain a muscle contraction, you can either electrically stimulate the muscle itself (direct stimulation) or you can stimulate the nerve (indirect stimulation), creating an action potential in the nerve. In both instances, your recording shows a latency period, a delay between the time of stimulation and the peak of the contraction. Do you expect the latency with direct stimulation to be greater or less than the latency with indirect stimulation? Explain briefly.

MAPS

1. Map the anatomical organization of skeletal muscle (see map in Anatomy Summary), then add functions where appropriate.

2. Use a map to relate the following words into a cohesive, orderly description of muscle contraction. You must use all the words. You may add other words to make the relationships clear.

acetylcholine   actin
action potential   binding site
calcium   crossbridge
dihydropyridine receptor   end plate potential
ion channel   myosin
myosin ATPase   power stroke
sarcoplasmic reticulum   swing
t-tubule   thick filament
thin filament   tropomyosin
troponin

BEYOND THE PAGES

FURTHER EXPLORATIONS

Muscle, Genes and Athletic Performance; *Scientific American* September 2000

The Mystery of Muscle; Men: The Scientific Truth- *Scientific American* Summer 1999

Mouse models of muscular dystrophy: Gene products and function. *News in Physiological Sciences* 7: 195-198, October 1992. (free access at http://nips.physiology.org)

The in vitro motility assay: A window into the myosin molecular motor. *News in Physiological Sciences* 11: 1-6, February 1996. (free access at http://nips.physiology.org)

Probing Nanometer Structures with Atomic Force Microscopy, *News in Physiological Sciences* 14: 142-149, 1999 Aug (free access at http://nips.physiology.org)

13

SUMMARY

What should you take from this chapter?

✓ A good review of nervous and autonomic reflexes, and a chance to review skeletal muscle contractions.
✓ A background in skeletal muscle reflexes. What are the structure and function of muscle spindles? Golgi tendon organs? Know the differences between alpha and gamma motor neurons.
✓ What are the differences between the three types of movement?

This chapter integrates all the information you've learned so far and then adds some. If the old material doesn't immediately click, now's the time to go back and review.

Remember the components of a neural reflex? If not, look in this chapter and back to Chapter 6 to see where it all began. Neural reflexes are classified in different ways. There are somatic reflexes and visceral reflexes, named for the neurons involved. There are spinal reflexes and cranial reflexes, named for the location where information is integrated. There are monosynaptic and polysynaptic reflexes, named for the number of neurons involved. Some neural reflexes are innate, others are learned. [◎ Go back to Chapter 9 and review the process of learning.] Neural activity can be altered by neuromodulators. Presynaptic modulation is more specific than postsynaptic modulation. Think about how modulation relates to divergence and convergence.

Some autonomic reflexes are spinal reflexes integrated in the spinal cord and modulated by the brain. Other reflexes are integrated in the brain itself, in the hypothalamus, thalamus, and brain stem. [◎ Go back to Chapter 9 and review CNS anatomy.] Many homeostatic reflexes are controlled by the brain. All autonomic reflexes are polysynaptic, and many exhibit tonic activity. [◎ Go back to Chapter 11 and review autonomic nervous system anatomy and physiology.]

Now for the new material. Remember that skeletal muscle contraction is controlled by somatic motor neurons. [◎ See Chapter 12, skeletal muscle contraction.] Contractile fibers are called extrafusal fibers, and they are controlled by alpha motor neurons. There are receptors within skeletal muscles that respond to stretch and length stimuli to protect the muscle from damage. Muscle spindles, made of intrafusal fibers, report information about length to the CNS. Sensory neurons wrap around the non-contractile centers of spindles, sending information to the CNS. Gamma motor neurons return commands to the contractile ends of the intrafusal fibers. Stretching the muscle fiber initiates a stretch reflex that creates contraction. Alpha-gamma coactivation ensures that the spindle stays active during contraction. Golgi tendon organs are found at the junction of muscle and tendon. They respond to both stretch and contraction, yielding a reflexive relaxation.

A myotatic unit is a set of synergistic and antagonistic muscles that control a single joint. Reciprocal inhibition is necessary to allow free movement by one member of the antagonistic pair. Flexion reflexes move a limb away from a harmful stimulus. Crossed extensor reflexes are postural reflexes that help maintain balance while one foot is off the ground. Central pattern generators, like those for breathing, are neural networks that spontaneously generate rhythmic muscle movements.

There are three categories of movement: reflex movements, voluntary movements, and rhythmic movements. Reflex movements are the least complex, and rhythmic movements are the most complex. The CNS coordinates and plans movements.

TEACH YOURSELF THE BASICS

NEURAL REFLEXES

1. List the steps in a neural reflex. _____

2. Compare the roles of negative feedback [∫ p. 194] and feedforward responses [∫ p. 195] in the control of body movement.

Neural Reflex Pathways Can Be Classified Different Ways (Table 13-1)

3. What is the difference between somatic reflexes and autonomic (visceral) reflexes?

4. What is the difference between a spinal reflex and a cranial reflex?

5. What is the difference between an innate reflex and a learned reflex?

6. What is the difference between a monosynaptic reflex (Fig. 13-1a) and a polysynaptic reflex? (Fig. 13-1b)

7. Compare convergence and divergence.

AUTONOMIC REFLEXES

8. Where are autonomic reflexes integrated? [∫ Fig. 11-3, p. 371]

9. Describe the influences that emotions and higher brain centers can have on autonomic reflexes.

10. Autonomic reflexes are (always monosynaptic / always polysynaptic / may be either?).

SKELETAL MUSCLE REFLEXES

11. What is the only way to inhibit skeletal muscle contraction?

12. What are proprioceptors? What are the three types found in the body?

13. What are alpha motor neurons?

14. What are extrafusal muscle fibers?

Muscle Spindles Respond to Muscle Stretch (Fig. 13-3)

15. What is the function of muscle spindles?

16. What is the difference between intrafusal and extrafusal muscle fibers?

17. What is the difference between alpha and gamma motor neurons?

18. What is muscle tone?

19. Describe the stretch reflex, using the standard steps of a reflex.
    Stimulus _____   Receptor _____
    Afferent path _____   Integrating center _____
    Efferent path _____   Effector _____
    Tissue response _____   Systemic response _____

20. Explain alpha-gamma coactivation. (Fig. 13-5)

21. What is the function of the muscle spindle reflex? (Fig. 13-6)

Golgi Tendon Organs Respond to Muscle Tension

22. Describe the structure of the Golgi tendon organs. (Fig. 13-3c)

23. Describe the Golgi tendon reflex, using the standard steps of a reflex.
    Stimulus _____   Receptor _____
    Afferent path _____   Integrating center _____
    Efferent path _____   Effector _____
    Tissue response _____   Systemic response _____

24. What is the function of this reflex? (Fig. 13-6)

Stretch Reflexes and Reciprocal Inhibition Control Movement Around a Joint

25. What is a myotatic unit?

26. Describe a monosynaptic stretch reflex, the knee jerk reflex, using the standard steps of a reflex. (Fig. 13-7)

Stimulus _____   Receptor _____
Afferent path _____   Integrating center _____
Efferent path _____   Effector _____
Tissue response _____   Systemic response _____

27. Describe reciprocal inhibition in the knee jerk reflex, using the standard steps of a reflex. (Fig. 13-7)

Stimulus _____   Receptor _____
Afferent path _____   Integrating center _____
Efferent path _____   Effector _____
Tissue response _____   Systemic response _____

28. How can a single stimulus, transmitted through a single sensory neuron, create two opposing responses?

Flexion Reflexes Pull Limbs Away from Painful Stimuli

29. Describe the flexion reflex (withdrawal reflex), using the standard steps of a reflex. There are two efferent pathways because this reflex involves reciprocal inhibition. (Fig. 13-8)

Stimulus _____   Receptor _____
Afferent path _____   Integrating center _____
Efferent path 1 _____   Effector 1 _____
Efferent path 2 _____   Effector 2 _____
Tissue response 1 _____   Tissue response 2 _____
Systemic response _____

30. Why does this reflex take longer than the knee jerk reflex?

31. Now describe the crossed extensor reflex that often accompanies the flexion reflex. (Fig. 13-8)

Stimulus _____   Receptor _____
Afferent path _____   Integrating center _____
Efferent path 1 _____   Effector 1 _____
Efferent path 2 _____   Effector 2 _____
Tissue response 1 _____   Tissue response 2 _____
Systemic response _____

32. What is a central pattern generator?

33. What role do central pattern generators play in movement?

THE INTEGRATED CONTROL OF BODY MOVEMENT

Movement Can Be Classified as Reflex, Voluntary, or Rhythmic (Table 13-2)

34. Skeletal muscles (can / cannot ?) communicate with each other.

35. Name and describe the three basic types of movement.

The CNS Integrates Movement

36. Movement is controlled at what three levels of the central nervous system? (Fig. 13-9, Table 13-3)

37. Describe the role of the following in planning and executing movement (Fig. 13-11 and Table 13-3):

    Thalamus   _____

    Cerebral cortex   _____

    Basal ganglia   _____

    Cerebellum   _____

38. Explain and give an example of a feedforward postural reflex. (Fig. 13-12)

Symptoms of Parkinson's Disease Reflect the Functions of the Basal Nuclei

39. What is the pathophysiology behind Parkinson's disease?

40. How did research into this disease shed light on the functions of the basal nuclei?

41. What are some current treatments?

CONTROL OF MOVEMENT IN VISCERAL MUSCLES

42. How does reflex control of visceral muscles differ from reflex control of skeletal muscles?

TALK THE TALK

alpha motor neuron	alpha-gamma coactivation	autonomic reflex or visceral reflex
basal ganglia	central pattern generator	convergence
corticospinal tract	cranial reflex	crossed extensor reflex
divergence	excitatory postsynaptic potential (EPSP)	extrafusal muscle fiber
extrapyramidal tract	feedforward postural reflex	flexion reflex
gamma motor neuron	Golgi tendon organ	inhibitory postsynaptic potential (IPSP)
intrafusal fiber	joint capsule mechanoreceptor	monosynaptic reflex
muscle spindle	muscle tone	myotatic unit
nervous reflex	neuromodulator	polysynaptic reflex
postsynaptic modulation	postural reflex	presynaptic modulation
pyramidal tract	reciprocal inhibition	rhythmic movement
somatic reflex	spinal reflex	stretch reflex

PRACTICE MAKES PERFECT

1. In the left-hand column, arrange the words below in the proper order:

   response, efferent path, afferent path, receptor, integrating center, effector

In the right-hand column, give the parts of any <u>biological</u> reflex discussed or demonstrated in the textbook except the knee jerk reflex.

Steps of a reflex	Example
Stimulus	

2. Proprioceptors monitor (circle the best one):
   a. limb and muscle state
   b. taste perception
   c. blood pressure in the carotid artery
   d. a. and c.

3. Look at the pathways diagramed in Fig. 13-10 (p. 441) and Fig. 13-11 (p. 442). Can you find examples of convergence, divergence, presynaptic or postsynaptic inhibition in these figures?

BEYOND THE PAGES

TRY IT

🖉 *PROPRIORECEPTION*

Proprioreceptors are special receptors in the muscles and joints that send messages to the central nervous system about the position of the body parts relative to each other. Proprioreception normally works with visual cues. These exercises will show you the effectiveness of proprioreception alone.

Get a partner and try the following exercises with your eyes closed.

1. Have your partner time how long you can stand on one leg with your eyes closed and arms extended. Note the extent of swaying. Repeat with the eyes open.

2. Extend your arms to the side at shoulder level, palms down. With your eyes closed and without bending your elbows, try to bring your arms together in front of you, palms down, so that the index fingers meet side by side. Repeat with your eyes open.

3. Extend your arms to the side again, palms facing front. With eyes closed, bend your elbows and try to touch the tips of your index fingers together in front of you. Repeat with your eyes open.

In all three tests, which was easier? Why? What can you conclude from these exercises?

FURTHER EXPLORATIONS

Controlling computers with neural signals. *Scientific American*, October 1996. Developing ways paralyzed people can use electrical impulses to command computers.

Transcranial Magnetic Brain Stimulation: a Tool to Investigate Central Motor Pathways, *News Physiol Sci* 16: 297-302, 2001.

Post-polio syndrome. *Science & Medicine* 6(3), 1999 May/Jun.

14

CARDIOVASCULAR PHYSIOLOGY

SUMMARY

This is a chapter full of new concepts. Here are some key points to watch for while studying this chapter:

✓ How do pressure, volume, resistance, vessel length, and fluid viscosity relate to fluid flow?
✓ How are action potentials generated in cardiac contractile and autorhythmic cells?
✓ How does cardiac action potential generation differ from AP generation in other excitable tissues?
✓ What are the electrical events of the cardiac cycle?
✓ What are the mechanical events of the cardiac cycle? How do they relate to the electrical events?
✓ How do pressure and volume change during a cardiac cycle?
✓ How is heart rate generated? regulated?
✓ What factors affect stroke volume? cardiac output (CO)?

This chapter discusses how the heart creates blood flow and examines the variables that influence blood flow through the circulatory system. Blood flow is a result of pressure gradients, resistance, volume, vessel length, and the viscosity of the fluid. The heart—the pump in this system—consists of striated contractile muscle cells and specialized myocardial autorhythmic cells that act as pacemakers. The most important pacemaker is the sinoatrial (SA) node, which sets the intrinsic heart rate by its firing rate. Depolarization of the SA node begins a transmission of action potentials along the heart's conduction system (AV node, bundle of His, Purkinjie fibers) to generate cardiac muscle contraction. Pacemaker activity is controlled by specialized ion channels and is influenced by the autonomic nervous system. Calcium, Na^+ and K^+ ions are involved in contraction of the myocardial contractile cells—compare the role of each ion in both skeletal muscle contraction and cardiac muscle contraction. The catecholamines, epinephrine and norepinephrine, affect the strength and duration of contraction by altering how much Ca^{2+} is available for binding to troponin.

The pumping action of the heart can be examined from both electrical and mechanical standpoints. An ECG records the electrical events and provides information about the mechanical events that follow. The mechanical pumping action of the heart is a result of the electrical signals produced by the autorhythmic cells. Blood flow through the heart during a cardiac cycle can be described in terms of pressure and volume changes created as the chambers contract and relax. See the pressure-volume graph (p. 477) and the Wiggers diagram (p. 479) to review the electrical and mechanical events of a cardiac cycle.

Cardiac output, the volume of blood pumped per ventricle per minute, is determined by heart rate and stroke volume. Heart rate is intrinsically controlled by the autorhythmic cells and is varied by autonomic influence. Stroke volume is influenced by length and tension generated in contractile cells (Frank-Starling law of the heart), venous return, and adrenergically mediated changes in contractility.

TEACH YOURSELF THE BASICS

OVERVIEW OF THE CARDIOVASCULAR SYSTEM
⁄ IP Cardiovascular System: Anatomy Review: The Heart
1. Why did organized cardiovascular systems become necessary as animals increased in complexity?

2. Describe the basic structure of a cardiovascular (CV) system. (Fig. 14-1)

3. Describe the general function of the cardiovascular system.

The Cardiovascular System Transports Material Throughout the Body
4. List at least five substances transported by the blood. (Table 14-1)

The Cardiovascular System Consists of the Heart and Blood Vessels
5. How do arteries differ from veins?
arteries carry blood away from the heart
veins return blood black [to] the heart

6. What ensures one-way flow of blood through the system?
ΔP- blood flows down a pressure gradient. The flow of blood follows the gr

7. Describe or diagram the structure of the heart.

8. Why do we say that the heart functions like two pumps pumping in series when, anatomically, the two sides of the heart are next to each other and look like they are pumping in parallel?

9. Trace a drop of blood from the left ventricle to the stomach and back to the left ventricle. (Fig. 14-1)

10. Compare the pulmonary circulation with the systemic circulation.

11. What is a portal system? *a specialized region of the circulation consisting of two sets of capillaries directly connected by a set of blood vessels*

12. Name the three portal systems of the body. [J p. 225]
    kidney
    digestive
    brain

hepatic pulmonary renal cardio neuro

13. Give the medical terms used for each of these organs: liver, lung, kidney, heart, brain

PRESSURE, VOLUME, FLOW, AND RESISTANCE

14. Liquids and gases flow from areas of __*high*__ pressure to areas of __*low*__ pressure.

15. How does the cardiovascular system create a region of higher pressure?

16. As blood moves away from the heart, what happens to the pressure? Why? *pressure decrease because of distance*

17. The highest pressure in the blood vessels is found in the __*arteries*__ and the lowest pressures are found in the __*veins*__. (Fig. 14-2)

The Pressure of Fluid in Motion Decreases over Distance

18. What is the difference between hydrostatic pressure and hydraulic pressure (Fig. 14-3)?
    - hydrostatic pressure is when fluid is not moving and force is exerted equally in all directions
    - hy

19. What units are used to measure pressure in the cardiovascular system?
    mm Hg = millimeters of mercury

Compressing a Fluid Raises its Pressure

20. What happens to the pressure inside a water-filled balloon when you squeeze on it? Why?

21. What is driving pressure?

22. What happens to pressure when the heart relaxes or the blood vessels dilate? _____

Blood Flows from an Area of Higher Pressure to One of Lower Pressure

23. What is a pressure gradient? (Fig. 14-4)

24. Fluid is flowing through two identical tubes. In tube A, the pressure at one end is 150 mm Hg and the pressure at the other end is 100 mm Hg. In tube B, the pressure at one end is 75 mm Hg and the pressure at the other end is 10 mm Hg. Which tube will have the greatest flow? (Answer at the end of the workbook.)

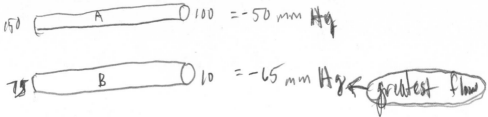

Resistance Opposes Flow

25. What two anatomical factors contribute to friction working against blood flowing through blood vessels?

26. Define resistance.

27. When resistance (R) increases, flow (increases / decreases?).

28. Express this relationship mathematically:

29. Name the three parameters that influence resistance for fluid flowing through a tube.

30. The relationship between these factors and resistance was expressed mathematically by Jean Poiseuille. Write the equation known as Poiseuille's law:

31. In humans, which of these factors are relatively constant and which play a significant role in determining resistance to blood flow?

32. When the radius of a tube decreases, what happens to the resistance of that tube? _____
What happens to flow through that tube? _____

33. Write the mathematical expression for the relationship between resistance and radius.

34. If the radius of a tube doubles, what happens to the resistance? (Fig. 14-5)

35. Define vasoconstriction and vasodilation in terms of diameter and resistance.

36. Write the mathematical expression for the relationship between flow, resistance, and the pressure gradient.

Velocity of Flow Depends on the Flow Rate and the Cross-Sectional Area
◎ *Table 14-2 summarizes the rules for blood flow.*

37. What is the difference between flow (flow rate) and the velocity of flow? (Give units.) (Fig. 14-6)

38. What factors have the biggest influence on the flow rate? On the velocity of flow?

39. Fluid is flowing through a tube at a constant rate of flow. What happens to the velocity of flow if the tube suddenly narrows?

40. Write the equation that expresses the relationship between the flow rate (Q), the velocity of flow (v), and the cross-sectional area (a) of a tube.

CARDIAC MUSCLE AND THE HEART
⚡ **IP Cardiovascular System: Cardiac Action Potential**

The Heart Has Four Chambers
41. The heart is a muscle that lies in the center of the ___pericardial___ cavity, surrounded by the ___pericardium___ membrane. (Fig. 14-7)

42. True ~~or false~~ – and explain: The base of the heart is the pointed end that angles downward.

43. The medical term for cardiac muscle is ___myocardium___.

44. The heart has (how many?) ___4___ chambers, separated by a wall known as the ___septum___.

45. The ___ventricles___ are the lower chambers and the ___atriums___ are the upper chambers. Which chambers have the thickest walls? _____

46. Outline or diagram the blood vessels that connect to each chamber and tell where they are bringing blood from or taking blood to.

47. Name the vessels that supply blood to the heart muscle itself. _____

48. Name two functions of the fibrous connective tissue rings that surround openings to major arteries and chambers (Fig. 14-7a).

Heart Valves Ensure One-Way Flow in the Heart

49. Outline or diagram the location of the heart valves. (Fig. 14-9)

50. What are the chordae tendineae and what is their function? (Fig. 14-9)

51. Compare and contrast the AV and semilunar valves.

Cardiac Muscle Cells Contract Without Nervous Stimulation

52. How are myocardial autorrhythmic cells different from myocardial contractile cells?

53. What is a pacemaker potential? [∫ p. 420]

54. What are intercalated disks?

55. What role do desmosomes play in myocardial cells? [∫ p. 65]

56. Compare the myocardial contractile cells to skeletal muscle cells.

57. Why do myocardial cells have a high rate of oxygen consumption?

58. What anatomical feature of myocardial cells allows coordinated contraction?

Cardiac EC Coupling Combines Features of Skeletal and Smooth Muscle

59. Contraction in contractile myocardium is most like that of smooth muscle or skeletal muscle?

60. Outline or diagram the Ca^{2+}-induced Ca^{2+} release mechanism for contraction in contractile myocardium. Is this more similar to skeletal or smooth muscle?

61. How is Ca^{2+} removed from the cytoplasm of a cardiac muscle cell?

Cardiac Muscle Contraction Can Be Graded

62. How do cardiac muscle cells create graded contractions?

63. How do catecholamines enhance the force of cardiac muscle contraction? [∫ p. 378]

64. What kind of (cholinergic / adrenergic?) receptors are found on the myocardium?

65. Signal transduction of epinephrine or norepinephrine uses what second messenger system? [∫ p. 180] (Fig. 14-12)

66. When voltage-gated Ca^{2+} channels are phosphorylated, their probability of opening is (increased / decreased?) and (more / less?) Ca^{2+} enters the cell.

67. What is phospholamban and what role does it play in altering cardiac muscle contraction?

When Cardiac Muscle Is Stretched, It Contracts More Forcefully

68. True or false? The force of cardiac muscle contraction depends on the length of the muscle fiber when contraction begins. [∫ p. 405] (Fig. 14-13)

69. In the intact heart, the length of the sarcomeres at the beginning of a contraction is a reflection of:

Action Potentials in Myocardial Cells Vary According to Cell Type

70. What ion is important in cardiac muscle action potentials but plays no significant role in skeletal muscle or neuronal action potentials?

Myocardial Contractile Cells (Fig. 14-4)

71. Do myocardial contractile cells have a stable or unstable membrane potential?

72. In the myocardial contractile cell, the rapid depolarization phase is due to the entry of _____ .

73. The repolarization phase is due to _____ (influx / efflux?).

74. In Fig. 14-14, what causes the small fall in the membrane potential between points 1 and 2? (Answer at the end of the workbook.)

75. Make a table that compares APs in a contractile myocardial cell to APs in a skeletal muscle cell or neuron.

Myocardial Autorhythmic Cells

76. Do myocardial autorhythmic cells have a stable or unstable membrane potential?

77. What happens when the pacemaker potential reaches -40 mV? (Fig. 14-16)

78. Why is the membrane potential in these cells unstable?

79. Describe the net ion movements that create the slow depolarization phase.

80. The rapid depolarization phase is due to the entry of _____ . How does this compare with a neuron?

81. The repolarization phase in autorhythmic cells is due to _____ (influx /efflux ?). How does this compare to a neuron?

Autonomic Neurotransmitters Modulate Heart Rate

82. How do the catecholamines affect the rate of depolarization in pacemaker cells? (Fig. 14-17)

83. To what kind of receptor are the catecholamines binding?

84. What happens to heart rate if the depolarization rate of autorhythmic cells decreases? If it increases?

85. The combination of which neurotransmitter and which receptor slows heart rate?

◎ *Table 14-4 compares AP generation in cardiac and skeletal muscle.*

THE HEART AS A PUMP

✔ **IP Cardiovascular System: Intrinsic Conduction System**
✔ **IP Cardiovascular System: The Cardiac Cycle**   ✔ **IP Cardiovascular System: Cardiac Output**

Electrical Conduction in the Heart Coordinates Contraction

86. Where do electrical signals in the heart originate? (Fig. 14-19)

87. If you cut all nerves leading to the heart, will it continue to beat? Explain.

88. What cell structures allow electrical signals to spread throughout the heart? (Fig. 14-19)

89. Starting at the sinoatrial (SA) node, describe, outline or map the spread of electrical activity through the heart. Be sure to include all the following terms. (Fig. 14-19)

atrial conducting system	atrioventricular (AV) node	AV node delay
bundle branches	bundle of His	left atrium
Purkinjie fibers	right atrium	septum
ventricle	internodal pathway	

90. What is the purpose of AV node delay?

Pacemakers Set the Heart Rate

91. If the SA node is damaged, will the heart continue to beat? At the same rate? Explain.

The Electrocardiogram Reflects the Electrical Activity of the Heart

92. What is an electrocardiogram (ECG)?

93. What information does an ECG show?

94. Does the ECG show ventricular contraction?

95. Define cardiac cycle.

96. What is Einthoven's triangle? (Fig. 14-20)

97. Name the waves of the ECG, tell what electrical event they represent, and with what mechanical event each wave is associated. (Fig. 14-21, 14-22)

98. In some leads of an ECG, the R wave goes down instead of up. Does this mean that the ventricles are repolarizing instead of depolarizing?

99. What are the medical terms for rapid and slow heart rate?

100. What is a normal range for heart rate?

101. When looking at an ECG, how can you determine the heart rate?

102. Why is it important to see that the P-R segment on an ECG has a constant duration?

103. Explain how you would identify an arrhythmia on an ECG.

***The Heart Contracts and Relaxes Once During a Cardiac Cycle* (Fig. 14-25)**
104. Define systole and diastole.

105. Is the heart in atrial and ventricular systole at the same time? Explain.

(Fig. 14-25, Step 1)
106. When both the atria and ventricles are relaxing:

107. Which valves are open?

108. Is blood flowing into the heart? Which chambers?

(Fig. 14-25, Step 2)
109. In a person at rest, how much of ventricular filling depends on atrial contraction?

110. Is there a valve between the atria and the veins emptying into them?

(Fig. 14-25, Step 3)
111. What electrical event precedes ventricular systole?

112. As the ventricles contract, why do the AV valves close?

113. What creates the heart sounds?

114. Explain what is happening during isovolumic ventricular contraction.

115. What happens to pressure within the ventricles during isovolumic ventricular contraction?

116. What is happening to the atria during this phase of the cycle?

(Fig. 14-25, step 4)
117. Why do the semilunar valves open, allowing blood to be ejected into the arteries?

118. Blood flows out of the ventricles, therefore you know that ventricular pressure must be (lower / higher ?) than arterial pressure.

(Fig. 14-25, step 5)
119. As the ventricles relax, the ventricular pressure (increases / decreases ?)

120. Why do the semilunar valves close?

121. What creates the second heart sound?

122. During this phase, are the AV valves open or closed? Explain.

123. When do the AV valves open?

Pressure-Volume Curves Represent One Cardiac Cycle
124. Answer the following questions using the pressure-volume loop shown in Fig. 14-26.

125. At point A, is the atrium relaxed or contracting?

126. Is the ventricle relaxed or contracting?

127. From point A to point B, the ventricular volume is increasing. Why doesn't ventricular pressure also increase substantially?

128. Define end-diastolic volume (EDV). What is the EDV for our 70-kg man at rest?

129. What event begins at point B and continues until point D?

130. From point B to point C, why does pressure increase without a change in ventricular volume?

131. What factors are affecting pressure and volume from point C to point D?

132. At point D, why does the aortic valve close?

133. Define end systolic volume (ESV). What is the ESV for our 70-kg man at rest?

134. At what point(s) on the graph are both the aortic and mitral valves closed?

◎ *The Wiggers diagram (Fig. 14-27) summarizes electrical and mechanical cardiac events.*

Stroke Volume Is the Volume of Blood Pumped by One Ventricle in One Contraction
135. Define stroke volume. (Give units!)

136. How do you calculate stroke volume?

137. If the end-diastolic volume increases and the end-systolic volume decreases, has the heart pumped more or less blood? Make up an example.

Cardiac Output Is a Measure of Cardiac Performance
138. Define cardiac output (CO). (Give units!)

139. What information does CO tell us? What does it not tell us?

140. What are average values for stroke volume and cardiac output in the 70 kg man at rest?

141. True or false? Defend your answer.
The right side of the heart pumps blood only to the lungs, so its cardiac output is less than that of the left side of the heart, which must pump blood to many more tissues.

Heart Rate Is Varied by Autonomic Neurons and Catecholamines
142. Explain the antagonistic control of heart rate by sympathetic and parasympathetic neurons. (Fig. 14-28)

143. If you were to block all autonomic input to the heart, what would happen to heart rate?

144. Name the parasympathetic and sympathetic neurotransmitters and their receptors at the SA node.

Multiple Factors Influence Stroke Volume
145. Stroke volume is directly related to the _____ generated by cardiac muscle during contraction.

146. Force is affected by these two factors:

147. Define contractility.

Length-Tension Relationships and Starling's Law of the Heart
148. As sarcomere length increases, what happens to force of contraction?

149. In the intact heart we cannot measure sarcomere length directly. What parameter do we use as an indirect indicator of sarcomere length?

150. State the Frank-Starling law of the heart. (Fig. 14-29)

Stroke Volume and Venous Return
151. Define venous return.

152. Venous return is best indicated by (end-systolic volume / end-diastolic volume ?).

153. Explain pre-load and its relationship to venous return.

154. List and explain three factors that enhance venous return.

Reflex Control of Contractility
155. What is an inotropic agent?

156. What effect does a positive inotropic agent have on the heart? Name two.

157. At the cellular level, an increase in contractility occurs when _____ increases.

158. Explain how Fig. 14-30 shows that contractility is distinct from length-tension relationships in cardiac muscle.

◎ Review Fig. 14-31, p. 437 for a map of the factors that affect cardiac output.

TALK THE TALK

acetylcholine (ACh)

aorta

artery

atrium

AV node delay

bradycardia

Ca^{2+} permeability

Ca^{2+}-induced Ca^{2+} release

cardiac cycle

cardiovascular system

complete heart block

cross-bridge formation

desmosome

driving pressure

electrocardiogram, or ECG

end-diastolic volume (EDV)

excitation-contraction coupling

flow

gap junction

heart

hepatic portal vein

I_f channel

internodal pathway

isovolumic ventricular contraction

millimeters of mercury (mm Hg)

myocardium

norepinephrine

pacemaker potential

pericarditis

Poiseuille

pressure

pulmonary artery

pulmonary valve

QRS complex

respiratory pump

septum

stenosis

systemic circulation

tachycardia

thoracic cavity

troponin

vein

venous circulation

viscosity

β_1 adrenergic receptor

action potential, contractile cell

aortic valve

atrioventricular node (AV node)

auscultation

bicuspid valve

bundle branch

Ca^{2+} spark

calcium

cardiac glycoside

catecholamine

contractility

cyanosis

diastole

ectopic pacemaker

electroencephalogram, or EEG

end-systolic volume (ESV)

fibrillation

flow rate

graded contraction

heart attack

hydrostatic pressure

inotropic agent

ischemia

length-force relationship

mitral valve

Na^+-Ca^{2+} exchanger

ouabain

pacemakers, cardiac

pericardium

portal system

pressure gradient (ΔP)

pulmonary circulation

pulmonary vein

refractory period, cardiac muscle

second heart sound

sinoatrial node (SA node)

sternum

systole

tetanus

torr

vasoconstriction

velocity of flow

venous return

voltage-gated Na^+ channel

action potential, autorhythmic cell

arrhythmia

atrioventricular valve

autorhythmic cell

blood

Bundle of His ("hiss")

Ca^{2+}-ATPase

capillary

cardiac output

chordae tendineae

coronary artery

cyclic AMP

digitoxin

Einthoven, Walter

electromyelogram, or EMG

epinephrine

first heart sound

foxglove

Harvey, William

heart rate, control of

hypoxia

intercalated disk

isovolumetric relaxation

mechanical events of cardiac cycle

myocardial infarction

Na^+-K^+-ATPase

P wave

papillary muscle

phospholamban

pre-load

prolapse

pulmonary trunk

Purkinje fiber

resistance

semilunar valve

Starling's law of the heart

stroke volume

T wave

tetrodotoxin

tricuspid valve

vasodilation

vena cava

ventricle

Wiggers diagram

QUANTITATIVE THINKING

Flow $\propto \Delta P$ where $\Delta P = P_1 - P_2$
$F \propto 1/R$ where $R = 8L\eta/\pi r^4$ and in most cases, $R = 1/r^4$
Flow $\propto \Delta P/R$ or Flow $\propto \Delta Pr^4$
stroke volume = EDV - ESV
cardiac output (CO) = heart rate x stroke volume

1. If the small intestines need more blood, what should happen to the resistance and radius of the blood vessels supplying their blood?

2. Compare the flow rates between tubes A and B below. L= length, r = radius, P1 = pressure at one end of the tube and P2 is the pressure at the other end.

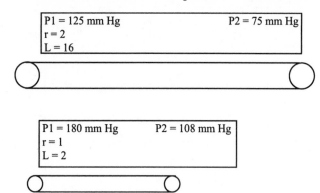

P1 = 125 mm Hg   P2 = 75 mm Hg
r = 2
L = 16

P1 = 180 mm Hg   P2 = 108 mm Hg
r = 1
L = 2

3. At rest, Juliet's heat rate is 72 beats/min and her cardiac output is 5.0 L/min. However, when she sees Romeo, her heart rate increases to 120 beats/min and her cardiac output reaches 15 L/min. What is Juliet's stroke volume before and after seeing Romeo?

PRACTICE MAKES PERFECT

1. Write out the full words for the following abbreviations:

ACh _____

AV (node or valves) _____

CO _____

ECG _____

EDV _____

ESV _____

SA (node) _____

SV _____

2. Describe the electrical and mechanical events associated with the electrocardiogram.

	Electrical Event	Mechanical Event
P wave		
QRS complex		
T wave		
PQ segment		
ST segment		
TP segment		

3. In a person at rest, only 20% of ventricular filling depends on atrial contraction. If heart rate speeds up, would this percentage become greater or less? Explain.

4. Compare the action potentials of cardiac and skeletal muscles.

	Skeletal muscle	Contractile myocardium	Autorhythmic myocardium
Membrane potential			
Events leading to threshold potential			
Rising phase of action potential			
Repolarization phase			
Hyperpolarization			
Duration of action potential			
Refractory period			

5. What happens to the kinetic energy of blood flow as it leaves the heart and travels through the blood vessels of the circulatory system?

6.   You need to design two different drugs, one that increases and another that decreases the force of a cardiac muscle contraction. What molecular and cellular mechanisms of the cardiac muscle cell might you try to alter with these drugs? (There are several possible answers; be creative. You are not limited to what has already been developed.)

7. Explain how Starling's Law, venous return and input from the autonomic nervous system affect cardiac output.

8. Below is an outline of the heart. Draw and label the atrioventricular node, atrial conducting system, bundle of His, Purkinje fibers, sinoatrial node. Show the direction of current flow.

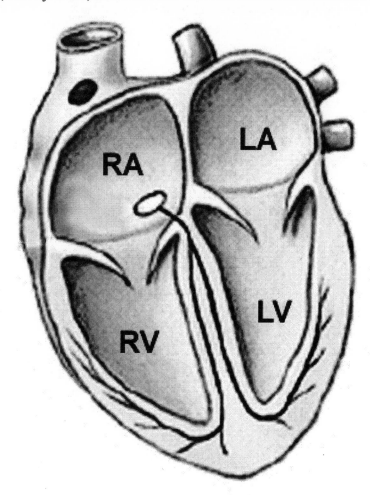

9. The total amount of blood in the circulatory system is about 5 liters. If the cardiac output of the left ventricle is 4.5 L/min at rest, what would be the cardiac output of the right ventricle? Explain your answer.

10. Answer the following questions using the pressure-volume loop shown in Fig. 14-26, p. 432.

    At point A, what can you say about atrial pressure relative to ventricular pressure? _____

    At what point on the curve does ventricular pressure match aortic pressure?
    _____

    Estimate the highest pressure in the aorta. _____

11. Draw a graph that has end diastolic volume (EDV) on the x-axis and stroke volume on the y-axis. Draw a point that represents a stroke volume at rest of 70 mL with an EDV of 135 mL. Draw a curve that would represent an increase in stroke volume with the same EDV.

MAPS

1. Construct a flow chart using the following terms to trace a drop of blood through the cardiovascular system:

artery	aorta	arteriole
capillary	left atrium	left ventricle
pulmonary artery	pulmonary vein	right atrium
right ventricle	vein	vena cava
venule		

2. The cardiovascular control center located in the medulla oblongata signals that an increase in cardiac output is required. Use the terms below to trace the sequence of events that would produce an increase in cardiac output.

β_1 receptors   acetylcholine   cardiac output
end diastolic volume   epinephrine   heart rate
parasympathetic activity   stroke volume   sympathetic activity

3.   Construct a diagram or map that provides the sequence of events that occurs during a cardiac cycle. Include in your answer the following: all electrical events, opening and closing of the valves, atrial and ventricular filling, atrial and ventricular systole and diastole, isovolumetric ventricular contraction, ventricular pressure increase, ventricular ejection, and isovolumetric relaxation.

4. Construct a flow chart or map that outlines the sequence of events leading to and occurring during excitation-contraction coupling in cardiac cells. Include membrane events, second messenger systems, the role of ions and the contractile proteins in your answer. How is the contractile process modulated?

BEYOND THE PAGES

✒ TRY IT: William Harvey's Experiments

Duplicate William Harvey's experiment that led him to believe that blood circulated in a closed loop: (1) Take your resting pulse. (2) Assume that your heart at rest pumps 70 mL per beat and that 1 mL of blood weighs 1 gram. Calculate how long it would take your heart to pump your weight in blood. (1 kilogram = 2.2 pounds).

FURTHER EXPLORATIONS

Construction of a model demonstrating cardiovascular principles. *Advan. Physiol. Edu.* 277: S67-S83, 1999.

William Harvey and the Circulation of the Blood: The Birth of a Scientific Revolution and Modern Physiology. *News Physiol Sci* 17: 175-180, 2002. October

The Heart as a Suction Pump. Scientific American 254 (6):84-91, 1969.

Have a heart. Tissue-engineered valves may offer a transplant alternative. Scientific American. 272(6):46, 1995 June.

The physiology of heart-lung transplantation in humans. News in Physiological Sciences. 5: 71-74, 1990.

15

BLOOD FLOW AND
THE CONTROL OF BLOOD PRESSURE

SUMMARY

Be sure to learn the pathways presented in this chapter. They'll be around for the rest of the book. Also become familiar with hydrostatic and osmotic pressures and their roles in bulk fluid flow. Here are some concepts to watch for in this chapter:

✓ How do the different blood vessels vary in structure and function?
✓ What factors determine blood pressure?
✓ Where is the primary site of variable resistance in the systemic circulation?
✓ What factors affect resistance?
✓ How is exchange at the capillaries accomplished?
✓ What are the functions of the lymphatic system?
✓ What are the components of the baroreceptor reflex?
✓ What are the risk factors for developing cardiovascular disease?

Blood vessels are composed of an inner layer of endothelium, surrounded by elastic and fibrous connective tissues and smooth muscle. Not all blood vessels have the same characteristics. For example, arterioles contain more smooth muscle than veins, and capillaries of the kidney are more porous than those of the brain. Form and function are directly related, as usual. More smooth muscle indicates a greater role in resistance and blood pressure regulation; a more porous endothelium indicates participation in filtration and fluid balance, etc. Movement across the endothelium of capillaries is accomplished by diffusion, transcytosis, and bulk flow. Filtration and absorption take place at the capillaries. Net filtration (bulk flow) is a result of the interaction of the hydrostatic and osmotic forces that exist in the capillaries and the interstitial space. The lymphatic system plays an important role in restoring fluid lost through capillary filtration in addition to its immune system function.

Blood pressure is a result of the pressure and volume changes associated with cardiac function as well as the physical properties of the blood vessels (vessel diameter, total cross-sectional area, composition of vessel structure, etc.). The main factors influencing mean arterial pressure (MAP) are cardiac output (CO) and peripheral resistance. CO is determined by stroke volume and heart rate (review Ch 14 for the factors affecting CO). Peripheral resistance is variable—affected by vasoconstriction and vasodilation of the arterioles (primarily). Various chemicals such as norepinephrine, epinephrine, and angiotensin II control vasodilation and vasoconstriction. The medullary cardiovascular control center (CVCC) integrates sensory information from carotid and aortic baroreceptors and regulates blood pressure through autonomic activity at the heart, vascular smooth muscle, and kidneys. (Here's a good chance to apply your knowledge of tonic and antagonistic control of homeostasis!) The baroreceptor reflex is the primary homeostatic control for blood pressure. However, paracrines can also have significant local control over blood pressure.

TEACH YOURSELF THE BASICS

1. Trace a drop of blood from the vena cava to the aorta, naming all major structures the drop of blood passes.

2. If blood flow through the aorta is 5 L/min, what is blood flow through the pulmonary artery?

THE BLOOD VESSELS
✐ **IP Cardiovascular -- Anatomy Review: Blood Vessel Structure & Function**

3. Name the four different tissue layers found in blood vessel walls, starting with the layer closest to the lumen.

Blood Vessels Contain Vascular Smooth Muscle
4. What is vascular smooth muscle?

5. What is the term for a decrease in the diameter of a blood vessel?

6. What is the term for an increase in the diameter of a blood vessel?

7. What is muscle tone?

Arteries and Arterioles Carry Well-Oxygenated Blood to the Cells
8. Describe the physical characteristics of the aorta and major arteries. (Fig. 15-2)

9. Blood flow from arteries to arterioles is best described as (divergent / convergent?).

10. Describe the key characteristic of arterioles.

11. How do metarterioles differ from arterioles? (Fig. 15-3)

12. What is the function of metarterioles?

13. What vessels make up the microcirculation?

Exchange Between the Blood and Interstitial Fluid Takes Place in the Capillaries
14. Describe the capillary wall and explain how this structure allows the capillaries to carry out their function. [∫ p. 67]

15. How do the capillaries of the blood-brain barrier differ from those in the rest of the systemic circulation?

Blood Flow Converges in the Venules and Veins

16. Blood flow from capillaries to venules is best described as (divergent / convergent?).

17. Compare the walls of veins with those of arteries.

18. How much of the blood in the circulatory system is found in the veins?

19. Are the bluish blood vessels you see under the skin arteries or veins?

Angiogenesis Creates New Blood Vessels

20. Define angiogenesis.

21. What is the reason for angiogenesis in children? in adults?

22. If we can find a way to stop angiogenesis, why might this become useful in treating cancer?

23. In coronary artery disease, what happens to the arteries? Why would a drug that stimulates angiogenesis be useful for treating this condition?

24. List some of the key substances involved in angiogenesis and antiangiogenesis?

BLOOD PRESSURE

⁄ IP Cardiovascular: Measuring blood pressure

25. What property of artery walls plays a key role in the ability of arteries to sustain the driving pressure created by the heart? (Fig. 15-4)

Systemic Blood Pressure Is Highest in the Arteries and Lowest in the Veins

26. Why does blood pressure decrease as blood flows through the circulatory system? (Fig. 15-5)

27. Define systolic pressure and give an average value for systolic arterial pressure.

28. Define diastolic pressure and give an average value for diastolic arterial pressure.

29. True or false, and explain: The pulse is created by a wave of blood flowing through the arteries.

30. The pulse amplitude (increases / decreases?) over distance from the heart due to what factor(s)? (Fig. 15-5)

31. What is pulse pressure and how do you calculate it?

32. How can low-pressure venous blood in the feet flow "uphill" against gravity to get back to the heart? (Fig. 15-6)

Arterial Blood Pressure Reflects the Driving Pressure for Blood Flow

33. To what does the term "blood pressure" refer?

34. Why is blood pressure such an important parameter to know?

35. Explain mean arterial pressure (MAP).

36. Write the calculation for MAP:

37. What kinds of problems may result when blood pressure is too low? too high?

Blood Pressure is Estimated by Sphygmomanometry

38. Explain how a sphygmomanometer is used to estimate arterial pressure of the radial artery. (Fig. 15-7)

39. What makes Korotkoff sounds?

40. Define systolic pressure.

41. Define diastolic pressure.

42. Explain a blood pressure of 100/70.

43. What is an average value for blood pressure?

44. Blood pressure is considered too high if systolic pressure is chronically over _____ mm Hg or diastolic pressure chronically exceeds _____ mm Hg. The medical term for high blood pressure is _____.

Cardiac Output and Peripheral Resistance Determines Mean Arterial Pressure
45. What two main factors determine mean arterial pressure (MAP)? (Fig. 15-8)

46. If blood flow into the arteries increases but there is no change in blood flow out of the arteries, MAP will (increase / decrease ?).

47. What happens to MAP if peripheral resistance increases?

48. What mathematical relationship represents blood flow into the arteries?

Changes in Blood Volume Affect Blood Pressure
49. If the volume of blood circulating through the system decreases, blood pressure (increases / decreases?)

◉ *As an analogy for blood volume exerting pressure, think of the tension on the wall of a water-filled balloon. One way to adjust pressure is to add or remove water from the balloon.*

50. What organ is responsible for decreasing blood volume?

51. The homeostatic regulation of blood pressure is accomplished by what two systems of the body? (Fig. 15-9)

52. True or false? If blood volume decreases, the kidneys can increase blood volume by reabsorbing water. Explain.

53. Name two ways the cardiovascular system tries to compensate for a decrease in blood volume. [∫ p. 480]

54. If arterial pressure falls, venous constriction mediated through the (sympathetic / parasympathetic) division will have what effect on blood distribution and blood pressure?

◉ *See Fig 15-10 for a summary map of factors affecting MAP.*

RESISTANCE IN THE ARTERIOLES
✗ **IP Cardiovascular: Factors that Affect Blood Pressure**
55. Which vessels are the main site of variable resistance in the systemic circulation?

56. What property of these vessels permits them to change resistance?

57. Write the mathematical expression for the relationship between radius (r) and resistance (R).

58. What are the goals of local control of arteriolar resistance?

59. What are the goals of reflex control of arteriolar resistance?

60. What are the goals of hormonal control of arteriolar resistance?

Myogenic Autoregulation Automatically Adjusts Blood Flow
61. What is myogenic autoregulation?

62. Describe or diagram the mechanism of myogenic autoregulation?

63. When blood pressure in an arteriole increases, myogenic regulation causes the arteriole to
_____.

Paracrines Alter Vascular Smooth Muscle Contraction
64. Tissue and endothelial paracrines locally control arteriole resistance. List some vasoactive
paracrines (Table 15-1):

65. Diagram the pathway for active hyperemia. (Fig. 15-11a)

66. Diagram the pathway for reactive hyperemia. (Fig. 15-11b)

The Sympathetic Division Is Responsible for Most Reflex Control of Vascular Smooth Muscle

67. Most systemic arterioles are innervated by sympathetic neurons. A notable exception is the erection reflex of the _____ and _____. This reflex is controlled by:

68. Norepinephrine + ____ receptors = tonic myogenic tone (Fig. 15-2)

69. Epinephrine + ____ receptors = reinforcement of vasoconstriction

70. Which catecholamine is favored by α receptors? [∫ p. 378]

71. Fight-or-flight: epinephrine + ___ receptors

DISTRIBUTION OF BLOOD TO THE TISSUES
72. Why don't all tissues get equal blood flow at all times?

73. At rest, which four organ systems receive most blood flow? (Fig. 15-13)

74. Are arterioles arranged in series or parallel? (Fig. 15-1)

75. At any given moment, the total blood flow through all arterioles = _____.

76. Flow through individual arterioles depends on (Fig. 15-15):

77. When resistance of an arteriole increases, its blood flow (increases / decreases?) (Fig. 15-14)

78. When blood flow decreases through one set of arterioles, where does that blood go?

79. Capillary blood flow can be regulated by precapillary _____.

EXCHANGE AT THE CAPILLARIES
80. What determines capillary density in a tissue?

81. Compare the structure and function of continuous and fenestrated capillaries. (Fig. 15-16)

82. Which three tissues don't have traditional capillaries? What do they have?

The Velocity of Blood Flow Is Lowest in the Capillaries
83. Explain the relationship between total cross-sectional area and velocity of flow in the circulatory system. Specifically, how does the total cross-sectional area of capillaries compare to that of larger-diameter blood-vessels? (Fig. 15-17)

Most Capillary Exchange Takes Place by Diffusion and Transcytosis
84. What are the options for exchange at the capillary?

85. For substances that diffuse freely across capillary walls, what factor is most important for determining the rate of diffusion?

86. The pores of capillaries are too small to allow proteins to pass through them. How then do protein hormones and other essential proteins move out of the blood and into the interstitial fluid?

Capillary Filtration and Reabsorption Take Place by Bulk Flow
87. Define bulk flow.

88. Distinguish between filtration and absorption in capillaries.

89. What forces create capillary bulk flow?

90. Hydrostatic pressure pushes fluid (in / out?) through capillary pores. This pressure decreases along the length of the capillary as energy is lost to _____.

91. What creates the osmotic pressure gradient between the blood and the interstitial fluid?

92. What is colloid osmotic pressure (π)?

93. What happens to colloid osmotic pressure along the length of the capillary?

94. Is filtration in capillaries exactly equal to absorption? Explain. (Fig. 15-18a)

95. How is net fluid flow determined?

THE LYMPHATIC SYSTEM
96. Name the three systems with which the lymphatics interact and explain the role of the lymphatics in each system.

97. Compare the anatomy of the lymphatic system to that of the circulatory system. (Fig. 15-18b, 15-19)

98. Bulk flow of fluid, proteins, and bacteria is (into / out of ?) lymph capillaries.

99. What is lymph? What are lymph nodes?

100. Where does lymph rejoin the blood?

101. Name the factors that influence fluid flow through the lymphatics. (Does the lymph system have a pump like the heart?)

102. What is edema?

103. Explain why disruption of the osmotic gradient between the plasma and the interstitial fluid causes edema.

Edema Is the Result of Alterations in Capillary Exchange
⫡ IP Fluids & Electrolytes: Electrolyte Homeostasis, Edema

104. Outline the mechanisms behind two different causes of edema.

REGULATION OF BLOOD PRESSURE
⫡ IP Cardiovascular: Blood Pressure Regulation

105. In what part of the brain is the neural control center for blood pressure homeostasis found?

The Baroreceptor Reflex Is the Primary Homeostatic Control for Blood Pressure
106. What type of sensory receptor responds to changes in blood pressure?

107. Where are the two main receptors for blood pressure located? What is significant about these locations?

108. If you are monitoring the electrical activity of the sensory neurons linking these baroreceptors to the cardiovascular control center, would you observe any electrical activity when a person's blood pressure is in the normal range? Are these receptors tonic or phasic?

109. List the components of the baroreceptor reflex. (Fig. 15-21, 15-22):

   Stimulus:

   Receptor(s):

   Afferent path:

   Integrating center:

   All efferent pathways

   All effectors. Match the effectors to their efferent pathways.

   Responses of the effectors:

   Systemic response:

110. A decrease in blood pressure results in (increased / decreased?) sympathetic activity and (increased / decreased?) parasympathetic activity.

111. An increase in sympathetic activity will have what effect on heart rate, force of contraction, and arteriolar diameter?

112. An increase in parasympathetic activity will have what effect on heart rate, force of contraction, and arteriolar diameter?

113. Vasoconstriction will (increase / decrease?) peripheral resistance and (increase / decrease?) blood pressure.

114. Explain the integration of breathing and cardiac output.

Orthostatic Hypotension Triggers the Baroreceptor Reflex
115. Why does blood pressure initially fall when standing up after lying flat?

116. What is the name given to this transient decrease in blood pressure?

117. Map the reflex response to orthostatic hypotension. (Fig. 15-23) Be sure to include all the steps of the reflex pathway (stimulus, receptor(s), afferent path, integrating center, efferent pathways, all effectors matched to their efferent pathways, responses of the effectors, systemic response)

CARDIOVASCULAR DISEASE
118. What is coronary heart disease (coronary artery disease) and why are millions of dollars yearly spent trying to find its cause and optimal treatment?

Risk Factors for Cardiovascular Disease Include Gender, Age, and Inheritable Factors
119. List the uncontrollable risk factors for cardiovascular disease.

120. List the controllable risk factors for cardiovascular disease.

121. What is atherosclerosis? Describe how it arises. (Fig. 15-24)

122. Compare stable plaques and vulnerable plaques and describe their role in cardiovascular disease.

123. What is LDL-cholesterol and what is its normal function?

124. Why is elevated LDL-cholesterol in the blood undesirable?

125. What is HDL-cholesterol and why is it treated differently than LDL-cholesterol?

Hypertension Represents a Failure of Homeostasis
126. Hypertension means chronically elevated blood pressure, with systolic pressures greater than _____ mm Hg or diastolic pressures greater than _____ mm Hg.

127. Differentiate between essential (primary) hypertension and secondary hypertension.

128. Explain why we say that hypertension represents failure of homeostasis.

129. How does the adaptation of sensory receptors [∫ p. 328] relate to hypertension?

130. How does hypertension contribute to atherosclerosis?

131. Why does high arterial blood pressure put additional strain on the heart?

132. How do you explain the fact that stroke volume remains constant in hypertensive patients?

133. What is congestive heart failure? How does it arise, and what are its effects on the body?

134. List some of the common treatments for hypertension.

TALK THE TALK

absorption	active hyperemia	adenosine
alpha receptor	angiogenesis	angiotensin II
arteriole	artery	atherosclerosis
atrial natriuretic peptide	baroreceptor reflex	beta (ß2) receptor
bulk flow	capillary	cardiac output
cardiovascular disease	colloid osmotic pressure	continuous capillary
coronary artery disease	diastolic pressure	discontinuous capillary
edema	elastic connective tissue	endothelin
endothelium	epinephrine	fenestrated capillaries
fibrous connective tissue	filtration	high-density lipoprotein (HDL)
histamine	hydraulic pressure	hydrostatic pressure
hypertension	kinin	Korotkoff sound
low-density lipoprotein (LDL)	lymph	lymph node
lymphatic system	mean arterial pressure (MAP)	medullary cardiovascular control center (CVCC)
metarteriole	microcirculation	muscle tone
myogenic autoregulation	norepinephrine	orthostatic hypotension
peripheral resistance	pre-capillary sphincter	pulse pressure
reactive hyperemia	serotonin	smooth muscle
sphygmomanometer	stroke	systolic pressure
thrombus	transcytosis	vasoconstriction
vasodilation	vein	venule

QUANTITATIVE THINKING

MAP = Diastolic P + 1/3 (Systolic P - Diastolic P)

Pulse pressure = Systolic pressure - Diastolic pressure

MAP $\propto$ Cardiac output x Resistance $_{arterioles}$

Flow $_{arteriole}$ $\propto$ 1/R $_{arteriole}$

1. At age 20, Missy had a blood pressure of 110/70. At 60 years old, she has a blood pressure of 125/82.

   a) In what units are these blood pressures measured?

   b) What are Missy's pulse pressures and mean arterial pressures at 20 and 60 years of age?

   c) Missy does not smoke and does not have other controllable risk factors for cardiovascular disease. Why did her pulse and mean arterial pressures change with age?

2. If the radius of an arteriole increases from 2 to 3 millimeters, how does this affect resistance and blood flow? Explain your answer using qualitative and quantitative terminology.

3. If total peripheral resistance increases and cardiac output does not change, how is MAP affected?

4. Chris has been in training for a triathlon. The Kinesiology Department decided to study his endurance and put him through some tests. His end-systolic volume was 50 mL, his end-diastolic volume was 160 mL, his heart rate was 140 beats/min, and his arterial blood pressure was 135/78. What was his cardiac output?

PRACTICE MAKES PERFECT

1. Match the blood vessel with its main characteristics.

    _____ arteries   A. lots of smooth muscle

    _____ arterioles   B. low compliance and high recoil

    _____ capillaries   C. high compliance and high recoil

    _____ veins   D. high compliance and low recoil

                                        E. contains endothelium only

2. Complete the table below. Your answer should include the relative amounts of the various types of tissues that each vessel contains.

Blood Vessel	Physical Characteristics	Function (s)
arteries		
arterioles		
capillaries		
veins		

3. A 45 year-old woman has a ventricular systolic pressure of 130. How high must you inflate the cuff of a sphygmomanometer on her left arm in order to stop blood flow through the brachial artery? Explain your reasoning?

4. Compare and contrast the response of a healthy artery with a diseased artery (arteriosclerosis) during systole and diastole. How would pulse pressure be affected by atherosclerosis?

5. Even though the radius of a single capillary is smaller than that of an arteriole, the peripheral resistance to blood flow through the capillaries is less than that of blood flow through the arterioles. Explain why this is true.

6. During exercise, blood flow to skeletal muscles to increased, but flow to the digestive system is decreased. How is this achieved?

7. Match the neurotransmitter/neurohormone and receptor with its target(s). Answers may be used more than once and more than one answer may apply to any target.

A - norepi on α receptors   B - ACh on nicotinic receptors   C - epi on β₂ receptors
D - ACh on muscarinic receptors   E - norepi on β₁   F - none of the above

SA node _____   ventricular myocardium _____   skeletal muscle capillary _____

cardiac vasculature _____   renal arterioles _____   brain arterioles _____

8. The arterioles of the kidneys constrict as a result of local control mechanisms. Assuming that no compensatory homeostatic mechanisms are triggered, what happens to each of the following? (*increases, decreases, no change*) Be able to defend your answer.

      blood flow through the kidneys? _____
      mean arterial pressure? _____
      blood flow through skeletal muscle arterioles? _____
      cardiac output? _____
      total peripheral resistance? _____
      blood flow through the venae cavae? _____
      through the lungs? _____

9. True/False and explain: In a fight-or-flight reaction, epinephrine from the adrenal cortex will combine with β₁ receptors in the heart and cause vasodilation.

10. You are a doctor and have just prescribed a calcium-channel blocking drug for a patient with high blood pressure. The patient asks how the drug works at a molecular and cellular level. How would you answer?

11. The figure below shows the cardiovascular center (CVCC) in the medulla oblongata, the heart, aortic arch, and carotid artery and carotid sinus, and an arteriole with a capillary bed. Cardiac output can be influenced by reflexes that alter heart rate, force of contraction, and peripheral resistance. Draw the anatomical components of the reflex pathways, including sensory receptors, sensory neurons, integrating centers, and efferent neurons that control cardiac function and peripheral blood pressure. Use different colors to represent different parts of the system. Where neurons terminate on targets, write in the appropriate neurotransmitters and receptors.

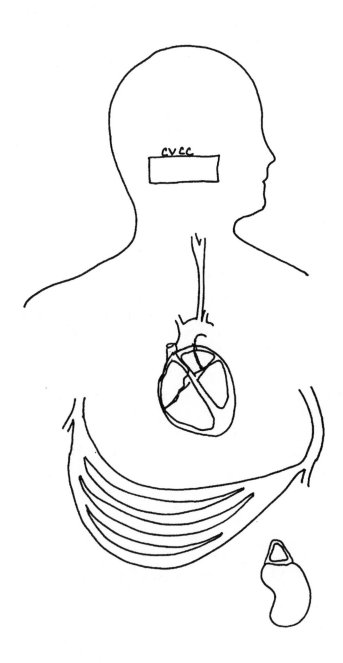

12. Fill in the following reflex pathway.

   Stimulus: Increased blood pressure

   Receptor(s): _____

   Afferent path: _____

   Integrating center:

   _____

   Efferent pathway 1:

   _____

   Effector(s) 1: ____ _____

   Tissue/organ response(s): _____

   Efferent pathway 2:

   _____

   Effector(s) 2:

   _____

   Tissue/organ response(s) 2:

   _____

   Systemic response: ___decreased blood pressure_____

13. A man has developed thromboangiitis obliterans, a condition in which the arteries in his legs (only)
have become calcified and partially obstructed. He comes to his physician complaining of pain when
walking; the pain subsides when he stops walking and rests. The man's blood pressure, taken in his left
arm, is normal.

   a) What is the blood flow in his legs compared to normal? On the basis of this answer, explain why
   he has pain when walking but not at rest.

   What would happen to blood flow in this man's legs if you: (answer and explain your reasoning)

   b) administer a peripheral vasodilator?

   c) cut the sympathetic nerves innervating the blood vessels in his legs?

MAPS

Reckless Ronnie was brought to the Emergency Room following a motorcycle accident. His blood pressure was 80/25 and pulse was 135/min. Tests showed the presence of intra-abdominal bleeding. Draw a **COMPLETE reflex map** that explains all Ronnie's physical findings, beginning with bleeding as the stimulus. Use the following terms and add any additional terms you wish to add.

α receptor	β₁ receptor	β₂ receptor
acetylcholine	aorta	baroreceptor
cardiac output	cardiovascular control center	carotid artery
decreased blood pressure	decreased blood volume	end diastolic volume
heart rate	hemorrhage	increased blood pressure
norepinephrine	parasympathetic activity	peripheral resistance
sensory neuron	stroke volume	sympathetic activity
vasoconstriction	venous return	

BEYOND THE BASICS

🖉 TRY IT: Reactive Hyperemia

Reactive hyperemia, a temporary increase in blood flow into a tissue that has been deprived of flow, can be easily demonstrated without any equipment. Wrap the fingers of your right hand around the base of your left index finger. Squeeze tightly for at least one minute to shut off blood flow into the finger. It is important to shut off as much arterial flow as you can. After one minute, release the finger and watch for color changes. It should flush red for a few seconds, then gradually fade to normal color as the vasodilators are washed away by the restored blood flow.

🖉 TRY IT: The Baroreceptor Reflex

You can demonstrate the baroreceptor reflex easily with a friend. Find the subject's pulse at the radial artery of the wrist. While monitoring the pulse, have the subject find the pulse point in the carotid artery (just to the side of the Adam's apple) and press gently on it for a few seconds. You should notice a decrease in the subject's pulse as the increased pressure created by pressing on the carotid artery is sensed by the cardiovascular control center. The baroreceptor reflex is one reason that taking a carotid pulse in an exercise class is not the most accurate indicator of heart rate.

FURTHER EXPLORATIONS

Excimer laser coronary angioplasty. Science & Medicine, January/February 1996.

Three-dimensional arterial imaging. Science & Medicine, March/April 1996.

Gene therapy: Anti-angiogenesis. Science & Medicine 6(4):4-5, 1999 Jul/Aug.

A is for ...Homocysteine. Science & Medicine 5(3), 1998 May/Jun.

Chronic infection and coronary disease. Science & Medicine 5(6), 1998 Nov/Dec.

Angiogenesis. Science & Medicine 6(3), 1999 May/Jun.

16

SUMMARY

What do you need to know about blood?

✓ Blood is composed of plasma, red blood cells (RBCs), white blood cells (WBCs), and platelets.

✓ Plasma is what's left of blood if you were to remove the cellular elements.

✓ All blood cells are descendants of pluripotent hematopoietic stem cells, and the production of blood cells (hematopoiesis) is under chemical control.

✓ WBCs carry out immune functions.

✓ RBCs transport O_2 from lungs to tissues and CO_2 from tissues to lungs.

✓ Hemoglobin (Hb) is the O_2-binding portion of the RBC.

✓ Hemostasis is achieved by activated platelets and the coagulation cascade.

This chapter gives some detail about our blood, its components and their functions. To help you organize these details, consider making a large map where the main headings are the components of blood (e.g., plasma, RBCs, WBCs, platelets).

Plasma resembles interstitial fluid except that it contains plasma proteins. Plasma proteins include albumins, globulins, fibrinogen, and immunoglobulins. Plasma proteins raise the osmotic pressure of plasma, thus pulling water from the interstitial fluid into the capillaries [∫ p. 506].

Red blood cells (RBCs, erythrocytes) transport O_2 and CO_2 between the lungs and tissues with the help of hemoglobin (Hb). Hb production requires that iron be ingested in the diet. Mature RBCs are biconcave disks that lack a nucleus and membranous organelles. Thus, they are essentially membranous "bags" filled with enzymes and Hb. Because RBCs lack a nucleus, they cannot make new proteins or membrane molecules and therefore die after about 120 days. Their flexible membrane and flattened shape allow RBCs to change shape in response to osmotic fluctuations.

White blood cells (WBCs, leukocytes) consist of five mature cell types: lymphocytes, monocytes, neutrophils, eosinophils, and basophils. Neutrophils and monocytes (macrophage precursors) are collectively called phagocytes because of their ability to ingest foreign particles. Basophils, eosinophils, and neutrophils are called granulocytes because of cytoplasmic inclusions that give a granular appearance.

Platelets are anuclear cell fragments that have broken off from megakaryocytes in the bone marrow. Platelets are always present in the blood, but they are inactive unless there is damage to the circulatory system. Ruptured blood vessels expose collagen fibers that activate platelets, and the activated platelets initiate coagulation with the goal of hemostasis.

All blood cells are derived from pluripotent hematopoietic stem cells that develop according to chemical signals into the mature cells already discussed. These chemical signals include cytokines [∫ p. 173], growth factors, and interleukins. Table 16-2 (p. 529) lists some of these chemicals and how they affect blood cell development. Some examples include erythropoietin, which influences erythropoiesis; various colony-stimulating factors, which influence leukopoiesis; and thrombopoietin, which influences platelet production.

TEACH YOURSELF THE BASICS

PLASMA AND THE CELLULAR ELEMENTS OF BLOOD

Plasma Is Composed of Water, Ions, Organic Molecules, and Dissolved Gases

1. What is plasma?

2. Describe the composition of plasma.

3. Compare plasma with interstitial fluid.

4. Where are most plasma proteins made?

5. Name three main groups of plasma proteins and give their functions. (Table 16-1)

6. What role do plasma proteins play in capillary filtration? [∫ p. 506]

The Cellular Elements Include Red Blood Cells, White Blood Cells, and Platelets

7. List the three main cellular elements of the blood and describe their primary function(s).

8. Why do we call them "cellular elements" rather than "cells?"

9. What are the "formal" names for red blood cells and white blood cells?

10. What are the parent cells of platelets called?

11. List the five mature WBCs found in blood and give the function(s) of each type.

12. Which of the WBCs are known as phagocytes, and why are they given that name? [∫ p. 144]

13. Why are lymphocytes also called immunocytes?

14. Which WBCs are called granulocytes and why?

BLOOD CELL PRODUCTION

15. What are pluripotent hematopoietic stem cells? (Fig. 16-3)

16. Describe the differentiation of the pluripotent hematopoietic stem cells.

Blood Cells Are Produced in the Bone Marrow

17. Define hematopoiesis. Where does it take place in embryos, children, and adults?

18. Describe red bone marrow.

19. Describe yellow bone marrow.

20. Of all blood cells produced, _____% will become RBCs and _____% will become WBCs.

21. Compare the lifespans of RBCs and WBCs.

Hematopoiesis Is Controlled by Cytokines, Growth Factors, and Interleukins

22. What are cytokines? [∫ p. 173]

23. What are some cytokines involved in hematopoiesis?

◉ *Table 16-2 lists some cytokines involved in hematopoiesis.*

Colony-Stimulating Factors Regulate Leukopoiesis

24. Where are the CSFs that regulate reproduction and development of WBCs made?

25. How do WBCs participate in the regulation of leukopoiesis? Why is this clever?

26. What is leukemia?

27. What is neutropenia?

Thrombopoietin Regulates Platelet Production

28. What is thrombopoietin (TPO) and where is it made?

Erythropoietin Regulates Red Blood Cell Production
29. What is RBC production called?

30. What is erythropoietin (EPO) and where is it made?

31. What is the stimulus for EPO synthesis and release?

◎ Share your thoughts on the potential therapeutic value of various recombinant hematopoietic cytokines (like EPO, filgrastim or sargramostim).

RED BLOOD CELLS
32. What is the red blood cell count of a μL of whole blood?

33. Define hematocrit? (Fig. 16-2)

Mature Red Blood Cells Lack a Nucleus
34. Name two immature forms of an erythrocyte. How are they different from the mature RBC? (Fig. 16-5)

35. Describe the structure and contents of the mature RBC. (Fig. 16-6a)

36. What is hemoglobin?

37. Without mitochondria, RBCs cannot carry out (anaerobic / aerobic?) metabolism.

38. What is the primary energy source for mature RBCs?

39. How is the lack of a nucleus related to the limited life span of the RBC?

40. What holds the RBC in its unique shape? (Fig. 16-6)

41. When placed in a hypotonic solution, a cell will do what? [∫ p. 154]

Hemoglobin Synthesis Requires Iron
42. Describe or draw the structure of hemoglobin (Hb). (Fig. 16-7)

43. How does fetal Hb differ structurally from adult hemoglobin?

44. Why must we have adequate iron in the diet in order to make hemoglobin? (Fig. 16-8)

45. What are the differences in function and location of transferrin and ferritin?

46. Where is heme made?

Red Blood Cells Live About Four Months
47. What is the average life span of an RBC?

48. How are old RBCs destroyed and what happens to the RBC components?

49. What is the relationship between heme, bilirubin, and bile?

50. How are bilirubin and its metabolites excreted?

51. What is jaundice?

Red Blood Cell Disorders Decrease Oxygen Transport
52. List four common causes of anemia. (Table 16-3)

53. Why are people with anemia often weak and fatigued?

54. Anemias in which the RBCs are destroyed at a high rate are called _____
    anemias.

55. Lack of adequate iron in the diet results in _____
    anemia.

56. Smaller-than-normal RBCs are said to be _____, while paler-than-normal
    RBCs are said to be _____.

57. What makes the hemoglobin of sickle cell disease abnormal? (Fig. 16-9)

58. In polycythemia vera, patients have higher than normal RBC production. Why is this harmful? [∫ p.
    454]

PLATELETS AND COAGULATION
59. In order to repair broken blood vessels, blood flow through the vessel should be (increased /
    decreased?).

60. What temporarily seals the hole in a broken blood vessel until it can be repaired?

Platelets Are Small Fragments of Cells
61. Describe how platelets are formed from megakaryocytes.

62. What intracellular components do platelets contain?

63. What is the typical lifespan of a platelet?

64. How do megakaryocytes get multiple nuclei? (Fig. 16-10)

65. What prevents platelets from constantly forming clots throughout the circulatory system?

Hemostasis Prevents Blood Loss from Damaged Blood Vessels
66. Define hemostasis.

67. What is the difference between platelet adhesion and platelet aggregation?

68. Briefly describe or diagram the main steps that take place when a blood vessel breaks and is repaired.
69. (Fig. 16-11)

70. Describe or diagram the relationship between thrombin, fibrin, fibrinogen, plasmin, coagulation, and fibrinolysis.

Platelet Activation Begins the Clotting Process
71. Describe how platelets are activated. (Fig. 16-11, 16-12; Table 16-4)

72. Activated platelets release chemicals that activate additional platelets. This is an example of what kind of pathway?

73. How is formation of the platelet plug restricted to the damaged region?

Coagulation Converts the Platelet Plug into a More Stable Clot
74. Define and describe coagulation.

75. How does initiation of the intrinsic pathway differ from that of the extrinsic pathway? (Fig. 16-13)

76. The intrinsic and extrinsic pathways unite at the common pathway to initiate _____ formation. (Fig. 16-14)

77. Why is it necessary to cross-link fibrin?

78. Is plasmin a free enzyme or a bound enzyme? Where would you expect to find it? How does plasmin accomplish fibrinolysis?

Anticoagulants Prevent Coagulation
79. What are anticoagulants?

80. Describe two ways anticoagulants can work.

81. List some known anticoagulants, both those produced by our body and others—indicate whether each is endogenous or exogenous.

82. What is hemophilia? What are some causes of the disorder?

TALK THE TALK

acetylsalicylic acid (aspirin) adipocyte   albumin
anemia   anticoagulant   basophil
bile   bilirubin   blood
blood cell culture   blood sinus   bone marrow
clot   coagulation   coagulation cascade
collagen   colony-stimulating factor   cytokine
                                (CSF)

cytoskeleton   differential white cell count endothelium
eosinophil   erythroblast   erythrocyte
erythropoiesis   erythropoietin (EPO)   extracellular matrix
extrinsic path   factor   ferritin
fetal hemoglobin   fibrin   fibrinogen
fibrinolysis   fibroblast   globulin
granulocyte   hematocrit   hematopoiesis
heme group   hemoglobin   hemolytic anemia
hemophilia   hemostasis   hereditary spherocytosis
hydroxyurea   hypertonic   hypochromic
hypotonic   immunocyte   immunoglobulin
infarct   interleukin   intrinsic path
iron-deficiency anemia   jaundice   leukemia
leukocytes   lymphocyte   macrophage
megakaryocyte   microcytic   monocyte
multipotent progenitor   neutropenia   neutrophil
nitric oxide   phagocyte   phagocytosis
plasma   plasma protein   plasmin
platelet   platelet adhesion   platelet aggregation
platelet plug   polycythemia vera   prostacyclin
recombinant DNA technology   reticular fiber   reticulocyte
sickle cell disease   stem cell   streptokinase
stroma   thrombin   thrombocyte
thrombopoietin   thrombus   tissue factor
tissue plasminogen activator (TPA) transferrin   umbilical cord blood
urokinase   vasoconstriction   venesection
William Harvey

PRACTICE MAKES PERFECT

1. Describe two different major functions of blood.

2. Give at least two characteristics that are used to identify different types of leukocytes.

3. A blood sample from a patient shows normal white cell count, low red cell count, and more than normal reticulocytes present in the blood. Would you suspect that this person's problem is a result of a defect in the bone marrow or a problem with the circulating red blood cells? Defend your choice.

4. A person has a total blood volume of 4.8 L and a hematocrit of 40%. What is her plasma volume?

5. Which ONE of the following is NOT TRUE?

   Neutrophils, eosinophils, and basophils:
   a) are leukocytes
   b) are lymphocytes
   c) are granulocytes
   d) are polymorphonuclear (have bi-lobed or tri-lobed nucleus)

6. Erythropoietin (EPO) is traditionally considered to be a hormone. Based on what you have learned about EPO, is it most accurately classified as a hormone or as a cytokine?

MAPS

1. Create a map showing hemostasis and coagulation. Include the terms below and any others you wish to add.

blood	clot	coagulation
coagulation cascade	collagen	cytokine
endothelium	extracellular matrix	extrinsic path
factor	fibrin	fibrinogen
fibrinolysis	hemostasis	intrinsic path
plasmin	platelet	platelet adhesion
platelet aggregation	platelet plug	prostacyclin
thrombin	thrombocyte	thrombus
tissue factor	tissue plasminogen activator (TPA)	vasoconstriction

2. Create a map of the blood cells, their synthesis, and their basic functions, using the terms below and any others you wish to add.

basophil	blood	bone marrow
colony-stimulating factor (CSF)	cytokine	eosinophil
erythroblast	erythrocyte	erythropoiesis
erythropoietin (EPO)	granulocyte	hematopoiesis
immunocyte	immunoglobulin	interleukin
leukocyte	lymphocyte	macrophage
megakaryocyte	monocyte	multipotent progenitor
neutrophil	phagocyte	phagocytosis
platelet	reticulocyte	stem cell
stroma	thrombocyte	thrombopoietin
umbilical cord blood		

3. Create a map for red blood cell synthesis and destruction, using the terms below and any others you wish to add.

amino acids   bile   bilirubin
erythroblast   erythrocyte   erythropoiesis
erythropoietin (EPO)   ferritin   fetal hemoglobin
hematopoiesis   heme group   hemoglobin
iron   jaundice   protein
transferrin

BEYOND THE BASICS

FURTHER EXPLORATIONS

Snake venoms and the hemostatic system. Toxicon 36(12):1749-800, 1998 Dec.

Antiplatelet therapy. Science & Medicine, July/August 1996.

Blood substitutes. Science & Medicine, March/April 1997.

Discovery of heparin: Contributions of William Henry Howell and Jay McLean. News in Physiological Sciences 7: 237-242, October 1992.

The molecular genetics of hemophilia. Scientific American, March 1986.

The stem cell. Scientific American, December 1991.

Hormones that stimulate the growth of blood cells. Scientific American, July 1988.

Gene therapy: Hemophilia. Science & Medicine 5(4), 1998 Jul/Aug.

Gene therapy: Factor IX deficiency. Science & Medicine 6(3), 1999 May/Jun.

17

MECHANICS OF BREATHING

SUMMARY

Many basic principles governing blood flow in the circulatory system apply to air flow in the respiratory system. Look for themes to be repeated in this chapter.

> ✓ Air movement during breathing occurs because of pressure gradients created by volume changes.
> ✓ Total cross-sectional area is greater for smaller airways than for larger airways.
> ✓ Alveolar ventilation and blood flow are matched to ensure efficiency.

Cellular respiration, which you studied in Chapter 4, refers to the metabolic processes that consume oxygen and nutrients and produce energy and CO_2. External respiration is the exchange of gases between the atmosphere and the cells. Ventilation (breathing) is the process by which air is moved into and out of the lungs. O_2 is transported via the blood to cells, and CO_2 is removed by the blood and taken to the lungs.

Air movement in the respiratory system highlights its anatomy: air goes from nasopharynx to trachea to bronchi, bronchioles, and finally alveoli. The lungs are contained within the thoracic cage. Each lung is surrounded by a double-walled pleural sac, and the pleural fluid that exists between the pleural membranes holds the lungs against the thoracic wall. This pleural fluid also helps the membranes slip past each other as the lungs move during respiration. The diaphragm, a sheet of skeletal muscle, forms the bottom of the thoracic cage, and its movement creates volume changes that in turn create air movement. The other muscles involved in respiration include the intercostal muscles, the scalenes, the sternocleidomastoids, and the abdominals.

Air moves according to a set of physical laws collectively known as the gas laws. Boyle's law describes how, in a closed system, volume increases as pressure decreases (and vice versa). Air moves from areas of higher pressure to areas of lower pressure. Therefore, when the thoracic volume is increased by respiratory muscle movement, the pressure in the thoracic cavity drops and air moves in down its pressure gradient (inspiration). Likewise, as thoracic volume decreases, the alveolar pressure increases and air moves out of the body (expiration). Movement of individual gases depends on their partial pressure gradients. Just as water and solutes move down their concentration gradients, so do gases. Dalton's law describes how the total pressure of a gaseous mixture is the sum of the pressures of the individual gases. The pressure of an individual gas is called a partial pressure, and gases move from higher partial pressures to lower partial pressures. Blood flow and alveolar ventilation are closely matched, with partial pressures serving as primary stimuli, to ensure efficient delivery and removal of gases.

Other respiratory functions include pH regulation, vocalization, and protection from foreign substances. Be sure you understand the graphs of this chapter. They will help you create a visual explanation of respiratory function. Also, be sure you understand the ways in which the cardiovascular system and respiratory system are integrated.

TEACH YOURSELF THE BASICS

1. List four key functions of the respiratory system.

2. What is lost from the body through the respiratory system besides carbon dioxide?

THE RESPIRATORY SYSTEM
⁄ IP RESPIRATORY SYSTEM: ANATOMY REVIEW

3. Distinguish between cellular respiration [∫ p. 105] and external respiration. (Fig. 17-1)

4. List the four integrated processes of external respiration (three exchanges and one transport).

5. Distinguish between inspiration and expiration.

6. Name the three major components of the respiratory system. (Fig. 17-2)

7. Name the structures of the upper and lower respiratory system.

The Bones and Muscles of the Thorax Surround the Lungs
8. What bones and muscles form the walls of the thoracic cage? The floor? (Fig. 17-2a)

9. Name the two additional sets of muscles associated with the thoracic cage.

10. Name the three sacs enclosed within the thorax. What is in each sac? (Fig. 17-2d)

11. What thoracic structures are not contained within these three sacs?

Pleural Sacs Enclose the Lungs
12. The lungs are light, spongy tissue mostly occupied by _____-filled spaces. (Fig. 17-2b)

13. What is the relationship between the lungs, the pleura, and the pleural fluid? (Fig. 17-3)

14. What are the functions of pleural fluid?

The Airways Connect Lungs to the Environment
15. Following an oxygen molecule from the air to the exchange epithelium of the lung, name each structure the molecule passes. (Fig. 17-2b, e)

16. As the molecule moves into the airways, the diameter of the airways gets progressively smaller and the total cross-sectional surface area of the airways (increases / decreases?). (Fig. 17-4)

17. The velocity of air flow is highest in the _____ and lowest in the _____. [∫ p. 455]

The Alveoli Are the Site of Gas Exchange
18. Describe the structure of the alveoli. (Fig. 17-2f, g)

19. Describe and give the functions of the two types of epithelial cells in alveoli.

20. Describe the composition of the alveolar walls and surrounding connective tissue.

21. Describe the association of the alveoli and the circulatory system. (Fig. 17-2f)

The Pulmonary Circulation Is a High-Flow, Low-Pressure System
22. Trace a drop of blood through the pulmonary circulation from the (left/ right ?) ventricle to the (left / right?) atrium.

23. Compare the following aspects of the pulmonary circulation to those of the systemic circulation:

Volume of blood in the pulmonary vessels _____

(Of this volume, how much is participating in gas exchange at any moment? _____)

Total blood flow through the lungs in liters per minute _____

Pulmonary arterial pressure _____

What effect does lower mean pulmonary blood pressure have on capillary fluid exchange? [∫ p. 506]

GAS LAWS ◎ *Gas laws are given in Table 17-1*
✗ IP RESPIRATORY SYSTEM: PULMONARY VENTILATION

24. Although we can draw many comparisons between air flow and blood flow, air and blood differ significantly in what way?

25. When we use an atmospheric pressure of 0 mm Hg, what is that value equivalent to? Why do we use this convention?

Air Is a Mixture of Gases
26. State Dalton's Law.

◎ *Table 17-2 summarizes partial pressures of atmospheric gases.*

27. How do you calculate the partial pressure of a single gas in a mixture?

28. What happens to the partial pressures of individual gases if dry air is suddenly humidified?

Gases Move from Areas of Higher Pressure to Areas of Lower Pressure
29. Air flows from regions of _____ to regions of _____.

30. What role does muscle contraction play in the creation of air flow in the respiratory system?

Boyle's Law Describes Pressure-Volume Relationships of Gases
31. What factors contribute to gas pressure in a closed container?

32. State Boyle's Law. (Fig. 17-5)

33. For gases in a closed container, as volume (increases / decreases?), pressure (increases / decreases?).

34. How does the respiratory system create volume changes?

VENTILATION
⟋ IP RESPIRATORY SYSTEM: PULMONARY VENTILATION

35. Define ventilation.

The Airways Warm, Humidify, and Filter Inspired Air
36. Describe three ways the upper airways condition air before it reaches alveoli.

37. What is the source of heat and water in the airways?

38. Explain how the airways filter air.

39. What kind of cell secretes mucus? (Fig. 17-6) [∫ p. 69]

40. What is the mucus escalator?

41. Why don't most pathogens trapped in the airway mucus make you sick?

42. Why do children with cystic fibrosis have so many lung infections?

During Ventilation, Air Flows Because of Pressure Gradients
43. Name the primary muscles involved in quiet breathing.

44. What happens in forced breathing?

45. As the pressure gradient increases, air flow _____.

46. As resistance of the airways increases, air flow _____.

47. Express the above relationships mathematically.

48. What are the differences between intrapleural pressure and alveolar pressure?

49. What is a respiratory cycle?

50. Compare the direction of air flow in the respiratory system to the direction of blood flow in the circulatory system.

Inspiration Occurs When Alveolar Pressure Decreases
51. Outline the role of the diaphragm and inspiratory muscles in inspiration. (Fig. 17-7, -8, -9)

52. Between breaths, is there air flow? _____ Therefore, alveolar pressure must be equal to
_____. (Fig. 17-9, point A_1)

53. When thoracic volume increases during inspiration, what happens to alveolar pressure? _____

54. At what point in the respiratory cycle is alveolar pressure lowest? _____

Expiration Occurs When Alveolar Pressure Exceeds Atmospheric Pressure
55. When thoracic volume decreases during expiration, what happens to alveolar pressure? _____

56. At what point in the respiratory cycle is alveolar pressure highest? _____

57. Are the following muscles contracting in passive expiration?

    External intercostal muscles _____ Internal intercostal muscles _____

    Diaphragm _____ Abdominal muscles _____

58. Are the following muscles contracting in active expiration?

    External intercostal muscles _____ Internal intercostal muscles _____

    Diaphragm _____ Abdominal muscles _____

59. What property of the respiratory system is responsible for passive expiration?

60. What happens to air flow? _____

61. Internal and external intercostals are _____ muscle groups. [∫ p.
390]

Intrapleural Pressure Changes During Ventilation
62. Define intrapleural pressure.

63. Explain why the intrapleural pressure is always subatmospheric. (Fig. 17-10)

64. Explain why puncturing the pleural membrane causes the lung to collapse and the rib cage to move
out. (Fig. 17-10)

65. Outline or diagram intrapleural pressure changes during the respiratory cycle.

Lung Compliance and Elastance May Change in Disease States
66. Define compliance.

67. A high-compliance lung (requires additional force to stretch it / is easily stretched?).

68. Define elastance.

69. True or false? A high compliance lung always has high elastance. Explain.

70. What happens to compliance and elastance in emphysema?

71. Diseases in which compliance is reduced are called _____ lung diseases.

Surfactant Decreases the Work of Breathing
72. What creates resistance to stretch in the lung?

73. State the Law of LaPlace and relate it to surface tension in alveoli.

74. According to the Law of LaPlace, if two bubbles have equal surface tension, the (larger / smaller ?) will have a higher internal pressure. (Fig. 17-11)

75. What is the function of surfactants?

76. Which will have a higher concentration of surfactant, a large alveolus or a small one? Explain.

77. What cells in the lung secrete surfactant?

78. What type of biomolecule comprises lung surfactant?

79. What happens in premature babies who have not produced surfactant?

Airway Diameter Is the Primary Determinant of Airway Resistance
80. Explain the relationship between resistance to air flow, length of airways (L), viscosity of air (η), and radius of airways (r) using Poiseuille's Law [∫ p. 454]. (Table 17-3)

81. In the respiratory system, which of these factors is usually the most significant? _____

82. Where in the airways does air flow normally encounter the highest resistance?

_____

83. What part of the respiratory system is the site of variable resistance? _____

84. Tell what role each of the following play in control of bronchiolar diameter (bronchodilation or bronchoconstriction?)

CO$_2$ _____   Histamine [∫ p. 173] _____

Parasympathetic neurons _____ What neurotransmitter and receptor? _____

Epinephrine _____ Binds to what type of receptor? _____

Pulmonary Function Tests Measure Lung Volume During Ventilation
85. What does a spirometer do? (Fig. 17-12)

Lung Volumes
86. Name, give the abbreviation for, and describe the four lung volumes. (Fig. 17-13)

Lung Capacities
87. What are lung capacities?

88. Name, give the abbreviation for, and describe the four lung capacities. (Fig. 17-13)

Auscultation of Breath Sounds
89. What is auscultation?

90. How is it useful in pulmonary diagnosis?

Rate and Depth of Breathing Determine the Efficiency of Breathing
91. Define total pulmonary ventilation in words and give the mathematical expression for it.

92. Give normal average values for breathing rate _____ and tidal volume _____ in an adult.

93. Using these values, what is an average value for total pulmonary ventilation? (Give units!)

94. Define anatomic dead space. (Fig. 17-14)

95. How is alveolar ventilation different from total pulmonary ventilation?

96. Why is alveolar ventilation a more accurate indicator of breathing efficiency? How is this volume calculated?

◎ *Table 17-4 compares alveolar ventilation differences with different breathing patterns. Table 17-5 describes various patterns of ventilation.*

Gas Composition in the Alveoli Varies Little During Normal Breathing
97. What happens to P_{O_2} and P_{CO_2} with increased alveolar ventilation? (Fig. 17-15)

98. What happens to P_{O_2} and P_{CO_2} with decreased alveolar ventilation? (Fig. 17-15)

99. During normal breathing, partial pressures in alveoli remain constant. Why?

Ventilation and Alveolar Blood Flow Are Matched
100. An alveolus with a normal P_{O_2} is no guarantee that adequate oxygen will get to the cells. Name two other factors that must be normal in order for oxygen to be picked up by blood at the alveoli.

101. Explain what is meant by the expression: "Ventilation is matched to perfusion in the lungs."

102. How are pulmonary capillaries different from other capillaries?

103. How does this property help the body meet a demand for additional oxygen, such as during exercise?

104. Local homeostatic mechanisms attempt to keep ventilation and perfusion matched in each section of the lung. (Fig. 17-16; Table 17-6)

105. When P_{CO2} of expired air increases, bronchioles (dilate / constrict ?). When P_{CO2} of expired air decreases, bronchioles (dilate / constrict ?).

106. When the tissue P_{O2} around pulmonary arterioles decreases, the arterioles (dilate / constrict ?). When the tissue P_{O2} around pulmonary arterioles increases, the arterioles (dilate / constrict ?).

107. Compare this response of pulmonary arterioles to that of systemic arterioles.

108. Will these homeostatic responses always be able to correct the initial disturbance? Explain.

TALK THE TALK

active expiration	aerobic metabolism	airway
alveolar pressure	alveolar ventilation	alveoli
anatomic dead space	antagonistic muscle groups	asbestos
atmospheric pressure	auscultation of breath sounds	Boyle's Law
bronchiole	bronchoconstriction	bronchodilation
carbon dioxide	cellular respiration	chest wall
chronic obstructive pulmonary disease	ciliated epithelium	collagen
compliance	conditioning of inspired air	cross-sectional area, airway
cystic fibrosis	Dalton's Law	diaphragm
dipalmitoylphosphatidylcholine	elastance	elastin
emphysema	endothelium	exchange epithelium
expiration	expiratory reserve volume	external respiration
fibroblast	fibrotic lung disease	forced breathing
friction rub	functional residual capacity	gas exchange
goblet cell	growth factor	humidity
hyperventilation	hypoventilation	inspiration
inspiratory capacity	inspiratory muscles	inspiratory reserve volume
intercostal muscle	intrapleural pressure	larynx
Law of LaPlace	lower respiratory tract	lung
lung capacities	lung volumes	maximum voluntary ventilation
mucus escalator	mucus layer	myasthenia gravis
obstructive lung disease	oxygen	partial pressure
passive expiration	perfusion, lung	pharynx
pleural fluid	pleural membrane	pleural sac
pneumothorax	Poiseuille's Law	polio
primary bronchi	pulmonary arterial blood pressure	pulmonary arteriole
pulmonary circulation	pulmonary edema	pulmonary function test
residual volume	resistance, pulmonary circulation	resistance, to air flow
respiratory cycle	respiratory distress syndrome	respiratory system
restrictive lung disease	scalene muscle	secondary bronchi
spirometer	sternocleidomastoid muscle	surface tension
surfactant	thoracic cage	thorax
tidal volume (V_T)	total lung capacity	total pulmonary ventilation
trachea	type I alveolar cell	type II alveolar cell
upper respiratory tract	velocity of air flow	ventilation
viscosity	vital capacity	vocal cords

QUANTITATIVE THINKING

1. The diagram below represents a spirometer tracing.

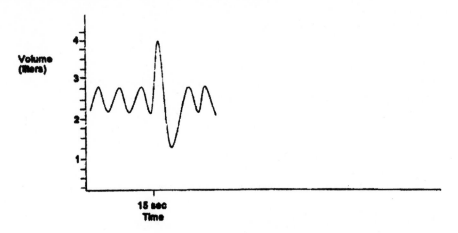

Using the tracing above, calculate the following:

Total lung capacity _____ Vital capacity _____

Expiratory reserve volume _____Residual volume _____

Total pulmonary ventilation, normal breathing (L/min) _____

2. If atmospheric pressure is 720 mm Hg and nitrogen is 78% of the atmosphere, what is the partial pressure of nitrogen?

3. A student breathes according to the following schedule (assume an anatomical dead space of 150 mL):
    tidal volume = 300 mL / breath   breath rate = 20 breaths / min
Calculate her pulmonary ventilation rate and her alveolar ventilation rate.

4. Patient A is breathing 12 times a minute with a tidal volume of 500 mL. Patient B is breathing 20 times a minute with a tidal volume of 300 mL. Which patient has better alveolar ventilation? Explain.

PRACTICE MAKES PERFECT

1. Spell out the words for the following abbreviations:

V_T _____

PO_2 _____

RV_____

IRV_____

2. Match the neurotransmitter/neurohormone and receptor with its target(s). Answers may be used more than once and more than one answer may apply to any target.

A - norepi on α receptors   B - ACh on nicotinic receptors   C - epi on β_2 receptors

D - ACh on muscarinic receptors   E - norepi on β_1

diaphragm _____   external intercostals _____

3. Blood flow to a small region of lung is blocked due to a blood clot in a small pulmonary artery.

     a) What happens to the PO_2 and PCO_2 of the alveoli that are associated with that artery?

     b) What happens to the tissue PO_2 and PCO_2 around the arterioles distal to the blockage?

     c) What is the response of the bronchioles and the arterioles in this region? Will either or both of these responses be effective in compensating for the blocked artery? Explain.

4. Alveolar air has an average P_{O2} of 100 mm Hg but expired air has an average P_{O2} of 120 mm Hg. If the lungs are taking oxygen into the body, why is there more oxygen in the expired air?

5. Compare the following pairs of items. Put the symbols below in the space provided.
     greater than >   less than <   same as or equal =

A - intrapleural pressure at the end of expiration
B - intra-alveolar pressure at the end of inspiration   A _____ B

A -blood flow in peripheral arterioles when surrounding tissue P_{O2} is 70 mm Hg
B -blood flow in pulmonary arterioles when interstitial P_{O2} is 70 mm Hg   A _____ B

A - resistance to air flow in the bronchioles
B - resistance to air flow in the trachea   A _____ B

A - compliance in alveoli with surfactant
B - compliance in alveoli without surfactant   A _____ B

MAPS

Create a map using the following terms:

Alveolar ventilation	Total pulmonary ventilation
Rate of breathing	Depth of breathing
Tidal volume	Dead space volume

BEYOND THE PAGES

Normal values in pulmonary medicine

Lung volumes and capacities (liters)	Men	Women
Tidal volume	0.5	0.5
Inspiratory reserve volume	3.3	1.9
Expiratory reserve volume	1.0	0.7
Residual volume	1.2	1.1
Total lung capacity	6.0	4.2

Total pulmonary ventilation -	6 L/min	Total alveolar ventilation	4.2 L/min
Max. voluntary ventilation	125-170 L/min	Respiration rate	12 -20 breaths/min

Blood gases

Arterial P_{O2}- 95 mm Hg (85-100)*	Arterial P_{CO2}- 40 mm Hg (37-43)	Arterial pH - 7.4
Venous P_{O2}- 40 mm Hg	Venous P_{CO2}- 46 mm Hg	Venous pH - 7.38

* Although we are considering arterial P_{O2} to be equal to alveolar P_{O2}, in reality the P_{O2} drops slightly after leaving the pulmonary capillaries. This is because a small amount of deoxygenated venous blood from the non-exchange portions of the respiratory tract and from the coronary circulation combines with oxygenated blood as it returns to the left side of the heart. The actual arterial P_{O2} value is closer to 95 mm Hg.

✎ TRY IT: Lung volumes and capacities

Calculate your volumes and capacities using the table below. What will happen to your predicted vital capacity when you are 70 years old?

H = height in cm, A = age in years (Source: Medical Physiology Syllabus, Univ. Texas Medical Branch, Galveston)

Lung volume (L)	Subject	Formula
Vital capacity	Men	(0.06 x H) - (0.0214 x A) - 4.65
	Women	(0.0491 x H) - (0.0216 x A) - 3.95
Total lung capacity	Men	(0.0795 x H) + (0.0032 x A) - 7.333
	Women	(0.059 x H) - 4.537
Functional residual capacity	Men	(0.0472 x H) + (0.009 x A) - 5.29
	Women	(0.036 x H) + (0.0031 x A) - 3.182
Residual volume	Men	(0.0216 x H) + (0.0207 x A) - 2.84
	Women	(0.0197 x H) + (0.0201 x A) - 2.421

FURTHER EXPLORATIONS

Why Doesn't the Elephant Have a Pleural Space? *News Physiol Sci* 17: 47-50, 2002. April

Breath tests in medicine. *Scientific American*, July 1992.

The human voice. *Scientific American*, December 1992.

Cystic fibrosis lung disease. *Science & Medicine* 6(3), 1999 May/Jun.

Gene therapy: Cystic fibrosis. *Science & Medicine* 6(1), 1999 Jan/Feb.

GAS EXCHANGE AND TRANSPORT

SUMMARY

✓ Gas exchange between lungs and blood or blood and tissues takes place because partial pressure gradients are created as the body consumes O_2 and releases CO_2.

✓ Hemoglobin binds O_2 and transports it to cells. Oxygen transport is affected by Po_2, temperature, pH, and metabolites.

✓ The reaction $CO_2 + H_2O \Leftrightarrow H^+ + HCO_3^-$ is an essential part of CO_2 transport in the blood.

✓ A central pattern generator in the brain stem is responsible for breathing patterns, but we can consciously control our breathing to some extent.

Recall from Chapter 17 that air moves from areas of higher pressure to areas of lower pressure. Therefore, when the thoracic volume is increased by inspiratory muscle movement, the pressure in the thoracic cavity drops and air moves in down its pressure gradient (inspiration). Likewise, as thoracic volume decreases, the alveolar pressure increases and air moves out of the body (expiration). Just as water and solutes move down their concentration gradients, so do gases. Movement of individual gases depends on their partial pressure gradients: gases move from higher partial pressures to lower partial pressures.

As the body consumes O_2 and releases CO_2, partial pressure gradients are created for each gas. Gas exchange is the result of simple diffusion down partial pressure gradients. The exchange surface in the lungs is the exchange epithelium of the alveoli. Blood flow and respiration are closely matched to ensure efficient delivery of gases. Hemoglobin (Hb) is the main facilitator of gas transport in the blood. Hb, a protein component of RBCs, consists of an iron molecule surrounded by a porphyrin ring embedded within a 4-subunit protein.

Hemoglobin binds O_2 and CO_2 and will carry either until a partial pressure gradient causes the gas to be released. Hemoglobin-binding ability is affected by pH, temperature, and 2,3-DPG. The relationship between Po_2 and Hb binding is shown by an oxyhemoglobin dissociation curve. Only 23% of CO_2 is transported bound to Hb. About 70% of CO_2 in venous blood is converted to H^+ and HCO_3^- inside the RBCs. Carbonic anhydrase is the enzyme that catalyzes this reaction: $CO_2 + H_2O \Leftrightarrow H^+ + HCO_3^-$.

A network of neurons in the pons and medulla oblongata controls respiration. This network is called a central pattern generator because it has intrinsic rhythmic activity. It is closely associated with two nuclei: the dorsal respiratory group and the ventral respiratory group. Somatic motor neurons of the dorsal respiratory group control inspiratory muscles; somatic motor neurons of the ventral respiratory group control muscles involved with active expiration and greater-than-normal inspiration.

Chemical factors also affect respiration. Central chemoreceptors respond to increases in H^+, due to elevated Pco_2, by increasing ventilation. Peripheral chemoreceptors monitor blood pH, Pco_2, and Po_2. We can control our respiration consciously to a certain extent, but chemoreceptors override conscious control.

TEACH YOURSELF THE BASICS

DIFFUSION AND SOLUBILITY OF GASES

1. By what mechanism do gases move between the alveoli and the plasma?

2. List the four rules for diffusion of gases. [∫ p. 134]

The Solubility of Gases in Liquids Depends on Pressure, Solubility, and Temperature

3. When a gas is placed in contact with a liquid, what three factors determine how much gas will dissolve in the liquid?

4. True or false, and explain. If a liquid is exposed to a P_{CO_2} of 100 mm Hg and a P_{O_2} of 100 mm Hg, equal amounts of oxygen and carbon dioxide will dissolve in the liquid. (Fig. 18-2)

5. The more soluble a gas is in a particular liquid, the (higher / lower?) the partial pressure required to force the gas into solution.

6. Gases move between liquid and gaseous phases until _____ is reached. (Fig. 18-2)

7. At equilibrium, the (concentration / partial pressure / both ?) of a gas will be equal in the air and gas phases.

8. Which is more soluble in body fluids: oxygen or carbon dioxide?

GAS EXCHANGE IN THE LUNGS AND TISSUES
⋀ IP Respiratory System: Gas Exchange

9. Give the following partial pressures in a normal person at sea level: (Fig. 18-3; Table 18-1)

◎ *Remember: Unless otherwise specified, the terms "arterial blood" and "venous blood" refer to blood in the systemic circulation.*

P_{O_2}: Alveoli = _____ Arterial blood = _____ Resting cells = _____ Venous blood = _____

P_{CO_2}: Alveoli = _____ Arterial blood = _____ Resting cells = _____ Venous blood = _____

10. If the alveolar P_{O_2} is 98 mm Hg, what will the departing arterial P_{O_2} be? Why?

11. Define hypoxia and hypercapnia.

12. What are the three categories of problems that result in low arterial content?

Decrease in Alveolar Po₂ Decreases Oxygen Uptake at the Lungs

13. If alveolar Po_2 is low, what two factors might have caused the decrease?

14. Explain the relationship between altitude and Po_2.

Changes in the Alveolar Membrane Alter Gas Exchange

15. What two cell layers must gases cross to go from the alveoli to the plasma?

16. Describe the pathological changes that adversely affect gas exchange. (Fig. 18-4)

17. Explain how emphysema can result in a loss of alveolar surface area.

18. Explain how fibrotic lung diseases can cause decreased oxygen exchange between alveoli and blood.

19. How much of the exchange epithelium must be incapacitated before arterial Po_2 drops?

20. What is pulmonary edema and how does it alter gas exchange?

21. Explain why some patients with pulmonary edema have low arterial Po_2 but normal arterial Pco_2.

GAS TRANSPORT IN THE BLOOD

↗ **IP Respiratory System: Gas Transport**

Hemoglobin Transports Most Oxygen to the Tissues

22. List two ways that gases are transported in the blood.

23. Total blood oxygen content = _____ + _____.

24. _____ % of oxygen in a given volume of blood will be carried bound to hemoglobin. (Fig. 18-6)

25. Compare the body's oxygen consumption at rest with the delivery of dissolved oxygen to the cells. Assume a cardiac output of 5 L/min.

26. How much additional oxygen per minute can be delivered by hemoglobin if each liter of blood carries 197 mL O_2 bound to hemoglobin?

27. The amount of O_2 bound to Hb depends on what two factors?

28. List three factors that establish the arterial P_{O_2}.

29. What determines the number of binding sites for oxygen?

30. What is mean corpuscular Hb?

Each Hemoglobin Molecule Binds Up to Four Oxygen Molecules

31. Hemoglobin molecules are composed of (how many?) _____ protein subunits, each with an O_2-binding _____ group. [∫ p. 532] This group is based around the element _____ that binds weakly to oxygen. Hb bound to O_2 is called _____ $(HbO_2)_{1-4}$.

32. Oxygen-hemoglobin binding obeys the law of _____.

33. Outline or diagram the steps followed by an oxygen molecule as it goes from the alveoli to its binding site on hemoglobin.

34. As dissolved O_2 diffuses into RBCs, what happens to the P_{O_2} of the surrounding plasma?

35. Therefore, as O_2 binds with Hb, (more / less?) O_2 can diffuse from alveoli into plasma.

36. Outline or diagram the steps followed by a molecule of oxygen as it diffuses from the plasma (and RBCs) and into a tissue.

37. As dissolved O_2 diffuses into a tissue, what happens to the P_{O_2} of the surrounding plasma?

38. Therefore, as O_2 enters a tissue, (more / less?) O_2 is released from Hb-binding to diffuse into the plasma.

Oxygen Binding Is Expressed as a Percentage

39. The amount of O_2 bound to Hb at any given PO_2 is shown as a percentage, called the:

40. At 100% saturation, all possible binding sites are (bound / free ?).

Po₂ DETERMINES HEMOGLOBIN BINDING OF OXYGEN

41. In the oxyhemoglobin dissociation curve (Fig. 18-8), the (Po_2 / percent saturation of Hb) determines the (Po_2 / percent saturation of Hb).

42. Adaptively, why is it important that the slope of the curve flattens out at Po_2 values above 60 mm Hg?

43. Below Po_2 of 60 mm Hg, where the curve is steeper, small changes in Po_2 cause relatively (small / large?) releases of O_2 from hemoglobin.

44. With respect to the oxyhemoglobin dissociation curve, describe how O_2 is delivered to metabolically active tissues.

Temperature, pH, and Metabolites Affect Oxygen-Hemoglobin Binding

45. Any factor that alters the hemoglobin protein may alter O_2-binding ability. (Fig. 18-9)

46. An increase in pH (increases / decreases ?) hemoglobin's affinity for oxygen.

47. An increase in temperature (increases / decreases ?) hemoglobin's affinity for oxygen.

48. An increase in PCO_2 (increases / decreases ?) hemoglobin's affinity for oxygen.

49. The metabolite 2,3-DPG (increases / decreases ?) hemoglobin's affinity for oxygen. (Fig. 18-10)

50. Fetal Hb has a/an (increased / decreased ?) affinity for oxygen. (Fig. 18-11)

51. A change in the O_2-binding affinity of hemoglobin is reflected by a shift in the O_2-Hb dissociation curve.

52. A left shift in the curve indicates (increased / decreased ?) binding affinity.

53. A right shift in the curve indicates (increased / decreased ?) binding affinity.

54. Why is it significant that a shift in the O_2-Hb dissociation curve is more pronounced at low Po_2 and less pronounced at higher Po_2?

55. Under what conditions is the cellular production of 2,3-DPG increased?

◎ *Fig. 18-12 summarizes all the factors that influence oxygen transport in the blood.*

Carbon Dioxide Is Transported Three Ways
56. Give two reasons that abnormally elevated P_{CO_2} can be toxic.

57. List the three ways that CO_2 is transported in the blood. (Fig. 18-13)

CO_2 and Bicarbonate
58. Write the equation in which CO_2 is converted in bicarbonate ion (HCO_3^-) and H+.

59. What enzyme catalyzes this reaction, and where in the blood is it found?

60. Explain why CO_2 forms HCO_3^- and H+ in the systemic capillaries, but HCO_3^- and H+ form CO_2 in pulmonary capillaries. (Fig. 18-13)

61. Why must H^+ and HCO_3^- be removed from RBC cytoplasm?

62. What is the chloride shift and what does it accomplish?

63. What is a buffer? [∫ p. 34]

64. Name two buffers found in the blood.

Hemoglobin and H^+
65. What is respiratory acidosis?

66. How does Hb help prevent this condition?

67. Constant removal of CO_2 from plasma (increases / decreases ?) P_{CO_2} and allows (more / less ?) CO_2 to leave cells.

Hemoglobin and CO_2
68. The name for hemoglobin bound to CO_2 is _____.

69. What facilitates the formation of carbaminohemoglobin? How?

CO_2 Removal at the Lungs

70. Describe or diagram the process(es) by which CO_2 moves from cells to plasma and from plasma into the alveoli? (Fig. 18-14)

◎ O_2 and CO_2 transport are summarized in Fig. 18-14.

REGULATION OF VENTILATION
∥ IP Respiratory System: Control of Respiration

71. Compare the rhythmicity and control of breathing to that of the heartbeat.

72. Compare the types of efferent neurons leaving the respiratory control center and the cardiovascular control center. (Fig. 18-15)

73. What is a central pattern generator? [∫ p. 437]

74. What role do each of the following play in the control of breathing?

    medulla oblongata:

    pons:

    cerebrum:

Neurons in the Medulla Control Breathing

75. Compare the functions of the dorsal and ventral respiratory groups of neurons in the medulla. (Fig. 18-15)

76. Which group is active during active expiration?

77. Which group is active during greater-than-normal inspiration?

78. Which group is active during inspiration?

79. Describe neural control of quiet respiration. (Fig. 18-16)

80. Describe the reciprocal inhibition between inspiratory and expiratory neurons.

Carbon Dioxide, Oxygen, and pH Influence Ventilation

81. For each group of respiratory chemoreceptors, list its location and the chemical factor(s) it monitors.

82. What is the primary chemical stimulus for changes in ventilation?

83. Explain the strategic significance of the location of the peripheral chemoreceptors. (Fig. 18-15)

The Carotid and Aortic Bodies

84. To what chemical signals do the carotid and aortic bodies respond?

85. Where do the sensory neurons leading from these receptors send their signals?

86. Describe or diagram the carotid chemoreceptor response to decreased Po_2. (Fig. 18-17)

87. Using the oxyhemoglobin dissociation curve in Fig. 18-8, explain the adaptive significance of the fact that the peripheral chemoreceptors do not respond to decreases in Po_2 until the Po_2 drops below 60 mm Hg.

Central Chemoreceptors

88. Describe or diagram how the central chemoreceptors respond to elevated blood Pco_2. (Fig. 18-18)

89. An increase in Pco_2 will trigger a/an (decrease / increase ?) in ventilation. (Fig. 18-19) How do central chemoreceptors respond to decreased Pco_2?

90. If Pco_2 is chronically elevated, the sensory receptors will _____ and the ventilation rates will (increase / decrease ?).

91. If a person has chronic hypercapnia and hypoxia, is CO_2 the primary chemical drive for ventilation? Why?

92. What will happen to ventilation if this person with chronic hypercapnia and hypoxia is given pure O_2 to breathe? Explain.

Protective Reflexes Guard the Lungs

93. Write the reflex response to an inhaled irritant.

Receptor _____

Afferent pathway _____

Integrating center _____

Efferent pathway (include chemicals and receptors) _____

Effector _____

Tissue response _____

Systemic response _____

94. Describe the Hering-Breuer inflation reflex.

Higher Brain Centers Affect Patterns of Ventilation

95. Give two examples of how higher brain centers can alter ventilation.

TALK THE TALK

2,3-diphosphoglycerate (2,3-DPG)	acidosis	aerobic metabolism
airway	alveolar pressure	beta$_2$ receptors, bronchioles
blood substitutes	blood-brain barrier	Bohr effect
buffer	carbaminohemoglobin	carbon dioxide
carbonic anhydrase	carotid and aortic bodies	cellular respiration
central chemoreceptor	central pattern generator	cerebrospinal fluid
chemical control of ventilation	chloride shift	chronic hypoxia
dopamine	dorsal respiratory group	endothelium
exchange epithelium	fetal hemoglobin	gas exchange
glomus cell	hemoglobin	Hering-Breuer inflation reflex
high-altitude acclimatization	hypercapnia	hypoventilation
hypoxia	inspiratory neuron	irritant receptor
medulla oblongata	oxygen	oxygen consumption
oxyhemoglobin	oxyhemoglobin dissociation curve	parasympathetic innervation of bronchioles
partial pressure	passive expiration	percent saturation of hemoglobin
peripheral chemoreceptor	pH regulation	pons
protective reflex	pulse oximeter	simple diffusion
solubility	solubility, carbon dioxide	solubility, oxygen
ventral respiratory group		

QUANTITATIVE THINKING

1. During exercise, a man consumes 1.8 L of oxygen per minute. His arterial oxygen content is 190 mL/L and the oxygen content of his venous blood is 134 mL/L. What is his cardiac output?

2. You are given the following data on a person:
   A. Arterial plasma P_{O2} = 95 mm Hg
   B. Blood volume = 4.2 liters
   C. Hematocrit = 38%
   D. Hemoglobin concentration = 13 g/dL whole blood
   E. Maximum oxygen-carrying capacity of hemoglobin = 1.34 ml oxygen/g hemoglobin
   F. At a P_{O2} of 95 mm Hg, plasma contains 0.3 mL oxygen per deciliter (dL) and hemoglobin is 97% saturated

Using the data above, calculate the total amount of oxygen that could be carried in the person's blood.

HINTS:
Total blood oxygen = amount dissolved in plasma + amount bound to hemoglobin
To determine amount of oxygen dissolved in plasma:
    What is this person's plasma volume? (use hematocrit to determine)
    What is the solubility of oxygen in plasma?
To determine the amount of oxygen bound to hemoglobin:
    How much hemoglobin is in this person's blood?
You are given total blood volume, hematocrit, and hemoglobin content/dL whole blood. Which of these
    parameters will you use?
Maximum oxygen-carrying capacity represents what percent saturation?
What is the percent saturation in this person's blood?

PRACTICE MAKES PERFECT

In the following questions, mark each answer as either true or false.

1. Oxygen
    a. is mainly transported in the blood while bound to the hemoglobin in red blood cells. _____
    b. is as soluble as carbon dioxide in plasma. _____
    c. is the primary chemical drive for ventilation. _____

2. Carbon dioxide
    a. is primarily transported as a gas dissolved in the plasma. _____
    b. binds to hemoglobin in erythrocytes. _____
    c. is converted to carbonic acid through the action of carbonic anhydrase. _____

3. The P_{O2} of the blood
    a. is a measure of the amount of oxygen dissolved in the plasma. _____
    b. is the most important factor determining the percent saturation of hemoglobin. _____
    c. is normal in anemia. _____
    d. is an accurate indicator of the total oxygen content of blood. _____
    e. determines P_{O2} of the alveoli. _____

Pick the single best answer:

4. Which of the following would decrease the ability of oxygen to diffuse across the alveolar/capillary membrane? (circle all that are correct)
    a. An increase in thickness of the alveolar membrane
    b. Increased hemoglobin concentration in erythrocytes
    c. An increase in the partial pressure of oxygen in the alveoli
    d. CNS depression by drugs or alcohol
    e. A decrease in the surface area of the alveoli

5. Compare the following pairs of items. Put the symbols below in the space.
    greater than >   less than <   same as or equal =

A- oxygen released from hemoglobin at a cell whose P_{O2} is 40 mm Hg when the plasma is at pH 7.4
B - oxygen released from hemoglobin at a cell whose P_{O2} is 40 mm Hg when the plasma is at pH 7.2   A _____ B

A - arterial oxygen transport in a person with a hemoglobin of 10 g Hb/dL blood and P_{O2} of 140 mm Hg
B - arterial oxygen transport in a person with a hemoglobin of 11 g Hb/dL blood and P_{O2} of 100 mm Hg   A _____ B

A - arterial P_{O2} in a person with anemia
B - arterial P_{O2} in a normal person   A _____ B

6. You are an astronomer who has been invited with colleagues to work for a week at the observatory on the summit of Mauna Kea, on the Big Island of Hawaii. The summit of this extinct volcano is 13,796 feet above sea level. Describe how each of the following parameters will change by the end of your journey to the summit, and explain the stimulus and pathway for each change.

a) Partial pressure of oxygen in the air _____

b) Barometric pressure _____

c) Arterial P_{O2} _____

d) Arterial P_{CO2} _____

e) Arterial pH _____

f) When you arrive at the observatory, you meet some resident astronomers who have been living there for years. How does the hemoglobin content of their blood compare with that of you and your colleagues?

g) Within a day of arrival, one of your colleagues complains of difficulty breathing and a severe headache. The emergency oxygen tank has run out of oxygen. What should you do?

h) When you first arrive at the observatory, you notice that you begin breathing more rapidly. But within a day, your breathing has returned to a more normal rate, although you know that your body has not had time to manufacture more hemoglobin. How could you explain this phenomenon?

7. A person hyperventilates. What effect will this have on the total oxygen content of her blood? Explain.

MAPS

1. Compile the following terms into a concept map showing the relationships between them.
   The major concept of your map is **total arterial O$_2$ content**. This should be your starting point.

# of RBCs	2,3-DPG	adequate perfusion of alveoli
airway resistance	alveolar ventilation	alveolar surface area
amount of interstitial fluid	composition of inspired air	diffusion distance
dissolved in plasma	hemoglobin (Hb) content	lung compliance
membrane thickness	number (#) of Hb binding sites	O$_2$ diffusion between alveoli and blood
pH	PO$_2$	rate and/or depth of breathing
temperature		

BEYOND THE PAGES

Total pulmonary ventilation -	6 L/min	Total alveolar ventilation	4.2 L/min
Max. voluntary ventilation	125-170 L/min	Respiration rate	12 -20 breaths/min

Blood gases

Arterial P$_{O2}$- 95 mm Hg (85-100)*	Arterial P$_{CO2}$- 40 mm Hg (37-43)	Arterial pH - 7.4
Venous P$_{O2}$- 40 mm Hg	Venous P$_{CO2}$- 46 mm Hg	Venous pH - 7.38

* Although we are considering arterial P$_{O2}$ to be equal to alveolar P$_{O2}$, in reality the P$_{O2}$ drops slightly after leaving the pulmonary capillaries. This is because a small amount of deoxygenated venous blood from the non-exchange portions of the respiratory tract and from the coronary circulation combines with oxygenated blood as it returns to the left side of the heart. The actual arterial P$_{O2}$ value is closer to 95 mm Hg.

✎ TRY IT: Demonstrations for chemical control of ventilation

Using what you have learned about the chemical control of ventilation, first make these predictions.

In which case can hold your breath the longest?
  a) after normal breathing
  b) after hyperventilating
  c) after breathing into a paper bag

Explain your reasoning:

Will your breathing rate increase or decrease after doing the following? (circle one answer)
  a) hyperventilating   increase / decrease
  b) breathing into paper bag   increase   / decrease

Explain your reasoning:

You can hyperventilate by increasing breathing rate or by taking deeper breaths at your usual breathing rate.

After which type of hyperventilation, do you think that you will be able to hold your breath longer?
  a) increasing breathing rate
  b) taking deeper breaths at your usual breathing rate

Explain your reasoning:

With a partner, do the following exercises. If you have time, repeat the sequence three times and take the average. Compare your results with your predictions above.

1. Normal breathing or **eupnea**
   Breathe normally. Have partner count and record the number of breaths per minute for three one-minute intervals.

2. No breathing or **apnea**
   Breathe normally for several minutes. After a normal inspiration, time how long you can hold your breath.

3. **Hyperventilation**: increased ventilation with no change in metabolic rate
   a) Increased rate
      Breathe normal volumes rapidly for 2 minutes. Record the rate. Immediately after hyperventilation, hold your breath from the end of a normal inspiration for as long as possible. Time.

   b) Increased volume
      Breathe maximum volumes for 2 minutes, trying to keep the rate as close to your normal rate as possible. *If you get dizzy, STOP! Note the time and extrapolate to 2 minutes.* Record the rate. Immediately after hyperventilation, hold your breath from the end of a normal inspiration for as long as possible. Time.

4. **Depressed blood carbon dioxide levels** (P_{CO_2})

Breathe deeply and rapidly for 1 minute. Stop sooner if you start to get dizzy. At the end of the 1 minute test, breathe naturally (normal volumes) for 3-4 minutes. Record the rate in the first 90 seconds of normal breathing. Try not to regulate the rate in any way.

5. **Elevated blood carbon dioxide levels**

Breathe normally into and out of a paper bag held over your nose and mouth. After 1 minute, record the breathing rate for the second minute. Then hold your breath for as long as possible. Time your breath-holding.

	Test #1	Test #2	Test #3	Average rate	Time for breath-holding
Normal breathing					
Increased rate, normal volume					
Increased volume, normal rate					
Increased rate and volume					
Breathe into paper bag					

FURTHER EXPLORATIONS

Mountain sickness. Scientific American, October 1992.

The physiology of decompression illness. Scientific American, August 1995.

19

SUMMARY

Key points to learn in this chapter:

✓ The nephron is the functional unit of the kidney.
✓ The three basic nephron processes are: filtration (F), reabsorption (R), and secretion (S). They are related to excretion (E) by the equation:

$$E = F - R + S$$

✓ Filtration rate can be controlled by altering the blood flow through the arterioles. There are three levels of control: myogenic response, tubuloglomerular feedback, and reflex control.
✓ Reabsorption and secretion involve transport and therefore exhibit saturation, specificity, and competition.
✓ Clearance is an abstract way of determining renal handling of a substance based on blood and urine analysis. Spend some time becoming familiar with the concept and with the math involved.

The urinary system consists of the kidneys, bladder, and accessory structures. The system produces urine and eliminates it to help the body maintain fluid and electrolyte balance. The kidneys have six functions: regulation of extracellular fluid volume, regulation of osmolarity, maintenance of ion balance, homeostatic regulation of pH, excretion of wastes and foreign substances, and production of hormones. There are four basic processes in the urinary system: filtration, reabsorption, secretion, and excretion.

The kidney is composed of nephrons, each nephron composed of vascular and tubular elements. Following the path of blood through the nephron, the anatomy is as follows: renal arteries, afferent arteriole, glomerulus, efferent arteriole, peritubular capillaries. Fluid filters out of the glomerulus into Bowman's capsule. It then moves into the proximal tubule, loop of Henle, distal tubule, collecting duct, and renal pelvis. After this point, the fluid will not be altered again, and it can be called urine. Urine drains into the urinary bladder via the ureters and is then eliminated in a process called urination (micturition).

One of the most important concepts to take from this chapter is that the amount of fluid excreted (E) is equal to the amount filtered (F), minus the amount reabsorbed (R), plus the amount secreted (S). Expressed mathematically, this becomes: $E = F - R + S$. Remembering this equation can often help you if you're in a bind trying to solve a problem.

Filtration is the movement of fluid from the blood of the glomerulus into the nephron lumen at Bowman's capsule. Filtered fluid composition is equal to that of plasma, minus blood cells and most proteins. Filtration occurs because the hydrostatic pressure exceeds the osmotic pressure, and the net driving force is 10 mm Hg in the favor of filtration.

Specialized epithelial cells in the capsule, called podocytes, and mesangial cells of the glomerulus form slits that can be manipulated to change the glomerular filtration rate (GFR). GFR is the amount of fluid that filters into Bowman's capsule per unit time; the average GFR is 125 mL/min (180 L/day).

Control of GFR includes the myogenic response, tubuloglomerular feedback, and reflex control. In the myogenic response, smooth muscle of the arteriole stretches as blood pressure increases, and this ultimately causes vasoconstriction. Tubuloglomerular feedback regulates arteriolar diameter by means of chemical communication between the macula densa cells and JG cells (together called the juxtaglomerular apparatus). Reflex control involves sympathetic neurons and alpha receptors on afferent and efferent arterioles.

Reabsorption is the movement of filtered material from the nephron lumen back into the blood supply. Bulk reabsorption takes place in the proximal tubule, but regulated reabsorption takes place in later tubule segments. Most reabsorption involves transepithelial transport (movement across the apical and basolateral membranes). Reabsorption of water and solutes depends on both active and passive transporting mechanisms. The transport of Na^+ into the extracellular fluid creates concentration gradients that allow movement of other substances. Transport involves protein-substrate interaction, so saturation, competition, and specificity are also involved. The renal threshold for a substance is the plasma concentration of that substance at which saturation occurs. At concentrations above renal threshold, substances that are normally reabsorbed are excreted in the urine.

Secretion is the transfer of molecules from the extracellular fluid into the nephron lumen. Secretion depends mostly on active membrane transport. As with reabsorption, secretion shows saturation, competition, and specificity.

Excretion is the result of the other three processes. It depends on filtration rate and on whether reabsorption or secretion is involved. Clearance is an abstract concept describing how many milliliters of plasma passing through the kidneys have been totally cleared of a substance in a given period of time. Clearance is used clinically to assess renal handling of a substance, based only on the analysis of the blood and urine. Spend some valuable time working through the examples in the chapter to get a grasp of this concept mathematically. It can be a little tricky, so be sure you give yourself plenty of time to work through it.

Micturition is the elimination of urine from the bladder. Two sphincters close off the opening between the ureters and the bladder. The external sphincter is skeletal muscle and can be consciously controlled. Micturition is a simple spinal reflex initiated by stretch in the bladder wall.

TEACH YOURSELF THE BASICS

FUNCTIONS OF THE KIDNEYS

1. State the law of mass balance. [∫ p. 9]

2. List the six functions of the kidneys:

    1. _____   2. _____

    3. _____   4. _____

    5. _____   6. _____

ANATOMY OF THE URINARY SYSTEM
The Urinary System Consists of Kidneys, Ureters, Bladder, and Urethra
◎ (Anatomy summary, Fig. 19-1)
✗ IP URINARY SYSTEM: ANATOMY REVIEW

3. Starting at the kidneys, follow a drop of urine to the external environment. (Fig. 19-1a)

4. Explain the term *retroperitoneal*.

5. Describe the vascular supply to the kidneys.

6. What is the function of the urinary bladder?

The Nephron Is the Functional Unit of the Kidney
7. The medulla is the (outer/inner?) layer and the cortex is the (outer/inner ?) layer of the kidney. (Fig. 19-1c)

8. What is a nephron?

Vascular Elements of the Nephron
9. Trace a drop of blood through the nephron from a renal artery to a renal vein. (Fig. 19-1g)

10. Describe the portal system of the nephron.

11. What takes place at the glomerulus?

Tubular Elements of the Nephron
12. Trace a drop of fluid through the tubule of the nephron, ending in the renal pelvis. (Fig. 19-1j, 19-2)

13. What occurs in the renal corpuscle?

14. Describe or diagram the relationship between the different segments of the nephron to the cortex and medulla of the kidney.

15. Describe the juxtaglomerular apparatus. (Fig. 19-9)

16. Fluid is considered urine when it enters the _____.

OVERVIEW OF KIDNEY FUNCTION
17. How much plasma on average enters the nephrons per day?

18. How much urine on average leaves the body per day as urine?

19. What happens to the fluid that doesn't leave in the urine?

The Three Processes of the Nephron Are Filtration, Reabsorption, and Secretion
20. Name the three processes of the kidney and describe them. (Fig. 19-2)

21. In which of these processes is fluid entering the external environment?

22. Which of these processes could be considered bulk flow?

23. Which of these processes uses transporting epithelia? [∫ p. 67]

Volume and Osmolarity Change as Fluid Flows Through the Nephron
24. Fluid entering Bowman's capsule is nearly _____osmotic with plasma. [∫ p. 524]

25. Fill in the blanks:

Location in Nephron	Volume of Fluid	Osmolarity of Fluid	What happens to the fluid in this nephric element?
Bowman's capsule	180 L/day	300 mOsM	
End of proximal tubule	54 L/day		
End of loop of Henle	18 L/day		
Distal tubule - end of collecting duct (final urine)	1.5 L/day		

26. Salt and water balance in the nephron is regulated by _____.

27. The final volume and concentration of the urine reflect what need(s) of the body?

28. What is excretion, and how is it different from secretion?

29. Describe the expression that relates excretion to the three processes of the nephron. (Fig. 19-3)

FILTRATION

30. Describe the composition of the filtrate that enters the lumen of the nephron.

The Renal Corpuscle Consists of the Glomerulus and Bowman's Capsule
/ IP URINARY SYSTEM: GLOMERULAR FILTRATION

31. List the three layers a water molecule will pass as it travels from the blood into the lumen of Bowman's capsule.

32. Describe the structure of glomerular capillaries and their pores. [∫ p. 504-508] (Fig. 19-4c, d)

33. Describe the structure and function of the basal lamina.

34. Describe the portion of Bowman's capsule that surrounds the capillaries of the glomerulus.

35. How do podocytes alter the glomerular filtration rate? How do podocytes compare to mesangial cells?

36. Define filtration fraction. (Fig. 19-5)

Filtration Occurs Because of Hydrostatic Pressure in the Capillaries

37. Glomerular filtration occurs because (fill in the blanks in the chart): (Fig. 19-6)

Pressure Type	Average Pressure Measurement	Favors movement of fluid from where to where
Glomerular capillary hydrostatic pressure (P_H)		
Colloid osmotic pressure (π)		
Bowman's capsule hydrostatic pressure (P_{fluid})		
Net pressure is:		

38. Compare the pressures involved in glomerular filtration to those involved in filtration out of systemic capillaries. [∫ p. 506]

Glomerular Filtration Rate Averages 180 Liters per Day

39. Define GFR.

40. What two factors influence GFR the most?

41. Name the components of the filtration coefficient.

42. An average value for GFR is _____ L / day or _____ mL/min.

43. The total body plasma volume is _____ L, which means that the kidneys filter the plasma _____ times each day.

Blood Pressure and Renal Blood Flow Influence GFR

44. What is the relationship between blood pressure and GFR? (Fig. 19-7)

45. Describe or diagram how GFR is controlled by the resistance at the renal arterioles. What happens when resistance increases or decreases at afferent or efferent arterioles? (Fig. 19-8)

GFR Is Subject to Autoregulation
46. What is autoregulation?

Myogenic Response
47. What is a myogenic response?

48. Describe the myogenic response of the afferent arteriolar smooth muscle to increased blood pressure.

49. Why is vasodilation not as effective as vasoconstriction in controlling GFR?

50. Why is a decrease in GFR when blood pressures fall below normal an adaptive response?

Tubuloglomerular Feedback
51. How does the distal tubule communicate with arterioles? (Fig. 19-9)

52. What does the abbreviation "JG" stand for?

53. Describe tubuloglomerular feedback as a result of increased blood pressure. (Fig. 19-10)

Hormones and Autonomic Neurons Also Influence GFR
54. In neural control of GFR, (sympathetic / parasympathetic ?) neurons release (ACh / norepi) onto (α, β_1, β_2 ?) receptors, causing (vasodilation / vasoconstriction) of renal arterioles.

55. Vasoconstriction of the afferent arteriole will (increase / decrease) its resistance, will (increase / decrease) hydrostatic pressure in the glomerular capillaries, and will (increase / decrease) GFR.

56. Vasoconstriction of the efferent arteriole will (increase / decrease) its resistance, will (increase / decrease) hydrostatic pressure in the glomerular capillaries, and will (increase / decrease) GFR.

57. Hormones that influence arteriolar resistance and GFR include
_____, a potent vasoconstrictor, and
_____, which are vasodilators.

58. What are other regulatory actions of hormones in the nephron?

REABSORPTION
✔ IP URINARY SYSTEM: EARLY FILTRATE PROCESSING

59. Bulk reabsorption in the nephron takes place in the _____.

60. Why is the kidney designed to filter such large volumes if 99% of what is filtered is reabsorbed?

Reabsorption May Be Active or Passive

61. To reabsorb molecules against their concentration gradient, the transporting epithelia of the nephron must use what process? [∫ p. 148]

62. Which ion plays a key role in bulk reabsorption in the proximal tubule?

Active Transport of Sodium

63. Filtrate entering proximal tubule has $[Na^+]$ similar to that of _____ and (higher / lower?) than the $[Na^+]$ inside cells.

64. Describe or diagram the transepithelial movement of Na^+ across proximal tubule cells. Include transporter proteins involved. (Fig. 19-11)

Secondary Active Transport: Symport With Sodium

65. List some molecules that are transported using Na^+-linked secondary active transport. [∫ p. 146]:

66. Describe or diagram the transepithelial transport of glucose in the nephron. Include transporter proteins.

Passive Reabsorption: Urea Reabsorption

67. Urea in the proximal tubule can only move by diffusion. If the urea concentration of filtrate is equal to the urea concentration of plasma, what creates the urea concentration gradient needed for diffusion? (Fig. 19-13)

Transcytosis: Plasma Proteins

68. Some of the smaller peptide hormones and enzymes can cross the filtration barrier at the glomerulus. What happens to those that are not reabsorbed intact?

69. For each of the following substances, tell how it crosses the apical and basolateral membranes of the proximal tubule cell and what form of transport it uses at each membrane (primary active, secondary active, facilitated diffusion, simple diffusion).

Molecule	Apical membrane	Type of transport?	Basolateral membrane	Type of transport?
Na^+				
glucose				
water				
urea				
proteins				

Saturation of Renal Transport Plays an Important Role in Kidney Function

70. List the three properties of mediated transport seen in all protein-substrate interactions. [∫ p. 138]

71. Explain what happens when transport is saturated.

72. Below saturation, the rate of transport is proportional to _____.

73. The rate of transport at saturation is also known as the _____.
(Fig. 19-14)

74. The plasma concentration of a substance at which the tubule reaches saturation is known as the
_____. (Fig. 19-15)

75. Filtration (does / doesn't ?) exhibit saturation. (Fig. 19-15a)

76. Normal plasma glucose concentrations are (lower than, equal to, higher than ?) the renal threshold
for glucose. Therefore, normally all glucose filtered is (excreted / secreted / reabsorbed ?).

77. What happens when the concentration of a substance in the plasma exceeds its renal threshold? (Fig.
19-15c,d)

78. What is the term for "glucose in the urine?"

79. If filtration of a substance > reabsorption, then the excess substance is _____.
(Fig. 19-15d)

◎ Remember! $E = F - R + S$

Peritubular Capillary Pressures Favor Reabsorption
80. How does fluid reabsorbed from the lumen of the nephron tubule system get reabsorbed into the
peritubular capillaries?

SECRETION
81. In renal secretion, molecules move from the _____ to the _____.

82. By what means of transport is most secretion accomplished?

83. What is the adaptive significance of secreting a substance in addition to filtering it?

Competition Decreases Penicillin Secretion
84. Describe competition in a mediated transport system, using penicillin and probenecid as your
example.

85. When probenecid is given at the same time as penicillin, what happens to the excretion rate of
penicillin?

EXCRETION
86. Does looking at the composition of urine tell us if a substance has been filtered? _____
reabsorbed? _____ secreted? _____ excreted? _____

87. To analyze how the renal tubule is handling a substance, we must know what information about a
substance?

Clearance Is a Noninvasive Way to Measure GFR

88. Define clearance and give its units. (Fig. 19-16)

89. Write the mathematical equation for clearance:

90. Why is inulin used to estimate GFR? Why is it not used more often in clinical settings? What substance is used instead?

91. Take some time to review the derivation of the concept of clearance. How do you calculate the filtration rate (filtered load)? When can you use a clearance rate to estimate GFR?

92. If you haven't done so yet, work the example in the concept check box on p. 616. Clearance can be tricky at first, so the more practice, the better!

Knowing the GFR Helps Us Determine How the Kidney Handles a Solute

93. Once a GFR is known, what two factors must be measured to allow you to analyze renal handling of a substance?

94. What two factors do you actually compare to determine how the nephron handled a substance? (Table 19-2)

95. What simple equation can you remember to help you analyze renal handling?

Clearance Can Be Used to Determine Renal Handling of a Substance

96. How can you use clearance values to determine renal handling of a substance? What's being compared against what?

97. What information about renal handling can clearance provide? What information about renal handling can clearance not provide? (Fig. 19-17)

98. Spend some time analyzing Fig. 19-17 to become comfortable with the concept of clearance.

MICTURITION

99. The urinary bladder can hold about _____ mL.

100. What prevents urine from leaving the bladder? _____

101. Describe the tonic control exerted by the CNS over the bladder. (Fig. 19-18)

102. Fill in the steps of the involuntary micturition reflex.

Stimulus _____

Receptor _____

Afferent pathway _____

Integrating center _____

Efferent pathway(s) _____

Effectors _____

Tissue responses _____

Systemic response _____

103. What neurotransmitters and receptors are involved in the tissue responses? [∫ pp. 373 (Fig. 11-5); 378; 400]

104. What role do higher brain centers play in micturition?

TALK THE TALK

active transport, kidney	afferent arteriole	Alexander Fleming
ascending limb, loop of Henle	basal lamina	benzoate
Bowman's capsule	clearance	collecting duct
cortex, renal	creatinine	descending limb, loop of Henle
diabetes mellitus	distal tubule	efferent arteriole
erythropoietin	excretion	extracellular fluid volume
fenestrated capillary	filtration	filtration fraction
filtration slit	fluid pressure	foot process
functional unit	GFR, autoregulation of	glomerular filtration rate (GFR)
glomerulus	glucosuria (glycosuria)	hemoglobin, in urine
hydrostatic pressure	inulin	juxtaglomerular apparatus
juxtaglomerular cell	kidney	law of mass balance
loop of Henle	macula densa	medulla, renal
mesangial cell	micturition	micturition reflex
myogenic response	Na^+-K^+-ATPase	Na^+-glucose co-transporter
nephron	osmotic pressure	parasympathetic neurons, bladder
passive reabsorption	penicillin	peritoneum
peritubular capillary	plasma volume	podocyte
probenecid	proximal tubule	renal artery
renal corpuscle	renal pelvis	renal threshold
renal vein	renin	retroperitoneal
saccharin	saturation	secondary active transport
secretion	sphincters, bladder	transcytosis, kidney
transepithelial transport	transport maximum (T_m)	transporting epithelium
tubuloglomerular feedback	urea	ureter
urethra	uric acid	urinary bladder
urinary system	urinary tract infection	urine
urine reabsorption	uroscopy	vasoconstriction

QUANTITATIVE THINKING

Excretion = Filtration - Reabsorption + Secretion

Filtered load of a substance (χ) = GFR 3 plasma concentration of χ

Clearance of χ = excretion rate of χ / plasma concentration of χ

Excretion rate of χ = urine flow rate 3 urine concentration of χ

---

1. Tamika goes in for a routine physical examination. Her urinalysis shows proteinuria but she has no other abnormalities upon physical exam. She weighs 60 kg and is 159 cm tall. Her lab data show:

      serum creatinine: 1.8 mg/dL   urine creatinine: 276 mg/dL

      urine volume: 1100 mL in 24 hours

Calculate Tamika's creatinine clearance and GFR.

2. Plasma concentration of inulin: 1 mg/mL

     Plasma concentration of X: 1 mg/mL

     GFR 125 mL/min

What is the filtration rate of inulin? of X?

What is the excretion rate of inulin? What is the excretion rate of X?

3. An alien willingly allows you to test its renal function. Answer the following questions about the alien kidney function (Remember: alien kidneys don't necessarily follow the same rules as human kidneys).

a) Tests show that the alien kidney freely filters glucose. Once in the lumen of the nephron, glucose is reabsorbed but not secreted. The renal threshold is determined to be 500 mg glucose/100 mL plasma, and the alien's glucose transport maximum is 90 mg/min.

Can you calculate the alien's GFR from this information? If so, what is it? If not, what other information do you need?

b) Additional tests show that creatinine gives an accurate GFR in this alien species. The alien transport maximum for the reabsorption of phenol red is 40 mg/min. Look at the following data:

GFR: 25 mL/min
Urine: creatinine = 5 mg/mL; phenol red = 5 mg/mL
Plasma: creatinine = 6 mg/mL; phenol red = 2 mg/mL
Urine flow: 2 mL/min

What is this alien's creatinine clearance? phenol red clearance?

4. Graphing question:

You are given a chemical Z and told to determine how it is handled by the kidneys of a mouse. After a series of experiments, you determine that 1) Z is freely filtered; 2) Z is not reabsorbed; 3) Z is actively secreted; and 4) the renal threshold for Z secretion is a plasma concentration of 80 mg/mL plasma, and the transport maximum is 40 mg/min. The mouse GFR is 1 mL/min. On the graph below, show how filtration, secretion, and excretion are related. One axis will be plasma concentration of Z (mg/mL) with a range of 0-140, and the other axis will show rates of kidney processes (mg/min) with a range of 0-140.

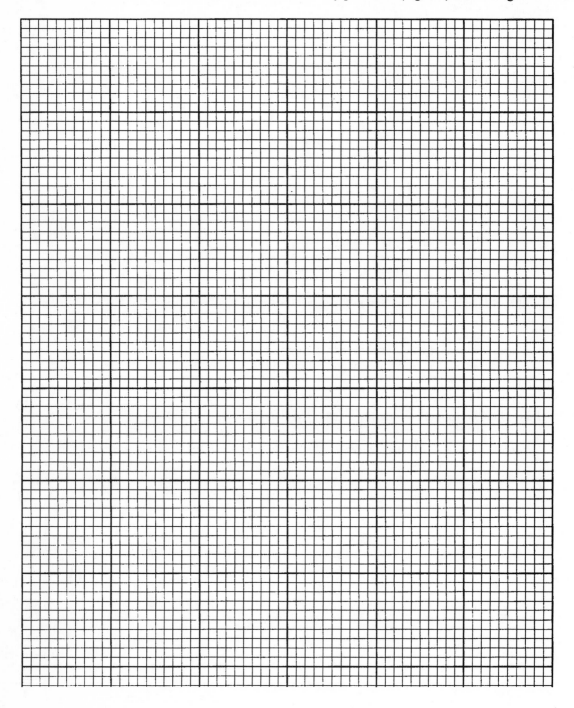

PRACTICE MAKES PERFECT

1. What has gone wrong with the nephron if a person has proteinuria (protein in the urine)?

2. Glucose is easily filtered by the kidneys. Why is glucose normally absent in the urine?

3. Diagram a nephron and label it. Next to each part name, write the processes or functions of that part.

4. Compare hydrostatic pressure, fluid pressure, osmotic pressure, and net direction of fluid flow in glomerular, peritubular, systemic, and pulmonary capillaries.

	Hydrostatic pressure	Fluid pressure	Osmotic pressure	Net direction of fluid flow
Glomerular capillaries				
Peritubular capillaries				
Systemic capillaries				
Pulmonary capillaries				

5. Define and give units for:

   a) renal threshold

   b) clearance

   c) GFR

   spell out "GFR"_____

6. Compare and contrast the following concepts:

   a) clearance and glomerular filtration rate

   b) renal threshold and transport maximum

7. Using what you know about K^+ concentrations in the filtrate and proximal tubule cells, figure out how the cell could reabsorb K^+ from the tubule lumen. See Tables 5-3 and 5-4 (p. 125 and 127) for a list of common transporters.

	Apical membrane	Type of transport?	Basolateral membrane	Type of transport?
K^+				

8. Trace a water molecule from a capillary in the hand directly to the kidney and out through the urine. Name all anatomical structures through which the water molecule will pass. Do not write sentences. Use only names connected by arrows.

9. Inulin clearance when mean arterial pressure = 100 mm Hg is (greater than / less than /the same as ?) inulin clearance when mean arterial pressure = 200 mm Hg.

10. Below is a graph of phenol red excretion in the bullfrog. You can assume that the structure of the frog kidney is like that of humans and that all four basic processes of human kidney function can occur. Based on this graph, answer the following questions:

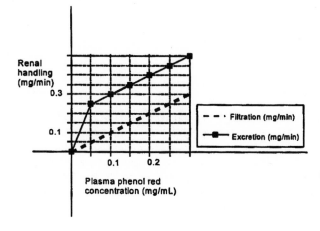

a) Circle the process or processes that allow excretion of phenol red by the bullfrog kidney:
   filtration   reabsorption   secretion

On the graph above, draw in lines for any missing processes. (This line(s) should not be estimated but rather calculated based upon the given data.)

b) What causes the slope of the excretion line at a plasma phenol red concentration of 0.05 mg/mL to change?

c) If a phenol red transport inhibitor was administered concurrently with phenol red to this bullfrog, the clearance rate of phenol red compared to normal would:

   increase   decrease   stay the same

BEYOND THE PAGES

◎ You can see a retroperitoneal kidney the next time you buy a whole chicken at the grocery. The abdominal organs are removed before the chicken is sold, but if you separate the chicken into breast and back halves by cutting through the ribs, you can see the paired kidneys lying alongside the backbone underneath the membranous lining of the abdomen.

ETHICS IN SCIENCE

Kidney transplants are now a very common procedure. How does organ availability affect our lives? Think about the "urban myth" that has spread through the Internet: a man visiting New Orleans was drugged following a wild party. The next morning he was found unconscious and bleeding, and doctors discovered that he was missing a kidney, removed for sale on the black market. Although this is just a folk tale, it brings up the question of whether people should be allowed to sell their organs. There have been reports of prison officials in China selling organs "to order" from prisoners who are to be executed. In the U.S., a new controversy is whether young women should be allowed to sell their ova (eggs) to infertile couples.

FURTHER EXPLORATIONS

Pathogenesis of diabetic nephropathy. Science & Medicine 7(1), 2000 Jan/Feb.

20

INTEGRATIVE PHYSIOLOGY II:
FLUID AND ELECTROLYTE BALANCE

SUMMARY

This is one of the most important chapters in the book because it integrates almost all of the concepts and details of previous chapters. It's loaded with information, and it really tests your understanding. Definitely plan on spending some serious time getting to know this material.

Here are some key points in this chapter:

- ✓ The kidneys regulate water and solute balance in the body by altering the concentration of the urine excreted.
- ✓ Vasopressin (ADH), from the posterior pituitary, controls water reabsorption in the collecting duct of the nephron.
- ✓ Aldosterone, from the adrenal cortex, controls Na^+ reabsorption in the distal tubule and collecting duct.
- ✓ Direct control of aldosterone release is increased plasma $[K^+]$. Indirect control involves ANGII from the RAAS pathway: decreased BP causes renin release, which ultimately allows the creation of ANGII.
- ✓ When dealing with a fluid-solute challenge, the body deals with osmolarity first.
- ✓ An essential equation in acid-base balance is $CO_2 + H_2O \Leftrightarrow H^+ + HCO_3^-$.
- ✓ Know how each scenario of acid-base imbalance affects the above equation.

Fluid and electrolyte balance are under homeostatic control involving the renal, respiratory, and cardiovascular systems. Respiratory and cardiovascular mechanisms are primarily under nervous control and are therefore more rapid than renal mechanisms, which are primarily under hormonal control.

Body osmolarity is homeostatically maintained at around 300 mOsM. Hypothalamic osmoreceptors sense changes in osmolarity and signal the kidneys to adjust urine concentration to correct for the changes. Kidneys must reabsorb water to make concentrated urine, and they must reabsorb Na^+ and not reabsorb water to make dilute urine. Water reabsorption takes place in the collecting duct of the neuron and is under the control of vasopressin released from the posterior pituitary. The presence of vasopressin increases the permeability of the collecting duct to water by inserting water pores into the apical membrane of the duct cell. Sodium reabsorption takes place in the distal tubule and collecting duct, and it is under the control of aldosterone from the adrenal cortex. Aldosterone initiates synthesis of Na^+-K^+-ATPase pumps on the basolateral membranes of P cells and thus allows Na^+ to be reabsorbed into the ECF.

Control of aldosterone release is complex. Secretion is controlled directly at the adrenal cortex by increased K^+ levels; secretion is inhibited by high osmolarity. Indirect control of aldosterone secretion involves renin produced in the juxtaglomerular cells of the kidney nephron. Renin secretion is directly or indirectly triggered by low blood pressure.

When secreted, renin converts angiotensinogen into angiotensin I (AGI). AGI is converted by angiotensin-converting enzyme (ACE) into angiotensin II (ANGII). ANGII causes release of aldosterone and widespread vasoconstriction, intended to contribute to an increase in blood pressure.

Changes in salt and water balance must be corrected, but it isn't always possible to correct the imbalances perfectly. In some instances, such as dehydration, integrating centers receive conflicting signals from different sensory pathways. When the body is faced with conflicting signals, the rule of thumb is to correct osmolarity imbalances first. Work through pp. 641-645 to get a full understanding of integrated salt and water balance. It would be especially helpful to your understanding for you to learn the integration of control well enough to be able to draw a map similar to the one on p. 645 without looking at any references.

Potassium balance is important to cell function, and is closely associated with Na^+ balance as well as with pH balance. Hyperkalemia and hypokalemia can cause problems with excitable tissues, especially the heart.

Acid-base balance is another homeostatic parameter that is crucial to body function. Remember that enzymes and other proteins are sensitive to pH changes. Acidosis is more common than alkalosis, but each requires compensation to restore homeostasis. The most important contributor to acidosis is CO_2 from respiration. Remember the equation: $CO_2 + H_2O \Leftrightarrow H^+ + HCO_3^-$. There are three compensations that the body uses to combat acid-base imbalances: buffers, ventilation, and renal excretion of H^+ and HCO_3^-. Ventilation removes CO_2 and therefore decreases H^+ production. The kidneys remove the excess acid or base directly by excreting H^+ or HCO_3^- into the urine. Intercalated cells of the collecting duct are responsible for the excretion of ions: type A cells secrete H^+ and reabsorb HCO_3^- during acidosis; type B cells secrete HCO_3^- and reabsorb H^+ during alkalosis.

Acid-base disturbances are classified according to the pH change they induce and by how the imbalance originated. There are four possibilities: respiratory acidosis, respiratory alkalosis, metabolic acidosis, and metabolic alkalosis. When learning about acid-base disturbances, pay careful attention to how each of the four possibilities change the CO_2, H^+ equation. Also, learn the hallmarks associated with each condition as well as its compensations. If you can remember how the equation is manipulated, then you will have an easier time working problems concerned with acid-base balance. Make charts, graphs, or whatever helps you the most.

TEACH YOURSELF THE BASICS

FLUID AND ELECTROLYTE HOMEOSTASIS

1.   Briefly describe mass balance.

2.   What role does each of the following organs play in maintaining mass balance?
       Kidneys:

       Lungs:

3.   How does behavior factor into the maintenance of fluid/electrolyte homeostasis?

4.   For that matter, why are we concerned at all with fluid/electrolyte homeostasis? Why is it important? Include a discussion of some of the regulated substances.

ECF Osmolarity Affects Cell Volume
◎ *If you need a refresher on osmolarity, now's the time to go back to Chapter 5 and review.*

5. What are some of the effects of osmolarity changes in the body?

Fluid and Electrolyte Balance Requires Integration Among Multiple Systems

6. What is the difference between respiratory and cardiovascular responses and renal responses? Compare response speed and reflex control. [∫ Ch. 6]

7. Cite some instances of overlap in the regulation of fluid/electrolyte balance. Why do you think such an extensive network exists for maintaining these parameters? (Fig. 20-1)

WATER BALANCE AND THE REGULATION OF URINE CONCENTRATION
✗ **IP Urinary System: Early Filtrate Processing, Late Filtrate Processing**

8. In a 70-kg man, how much water is in his entire body? _____
    intracellular fluid (ICF) ? _____ extracellular fluid (ECF) ? _____
    plasma? _____ interstitial fluid? _____ [∫ p. 150]

9. Now describe a woman's body water distribution.

Daily Water Intake and Excretion are Balanced
10. List the normal routes of water input and water loss for the body. (Fig. 20-2)

11. Which are the most significant? Put a star next to them.

12. What is insensible water loss?

13. Give some examples of pathological water loss.

The Kidneys Conserve Water
14. True or false? When body osmolarity goes up, the kidneys reabsorb water and bring osmolarity back to normal. (Fig. 20-3) Explain.

15. When water is lost from the body, how can it be restored?

Urine Concentration Is Determined in the Loop of Henle and Collecting Duct

16. By what process do the kidneys eliminate excess water?

17. By what process do the kidneys conserve water?

18. Describe or diagram how the concentration gradient in the medullary interstitium is established. Include ions, osmolarities, and tubule anatomy in your discussion. (Fig. 20-4)

Vasopressin Regulates Urine Osmolarity

19. How does the collecting duct alter its permeability to water and determine final urine concentration? (Fig. 20-5)

20. Is permeability absolute or graded? What does this accomplish?

Vasopressin and Aquaporins

21. What are aquaporins? Where are they stored?

22. Which is the aquaporin isoform regulated by vasopressin? Where is it found?

23. Describe or diagram vasopressin regulation of AQP2. What happens in low vasopressin concentrations? What is vasopressin's cellular mechanism of action? (Fig. 20-6)

24. What is the net result of vasopressin action?

Changes in Blood Pressure and Osmolarity are the Stimuli for Water Balance Reflexes

25. The two primary stimuli that trigger renal reflexes are: (Fig. 20-7)

26. Osmolarity changes are sensed by what type of sensory receptor? Where are these receptors found?

27. To what integrating center(s) are these receptors linked?

28. What efferent pathway(s) are linked to the integrating center(s)?

29. When osmolarity increases above _____ mOsM, vasopressin release is (stimulated / inhibited ?), leading to (increased / decreased ?) renal water reabsorption.

30. Which receptors respond to changes in blood volume or blood pressure?

31. How do these receptors influence vasopressin activity?

◎ *Fig. 20-7 shows integrated responses to blood volume/pressure changes.*

The Loop of Henle Is a Countercurrent Multiplier
32. What is the key to the kidney's ability to produce concentrated urine?

Countercurrent Systems Exchange Molecules or Heat
33. Describe a countercurrent exchange system. What are the requirements for such a system? What is the purpose of a countercurrent exchanger? (Fig. 20-9, 20-10)

34. Describe or diagram how the loop of Henle is a countercurrent exchange system and a countercurrent multiplier. (Fig. 20-10)

35. The descending limb of the loop is permeable to (water / solutes ?) and impermeable to (water / solutes ?). The ascending limb is permeable to (water / solutes ?) and impermeable to (water / solutes ?). As a result of the countercurrent system, fluid leaving the loop is (hypo- / iso- /hyper-) osmotic to the blood.

The Vasa Recta Removes Water
36. Define the vasa recta?

37. Describe or diagram solute/water movement in the descending and ascending components of the vasa recta. What factors contribute to solute/water movement? (Fig. 20-10)

38. How do the vasa recta participate in the countercurrent exchange/multiplier system?

Urea Increases Osmolarity of the Medullary Interstitium

39. Urea makes up what fraction of solute present in the medullary interstitial fluid?

40. How does urea cross cell membranes in the collecting duct? Does it move via active or passive transport?

SODIUM BALANCE AND THE REGULATION OF EXTRACELLULAR FLUID VOLUME
⁄ IP Urinary System: Late Filtrate Processing

41. What is normal body osmolarity?

42. The addition of NaCl to the body raises osmolarity. This stimulus triggers two responses, what are they?

43. Bringing increased osmolarity back into normal range often involves disrupting another set of homeostatic parameters. What are these parameters? (Fig. 20-11)

44. Sodium excretion is a function of the _____.

Aldosterone Controls Sodium Balance

45. Quick review: if aldosterone behaves like a typical steroid hormone, then describe how it's made, if it's stored, how it's transported to its target, and its cellular mechanism of action. [See Chapter 7 details, p. 218.]

46. What are the target cells for aldosterone, and where are they located? Describe or diagram their apical and basolateral membranes. (Fig. 20-12)

47. What effect does aldosterone have on its target cells? There's a faster early response and a slower response that comes later. Describe or diagram both. What's the net result of aldosterone action?

48. Compare water and sodium handling in the distal nephron versus the proximal tubule.

Blood Pressure, Osmolarity, and K⁺ Influence Aldosterone Secretion

49. What are the direct and indirect stimuli for aldosterone secretion? (Table 20-1)

The Renin-Angiotensin-Aldosterone Pathway (RAAS)

50. Arrange the following terms into a map of the RAAS pathway. (Fig. 20-13)

active	adrenal cortex	afferent arteriole
aldosterone	angiotensin converting enzyme (ACE)	angiotensin I (ANGI)
angiotensin II (ANGII)	angiotensinogen	endothelium
inactive	JG cells	liver
plasma protein	renin	

51. The stimuli that begin the RAAS pathway are all related directly or indirectly to what?

52. What is renin, and where is it secreted? (Fig. 20-13)

53. List three stimuli for renin secretion. (Fig. 20-14)

54. True or false? Na$^+$ retention immediately raises low blood pressure. Explain. (Fig. *20*-11)

Angiotensin II Influences Blood Pressure Through Multiple Pathways
55. List the effects of ANG II beyond stimulating aldosterone secretion. (Fig. 20-13)

Atrial Natriuretic Peptide Promotes Na$^+$ and Water Excretion
56. What is ANP, and where is it produced?

57. OK, this should be familiar by now—based on its structure, respond to the following: how is ANP made, is it stored, how is it transported, and what is its cellular mechanism of action. [See Chapter 7 for a review, p. 215.]

58. What is the stimulus for ANP secretion?

59. What is the net effect of ANP? How does ANP achieve its net effect? (Fig. 20-15)

60. What are some of the indirect effects of ANP? Do these enhance or inhibit its natriuretic effects?

61. How is it proposed that ANP increases GFR? [∫ p. 605]

62. ANP and related peptides are also secreted by neurons in the brain. Describe the targets and the effects of ANP in the brain.

POTASSIUM BALANCE

63. K$^+$ balance is important despite its relatively (high / low ?) ECF concentration. [∫ p. 262]

64. Hyperkalemia (increases / decreases ?) the K$^+$ concentration gradient across cell membranes and (depolarizes / hyperpolarizes ?) cells. This leads to (increased / decreased ?) excitability in excitable tissues and can lead to cardiac arrhythmias.

65. Compare this to hypokalemia.

66. How does the body compensate for increase K$^+$ levels?

67. Cite some possible sources for K$^+$ disturbances.

BEHAVIORAL MECHANISMS IN SALT AND WATER BALANCE

68. Drinking water is normally the only way to _____, and eating salt is the only way to _____.

Drinking Replaces Fluid Loss

69. Which receptors trigger thirst, and what is their threshold osmolarity?

70. How does the act of drinking alleviate thirst? What is the adaptive advantage of this?

Low Na$^+$ Stimulates Salt Appetite

71. Define salt appetite.

72. Where are the human salt appetite centers?

Avoidance Behaviors Help Prevent Dehydration

73. List some other behaviors that help prevent dehydration. What is the adaptive significance of each?

INTEGRATED CONTROL OF VOLUME AND OSMOLARITY

✔ IP Fluids & Electrolytes: Water Homeostasis

Osmolarity and ECF Volume Can Change Independently

74. What are some examples of extreme fluid loss?

75. Recreate the chart in Fig. 20-16 that represents the possible states of volume and osmolarity.

76. For each of the situations below, describe possible causes and in general terms explain the appropriate homeostatic response.
   Increased volume and increased osmolarity:

   Increased volume, unchanged osmolarity:

   Increased volume and decreased osmolarity:

   Normal volume with increased osmolarity:

   Normal volume with decreased osmolarity:

   Decreased volume and increased osmolarity:

   Decreased volume, unchanged osmolarity:

   Decreased volume and decreased osmolarity:

Dehydration Triggers Renal and Cardiovascular Responses
◎ *Table 20-2 summarizes pathways involved in volume/osmolarity homeostasis.*

77. When integrating centers receive conflicting information about regulation of volume and osmolarity, correction of _____ has priority.

78. In compensation for severe dehydration (Fig. 20-17):

79. What are the homeostatic challenges?

80. Carotid, aortic _____ respond to BP changes. The cardiovascular control center (increases / decreases ?) parasympathetic output and (increases / decreases ?) sympathetic output in an effort to (increase / decrease ?) blood pressure.

81. What effects do these autonomic neurons have on different effectors? Name the neurotransmitter and receptor as well as the specific target tissue. [Review the autonomic nervous system in Ch 11.]

82. What effect does severe dehydration have on GFR?

83. List all the stimuli that will cause renin release in this pathway.

84. What behavioral pathway(s) will be initiated?

◎ *Redundancy in control pathways ensures that four main compensatory mechanisms are activated.*

85. List the four main compensatory mechanisms in this severe dehydration example:

86. What is the net result of these compensatory measures? (Fig. 20-17)

87. If you haven't yet done it, make reflex pathways similar to Fig. 20-17 for the volume/osmolarity disturbances shown in Fig. 20-16. Use the pathways listed in Table 20-2.

ACID-BASE BALANCE
↗ **IP Fluids & Electrolytes: Acid/Base Homeostasis**

88. Define pH. [∫ p. 33; Appendix A]

89. A change of 1 pH unit = a _____-fold change in $[H^+]$.

90. An alkaline solution has a (higher / lower ?) H^+ concentration and a (higher / lower ?) pH than an acid solution.

Enzymes and the Nervous System Are Particularly Sensitive to Changes in pH

91. What are both the normal average pH and the normal range of pH in the human body?

92. Which body fluid is used clinically to indicate the body pH?

93. If the pH range compatible with life is 7.0-7.7, how can we survive stomach juices with a pH as low as 1 or urine with a pH ranging from 4.5 - 8.5?

94. If pH falls outside the normal range, what kinds of things go wrong?

95. Acidosis (increases / decreases ?) neuron excitability; alkalosis (increases / decreases ?) neuron excitability.

96. Disturbances in pH balance are often associated with changes in what other important ion (besides HCO_3^-)?

97. Name the membrane transporter that links movement of H^+ and this ion in the kidney.

98. This transporter moves the ions in (the same / opposite ?) directions, so that in acidosis, when H^+ is excreted, _____ is reabsorbed.

99. In alkalosis, when H^+ is excreted, _____ is reabsorbed.

Acids and Bases in the Body Come from Many Sources
100. In day-to-day functioning, the body is challenged by intake and production of _____ more than _____.

101. Maintaining mass balance requires what? (Fig. 20-18)

Acid Input
102. Cite examples of organic acids that contribute to $[H^+]$.

103. What is lactic acidosis? What is ketoacidosis? How can these states develop?

104. The biggest daily source of acid production is _____. How is this so?

105. Write the equation for the production of H_2CO_3 from $CO_2 + H_2O$:

106. What enzyme catalyzes the reaction above? [∫ p. 584]

Base Input

107. There are few significant sources of bases in the diet and metabolism. List a couple.

◎ Because of this, the body spends more time correcting acid disturbances.

pH Homeostasis Depends on Buffers, the Lungs, and the Kidneys

108. Name the three mechanisms used by the body to cope with minute-to-minute changes in pH. List the order in which these mechanisms are employed—which is the first line of defense, second, third…and tell why.

Buffer Systems Include Proteins, Phosphate Ions, and Bicarbonate Ions

109. Define a buffer. [∫ p. 34]

110. List some important buffers found in the human body.

111. Which is the most important extracellular buffer? Where does it come from, and how does it function? Include the equation for the reaction. [∫ p. 585, Fig. 18-13]

112. According to the law of mass action [∫ p. 97], an increase in CO_2 will cause a/an (increase / decrease ?) in H^+ and HCO_3^-.

113. What effect does an increase in $[H^+]$ due to production of metabolic acids have on pH, HCO_3^-, and CO_2?

114. Sometimes changes in HCO_3^- concentrations aren't observed clinically. Explain why this is true.

Ventilation Can Compensate for pH Disturbances

115. Because CO_2 and H^+ are linked in a dynamic equilibrium, P_{CO_2} changes will affect both H^+ and HCO_3^- levels.

If ventilation increases, plasma P_{CO_2} (↑ or ↓ ?), H^+ (↑ or ↓ ?) and HCO_3- (↑ or ↓ ?).

If ventilation decreases, plasma P_{CO_2} (↑ or ↓ ?), H^+ (↑ or ↓ ?) and HCO_3- (↑ or ↓ ?).

116. The body uses ventilation as a method for adjusting pH only if a stimulus associated with pH triggers the reflex response. Name the two stimuli that can do this: _____. (Fig. 20-19)

117. The carotid and aortic chemoreceptors respond to changes in _____ and initiate the following pathway:

118. The central chemoreceptors respond to changes in _____ and initiate the following pathway [∫ Fig. 18-18, p 590]:

Kidneys Excrete or Reabsorb H^+ and HCO_3^-

119. Describe the two ways that kidneys can alter pH:

120. How do the kidneys respond in times of acidosis? (Fig. 20-20)

121. What substances act as buffers in the kidneys?

122. Even with buffers, urine can become quite (acidic / basic ?).

123. How do the kidneys respond in times of alkalosis?

124. Renal compensations are (faster / slower ?) than respiratory compensations. Why?

125. Make a table that shows the membrane transporters involved in renal compensation of alkalosis. Describe cell membranes crossed, ion movement, and concentration gradients.

The Proximal Tubule: Hydrogen Ion Excretion and Bicarbonate Reabsorption

126. Most HCO_3^- is absorbed in the _____.

127. HCO_3^- is absorbed mostly by indirect methods because there are no transporters to do what?

128. Looking at Fig. 20-21, you'll see how the transporters function together to achieve HCO_3^- and H^+ movement. Outline, diagram, or describe how bicarbonate is reabsorbed and H^+ secreted in the proximal tubule.

129. Describe a second pathway for bicarbonate reabsorption/H^+ secretion. (Fig. 20-21)

The Distal Nephron: H^+ and HCO_3^- Handling Depend on the Acid-Base State of the Body

130. The distal nephron plays a significant role in the _____ of acid-base balance.

131. How do I cells compare to P cells? What does "I" stand for here?

132. I cells are characterized by high concentrations of _____ in their cytoplasm.

133. Describe or diagram the differences between type A and type B I cells.

134. Diagram, outline, or describe how type A cells work. Include the transporters and ions involved. (Fig. 20-22a)

135. Diagram, outline, or describe how type B cells work. Include the transporters and ions involved. (Fig. 20-22b)

136. How are acid-base disturbances related to K^+ balance? Discuss transporters and acid-base states when answering this question.

Acid-Base Disturbances May Be Respiratory or Metabolic in Origin
137. Describe the classification of acid-base disturbances. (Table 20-3)

138. By the time an acid-base disturbance shows up as a change in plasma pH, what has happened?

139. If the problem is of respiratory origin, only which homeostatic compensation is available?

140. On the other hand, in metabolic acid-base disturbances, which homeostatic compensations are available?

Respiratory Acidosis

141. What alteration in ventilation will cause a respiratory acidosis?

142. Name some conditions/situations in which this might occur.

143. What happens? (fill in ↑ or ↓)   _____ CO_2 + H_2O →→ _____ H^+ + _____ HCO_3^-

144. The hallmark of respiratory acidosis is:

145. What compensation mechanisms are available in this state?

146. As compensation occurs, the pH will (increase / decrease) and the HCO_3^- levels will be (greater than / less than / the same as ?) when the acidosis first occurred.

Metabolic Acidosis

147. Name some causes of metabolic acidosis.

148. What happens? (fill in ↑ or ↓)   _____ CO_2 + H_2O ←← _____ H^+ + _____ HCO_3^-

149. The hallmark of metabolic acidosis is:

150. What compensation mechanisms are available in this state?

151. The change in P_{CO_2} in this condition does what to ventilation?

152. What do the kidneys do to compensate for this condition?

153. Because compensation is almost instantaneous in this condition, the P_{CO_2} levels will often be (greater than / less than / the same as ?) normal.

Respiratory Alkalosis

154. Respiratory alkalosis occurs as a result of:

155. What happens? (fill in ↑ or ↓)   _____ CO_2 + H_2O ←← _____ H^+ + _____ HCO_3^-

156. What indicates a respiratory acid-base disorder?

157. What compensation mechanisms are available in this state?

158. The hallmark of respiratory alkalosis is:

Metabolic Alkalosis

159. What could cause metabolic alkalosis?

160. What happens? (fill in ↑ or ↓) _____ CO_2 + H_2O →→→ _____ H^+ + _____ HCO_3^-

161. The hallmark of metabolic alkalosis is:

162. What compensation mechanisms are available in this state?

163. The change in P_{CO_2} in this condition does what to ventilation?

164. The ventilatory compensation helps correct the pH problem but does what to HCO_3^- levels?

165. What do the kidneys do to compensate for this condition?

To distinguish a respiratory acidosis from a respiratory alkalosis, you should look primarily at the relative concentrations of (H^+ / CO_2 / HCO_3^- ?).

To distinguish a respiratory acidosis from a metabolic acidosis, you should look primarily at the relative concentrations of (H^+ / CO_2 / HCO_3^- ?).

To distinguish a respiratory alkalosis from a metabolic alkalosis, you should look primarily at the relative concentrations of (H^+ / CO_2 / HCO_3^- ?).

TALK THE TALK

acidosis	adrenal cortex	aldosterone
alkalosis	ammonia	angiotensin converting enzyme (ACE)
angiotensin II (ANGII)	antidiuretic hormone (vasopressin)	asthma
atrial natriuretic peptide	atrial stretch receptor	atriopeptin
bedwetting	bicarbonate	buffer
carbonic anhydrase	cardiovascular control center	carotid and aortic baroreceptor
carotid and aortic chemoreceptor	central chemoreceptor	chloride shift
chronic obstructive pulmonary disease (COPD)	CO_2 and acid-base balance	countercurrent heat exchanger
countercurrent multiplier	daily water intake	desmopressin
diarrhea	diuresis	ECF volume, role of sodium in determining
emphysema	enuresis	feedforward reflex: drinking
fibrosis	fluid and electrolyte balance	guanylin and uroguanylin
H^+-ATPase	H^+-K^+-ATPase	HCO_3^--Cl^- antiport
hemoglobin	hemorrhage	hyperkalemia
hyperventilation	hypokalemia	hypoventilation
insensible water loss	intercalated cell (I cell)	intravenous (IV) injection
juxtaglomerular granular cell (JG cell)	lactic acidosis	ketoacid
ketoacidosis	leak channels for Na^+ and K^+	law of mass balance
law of mass action	medullary chemoreceptor	loop of Henle
macula densa	metabolic alkalosis	membrane recycling
metabolic acidosis	Na^+-HCO_3 symport	Na^+-K^+-ATPase
Na^+-H^+ antiport	osmolarity	natriuresis
oropharynx receptor	phosphate ion	osmoreceptor
pH	principal cell (P cell)	pneumonia
potassium homeostasis	renin-angiotensin-aldosterone system (RAAS)	regulation of cell volume
renin	respiratory compensations to pH changes	respiratory acidosis
respiratory alkalosis	sweating	salt appetite
severe dehydration	tonicity	sympathetic neurons and the nephron
thirst	vasopressin	urine concentration
vasa recta	water excretion	vomiting

QUANTITATIVE THINKING

Osmotic Diuresis

When a diabetic's plasma glucose concentration exceeds the renal threshold for glucose reabsorption, the unreabsorbed glucose is excreted in the urine. The presence of this excess solute in the tubule lumen will cause additional water loss and create an **osmotic diuresis**. In the clinics, it is sometimes said that "the glucose holds the water in the urine." Physiologically, osmotic diuresis is based on simple amount/concentration relationships. The nephron can only concentrate urine to a maximum of 1200 mosmoles/liter. If there is more solute in the lumen (i.e., greater amount of solute) but the osmolarity cannot increase above 1200 mOsM, there will be a greater urine volume. To understand why this is so, work through the following problem.

The diagram shows a nephron. The numbers inside the nephron at points A, B, and C represent the concentration of the filtrate at those points. Assume for this example that vasopressin is present in amounts that allow maximal concentration of the urine and that there is no solute reabsorption in the distal parts of the nephron.

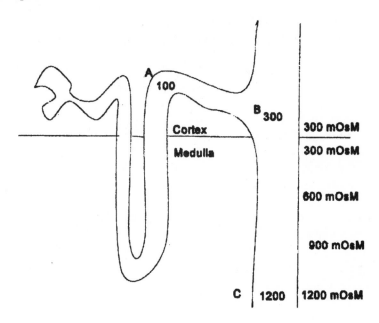

Assume that in a normal individual, 150 mosmoles of NaCl per day pass from the loop of Henle into the urine. Given the concentrations shown at points A-C, what volume of fluid passes those points in one day?

Point A _____   Point B _____   Point C _____

Now suppose the person suddenly becomes diabetic and is unable to reabsorb all filtered glucose. The 150 mosmoles of NaCl in the distal nephron are joined by 150 mosmoles of unreabsorbed glucose. Now the <u>amount</u> of solute leaving the loop of Henle has increased from 150 to 300 mosmoles.

Do you think the volume of fluid leaving the loop of Henle will be the same, greater or smaller? _____

Now do the calculations:

	Osmolarity	Volume
Point A	_____	_____
Point B	_____	_____
Point C	_____	_____

What happened to the volume of urine when the <u>amount</u> of solute entering the distal nephron doubled?

_____ . This shows you the process behind fluid loss in osmotic diuresis.

PRACTICE MAKES PERFECT

1. Compare the following pairs of items. Put the symbols below in the space.
   greater than >   less than <   same as or equal =

A - urine osmolarity in a normal person with maximal vasopressin
B - urine osmolarity in a diabetic who is excreting glucose with maximal vasopressin   A _____ B

A - aldosterone secretion when osmolarity is high and blood pressure low
B - aldosterone secretion when osmolarity and blood pressure are both low   A _____ B

A - plasma P_{CO_2} in respiratory acidosis
B - plasma P_{CO_2} in respiratory alkalosis   A _____ B

A - renal reabsorption of HCO_3^- in acidosis
B - renal reabsorption of HCO_3^- in alkalosis   A _____ B

A - ventilation in metabolic alkalosis
B - ventilation in metabolic acidosis   A _____ B

A - renin secretion when blood pressure is high
B - renin secretion when blood pressure is low   A _____ B

A - renal filtration of HCO_3^- in acidosis
B - renal filtration of HCO_3^- in alkalosis   A _____ B

2. What effect does a decrease in mean arterial blood pressure have on each item below?

   (a) Na^+ reabsorption in the proximal tubule _____

   (b) blood pressure in the afferent arteriole _____

   (c) atrial stretch _____

   (d) aldosterone secretion _____

   (e) angiotensinogen levels in the plasma _____

   (f) blood volume _____

3. The labels were left off the axes on the following graph. One axis is vasopressin concentration and one axis is plasma osmolarity. Which is which? Defend your answer.

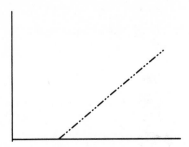

4. It's the night before your physiology test, and you awake from a crazy dream to find yourself still at your desk in a pile of books and papers. You remember that in your dream, you were walking through a peach orchard. As you were walking down the path, you noticed that all the trees on your left were turning into CO_2 and H_2O. Looking to your right, you noticed that all the trees on that side were turning into H^+ and HCO_3^-. Having thoroughly studied acid-base balance, you recognized that you were standing in the middle of the important acid-base equation. As you realize this, a funny new tree pops up. On one side of the tree there are green fruit, and on the other side there are red fruit. You are hungry from all your studying, so your subconscious picks a green fruit from the tree.

As you eat the green fruit, something strange happens (as if this isn't strange enough already!). The left side of the path (the $CO_2 + H_2O$ side) grows and grows until it looks as if it will topple on top of you. You suddenly realize that you have a touch pad in your hand that will enable you to set the proper compensatory mechanisms in action. What do you do to prevent your impending doom?

Write the equation of interest, show the imbalance that occurred, and describe what physiological mechanisms you employed to compensate for the imbalance. Why did you choose the way you did?

5. In a patient with an acid-base disturbance characterized by a plasma P_{CO_2} of 80 mm Hg and a plasma bicarbonate concentration of 33 mEq/L (normal = 24), you would expect to find:
 (Circle all correct answers):

    a) virtually complete renal bicarbonate reabsorption despite the elevated plasma bicarbonate

    b) urine pH less than 6.0

    c) stimulation of distal tubule H^+ secretion due to elevated plasma P_{CO_2}

    d) hypokalemia

6. Mr. Osgoode arrives at the hospital hyperventilating and disoriented. You order tests and receive these results: plasma pH 7.31; arterial P_{CO_2} = 30 mm Hg; plasma HCO_3^- = 20 mEq/L (normal = 24). What are the normal values for pH and P_{CO_2}? What is Mr. Osgoode's acid-base state, and how did you come to that conclusion?

7. Ari wants to play a trick on his friends, so he gets a long tube and hides in the bottom of a pond, breathing through the tube. After a few minutes, he feels that he is having trouble getting air and considers surfacing. If you tested his plasma pH, plasma HCO_3^-, and arterial P_{CO_2} at this time, would you expect each of them to be normal, above normal, or below normal? Explain your answers.

MAPS

1. Create a summary map showing the compensations for acid-base disturbances, using the following terms and any others you wish to add.

acidosis

bicarbonate

carotid and aortic chemoreceptor

CO_2

H^+-ATPase

hyperkalemia

hypoventilation

medullary chemoreceptor

Na^+-K^+-ATPase

pH

respiratory acidosis

secretion

alkalosis

buffer

central chemoreceptor

excretion

H^+-K^+-ATPase

hyperventilation

intercalated cell (I cell)

metabolic acidosis

Na^+-H^+ antiport

phosphate ion

respiratory alkalosis

ammonia

carbonic anhydrase

chloride shift

filtration

HCO_3^- -Cl^- antiport

hypokalemia

law of mass action

metabolic alkalosis

Na^+- HCO_3^- symport

reabsorption

respiratory compensation

2. Use the map on the renin-angiotensin pathway (Fig. 20-13, p. 637) as the basis for a large map. Fill in mechanisms and receptors and neurotransmitters—and anything else you can think of. Here's your chance to demonstrate mastery of physiology!

3. Take each of the following situations. Figure out:
   a. what changes will occur in the volume, osmolarity, and sodium concentration of the body.
   b. what homeostatic responses these changes will trigger and how
   c. describe *in as much detail as possible* the homeostatic response
   d. explain how the homeostatic response will bring the altered condition(s) back to normal

On large pieces of paper, map the detailed homeostatic pathways for each situation below.

   Example 1: Person ingests a large amount of salt and drinks enough water so that the result is as if
                  he/she drank a large volume of isotonic saline
   Example 2: Person drinks a large volume of pure water
   Example 3: Person loses water and salt, but more water than salt through sweating (loses hyposmotic
                  fluid).
   Example 4: Person loses a large volume of blood (hemorrhage)

HINTS FOR MAPPING VOLUME AND OSMOLARITY PROBLEMS

1. What are the possible stimuli? The primary stimuli are blood pressure and osmolarity (increased, decreased, or no change ...see the matrix). You should also consider $[Na^+]$, $[K^+]$, and blood volume.

2. Make a list of all receptors/tissues that respond to the stimuli in #1. Don't forget tissues that respond directly to the stimuli, such as the atrial cells that secrete ANP and the aldosterone-secreting cells of the adrenal cortex. Don't forget GFR and blood pressure homeostasis via the cardiovascular control center.

3. Once you have established which pathways will be stimulated/inhibited, draw out all reflex pathways through to the desired response, which should be the opposite of the stimulus. If you get to the end and have a response that is the same as the stimulus (i.e., stimulus was increased BP but the response increases BP), go back...you've done something wrong or forgotten a link. Be sure to look for places where pathways intersect.

4. Sometimes two pathways will have opposite effects on a single integrating center (i.e. one stimulates aldosterone, the other inhibits). Assume that the response that opposes the stimulus is dominant. Alternatively, remember that the body defends osmolarity before it defends volume.

BEYOND THE PAGES

✏ TRY IT: Kitchen Buffers

Your kitchen contains the necessary ingredients for a simple demonstration of the bicarbonate buffer system. Pour a couple of tablespoons of white or cider vinegar into a small bowl. Taste the vinegar and notice the sour or tart taste. The sensation of sour taste is directly proportional to the acidity of a solution. Now put a tablespoon of baking soda into another small bowl. Baking soda is sodium bicarbonate, the sodium salt of the bicarbonate buffer.

Remember the equation in which bicarbonate buffers acid:

$$CO_2 + H_2O \leftrightarrow H^+ + HCO_3^-$$

Based on this equation, what do you predict will happen when you pour the vinegar into the baking soda? If you taste the resulting solution, do you think the taste will be the same as it was before? Explain.

Now conduct your experiment. What happens when the vinegar and baking soda mix? This reaction has been used in baking for centuries. Allow the excess baking soda to settle to the bottom of the bowl and taste the remaining vinegar solution. Is it as sour as before? (see answers)

FURTHER EXPLORATIONS

 How good are all those sports drinks at keeping you hydrated during exercise? To find out, try a Google search (www.google.com) for *sports rehydration*.

 Articles

ACE inhibitors: Almost too good to be true. Science & Medicine, July/August 1994.

Progress in oral rehydration therapy. Scientific American, May 1991.

A is for...Aquaporin. Science & Medicine 6(5):64, 1999 Sep/Oct.

SUMMARY

This chapter is definitely full of information. Digestion concepts and details would work well as a series of charts connected by pathway maps. In other words, a concept map made with charts as well as other items.

> ✓ The anatomy and the contraction patterns of digestive smooth muscle are complex. What is the anatomy of GI smooth muscle? How is contraction generated? What are these complex contraction patterns, and what factors affect them?
> ✓ Food processing is traditionally divided into three phases: cephalic, gastric, and intestinal.
> ✓ There are four digestive processes: digestion, absorption, motility, and secretion. What factors affect each of these processes?
> ✓ There are three general control system categories for the GI tract: long reflexes (CNS), short reflexes (ENS), and GI peptides.
> ✓ There are the three families of GI peptides. (Table 21-2) How do GI peptides participate in the regulation of GI function?
> ✓ The digestive system secretes many different substances: enzymes, hormones, paracrines, and ions. Where are the different substances secreted? What are their functions?
> ✓ Many of the mechanisms for secretion and absorption will look familiar from your study of renal physiology.

If you trace food through the digestive system, it passes through the following structures: mouth, pharynx, esophagus, stomach (fundus, body, antrum), small intestine (duodenum, jejunum, ileum), large intestine, rectum, and anus. Exocrine secretions are added by the salivary glands, pancreas, and liver. The GI tract contains the largest collection of lymphoid tissue, called the gut-associated lymphoid tissue (GALT). The enteric nervous system (ENS) integrates and initiates GI reflexes. The ENS can act in coordination with or completely separate from the cephalic brain.

There are three phases of food processing: cephalic, gastric, and intestinal. There are four digestive processes that can take place during food processing: digestion, absorption, motility, and secretion.

Digestion of biomolecules takes place at various locations throughout the GI tract. Carbohydrates are digested in the mouth and small intestine by amylases and disaccharidases. Proteins are digested in the stomach and small intestine by endopeptidases and exopeptidases. Fat digestion begins in the mouth and small intestine with the help of lipases, but most fat digestion takes place in the small intestine via pancreatic lipase and colipase. Bile from the liver emulsifies fats, increasing the surface area exposed to enzyme action.

Absorption takes place mostly in the small intestine. Because the intestinal wall is composed of transporting epithelium, transepithelial transport mechanisms similar to those in the kidneys are observed. Glucose is transported across the apical membrane by a Na+-glucose symporter and across the basolateral membrane by the GLUT2-facilitated diffusion carrier. Amino acids are absorbed by a Na+-dependent cotransporter, while small peptides are absorbed by H+-dependent cotransporters or by transcytosis. Fat absorption is primarily by simple diffusion. In epithelial cell cytoplasm, monoglycerides and fatty acids are moved to the smooth ER where they combine with cholesterol and proteins to form chylomicrons. Chylomicrons are then transported out of the cells by exocytosis and moved into the lymphatic system—bypassing the liver and entering the venous blood just before it reaches the heart. Most nutrients are absorbed into the hepatic portal system by which they are delivered into the liver.

Motility is the movement of material through the digestive system. The muscles of the GI tract are single-unit smooth muscle whose cells are connected by gap junctions. Muscle contraction can be generated by nervous or chemical control, and some muscle cells generate spontaneous slow wave potentials. The wall of the intestinal tract is composed of an outer layer of longitudinal muscle and an inner layer of circular muscle. Peristaltic contractions are progressive waves of contraction that propel material from the esophagus to the rectum. Segmental contractions are mixing contractions that churn the material without propelling it forward. Material in the large intestine is moved forward by mass movement and is removed from the body by means of the defecation reflex. Each segment of the GI tract is separated by muscular sphincters that are tonically contracted except when food must move into the next segment or out of the body. Motility in each section of the GI tract is under multiple controls—both nervous and hormonal.

Various components of the digestive system contribute mucus, enzymes, hormones, and paracrines that make up the 7 L secreted by the body into the GI lumen. Digestive enzymes are secreted by either exocrine glands or epithelial cells in the mucosa of the stomach or small intestine (Table 21-1). Because enzymes are proteins, they are synthesized ahead of time, stored in secretory vesicles, and released on demand. To prevent autodigestion and provide an additional level of control, some enzymes are secreted as inactive zymogens that must be activated in the GI lumen. Mucus forms a protective coating over the GI mucosa and also provides lubrication for food movement. Large amounts of water and ions (Na^+, K^+, $Cl-$, H^+, and HCO_3^-) are also secreted. For example, the stomach secretes H^+-rich fluid while the pancreas secretes HCO_3^--rich fluid.

GI tract processes are governed by two types of neural reflexes: short reflexes, which take place entirely in the enteric nervous system, and long reflexes, which are integrated in the CNS. Stimuli for long reflexes may originate either inside or outside the GI tract. Peptides controlling GI processes can be grouped into three families: gastrin family, secretin family, and those not belonging to either. GI peptides can act locally or affect brain regions to influence behavior.

TEACH YOURSELF THE BASICS

FUNCTION AND PROCESSES OF THE DIGESTIVE SYSTEM

1. What is the function of the GI tract?

2. List two important challenges the GI tract must overcome to carry out this function.

3. List and define the four basic processes of the digestive system. (Fig. 21-1)

4. What happens to nutrients brought into the body through the digestive system?

5. Why does the GI tract have the most immune tissue of any organ?

6. What is the name given to the GI system's immune tissue?

ANATOMY OF THE DIGESTIVE SYSTEM

7. What are the first steps in digestion? Where do these steps take place?

8. The GI tract is a long tube lined with _____ epithelium and surrounded by _____ muscle. It is closed off by _____ muscle sphincters at the ends. (Fig. 21-2)

9. The combination of ingested food and digestive secretions forms a mixture known as _____.

The Digestive System Consists of the GI Tract and Accessory Glandular Organs

10. Trace a piece of food that enters the mouth through the digestive system, and follow its undigested portion until it is excreted. Include the sphincters the food passes. (Fig. 21-2)

11. List the three sections of the stomach.

12. List the three sections of the small intestine.

13. The digestive waste that leaves the body is called _____.

The GI Tract Wall Has Four Layers

14. List the four layers of the GI wall in the stomach and intestines, from inside to outside. (Fig. 21-2c-f)

The Mucosa

15. List and describe the three layers of the mucosa.

16. What anatomical modifications increase surface area facing the lumen of the stomach and intestine? Use the proper names given to these modifications. (Fig. 21-2g)

17. The tubular invaginations of the lumen that extend into supporting connective tissue are called
_____ in the stomach and _____
in the small intestine.

18. The surface area on the apical membrane of epithelial cells is increased by the presence of
_____. (Fig. 21-2g) [∫ p. 57-58]

19. List the types of epithelial cells found in the lumen of the GI tract. What is the function of each?

20. Compare cell-to-cell junctions of the stomach and intestine.

21. What is found in the layer known as the lamina propria? (Fig. 21-2c)

22. What are Peyer's patches? (Fig. 21-2a)

23. Describe the muscularis mucosa.

The Submucosa
24. What structures are found in the submucosa? (Fig. 21-2c)

The Muscularis Externa and Serosa
25. The outer intestinal wall consists of two smooth muscle layers. (Fig. 21-2c,d,e) Contraction of the
_____ layer decreases lumen diameter, while contraction of the _____ layer
shortens the length of the tube. The stomach has an incomplete third muscle layer, arranged
_____.

26. What is the myenteric plexus and where is it found?

27. What is the serosa and where is it found?

28. What are the peritoneum (peritoneal membrane) and mesentery?

MOTILITY
29. What are the two functions of motility?

30. Gastrointestinal motility is determined by what:

Gastrointestinal Smooth Muscle Contracts Spontaneously

31. Most of the intestinal tract is composed of _____-unit smooth muscle whose cells are electrically connected by _____ junctions. [∫ p. 414]

32. Distinguish between tonic and phasic contractions and tell where in the GI tract each contraction type can be found.

33. Describe how a slow-wave potential generates smooth muscle contraction in the GI tract. What roles do interstitial cells of Cajal and gap junctions play in this process? (Fig. 21-3)

GI Smooth Muscle Exhibits Different Patterns of Contraction

34. Describe or diagram the three general patterns of muscle contraction in the gut. What is the function of each? (Fig. 21-4)

35. What is a bolus?

36. What are some common motility disorders?

SECRETION

37. List the sources and volumes of fluid input into the GI tract. (Fig. 21-5)

38. What is the significance of this secreted volume?

Digestive Enzymes Are Secreted in the Mouth, Stomach, and Intestine

39. List the structures that secrete digestive enzymes.

40. Describe the synthesis, storage, and release of digestive enzymes. [∫ p. 146]

41. Enzymes secreted in inactive form are known collectively as _____.

42. What types of pathways control enzyme release?

Specialized Cells Secrete Mucus
43. Mucus is composed of glycoproteins called _____.

44. Name two functions of mucus.

45. Mucus is made by specialized cells: _____ cells in the stomach, _____ cells in the intestine, and _____ cells in the mouth.

46. List three different signals for mucus release.

The Digestive System Secretes Ions and Water
47. List the five major ions found in digestive secretions.

48. Movement of water and ions in the GI tract is very similar to water and ion movement in what other organ?

49. What are some of the transporters found on apical and basolateral membrane surfaces in GI epithelial cells?

DIGESTION AND ABSORPTION
50. How is digestion accomplished?

51. What is bile?

52. The pH at which different enzymes best function reflects what?

53. Where does most nutrient absorption take place?

Carbohydrates Are Digested to Monosaccharides
54. Name the enzyme that is responsible for the following reactions. (Fig. 21-6)

    maltose → monosaccharides _____

    starch → maltose _____

    sucrose → monosaccharides _____

    lactose → monosaccharides _____

55. Into what monosaccharides are the following disaccharides digested? (Fig. 21-6)
maltose → _____
sucrose → _____
lactose → _____

Proteins Are Digested to Small Peptides and Amino Acids

56. Name the type of enzyme that is responsible for each of the following reactions (Fig. 21-6) [∫ Fig. 2-16, p. 39]

Breaks interior peptide bonds to make smaller peptides _____
Breaks exterior peptide bonds to make single amino acids _____

57. Between 30% and 60% of the protein found in the intestinal lumen comes from what source?

Fat Digestion Is Assisted by Bile

58. Name five common forms of fat or fat-related molecules in the Western diet. [∫ Fig. 2-14, p. 37]

59. Why is it necessary to emulsify fats? [∫ p. 126]

60. What enzyme catalyzes triglyceride digestion? What are the products of this reaction? (Fig. 21-8)

Nucleic Acids Are Digested into Bases and Monosaccharides

61. What enzyme catalyzes the digestion of nucleic acids? What are the products of this reaction? [∫ Fig. 2-17, p. 40]

62. Describe the absorption of nucleic acids.

REGULATION OF GI FUNCTION

Overview of GI control mechanisms:

63. Classic neural reflexes:
Distinguish between long reflexes and cephalic reflexes (a special subset of long reflexes). Give examples of each.

Describe the autonomic influence in long reflexes.

64. Short reflexes integrated in the enteric nervous system
Contrast short reflexes with long reflexes. (Fig. 21-9)

The primary responses controlled by the ENS are related to:

Describe the nature and the functions of
Submucosal nerve plexus

Myenteric motor neurons

65. GI peptides
Describe the nature and location of action for GI peptide hormones and paracrines.

Which GI functions are under GI peptide control? Give examples. (Fig. 21-10)

The Enteric Nervous System Is Known As the Little Brain
66. Describe the similarities between the ENS and the brain.

GI Peptides Include Hormones, Neurocrines, and Cytokines

67. Name the three families of GI peptides and give examples of each.

68. What do the following abbreviations stand for? (Table 21-2)

CCK _____ VIP _____
GIP _____
GLP-1 _____

69. Where are the following GI peptides synthesized/secreted?

gastrin _____ secretin _____
CCK _____ GIP _____
motilin _____

◉ *Figure 21-11 is a summary figure for GI processes.*

70. Food processing is traditionally divided into three phases. Name those three phases.

THE CEPHALIC PHASE

71. What are some stimuli that cause anticipatory long reflexes during the cephalic phase? (Fig. 21-12)

72. List some feedforward GI responses to these anticipatory reflexes.

Chemical and Mechanical Digestion Begins in the Mouth

73. Describe the composition of saliva.

74. What controls saliva secretion?

75. List the functions of saliva.

76. Saliva begins chemical digestion with the secretion of which two enzymes? What digestive functions do these enzymes participate in?

77. What is the result of food processing in the oral cavity?

Swallowing Moves Food from the Mouth to the Stomach

78. What is the stimulus for the swallowing (deglutition) reflex? (Fig. 21-13)

79. Outline or diagram the swallowing reflex. (Fig. 21-13)

80. Describe how food enters the stomach.

81. Describe the structure and function of the esophageal sphincter.

THE GASTRIC PHASE

82. How many liters of food, drink, and saliva enter the fundus of the stomach each day?

83. Name and describe the three general functions of the stomach.

84. When does the gastric phase of digestion begin?

85. Are gastric phase reflexes long or short? Describe the factors involved in gastric phase reflexes.

The Stomach Stores Food

86. Compare upper stomach action to lower stomach action upon the arrival of food.

87. What is the importance of food storage in the stomach?

88. Enhanced gastric motility during a meal is primarily under _____ control and is stimulated by _____ of the stomach.

Digestion in the Stomach

89. Describe the actions of each of the following in the stomach:

Gastric acid (HCl):

Pepsin:

Gastric lipase:

Salivary amylase:

Secretion in the Stomach

90. The stomach secretes a variety of substances from an assortment of cells (Fig. 21-16).
Parietal cells (Fig. 21-14): Diagram or outline the cellular pathway for H^+ secretion

What is intrinsic factor, where is it from, and what is its significance?

Chief cells: What do they secrete? Does it have to be activated?

D cells: What do they secrete?

Enterochromaffin-like (ECL) cells: What do they secrete?

G cells: Where are they located? What do they secrete? What are the stimuli for its release?

Mucous cells: Where are they located? What do they secrete? What are the functions of their secretions? (Fig. 21-15)

The Stomach Balances Digestion and Protection

91. Outline or diagram the integrated stomach processes, as they function when you eat a meal. Start with food entering the mouth. (Fig. 21-17)

92. What normally protects the gastric mucosa from enzymes and acid? How is this protection compromised in Zollinger-Ellison syndrome?

93. What are other causes of excess acid secretion?

94. What are some therapies for dypepsia?

THE INTESTINAL PHASE

95. When does the intestinal phase begin?

96. Reflexes during the intestinal phase serve to regulate what? Are they hormonal, neural, or otherwise in their action? (Fig. 21-18)

97. Take the following stimuli and extrapolate the reflex initiated:
    The presence of acidic chyme in the duodenum:

A meal containing fats:

A meal containing carbohydrates:

Hyperosmotic solution in the intestine:

98. What is the net result of all three phases of gastric function?

Most Digestion and Absorption Occurs in the Intestine

99. Additional secretions are added to chyme as it passes through the small intestine. What structures are secreting these substances?

100. Describe how the small intestine and its accessory organs fulfill these roles:
    Protection and lubrication:

    Digestion of macromolecules:

    Motility:

    Absorption:

    Integration and coordination:

101. What is the significance of the hepatic portal system in intestinal absorption?

Secretions in the Small Intestine Include Bicarbonate
Enzyme secretion

102. Contrast pancreatic and intestinal enzymes with regard to their location and functionality. Include a discussion of the brush border and its role.

103. What are some of the enzymes secreted by the intestinal epithelium?

104. What are some of the enzymes secreted by the exocrine pancreas?

105. For enzymes secreted as zymogens, describe how they are activated. (Fig. 21-20)

106. What signals enzyme release for intestinal epithelial enzymes? for pancreatic enzymes?

107. The pancreatic reflex is mediated by:

Bicarbonate secretion
108. What function is served by the secretion of bicarbonate into the small intestine?

109. In what form does the pancreas secrete bicarbonate?

110. What are the stimuli for bicarbonate secretion?

111. As in the renal tubule cells and RBCs, bicarbonate production requires high levels of which enzyme? [∫ p. 585, p. 649]

112. On the diagram below, draw the appropriate channels on the correct membrane surface to achieve secretion of sodium bicarbonate. (Fig. 21-21, but try not to look first)

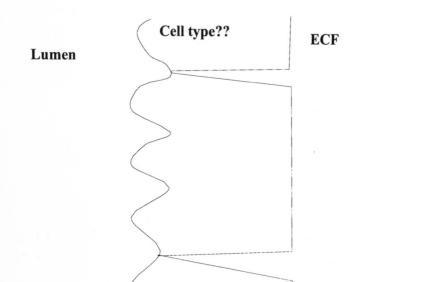

Cell type??   **ECF**

Lumen

Components to include:

pancreatic cell
carbonic anhydrase
Na^+-K^+ ATPase
Cl^--HCO_3^- antiporte
Na^+-H^+ antiporter
Na^+-K^+-$2Cl^-$ sympo1
CFTR chloride
channel
H^+, HCO_3^-,
Na^+, Cl^-, K^+
Paracellular movem
of Na^+ and water

113. What results from a defective CFTR channel, as in cystic fibrosis? [∫ p. 554]

Bile secretion
114. What is bile? (See Focus on the Liver, Fig. 21-22)

115. What are the components of bile?

116. Which cells secrete bile? Where is it stored? Through which duct does it enter the duodenum?

117. What is the function of bile? (Fig. 21-23)

118. Gall bladder contraction is stimulated by _____.

Carbohydrate Digestion and Absorption
119. Carbohydrate digestion in the small intestine converts digestible polysaccharides and disaccharides into _____ so that they can be absorbed.

120. What are the functions of the following:

    Pancreatic amylase:
    Maltase:
    Sucrase:
    Lactase:

121. What are the end products of carbohydrate digestion?

122. On the diagram below, supply transporters and other components to make cells that absorb
carbohydrates just like our intestinal epithelium (Fig. 21-24, but don't look first):

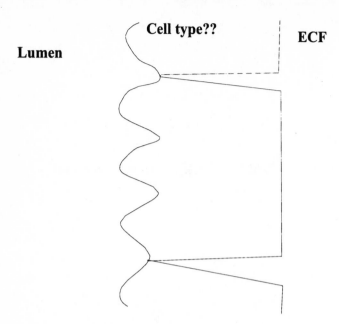

Cell type??

ECF

Lumen

Components to include:

glucose, fructose,
galactose
Na^+-glucose symporter
GLUT2 transporter
GLUT5 transporter
Na^+-K^+-ATPase
capillary

123. How do intestinal epithelial cells keep intracellular glucose concentrations high for facilitated
diffusion if glucose is the major metabolic substrate for aerobic respiration?

Protein Digestion and Absorption
124. How is pepsin inactivated?

125. How is protein digestion continued?

126. What are the primary products of protein digestion?

127. On the diagram below, show the three ways that proteins are absorbed (Fig. 21-25, but try not to look first).

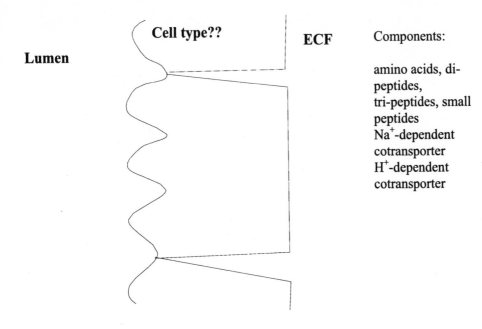

Cell type??   **ECF**   Components:

Lumen
                                                        amino acids, di-
                                                        peptides,
                                                        tri-peptides, small
                                                        peptides
                                                        Na^+-dependent
                                                        cotransporter
                                                        H^+-dependent
                                                        cotransporter

128. What are the two possible fates of absorbed di- and tri-peptides?

129. How does peptide absorption relate to food allergies and food intolerances?

130. How does the development of the intestinal epithelium relate to the development of food allergies? Cite some examples.

131. What therapeutic implications could come about from our knowledge of intact peptide absorption?

Fat Digestion and Absorption

132. In what form do fats enter the small intestine? (Fig. 21-26)

133. Define emulsion.

134. What is the role of bile salts in the duodenum?

135. What is the role of pancreatic lipase? colipase?

136. As digestion proceeds, fatty acids, bile salts, monoglycerides, phospholipids, and cholesterol form: [∫ p. 126]

137. How are most fats absorbed across the apical membrane? (Fig. 21-26)

138. How is cholesterol absorbed at the apical membrane?

139. Describe what happens to monoglycerides and fatty acids once inside the cell.

140. How do chylomicrons leave the cell? (Fig. 21-26)

141. How/where are chylomicrons absorbed once in the extracellular space? How do they make it into the venous circulation? Why aren't they just directly absorbed into the bloodstream? [∫ p. 508]

142. Why is it that some fatty acids go directly into the blood?

143. How are bile salts recycled? Why is this necessary?

144. What happens to bilirubin?

Vitamins and Minerals
145. What are the fat-soluble vitamins? How are they absorbed?

146. How are water-soluble vitamins absorbed?

147. How is vitamin B_{12} absorbed? What is required? Where is the B_{12} transporter found?

148. How does mineral absorption take place?

149. What is special about iron and calcium absorption?

Absorption of Ions and Water
150. Of the approximately 9 L/day of fluid that enters the small intestine, how much is reabsorbed?

151. Where does the absorption of organic nutrients mainly take place? What does the absorption of these nutrients create?

152. How is Na+ reabsorbed across the intestinal epithelium? Name the transporters. [∫ Fig. 19-11, p. 610]

153. By the end of the ileum, what amount of unabsorbed chyme remains?

154. Describe the movement of chyme into the large intestine. Include major anatomical landmarks.

The Large Intestine Concentrates Waste for Excretion
155. List the seven regions of the large intestine as they would be encountered by chyme entering from the small intestine. (Fig. 21-27)

156. The anus is closed by two sphincters. Describe those sphincters.

157. How does the wall of the large intestine differ from the wall of the small intestine? Describe the muscularis, the mucosa, and the luminal surface.

Motility in the Large Intestine

158. Chyme that enters the colon continues to be mixed by _____.

159. Describe mass movement, the unique colonic contraction. This type of contraction is associated with what reflex?

160. Outline or diagram the defecation reflex, beginning with the stimulus for defecation.

161. Describe some of the results that emotional influences can have on defecation.

Digestion and Absorption in the Large Intestine

162. How do bacteria in the large intestine participate in digestion?

163. What is flatus?

Secretion and Absorption of Fluid and Electrolytes

164. The colon is responsible for absorbing:

165. Of the 1.5 L/day that enter the large intestine, how much water is lost in the feces under normal conditions?

166. The colonocytes (absorb / secrete ?) NaCl and (absorb / secrete ?) K^+. (Fig. 21-28) This process is under the influence of _____, just as in the kidney. [∫ p. 636]

167. How is Cl^- secreted into the lumen of the intestine? (Fig. 21-29)

Diarrhea Can Cause Dehydration

168. What is diarrhea? What are some causes of the condition?

169. What is osmotic diarrhea? How does it occur?

170. What is secretory diarrhea? How does it occur?

171. How can diarrhea cause dehydration? What are the appropriate therapies?

IMMUNE FUNCTIONS OF THE GI TRACT
172. What are the GI tract's first lines of defense in fighting off pathogens?

173. Pathogens or toxic materials in the small intestine trigger sensory receptors and the immune cells of the _____. What are two common responses?

M Cells Sample the Contents of the Gut
174. Describe the components of the immune system of the intestinal mucosa.

175. What do M cells do?

176. How are antigens brought into the M cells? [∫ p. 145] What do M cells do with the antigens they've ingested? [∫ p. 524]

177. If the antigen is threatening, what responses does the immune system initiate?

178. What process is disrupted in inflammatory bowel diseases like ulcerative colitis and Crohn's disease?

179. How do certain pathogenic bacteria cross the barrier created by the intestinal epithelium?

Vomiting Is a Protective Reflex
180. What is vomiting? What does it accomplish?

181. Excessive vomiting can cause what condition? [∫ p. 652]

182. Outline or diagram the vomiting reflex.

TALK THE TALK

absorption	absorptive cell	amylase	anal sphincter
antrum	anus	bicarbonate secretion, stomach	bile
bile acid	bile salt	bilirubin	bolus
brush border	cell-to-cell junctions	cellulose	cephalic phase
chief cell	chloride secretion	cholecystokinin (CCK)	cholera toxin
cholesterol transport	chylomicron	chyme	Cl^--HCO_3^- antiporter
cobalamin	colipase	crypt	cystic fibrosis
cystic fibrosis transmembrane regulator (CFTR channel)	D cell	defecation reflex	deglutition
diarrhea	digestion	disaccharidase	disaccharide
duodenum	emulsion	endopeptidase	enteric nervous system
enterochromaffin-like (ECL) cell	enteropeptidase	enterostatin	enterotoxin
Escherichia coli	esophageal sphincters	esophagus	feces
fistula	flatus	food allergies	fructose
fructose absorption	fundus	G cell	gallbladder
gastric gland	gastric inhibitory peptide (GIP)	gastric phase	gastrin
gastrin-releasing peptide	gastrointestinal tract	glucagon	glucose
glucose transport	glucose-dependent insulinotropic peptide	GLUT transporter	gluten allergy
glycogen	goblet cell	gut-associated lymphoid tissue (GALT)	H^+-K^+-ATPase
H^+-peptide cotransport	heartburn	*Helicobacter pylori*	hepatic artery
hepatic portal system	hepatocyte	histamine	histamine receptor (H_2 receptor)
ileocecal sphincter	ileum	intestinal phase	intrinsic factor
jejunum	lactase	lactose	lactose intolerance
lamina propria	large intestine	leaky epithelium	lingual lipase
lipid digestion	liver	long reflex	M cell
maltase	maltose	mass movement	mastication
mesentery	micelle	microvilli	monosaccharide
motilin	motility	mucin	mucosa
mucus cell	muscularis mucosa	myenteric plexus	Na^+-K^+-2Cl- symporter
Na^+-K^+-ATPase	Na^+-amino acid cotransport	Na^+-glucose symporter	NSAIDs
nucleic acid digestion	Olestra	oral cavity	osmoreceptor
pancreas	paracrines in the GI tract	parietal cell	pepsin
pepsinogen	peptic ulcer	peptidase	peristaltic contraction
peristaltic reflex	peritoneal membrane	pernicious anemia	Peyer's patch
pharmacomechanical coupling	plicae	protease	pyloric sphincter
pylorus	receiving segment	rectum	reflux esophagitis
rugae	saliva	satiety	secretin
secretion	segmental contraction	serosa	short reflex
single-unit smooth muscle	slow wave potential	small intestine	somatostatin
sphincter	sphincter of Oddi	starch digestion	stomach
submucosal gland	submucosal plexus	sucrase	sucrose
tonic contraction	transcytosis	triglyceride	trypsin
trypsinogen	vagal reflex	vasoactive intestinal peptide (VIP)	villi
vitamin	vitamin B_{12}	zymogen	

PRACTICE MAKES PERFECT

1. Number the following structures of the gastrointestinal tract in the order which food passes:

_____ Stomach   _____ Ileum   _____ Esophagus

_____ Ascending colon   _____ Pyloric sphincter   _____ Duodenum

2. Why doesn't salivary amylase work in the stomach?

3. Pepsin is produced by the _____, and trypsin is produced by the
_____.

   Pepsin is active only at _____ H^+ concentrations, while trypsin is active at _____ H^+
   concentrations.

4. How does the digestive system prevent autodigestion?

5. True or false? Be able to defend your answer.

   a) The pathway from the intestinal lumen to the circulating blood for a short-chain fatty acid (<10
   carbon atoms) is intestinal mucosa cell to chylomicrons to capillary to systemic venous blood in the
   hepatic portal vein.

   b) Most of the bile salts secreted by the liver into the lumen of the intestine are excreted in the feces.

c) The amount of water that is reabsorbed from the intestinal tract in a day is equal to the amount of water that is ingested in a day.

d) If the blood supply to the small intestine decreases dramatically so that the cells become hypoxic, the absorption of glucose will decrease.

6. The parietal cells of the stomach secrete hydrochloric acid.

a) Based on your knowledge of acid secretion in the kidney, draw the mechanism of HCl secretion in the parietal cell.

b) Based on the model you just drew, what kind of acid-base disturbance would excessive vomiting of stomach contents cause? In one sentence, defend your answer.

7. Why is the enteric nervous system considered by some to be a third division of the nervous system that is equivalent to the CNS and peripheral nervous system?

8. Why do physicians recommend that parents not feed infants gluten-based cereals until they are several months of age?

9. Fill in the reflex pathway below. The stimulus and response are given.

Stimulus: test anxiety

Receptor(s): _____

Afferent pathway:_____

Integrating center: _____

Efferent pathway: _____

Effector(s): _____

Cellular response: _____

Tissue response: _____

Systemic response: acid stomach syndrome

10. In no more than two phrases per pair, compare/contrast the four processes of the urinary system to the four processes of the digestive system.

11. You have been doing some experiments in lingual and gastric lipase, but someone marked the test tubes with a marker that rubbed off. You know that one tube has the gastric enzyme and one tube has the lingual enzyme. What test could you do with the enzymes to tell which is which?

MAPS

1. Start with some sucrose and starch molecules in a candy bar. Follow these molecules through ingestion, digestion, and absorption as they move through the digestive tract.

2. Map digestive smooth muscle contraction, using the following terms and any others you wish to add.

circular layer	gap junction	longitudinal layer
motility	muscularis mucosa	myenteric plexus
paracrines in the GI tract	peristaltic contraction	peristaltic reflex
pharmacomechanical coupling	receiving segment	segmental contraction
short reflex	single-unit smooth muscle	slow wave potential
tonic contraction		

3. Map the long and short reflexes of the gastrointestinal system.

4. Create a map of stomach function.

5. Compile information from the entire chapter to create a map of small intestine function.

BEYOND THE PAGES

✎ TRY IT: **Digestion of starch by salivary amylase**

You can sense the changes that take place during starch digestion by chewing on a soda cracker and holding it in your mouth rather than swallowing it. For best results use a starchy, unflavored soda cracker like a Saltine®. Put it in your mouth and start chewing. What happens to the taste as you chew? Rather than swallowing the chewed cracker right away, keep it in your mouth for a minute or two and see if the taste continues to change. Your salivary amylase acts on the starch in the cracker, breaking it up into smaller glucose polymers and the disaccharide maltose. Maltose has about 40% of the sweetness of sugar, so you should notice the taste of the cracker changing as you chew.

Terminology
GI physiology is full of technical words for functions that go by much more common names. Impress your friends with these --- "Excuse me. I need to eructate."

mastication	= chewing
emesis	= vomiting
flatulence	= having intestinal gas (flatus)
borborygmi	= rumbling noises in the GI tract from intestinal gas
deglutition	= swallowing
eructation	= burping

Organizing study
This is another chapter that is top heavy with terminology and information that needs to be memorized. There are several ways that you can organize the information in the chapter for study. One is to go anatomically, section by section, and outline everything that happens in each section. Within a section, you can subdivide into the four processes of motility, secretion, digestion, and absorption. For the latter two sections, you can further subdivide according to nutrients. Another way to organize is to take the three major classes of biomolecules and follow them one at a time from ingestion through absorption. Whichever way you organize it, maps are a great method for putting lots of integrated information into a relatively compact space. You may want to buy some poster board for the maps in this chapter, though!

Here is an example of a chart to make:

	Carbohydrate	Fat	Protein
List ALL places in the digestive tract where significant digestion of this takes place. What enzymes?			
In what form is this group of foods absorbed? (i.e. What is the product of digestion?)			
Describe the process of absorption.			

FURTHER EXPLORATIONS

Alcohol and the liver. Science & Medicine, March/April 1995.

Genetics of colon cancer. Science & Medicine, July/August 1997.

Peristalsis. Science & Medicine, November/December 1994.

The artificial liver. Science & Medicine, May/June 1995.

The enteric neuroimmune system. News in Physiological Sciences 12: 245-246, October 1997.

The bacteria behind ulcers. Scientific American, February 1996.

The gastrointestinal tract in growth and reproduction. Scientific American, July 1989.

Olestra and the FDA. New England Journal of Medicine 334 (15): 984-986. 1996 Apr 11.

Are we ready for fat-free fat? Time 147 (2): 52. 1996 Jan 8.

Letting the chips fall where they may. Tufts University Diet & Nutrition Letter 14 (1): 2. 1996 March.

Virtual colonoscopy. Science & Medicine 6(5):56-63, 1999 Sep/Oct.

Edible vaccines. Science & Medicine 5(6), 1998 Nov/Dec.

22

METABOLISM AND ENERGY BALANCE

SUMMARY

Don't wait until the last minute to learn the information in this chapter. As with Chapter 20 (Fluid and Electrolyte Balance), this chapter presents material that integrates all the concepts and details of the previous chapters. Spend quality time (not stressed, last minute cramming) on this material.

> ✓ Anabolic and catabolic metabolic states are balanced to ensure that the body (especially the brain) has an adequate supply of fuel.
> ✓ Control of metabolic states is largely under endocrine control. Hour-to-hour control of metabolism is determined by the ratio of insulin to glucagon.
> ✓ Abnormalities in insulin production or activity can lead to a condition called diabetes mellitus. Allow plenty of time to learn and understand the pathways in this condition!! Diabetes involves almost every pathway you've encountered throughout this textbook.

Metabolism is the sum of the chemical reactions in your body that extract and use energy or store it for later use. There are two general types of metabolic reactions: anabolic (synthesis) and catabolic (breakdown). Normally, these reactions are balanced so that energy intake equals energy output. Energy is used to fuel biological work such as transport work, mechanical work, and chemical work. Body temperature regulation is also closely linked with metabolism.

Metabolism is divided into two states: fed (absorptive) and fasting (postabsorptive). The fed state is predominantly anabolic and the fasting state is predominantly catabolic. During the fed state, energy storage compounds are made. These include glycogen (liver, skeletal muscles) and fat (adipose). When the body enters the fasting state, these compounds are broken down to provide energy. Reactions involved in glycogen processing are glycogenesis (glucose → glycogen) and glycogenolysis (glycogen → glucose). Glucose can also be synthesized from noncarbohydrate precursors. Fats and proteins are converted into glucose through a process called gluconeogenesis. Different enzymes control the forward and reverse reactions in these processes, adding an additional level of control to metabolism called push-pull control. The goal of all this is to maintain plasma glucose concentrations so that the brain receives enough glucose.

The hour-to-hour control of glucose concentration depends on the ratio of insulin to glucagon. These are hormones secreted by islets of Langerhans cells in the endocrine pancreas: beta cells produce insulin and alpha cells produce glucagon. Insulin and glucagon work antagonistically (remember hormone interactions from Chapter 6?) to maintain plasma glucose. Insulin dominates during the fed state, and glucagon dominates during the fasted state. Insulin lowers glucose levels by facilitating glucose uptake and utilization primarily in liver, adipose, and skeletal muscle cells. Glucagon has the opposite effect from that of insulin. It raises plasma glucose by initiating glycogenolysis and gluconeogenesis and increasing hepatic glucose output.

Diabetes mellitus is a collection of diseases marked by abnormal secretion or activity of insulin. BEWARE: This one topic integrates almost every control pathway you have learned in this course! Be sure to give yourself plenty of time to learn and understand every pathway involved. Once you have mastered the integration of diabetes, you can rest assured that you have reached a new level in understanding human physiology. Insulin-dependent diabetes (type 1) is the more severe of the diabetes mellitus conditions. With type 1 diabetes, despite high plasma glucose concentrations, lack of insulin prevents most cells from taking up glucose. Therefore, the body is tricked into thinking it is in a constant state of fasting. The cells are breaking down proteins and fats, leading to muscle wasting and ketoacidosis. Suprathreshold glucose concentrations lead to glucosuria, which in turn causes osmotic diuresis and polyuria. Fluid loss leads to dehydration, which triggers homeostatic renal and cardiovascular reflexes. If all these problems aren't resolved, coma and death are inevitable. However, insulin injections and electrolyte therapy can correct the imbalances and prevent death. Study Figure 22-15 on p. 713 to see the integration of diabetes control. All the pathways are there, but there are some details left out (on purpose). See if you can supply additional detail to this map.

TEACH YOURSELF THE BASICS

The Brain Controls Food Intake
1. Our current model of the control of food intake is based on:

2. Distinguish between the feeding center and the satiety center:

3. Contrast the glucostatic theory and the lipostatic theory.

4. Describe some of the peptides involved in food regulation. (Fig. 22-1; Table 22-1)

ENERGY BALANCE
5. Define metabolism.

Energy Input Equals Energy Output
6. The first law of thermodynamics states that:

7. Energy input into the body comes in the form of:

8. Energy output by the body takes one of two forms:

9. List the three kinds of biological work and give an example of each [∫ p. 85]:

Energy Balance Is Reflected by an Individual's Oxygen Consumption
◎ We must be able to estimate energy intake (food) and energy output (heat loss, work).

Oxygen Consumption Can Be Equated to Metabolic Rate
10. What is direct calorimetry? How is the energy measured experimentally?

11. List the metabolic energy content of carbohydrates, proteins, and fats. How would you determine the kilocalories for a particular food that contains a variety of biomolecules?

12. True or false? The metabolic energy content of food is equal to the content measured by direct calorimetry. (Defend your answer.)

13. What are some ways to measure the metabolic rate?

Many Factors Influence Metabolic Rate
14. What is the basal metabolic rate (BMR)?

15. What is the most accurate way to measure a person's BMR? What is the most practical way to measure a person's BMR?

16. What are some factors that influence metabolic rate?

17. What is meant by diet-induced thermogenesis? What factors are involved?

18. What behavioral changes can we make to influence our metabolic rate?

Energy Is Stored in Fat and Glycogen
19. How is our daily energy requirement expressed?

20. Compare glycogen versus fats for energy storage. Which holds more energy? Which is easier to access?

METABOLISM
21. Define metabolism.

22. Distinguish between anabolic and catabolic pathways.

23. What are the two states of metabolism? Which is catabolic and which is anabolic?

Energy from Ingested Nutrients May Be Used Immediately or Stored
24. What three possible fates do biomolecules meet in the body?

25. Most fats enter the energy production pathways as _____ and _____
    (Fig. 21-5).

26. Most carbohydrates are absorbed in the form of _____. Most proteins are absorbed in the
    form of _____.

27. The plasma concentration of which biomolecule is most closely regulated?

28. The amino acid pool of the body is used primarily for:

29. Define the following terms:
    glycogenesis _____
    glycogenolysis _____
    gluconeogenesis _____
    lipogenesis _____
    lipolysis _____

Hormones Control Metabolic Pathways by Changing Enzyme Activity
30. Review Fig. 22-3 to examine the biological pathways important for energy production and how they
    interact.

31. Describe dual control of metabolic reactions and give an example. Why is dual control important?
    (Fig. 22-4)

Anabolic Metabolism Dominates in the Fed State
32. Review the fates of nutrients during the fed state as outlined in Table 22-2.

Carbohydrates Provide Energy
33. Anatomically, what is the path of glucose absorption?

34. On the cellular level, how/where is glucose absorbed?

35. What are the potential fates for absorbed glucose?

36. How is unused glucose stored?

New Proteins Are Made from Amino Acids
37. Anatomically, what is the path of amino acid absorption?

38. What are the potential fates of absorbed amino acids?

Fats Store Energy
39. Anatomically, what is the path of fat absorption? (Fig. 22-5)

40. How are fats absorbed into cells?

41. What are the potential fates of fats in the body?

42. What's the difference between "good" cholesterol and "bad" cholesterol?

43. What are the roles of lipoproteins in cholesterol metabolism?

44. What are apoproteins?

Catabolic Metabolism Dominates in the Fasted State
45. What is the signal for a shift in metabolic state?

46. What is the goal of the fasted state?

47. Which organ is the primary source of glucose production during the fasted state (Fig. 22-6)? How does it contribute to available glucose levels?

48. What are other sources of energy during the fasted state?

49. What is beta-oxidation? What are the potential dangers of beta-oxidation?

HOMEOSTATIC CONTROL OF METABOLISM

50. Hour-to-hour regulation of metabolism depends on what ratio?

The Pancreas Secretes Insulin and Glucagon

51. Each cell type within the Islets of Langerhans secretes a different peptide (Fig. 22-7):
    α cells: _____
    β cells: _____
    D cells: _____
    PP cells or F cells: _____

52. Like all endocrine glands, the islets are closely associated with _____.

53. Nervous control of the endocrine pancreas involves which neurons? Would you expect antagonistic or tonic nervous control?

The Insulin-to-Glucose Ratio Regulates Metabolism

54. Insulin and glucagon are (synergistic / antagonistic / permissive ?) hormones. [∫ p. 226]

55. What controls which of these hormone dominates?

56. Which hormone is dominant during the fed state (Fig. 22-8a)? What is the net metabolic effect?

57. Which hormone is dominant during the fasted state (Fig. 22-8b)? What is the net metabolic effect?

58. Describe the fluctuations of glucose, glucagons, and insulin concentrations during the course of a day. (Fig. 22-9)

Insulin Is the Dominant Hormone of the Fed State

59. How does insulin behave like a typical peptide hormone? (Table 22-3) [∫ p. 216]

60. List and briefly describe the factors that influence insulin secretion:

61. What is the mechanism by which increased glucose concentration causes insulin secretion? [∫ Fig. 5-42; p. 163]

Insulin Promotes Anabolism

62. Which receptor type is involved in the signal transduction pathway for insulin? [∫ p. 162]

63. What are the primary targets for insulin (Table 21-2)? How does glucose enter these cells?

64. Which tissues do not require insulin for glucose uptake?

65. What is the cellular mechanism for insulin activity:
    a. In adipose and muscle tissues? (Fig. 22-11)

b. In hepatocytes? (Fig. 22-12)

66. Insulin is considered to be (catabolic / anabolic ?). Which metabolic pathways are activat
which are inhibited? (Fig. 22-13)

67. List the four categories of insulin action.

Glucagon Is Dominant in the Fasted State
68. How is glucagon antagonistic to insulin? (Table 22-5)

69. Is it always present, or is it secreted only upon demand? (Fig. 22-9)

70. What factors trigger glucagon release?

71. What is the target of glucagon? (Fig. 22-9; Table 22-5)

72. What metabolic pathways does glucagon trigger?

Diabetes Mellitus Is a Family of Metabolic Diseases
73. Distinguish between type 1 and type 2 diabetes mellitus.

74. What are some of the causes of diabetes?

Type 1 Diabetics Are Ketosis-Prone

75. Explain the physiology behind each of the symptoms of untreated type 1 diabetes mellitus (Fig. 22-15):

glucose in the urine [∫ p. 612] _____

ketone production [∫ p. 646] _____

muscle wasting _____

excessive urination _____

metabolic acidosis [∫ p. 652] _____

excessive thirst _____

polyphagia _____

osmotic diuresis _____

hyperglycemia _____

increased ventilation [∫ p. 589] _____

lactic acidosis _____

76. What is the treatment for type 1 diabetes mellitus?

◎ Type 1 diabetes integrates just about everything you've learned so far in physiology. Spend some more time learning the pathways affected by this disease before you move on.

Type 2 Diabetics Often Have Elevated Insulin Levels

77. Why do type 2 diabetics often have elevated insulin levels?

78. Explain the glucose tolerance test and its role in diagnosing diabetes.

79. Why do patients with untreated type 2 diabetes usually not develop ketosis?

80. What are the major complications of type 2 diabetes?

81. What are the therapy options for type 2 diabetes?

REGULATION OF BODY TEMPERATURE
Body Temperature Is a Balance Between Heat Production, Gain, and Loss (Fig. 22-17)
82. How is metabolic efficiency related to obesity?

83. What is meant by homeothermic?

84. What is the normal body temperature range of humans (in °C)?

85. List factors that can affect body temperature:

86. When during the day is body temperature generally highest?

Heat Gain and Loss Are Balanced
87. List two sources of internal heat production (Fig. 22-18):

88. List the sources of external heat input:

89. Describe the four different kinds of heat loss:

Body Temperature Is Homeostatically Regulated
90. What is the thermoneutral zone?

91. What is the temperature range for the human thermoneutral zone? What happens as body temperature goes above or below this range?

92. The greatest physiological challenge to homeostasis comes from (hot / cold ?) temperatures.
93. The integrating center for control of body temperature is located in the _____.
   (Fig. 22-19)
94. The body's thermoreceptors monitor temperatures in what locations?

95. Heat loss is achieved by what two mechanisms?

96. Heat generation is achieved by what two mechanisms?

Alterations in Cutaneous Blood Flow Conserve or Release Heat

97. Does blood flow through cutaneous blood vessels increase or decrease to achieve heat loss? To achieve heat conservation?

98. Outline the mechanisms for regulation of cutaneous responses to body temperature fluctuations (to both rising and falling temperatures).

Sweat Contributes to Heat Loss

99. Describe the anatomy of a sweat gland and the composition of sweat.

100. How is sweat produced?

101. How does sweat contribute to surface heat loss?

The Body Produces Heat Through Movement and Metabolism

102. Describe shivering thermogenesis (include the mechanism).

103. Describe nonshivering thermogenesis (include the mechanism).

◎ Responses to high/low temperatures are shown in Fig 22-20.

The Body's Thermostat Can Reset

104. List some physiological causes for temperature variation.

105. List some pathological causes for temperature variation.

106. What are some of the cytokines that influence body temperature? How do they work?

107. What is the mechanism behind malignant hyperthermia?

TALK THE TALK

absorptive state (fed state)
adipose tissue
amylin
apolipoprotein
apoproteins
beta cell
bradykinin
catabolism
chromium
conductive heat gain
diabetes mellitus
direct calorimetry
essential amino acid
fatty acid
fever
ghrelin
glucose tolerance factor
glucosuria
glycogenesis
high density lipoprotein (HDL)
hypercholesterolemia
hypoglycemia
indirect calorimetry
islets of Langerhans
ketosis
lipoprotein lipase
malignant hyperthermia
metabolism
obese (ob) gene
oxidation
Paul Langerhans
post-absorptive, state (fasted state)
push-pull control
receptor-mediated endocytosis
satiety center
sweat gland
thermography
thermoregulation
type 2 diabetes mellitus
uncoupling protein

acetoacetic acid
alpha cell
anabolism
apoprotein B
appetite
beta-adrenergic receptor
brown adipose tissue
CCK theory of feeding
chylomicron
convective heat loss
diabetic ketoacidosis
energy balance
evaporative heat loss
feedforward
first law of thermodynamics
glucagon
glucose tolerance test
GLUT transporter
glycogenolysis
homeothermy
hyperglycemia
hypothalamic thermostat
insulin
ketoacidosis
kilocalorie (kcal)
lipostat theory
mechanical work
microtubule assembly
orexins
oxygen consumption
polyphagia
postprandial period
pyrogen
renal threshold for glucose
shivering thermogenesis
sympathetic vasodilator neuron
thermoneutral zone
transport work
tyrosine
very low density lipoprotein (VLDL)

active vasodilation
amino acids, metabolism of
anorexia nervosa
apoprotein E
basal metabolic rate (BMR)
bomb calorimeter
carbohydrates, as energy source
chemical work
chylomicron remnant
cutaneous blood flow
diet-induced thermogenesis
enterostatin
fat, as energy source
feeding center
gastric inhibitory peptide (GIP)
gluconeogenesis
glucostatic theory of feeding control
glycogen, as energy source
heat index
hot flashes
hypocretins
hypothermia
insulin-receptor substrate
ketone body
leptin
low density lipoprotein (LDL)
metabolic acidosis
non-shivering thermogenesis
osmotic diuresis
pancreatic polypeptide
polyuria
PP cell
radiant heat loss
respiratory quotient (RQ)
sweat
thermogenin
thermoreceptor
type 1 diabetes mellitus
tyrosine kinase
wind chill factor

QUANTITATIVE THINKING

Body Mass Index: The **body mass index** (BMI) has been shown to correlate well with how much body fat a person has, and it can be calculated without special equipment or testing. The 1995 NIH guidelines define a BMI below 25 as healthy.

To calculate: $BMI = w/h^2$

w = weight in kilograms or weight in pounds divided by 2.2
h = height in meters or height in inches divided by 39.4

Calculate your BMI: weight = _____ lbs. 4 2.2 = _____ kg

height = _____ in. 4 39.4 = _____ m

$BMI = $ weight (kg) / height^2

PRACTICE MAKES PERFECT

1. Circle the letter of each pair representing an INCORRECT cause:effect relationship:

    a) epinephrine : increased glycogenolysis in the liver
    b) insulin : increased protein synthesis
    c) glucagon : decreased gluconeogenesis

2. TRUE/FALSE and explain: The heat produced by an organism is one way of defining (or measuring) metabolism.

3. Classify each of the following hormones as anabolic (A) or catabolic (C).

    glucagon _____   insulin _____

4. If you go on a no-carbohydrate diet, why doesn't the brain starve to death for lack of glucose?

5. Compare insulin secretion when glucose is given orally to insulin secretion after the same amount of glucose is given intravenously.

6. Generally insulin and glucagon are released by opposing stimuli and have opposing effects on metabolism. However, *both* hormones are released by the stimulus of an increase in blood amino acids. Circle all the answers below that explain correctly why this occurs.

    a) Glucagon will prevent hypoglycemia following ingestion of a pure protein meal.
    b) Both insulin and glucagon promote amino acid absorption at the small intestine.
    c) Amino acids are present in the blood during both anabolism and catabolism.
    d) Glucagon release is part of a positive feedback loop.
    e) Amino acids stimulate the release of insulin that stimulates the release of glucagon.
    f) Glucagon stimulates transcription and translation of amino acid transporters at the cell membrane.

7. Analyze the food label below for fat content (% of total calories) and critique the labeling. Is this a "good" food according to current guidelines on recommended fat intake (30% or fewer calories from fat)?

Calories per serving:	190
Total fat	7 g
Total carbohydrate	25 g
Total protein	9 g

8. Mice with leptin deficiency become obese, but obese humans have elevated levels of leptin in their blood. Can you think of an alternate explanation for leptin-related obesity in humans that fits these findings?

9. True or false? Explain your reasoning.

    a) Glucagon promotes glycogenolysis, gluconeogenesis, and ketogenesis.

    b) Insulin promotes transport of glucose into liver.

    c) Glucose transport in all cells of the body is via a mediated transport system that exhibits saturation.

10. Why are body-builders wasting their money if they take amino acid supplements in addition to a balanced diet?

MAPS

1. Map in detail the physiological complications arising from insulin-dependent diabetes mellitus. Include all homeostatic controls, all hormones, neurotransmitters, receptors, integrating centers, effector tissues, etc. Be very SPECIFIC. This map will require a large sheet of paper or a poster board.

BEYOND THE PAGES

FURTHER EXPLORATIONS

Diet and cancer. Scientific American, November 1987.

Encapsulated cell therapy. Science & Medicine, July/August 1995.

Gaining on fat. Scientific American, August 1996.

Glucose transport and glucose homeostasis: New insights from transgenic mice. News in Physiological Sciences 10: 22-29, February 1995.

How does the fetus cope with thermal challenges? News in Physiological Sciences 11: 96-100, April 1996.

Mouse models of human obesity. Science & Medicine, May/June 1997.

Reaching out: Nutrition quackery. Science & Medicine, May/June 1997.

The obese gene (ob) and human obesity. News in Physiological Sciences 11: 147-148, June 1996.

Temperature and proteins: Little things can mean a lot. News in Physiological Sciences 11: 72-76, April 1996.

The fish oil puzzle. Science & Medicine, September/October 1996.

Treating diabetes with transplanted cells. July 1995.

Vitamin E is nature's master. Science & Medicine, March/April 1994.

What causes diabetes? Scientific American, July 1990.

CHAPTER 23

ENDOCRINE CONTROL OF GROWTH AND METABOLISM

SUMMARY

✓ Long-term metabolic control involves cortisol (adrenal cortex), thyroid hormones (thyroid gland), and growth hormone (anterior pituitary).

✓ Endocrine pathologies are generally the result of disturbances in hormone control pathways – too much or too little hormone produced, or abnormal tissue responsiveness. Pathologies are characterized by the nature of the disturbance and by the portion of the control pathway affected. [∫ p. 227-230]

✓ Cortisol is essential for life; its metabolic effects are all aimed at preventing hypoglycemia.

✓ Thyroid hormones affect quality of life: their overall effect in adults is to provide substrates for oxidative metabolism.

✓ Growth hormone is necessary for normal growth in children. Growth hormone, interacting with insulin, IGFs, thyroid hormones, and sex hormones, controls growth of bone and soft tissue. In adults it interacts with IGFs and other factors to stimulate soft tissue growth.

✓ Bone is dynamic tissue—always being formed and resorbed. This is primarily to ensure adequate levels of free calcium. Hormones involved in calcium balance are: parathyroid hormone, calcitriol, and calcitonin.

Recall from Chapter 22 that metabolism is the sum of the chemical reactions in your body that extract and use energy or store it for later use. There are two general types of metabolic reactions: anabolic (synthesis) and catabolic (breakdown). Insulin and glucagon are the primary hormones of minute-to-minute metabolic control.

Other hormones play roles in the long-term regulation of metabolism. The main hormones involved in long-term metabolic regulation are: cortisol (from the adrenal cortex), thyroid hormones (thyroid gland), and growth hormone (anterior pituitary).

Cortisol is essential for life; it's overall effects are aimed at preventing hypoglycemia. Cortisol and the other adrenal glucocorticoids (like the catecholamines) are known as stress hormones because of their roles in mediating long-term stress. Cortisol also has immunosuprresant effects, making it a useful therapeutic drug.

Thyroid hormones affect the quality of life. Their overall effect in adults is to provide substrates for oxidative metabolism. In children, thyroid hormones are necessary for full-expression of growth hormone.

Growth hormone is secreted throughout our lifetime, but peak GH secretion is around the time of puberty. Normal growth requires adequate amounts of growth hormone, thyroid hormones, insulin, and sex hormones. Growth hormone controls the release of insulin-like growth factors (IGFs) from the liver, which in turn stimulate bone and soft tissue growth.

The extracellular matrix of bone contains large amounts of calcium phosphate. Calcium is extremely important to our physiology, so the calcium stored in bones serves as a reservoir that can be tapped when free plasma calcium levels drop. Bone is constantly being formed and resorbed depending on calcium needs. Hormone control of calcium levels involves parathyroid hormone, calcitriol, and calcitonin.

TEACH YOURSELF THE BASICS
REVIEW OF ENDOCRINE PRINCIPLES
1. Take some time to review the endocrine principles first presented in Chapter 7.

ADRENAL GLUCOCORTICOIDS
2. Distinguish between the adrenal cortex and the adrenal medulla? (Fig. 23-1)

The Adrenal Cortex Secretes Steroid Hormones
3. Which hormones does the adrenal cortex secrete? In which cortical zone (layer) is each produced? (Fig. 23-1)

◉ All steroid hormones are synthesized from cholesterol. (Fig. 23-2)

Cortisol Secretion Is Controlled by ACTH
4. Describe or draw the cortisol control pathway. (Fig. 23-3)

5. Describe the diurnal secretion pattern of cortisol. (Fig. 23-4)

6. If cortisol is a typical steroid hormone, answer the following [∫ Fig. 7-6, 7-7; pp. 217-218]:
   Where (which organelle) in the cell would you expect it to be produced? _____
   How is it stored? (explain) _____
   When/how is it secreted and transported? _____
   Where are the receptors at its target cell? _____
   How does it elicit its cellular action? _____

Cortisol Is Essential for Life
7. List the net effects of cortisol action.

8. What is cortisol's most important metabolic effect? What role does it play in glucagon activity?

Cortisol Is a Useful Therapeutic Drug
9. What are cortisol's immunosuppressant effects?

10. What group of drugs has dimished the use of glucocorticoids for treating minor inflammatory problems?

11. What negative feedback effect does exogenous cortisol administration have?

Cortisol Pathologies Result from Too Much or Too Little Hormone
Hypercortisolism "Cushing's syndrome"
12. What are the effects of hypercortisolism? (Fig. 23-5)

13. What are three causes of Cushing's syndrome?

Hypocortisolism "Addison's disease"
14. What are the cause(s) and effects of hypocortisolism?

CRH and ACTH Have Additional Physiological Functions
15. The association between stress and immune function appears to be mediated through the HPA pathway. What evidence supports this?

CRH Family
16. The CRH family includes:

17. What are some physiological effects of CRH?

ACTH and Melanocortins
18. ACTH is synthesized from a large glycoprotein called pro-opiomelanocortin (POMC). What, other than ACTH, is made from POMC? What are the physiological effects of these other substances? (Fig. 23-6)

19. How many different melanocortin receptors have been identified?

THYROID HORMONES

20. List the distinct cell types within the thyroid gland and give the hormones they secrete. (Fig. 23-7)

Thyroid Hormones Contain Iodine

21. Thyroid hormones belong to which class of hormones? Which characteristics of thyroid hormones are different from most hormones in that class? (Fig. 23-8)

22. Describe the structure of thyroid follicles and the composition of colloid. (Fig. 23-7)

23. Outline or diagram the process of thyroid hormone synthesis and secretion. (Figs. 23-9, 23-10)

24. Which is the more active thyroid hormone?

Thyroid Hormones Affect Quality of Life

25. List the actions of thyroid hormones in adults. (Table 23-2)

26. What additional actions do they have in children?

Hyperthyroidism

27. What are the effects of hyperthyroidism?

28. People with hyperthyroidism often have a rapid heartbeat. Explain how thyroid hormones cause this.

Hypothyroidism

29. What are the effects of hypothyroidism?

TSH Controls the Thyroid Gland

30. Outline or diagram the thyroid hormone control and feedback pathways (Fig. 23-12)

31. Describe goiter formation by means of a primary hypothyroidism and compare that to goiter formation by means of a primary hypersecretion. (Fig. 23-13, 23-14)

32. List the therapies for thyroid disorders.

GROWTH HORMONE

33. What factors are important for normal growth?

Growth Hormone Is Anabolic

34. Is growth hormone (GH) secreted throughout a lifetime?

35. When is peak GH secretion observed in humans?

36. What factors regulate the release of GH?

37. When is the daily GH peak observed?

38. To which class of hormones does GH belong? Is it an exact fit to the model? Explain. Fill in the blanks: [See Chapter 7, p. 215]

> Made in what organelle?
> Stored? (explain)
> How is it transported in the blood? Is this typical? Explain.

> Where at its target are the receptors located?
> What is the general cellular response to hormone-receptor activation?

39. What are the metabolic effects of GH?

40. What are IGFs, and what role do they play? (Fig. 23-16)

Growth Hormone Is Essential for Normal Growth in Children
41. What are the effects of GH hypersecretion? (Fig. 23-17)

42. What are the effects of GH hyposecretion?

43. Draw the growth hormone control pathway.

Genetically Engineered Human Growth Hormone Created Ethical Dilemmas
◎ Take a moment to consider the ethical considerations involved with GH therapy.

TISSUE AND BONE GROWTH
44. What are the two general areas of growth, and how are they measured?

Tissue Growth Requires Hormones and Paracrines
45. What hormones/paracrines are required for soft tissue growth?

46. Define hypertrophy and hyperplasia.

47. Describe the role of thyroid hormones in growth.

48. Describe the role of insulin in growth.

Bone Growth Requires Adequate Amounts of Calcium in the Diet
49. Describe the extracellular matrix of bone.

50. Why is bone considered a dynamic tissue? What do we mean by resorbed?

51. What are the two forms of bone. (Fig. 23-18)

52. Outline or diagram the process of bone growth. (Fig. 23-19) Be sure to explain the differences between osteoblasts, osteoclasts, and osteocytes.

53. What factors control bone growth?

CALCIUM BALANCE
⁄ IP Fluids & Electrolytes: Calcium Balance

54. Where is most of the body's calcium found?

55. Compare extracellular Ca^{2+} concentration to intracellular Ca^{2+} concentration.

56. List eight important functions of Ca^{2+} in the body (Table 23-4)

57. If Ca^{2+} concentrations move outside the normal range, which of the functions in the previous question is most likely to experience significant problems?

Calcium Concentrations in the Blood Are Closely Regulated
58. Describe how Ca^{2+} concentrations are regulated in terms of intake, output, and total body calcium.

59. Where does the body maintain a Ca^{2+} reservoir? How does it tap into this reservoir?

60. Describe or diagram osteoclast activity in bone resorption (Fig. 23-21).

Three Hormones Control Calcium Balance
61. Which three hormones regulate Ca^{2+} movement between bone, kidney, and intestine? (Fig. 23-20)

62. Why are the parathyroid glands so important? Where are they found? (Fig. 23-22)

Parathyroid Hormone
63. What is the stimulus for parathyroid hormone (PTH) secretion?

64. What are the three actions of PTH? (Table 23-5)

65. If osteoclasts have no PTH receptors, how then are they directed in bone resorption?

Calcitriol
66. How does calcitriol enhance intestinal Ca^{2+} absorption? (Table 23-6)

67. How/where is calcitriol made? (Fig. 23-23)

68. How/where is calcitriol regulated?

Calcitonin

69. Where is calcitonin made and what is the nature of its structure? (Table 23-7)

70. What is calcitonin's role in the body?

71. What is a therapeutic benefit of calcitonin?

Calcium and Phosphate Homeostasis Are Linked

72. What functions, other than bone formation, involve phosphate?

73. What aspects of phosphate homeostasis are linked with calcium homeostasis?

Osteoporosis Is a Disease of Bone Loss

74. What is osteoporosis, and what are the effects of the disease? (Fig. 23-24)

75. Who in the population are more likely to develop osteoporosis?

76. List the risk factors for osteoporosis.

77. Which osteoporosis treatment is currently preferred? What is the mechanism of action for these drugs?

78. Why has estrogen/progesterone hormone replacement therapy been replaced as the leading osteoporosis therapy?

79. List preventative measures that young women should take to help stave off osteoporosis later in life?

TALK THE TALK

1,25-dihydroxycholecaliferol (1,25(OH)$_2$D$_3$)

acromegaly

adrenal cortex

adrenal gland

adrenal medulla

adrenocorticotropic hormone (ACTH)

agouti mouse

aldosterone

androgen

bradykinin

brown adipose tissue

C cells (thyroid gland)

calcitonin

calcitriol

calcium phosphate

catecholamine

chondrocyte

circadian rhythm, cortisol

colloid

compact bone

corticotropin releasing hormone (CRH)

cortisol

cortisone

cretinism

D cell

deiodinase

diaphysis

diiodotyrosine (DIT)

dwarfism

epiphyseal plate

epiphysis

estrogen

estrogen replacement therapy

failure to thrive

follicle, thyroid

giantism

glucocorticoid

goiter

Graves' disease

growth

growth hormone

growth hormone binding protein

growth hormone-inhibiting hormone

growth hormone-releasing hormone (GHRH)

hydroxyapatite

hypercalcemia

hyperplasia

hyperthyroidism

hypertrophy

hypocalcemia

hypothyroidism

insulin-like growth factor

iodine

kyphosis

melanocortin

melanocortin receptors (MC-R)

mineralocorticoid

monoiodotyrosine (MIT)

osteoblast

osteoclast

osteocyte

osteoid

osteoporosis

Paget's disease

parathyroid glands

parathyroid hormone (PTH)

pro-opiomelanocortin POMC

receptor-mediated endocytosis

resorption of bone

sodium-iodide cotransporter

somatomedin

somatostatin

somatotropin

thyroglobulin

thyroid gland

thyroid-stimulating immunoglobulin (TSI)

thyrotropin, thyroid-stimulating hormone (TSH)

thyrotropin-releasing hormone (TRH)

thyroxine-binding globulin (TBG)

triiodothyronine (T$_3$)

up-regulation

vitamin D$_3$

zona fasciculata

zona glomerulosa

zona reticularis

_-MSH

_-endorphin

ETHICS

Should athletes be allowed to take prohormones like DHEA or androstenedione and synthetic growth hormone? Should children who are genetically short but have normal growth hormone secretion be given growth hormone? What are the potential risks of taking hormones if a person's own hormone production is normal?

PRACTICE MAKES PERFECT

1. The active hormone of the thyroid gland is:
    a. thyroglobulin
    b. thyroxine
    c. diiodotyrosine

2. Classify each of the following hormones as anabolic (A) or catabolic (C).

    cortisol _____   growth hormone _____

3. True or false? Explain your reasoning.

    a) When we hear of athletes and body-builders taking "anabolic steroids," we know that they are taking glucocorticoids.

    b) A child who has a vitamin D deficiency will develop rickets (poor bone formation) because vitamin D plays a major role in the precipitation of calcium phosphate into bone.

4. The diagram below represents calcium balance in the human body. The labeled arrows represent calcium movement of calcium between the compartments. Answer the questions below that refer to the letters on the diagram.

a) What hormone(s) directly or indirectly regulate movement at arrow A?

_____
_____
_____

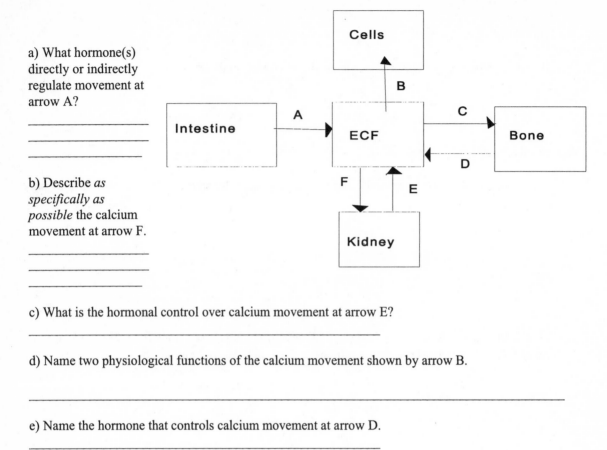

b) Describe *as specifically as possible* the calcium movement at arrow F.

_____
_____
_____

c) What is the hormonal control over calcium movement at arrow E?

_____

d) Name two physiological functions of the calcium movement shown by arrow B.

_____

e) Name the hormone that controls calcium movement at arrow D.

_____

5. On axis (A) below, plot the effect of plasma parathyroid hormone concentration on plasma Ca^{2+} concentration. On axis (B) below, plot the effect of plasma Ca^{2+} concentration on plasma parathyroid hormone concentration. Be sure to label the axes of each graph!

A

B

6. A patient comes in with a diagnosis of alpha-cell hyperplasia due to a pancreatic tumor. You draw a blood sample and send it out for analysis. Before it comes back, predict what changes you expect to see in the following parameters (up, down, no change) and explain your rationale.

Plasma concentration	Change: ↑, ↓, or N/C	Rationale for your answer
glucose		
insulin		
amino acids		
ketones		
K^+		

MAPS

1. Create pathway maps for each hormone introduced in this chapter. You should have details about trophic hormones and control pathways, as well as details at the cellular level where appropriate. The hormones presented were: cortisol, thyroid hormone, growth hormone, parathyroid hormone, calcitriol, and calcitonin.

BEYOND THE PAGES

✐ TRY IT: Can you tie a bone in a knot? Place the leg bone of a chicken in commercial white vinegar and monitor what happens. The vinegar will dissolve the calcium phosphate of the bone in vinegar, leaving behind the soft organic matrix. This is similar to the way osteoclasts secrete acid to dissolve bone in the body.

FURTHER EXPLORATIONS

⬟ Osteoporosis and Bone Physiology - http://courses.washington.edu/bonephys/opnew.html

 Articles

Born Again Bone: Tissue Engineering for Bone Repair, *News Physiol Sci* 16: 208-213, 2001 October

Species specificity of the primate growth hormone receptor. *News Physiol Sci* 11: 157-160, August 1996.

24

SUMMARY

This is another chapter packed with information. In other words, don't wait until the last minute to learn this. One suggestion: break the material up into types of responses, then types of cells involved in those responses, then cellular components involved in those responses, and so forth. But first, learn the vocabulary.

Here are the main concepts presented in this chapter:

✓ The immune system is spread throughout the body. It consists of primary and secondary lymphoid tissue and immune cells.

✓ There are six types of immune cells, and each plays a different role in the immune system.

✓ There are two types of immune responses: innate and acquired. Innate is nonspecific; acquired is highly specific.

✓ There are two types of acquired responses: humoral immunity and cell-mediated immunity. Humoral immunity involves antibodies from B cells; cell-mediated immunity is under the direction of T cells.

✓ Secondary responses are stronger and more rapid than primary responses.

✓ The immune system handles different pathogens in different ways.

✓ The immune system recognizes self from non-self. Major histocompatibility complexes play an integral role in determining self and non-self.

✓ The immune system is linked to the nervous and endocrine systems.

Immunity is the ability of the body to protect itself from pathogens. Anything that elicits an immune response is called an antigen, while a pathogen is anything that creates a pathophysiological condition. As you're probably beginning to see, the first step to understanding the immune system is conquering its vocabulary.

The immune system is spread throughout the body. The primary lymphoid tissues are the thymus and the bone marrow. These are places where immune cells are produced and mature. Secondary lymphoid tissues include encapsulated tissues (spleen and lymph nodes) and unencapsulated tissues (tonsils, GALT, skin and respiratory clusters). There are several types of immune cells: eosinophils, basophils, neutrophils, monocytes, lymphocytes, and dendritic cells. Learn how each plays a different role in the immune response.

There are two types of immune responses: innate immunity and acquired immunity. Innate immunity is a nonspecific immune response that reacts to all foreign particles. The inflammatory response is the hallmark of the innate immune response. If an antigen should get past the body's physical defenses, then it will initiate an inflammatory response and ultimately meet one of the following fates: it could be phagocytized by tissue macrophages or neutrophils, or it could be destroyed via the complement system. At the site of antigen entry, chemicals are released by local cells that result in the attraction of immune cells and the formation of a warm, red, swollen area. You should learn the steps and chemicals involved in the inflammatory response (Table 24-2).

Acquired immunity involves two responses: humoral immunity, brought about by B lymphocytes; and cell-mediated immunity, brought about by T lymphocytes. B lymphocytes (B cells) secrete antibodies (immunoglobulins) that recognize specific sites (epitopes) on specific antigens. B cells that have never been exposed to an antigen are called naive B cells. Once naive cells have encountered their antigen, they divide and produce memory cells and plasma cells in a process called clonal expansion. Memory cells stick around in the body and are responsible for the phenomenon of secondary immune response. Plasma cells secrete antibodies (Ab) into the "humors" or body fluids (hence the name humoral immunity). The primary function of Ab's is to bind B cells and antigens and cause the production of more Ab's, but Ab's also have many secondary functions that target an antigen for destruction (Fig. 24-13). Ab's are Y-shaped protein structures: the arms recognize the antigen, and the stem can attach to cell membranes. There are five classes of Ab's: IgG, IgE, IgD, IgM, IgA.

T cells develop in the thymus. There, T cells that bind self proteins are destroyed. Mature T cells must have contact with their target cells to initiate cell-mediated immunity. T cell receptors (related, but not equivalent to Ab's) must bind to a major histocompatibility complex (MHC) bearing a specific antigen fragment on a target cell surface. MHCs display protein fragments (either self or nonself) on the cell surface. If a T cell recognizes a foreign protein displayed in an MHC, it will initiate a response that either kills that cell or activates other immune cells. There are two types of MHC proteins: MHC-I is found on all nucleated cells; MHC-II is found only on antigen-presenting cells (APCs). There are three subtypes of T cells: cytotoxic T cells, helper T cells, and natural killer cells (possibly also suppressor T cells). Cytotoxic T cells kill a target cell by apoptosis when they recognize an MHC-antigen complex. When helper T cells recognize an MHC-antigen complex, they secrete cytokines that activate other T and B cells. Natural killer cells are actually a distinct cell line. If they recognize an MHC-antigen complex on a cell, they will kill that cell. However, they can also kill an Ab-coated cell through a nonspecific process called antibody-dependent cell-mediated cytotoxicity.

That's a mouthful! We suggest making charts that show the differences between 1) innate and acquired immunity, and 2) humoral and cell-mediated immunity. Be sure to include information about the different types of cells and Ab's involved.

Beginning on p. 768, the different types of immune response pathways are discussed. Learn how the immune system responds differently to different types of antigens (bacterial, viral, allergenic).

The same processes we discussed earlier also apply to the body's recognition of self and non-self tissues. With RBC recognition, it involves surface antigens (because RBCs don't have MHC proteins). With other cases, like organ transplants, foreign MHCs and/or MHC-antigen complexes can cause an immune response that results in tissue rejection.

Finally, we are learning that the immune system is closely linked with the nervous and endocrine systems. It seems that some cytokines, neuropeptides, and hormones are secreted by some or all of these systems. Therefore, they all exert an integrated control over each other. Neuroimmunomodulation is the field that studies the brain-immune system interaction.

TEACH YOURSELF THE BASICS

OVERVIEW OF IMMUNE SYSTEM FUNCTION

1. Define immunity.

2. List three major functions of the immune system:

3. Immune pathologies typically fall into one of these categories:

PATHOGENS OF THE HUMAN BODY

4. List the types of infections common in the USA.

5. List the types of infections common in the world.

Bacteria and Viruses Require Different Defense Mechanisms
6. Fill in the following table on the differences between bacteria and viruses (Table 24-1):

	Bacteria	Viruses
Structure		
Living conditions		
Reproduction		
Susceptibility to antibiotics		

Viruses Must Reproduce Inside Host Cells
7. Briefly describe ways that virus particles can enter a host cell.

8. Next, describe how a virus takes over host cell resources. (Fig. 24-1b)

9. Describe two ways viruses are released from host cells.

10. Give two examples of viral damage to host cells.

THE IMMUNE RESPONSE
11. List the four basic steps of all internal immune responses.

12. What are the two categories of the human immune response? Describe them.

13. A distinguishing feature of the immune system is that it uses what kind of signaling?

14. What are cytokines? [∫ p. 173]

ANATOMY OF THE IMMUNE SYSTEM
Lymphoid Tissues Are Distributed Throughout the Body
15. Name the 2 primary lymphoid tissues. (See Focus box, p. 756 and Fig. 24-2)

16. List the two types of secondary lymphoid tissues.

17. Describe the following encapsulated lymphoid tissues:
     Spleen (Fig. 24-2, 24-3)

     Lymph nodes (Fig. 24-2b) [∫ lymphatic circulation, p. 508]

18. Identify and describe diffuse lymphoid tissues (Fig. 24-2):

19. What is the GALT?

Leukocytes Are the Primary Cells of the Immune System
20. List four ways that leukocytes (WBCs) differ from RBCs. [∫ p. 524]

21. List and briefly describe the six basic groups of immune cells:

22. How are immune cells distinguished from one another in stained tissue samples?

Immune Cell Names Reflect Cell Function or Appearance
23. Know the classification systems for immune cells. (Fig. 24-4)

24. What are granulocytes? Describe the different types of granulocytes.

25. What are phagocytes? What cells belong to this group?

26. Explain the following terms:

   a. cytotoxic cell

   b. antigen-presenting cell (APC)
   ◉ *B lymphocytes are the APC lymphocytes.*

   c. reticuloendothelial system

27. What is the contemporary terminology for the reticuloendothelial system?

Eosinophils Fight Parasites and Contribute to Allergic Reactions
28. Describe eosinophils. Include their relative abundance, location in the body, and their role(s) in the immune system. What is the physiological significance of their granules?

Basophils Release Histamine and Other Chemicals
29. Describe basophils. Include their relative abundance, location in the body, lifespan, and their role(s) in the immune system. What is the physiological significance of their granules?

Neutrophils Eat Bacteria and Release Cytokines
30. Describe neutrophils as you've done for the other groups.

Monocytes Are Tissue Scavengers
31. Describe monocytes and macrophages.

32. Why are monocytes/macrophages called antigen-presenting cells? (Fig. 24-5)

Lymphocytes Mediate Acquired Immunity
33. Describe lymphocytes and plasma cells.

Dendritic Cells Activate Lymphocytes
34. Describe dendritic cells.

INNATE IMMUNITY: NONSPECIFIC RESPONSES
◎ Innate immunity either clears the infection or contains it until the acquired response is activated.

Physical and Chemical Barriers Are the Body's First Line of Defense
35. Describe three examples of physical barriers against foreign invaders. [∫ p. 78]

36. Describe the specialized physical barriers of the:
    a. respiratory system [∫ p. 554]

    b. stomach

    c. tears

37. Lysozyme can only attack which type of bacterial cell wall?

38. What is the two-fold response strategy of the innate immune cells?

39. What are chemotaxins? Give some examples.

Phagocytes Recognize Foreign Material and Ingest It
40. What are the primary phagocytic immune cells?

41. What is extravasation?

42. Describe the process of phagocytosis. (Fig. 24-6) [∫ p. 144]

43. Some bacteria have evolved ways to "hide" from phagocytes. How have they accomplished this?

44. What are opsonins?

45. What happens to particles ingested by phagocytes? (Fig. 24-7)

46. Why do sites of bacterial infection develop pus?

Natural Killer Lymphocytes Eliminate Virally Infected and Tumor Cells
47. What is another name for natural killer cells?

48. How do NK cells work?

49. Define interferon and distinguish between the alpha, beta, and gamma interferons.

Chemical Mediators Create the Inflammatory Response
50. What signs and symptoms suggest an inflammation?

51. What are three roles inflammation has in fighting infection?

52. What cells create the inflammatory response?

53. What role do cytokines play in this response? (Table 24-2)

Acute Phase Proteins Are Released Early in the Immune Response
54. When do we see an increased presence of acute phase proteins?

55. What are acute phase proteins and where do they originate? Include examples.

56. What happens to the level of acute phase proteins after an acute infection?

57. What happens to the level of acute phase proteins in cases of chronic infection?

Histamine Initiates Inflammation
58. Describe the chemical structure of histamine. [∫ p. 173]

59. Where do we find histamine in the body?

60. Describe the histamine reaction.

61. What is the purpose of the histamine reaction in the larger immune response?

62. How do antihistamines work?

Interleukins Have Widespread Systemic Effects
63. What are interleukins? What is their role in the immune response?

64. As an example, interleukin-1 (IL-1) is secreted by:

Its overall role is:

Four specific actions of IL-1 include:

Bradykinin Stimulates Pain Receptors

65. What are kinins?

66. What is the physiological action of bradykinin?

Complement Proteins Are Opsonins and Chemotaxins

67. Complement is a collective term for:

68. Briefly describe the complement pathway. [∫ coagulation cascade, p. 538]

69. What is membrane attack complex, and how does it cause cell lysis? (Fig. 24-8)

ACQUIRED IMMUNITY: ANTIGEN-SPECIFIC RESPONSES

70. How does acquired immunity differ from innate immunity?

71. Which immune cells primarily mediate the acquired response?

72. There are three main types of lymphocytes: _____ lymphocytes secrete antibodies while _____ lymphocytes and _____ attack and destroy foreign cells.

73. Describe the difference between active and passive immunity.

Lymphocytes Are the Primary Cells Involved in the Acquired Immune Response

74. What gives different lymphocytes specificity for specific pathogens? (Fig. 24-9)

75. What are lymphocyte clones? (Fig. 24-9, 24-10)

76. Outline or map the lymphocyte life cycle, using the following terms: antigen, clonal expansion, effector cells, naive lymphocytes, memory cells, primary response, secondary response

77. How do memory cells differ from effector cells?

B Cells Differentiate into Plasma Cells and Memory Cells

78. Where do B lymphocytes (B cells) develop?

79. What is the primary function of B cells?

80. What are plasma cells?

81. What role do surface antibodies on B cells serve? (Fig. 24-9)

82. What role do memory cells play?

83. Draw and label a graph that shows plasma antibody concentration during a primary response and during a secondary response. (Fig. 24-11)

84. Based on your graph and what you know so far, why do immunizations help fight against infection?

Antibodies Are Proteins Secreted by Plasma Cells

85. There are five general classes of Ab's: IgG, IgA, IgE, IgM, IgD. Match the antibody group to its functions.

Ig _____: Allergic response

Mast cell + Ig ___ + antigen = degranulation and histamine release

Ig _____: B lymphocyte surface; an unclear physiological role

Ig _____: Found in external secretions (saliva, tears, mucus, breast milk)

Disables pathogens before body entry

Ig _____: Produced in secondary immune responses

75% of adult serum Ab's
Can cross placenta and provide the initial immunity for the infant

Ig _____: B lymphocyte surface; primary immune responses; reacts to blood group antigens

86. Define gamma globulins.

Antibodies are Y-Shaped Proteins

87. Sketch a picture of the typical antibody molecule. Label all the parts and briefly describe the relevance of each part.

Antibodies Have Multiple Functions

88. Where are most antibodies found? They account for what percentage of plasma proteins in healthy individuals?

89. These antibodies are most effective against:

90. How do antibodies make antigens more visible to the immune system? (Fig. 24-13)

91. What is antibody-dependent cell-mediated cytotoxicity?

Antigen-Binding to Antibodies on B Cells Activates the B Cells

92. Describe the binding of antibodies to the surface of B cell membranes.

93. How are B cells activated? (Fig. 24-13)

94. What role do these antibodies play?

T Lymphocytes Must Make Direct Contact with Their Target Cells

95. Where do T lymphocytes (T cells) form? (Fig. 24-14)

96. T cells are responsible for which type of immunity?

97. What must T cells do before acting against an antigen?

98. T cells bind to targets using what type of receptor? (Fig. 24-15)

99. Describe T-cell binding.

Major Histocompatibility Complexes Incorporate Antigen Fragments

100. Define and describe major histocompatibility complexes (MHC).

101. Where do we find MHCs?

102. What is the function of MHC molecules?

103. Why do MHC proteins vary from person to person? What about MHCs in identical twins?

104. We see the importance of MHCs with transplants and in some autoimmune diseases. What roles do MHC proteins play in these two cases?

105. Describe how MHCs work. (Figs. 24-5)

106. Name the two types of MHC molecules and describe the differences between the types.

Cytotoxic T Cells Kill Their Targets

107. What are the subtypes of cells that develop from T cell precursors? (Fig. 24-16)

108. Describe the action of cytotoxic T cells. Include the following terms: apoptosis, granzymes, perforin, channels

109. Describe the action of helper T cells.

110. List four cytokines secreted by helper T cells.

IMMUNE RESPONSE PATHWAYS

◎ *Once you've worked through these pathways the first time, go back and see if you can describe them completely without looking.*

111. Describe how the body responds to 4 challenges:
       a.   Extracellular bacterial infection
       b.   Viral infection
       c.   Allergic response to pollen
       d.   Transfusion of incompatible blood

◎ These pathways show how the innate and acquired immune responses are interconnected processes.

Inflammation Is the Typical Response to Bacterial Invasion

112. Outline the integrated response to bacterial entry into the ECF (Fig. 24-17). Feel free to do this as a map, but don't directly copy the one in the book (this is for your own good). Be sure to use all the following terms:

acute phase proteins	antibodies	antigen
B lymphocytes	bacteria, encapsulated	bacteria, not encapsulated
capillary permeability	chemotaxin	complement
diapedesis	histamine	leukocyte
lyse	lysozyme	mast cell
membrane attack complex	memory B cells	opsonins
phagocytes	plasma cells	plasma protein

Intracellular Defense Mechanisms Are Needed to Fight Viral Infections

◎ *Before viruses enter host cell, innate and humoral defenses both control infection.*

113. After viral entry into a host cell, what cell type is the main line of defense?

114. Map the steps of viral infection, assuming previous viral exposure/presence of Abs (Fig. 24-18).
      Again, don't directly copy the figure in the book. Be sure to use all the following terms:

γ-interferon	acute phase proteins	antibodies
antigen	apoptosis	B lymphocytes
cytokines	cytotoxic T cell	granzymes
helper T cell	host cell	lyse
macrophage	MHC-I	MHC-II
NK cell	opsonins	perforin
phagocytosis	T cell receptor	virus

Antibodies Against a Virus May Not Work in Subsequent Infections

115. Why might Abs from one viral infection not be effective against subsequent viral infections? Give some examples of viruses for which this is true.

Allergic Responses Are Inflammatory Responses Triggered by Specific Antigens
116. Define allergy and allergen.

117. How do immediate hypersensitivity and delayed hypersensitivity reactions differ?

118. What kinds of molecules can be allergens? Name some common allergens.

119. How are people exposed to allergens?

120. Name three effects of massive histamine release that cause the condition known as anaphylactic shock or anaphylaxis.

121. Map the steps in allergy development (Fig. 24-19). Include the following terms:

allergen	antibodies	antigen-processing cell
B lymphocyte	complement	cytokines
first exposure	helper T cell	histamine
Ig __?__	inflammation	mast cell
memory cell	MHC-I	plasma cell
re-exposure	T cell receptor	

MHC Proteins Allow Recognition of Foreign Tissue

122. Which cell surface markers determine tissue compatibility?

123. Use blood transfusion as example of compatibility. Make a chart or table with the four blood groups, tell what antigens and antibodies a person with each group will have, and tell which groups will be compatible and incompatible for transfusions.

Recognition of Self Is an Important Function of the Immune System

124. Define self-tolerance.

125. How does self-tolerance arise?

126. What happens if self-tolerance fails?

Immune Surveillance Allows the Body to Remove Abnormal Cells

127. Briefly describe the immune surveillance theory.

128. If this theory is accurate, how can cancer cells escape detection and destruction?

NEURO-ENDOCRINE-IMMUNE INTERACTIONS

129. Define neuroimmunomodulation and describe some examples of current research into the area. (Fig. 24-22)

130. Describe the three known links between the immune, nervous, endocrine systems. (Fig. 24-21)

Stress Alters Immune System Function

131. Define stress and describe the stress response. [∫ p. 730]

132. Where are most physical and emotional stressors integrated?

133. The nervous system responds to acute stress. Hormonal responses attend to chronic stresses. Based on what you learned in Chapter 6, why does this make sense?

134. Why is study of the stress response difficult?

TALK THE TALK

ABO blood group	acquired immunity	ACTH
acute phase protein	adrenal gland	agglutinin
AIDS (acquired immune deficiency syndrome)	allergen	allergy
amyloid protein	anaphylaxis	antibiotic
antibody	antibody-dependent cell-mediated cytotoxicity	antigen
antigen-presenting cell	antihistamine	apoptosis
autoimmune disease	B lymphocyte	bacteria
basophil	beta adrenergic receptor	blood transfusion
bone marrow	bradykinin	brown adipose tissue
cancer	capsule, bacterial	cell-mediated immunity
chemokine	chemotaxin	clonal expansion
clone	complement	corticotropin releasing hormone (CRH)
cytokines	cytotoxic cells	cytotoxic T cell
degranulation	delayed hypersensitivity reaction	dendritic cell
diapedesis	diffuse lymphoid tissue	diphtheria
DNA	edema	effector cell
electrophoresis	encapsulated lymphoid tissue	envelope, viral
eosinophil	Fab region	Fc region
fight-or-flight reaction	gamma globulin	gamma-interferon (interferon-γ)
general adaptation syndrome	glucocorticoid	granulocyte
granzyme	growth hormone	gut-associated lymphoid tissue (GALT)
helper T cell	hemolysin	heparin
herpes virus	histamine	histiocyte
histoplasmosis	human leukocyte antigen (HLA)	humoral immunity
hypersensitivity	IgA	IgD
IgE	IgG	IgM
immediate hypersensitivity reaction	immune surveillance	immunity
immunization	immunocyte	immunoglobulin
inflammation	innate immunity	insulin-dependent diabetes mellitus
interleukin	interleukin-1 (IL-1)	keratinocyte
killer T cell	kinin	Kupffer cell
large granular lymphocyte	leukocyte	life cycle of a virus
lymph node	lymphatic circulation	lymphocyte
lymphoid tissue	lymphoma	lysozyme
macrophage	major histocompatibility complex	malaria
mast cell	melatonin	membrane attack complex
memory cell	MHC class I molecule	MHC class II molecule
microbe	microglia	monocyte
mononuclear phagocyte system	mucus escalator	naive lymphocyte
natural killer cell	neuroimmunomodulation	neutrophil
oncogenic virus	opiate receptor	opsonin
osteoclast	parasite	pathogen
perforin	peroxide	phagocyte
phagocytosis	phagosome	pineal gland
placebo effect	plasma cell	polymorphonuclear leukocyte
precipitin	primary immune response	prolactin
psychosomatic illness	pus	pyrogen
recognition of self	reticuloendothelial cell	reticuloendothelial system
retrovirus	reverse transcriptase	Rh antigen
RNA	secondary immune response	self-tolerance
Selye, Hans	spleen	stress
substance P	superoxide anion	T lymphocyte
T-cell receptor	thymopoietin	thymosin
thymulin	thymus gland	thyrotropin (TSH)
tonsil	transplantation of organs	valley fever
viral capsid	virus	

ETHICS IN SCIENCE

A mother brings her ill child to the doctor, who diagnoses a viral illness and sends the child home with instructions for his care. The mother is convinced that only antibiotics will cure her son, so she keeps calling and pestering the doctor's staff until the doctor finally prescribes antibiotics, despite knowing that they will not be effective. How is this scenario related to the development of drug-resistant strains of bacteria? What should doctors and the public be doing to prevent the development of more drug-resistant strains?

PRACTICE MAKES PERFECT

1. From the following list, place one appropriate letter in each blank:

   a) neutrophil   b) eosinophil   c) basophil   d) erythrocyte   e) monocyte   f) lymphocyte

   _____ produces antibodies; has large round nucleus with very little surrounding cytoplasm

   _____ phagocytic; has nucleus with 3-5 segments, pale pink granules in cytoplasm

   _____ releases histamine and heparin; dark blue-staining granules in cytoplasm

2. Match the cell surface markers/receptors with the cells on which they are found.

   a) MHC-I   b) MHC-II   c) T-cell receptors   d) glycoprotein markers
   e) antibodies   f) no receptors

   _____ macrophage   _____ red blood cell

   _____ B lymphocyte   _____ natural killer cell

   _____ liver cell   _____ cytotoxic T cell

   _____ plasma cell   _____ helper T cell

3. List three functions of macrophages.

4. Can a mother with blood type A and a father with blood type B have a baby with blood type O? Explain. (Remember that each parent carries two alleles for the RBC surface antigens.)

5. A technician runs an ABO blood type test on Aparna's blood. Her blood agglutinated with anti-B serum but not with anti-A serum.

    a. What is Aparna's blood type? _____

    b. To what other ABO groups can she donate blood? _____

    c. From what ABO groups can she receive blood? _____

6. You are walking barefoot through the cool spring grass, and you unconsciously step on a plant to which you are allergic. Your feet swell up in response. When you consider the physiology behind this reaction, you realize that there are seven kinds of leukocytes involved in this hypersensitivity reaction. Name these blood cells.

7. Where do B lymphocytes develop? _____ T lymphocytes? _____

8. Your friend Elizabeth knows that she is ABO blood type O. Why is the blood bank always calling her to ask her for a blood donation?

9. You are the microscopic ace reporter for the news station Plasma 1, and you have just been alerted to a bacterial entry at the index finger. As you arrive on the scene, describe the events you observe.

10. What is the hallmark of the innate response?

11. Peng-Chai is feeling bad and thinks he is coming down with the flu virus that has been going around school, so he takes some old antibiotics that he has left over from a previous sinus infection (not something anyone should ever do!). Will the antibiotics help his viral infection? Explain.

12. What role do acute phase proteins play in an innate response?

13. What is the result of the terminal step in the complement system?

14. What is the difference between the Fc region and the Fab region of an antibody?

15. What is a major histocompatibility complex (MHC)? Describe the differences between the functions of type I MHC and type II MHC.

16. How do the body's white blood cells know to attack and destroy old red blood cells but not new ones?

MAPS

1. Create a map showing the process of clonal expansion.

2. Map the different groups of white blood cells, their structure and their function.

BEYOND THE PAGES

FOCUS ON PHYSIOLOGY

Biotechnology Focus: Stealth® Liposomes

Early in their history, liposomes seemed to be the ideal vehicle for drug delivery: "magic bullets" that could deliver drugs wherever they were needed. But the first animal trials were disappointing, since liposomes injected intravenously disappeared rapidly from the circulation without reaching their target cells. The body's immune system recognized them as foreign even though they were composed of biological phospholipids, and macrophages gobbled them up and digested them. The solution that occurred to researchers was to make the liposomes invisible to the immune system somehow so that they could slip by the macrophages and reach their intended targets. The first type of "invisible" liposome relied on carbohydrate groups attached to the liposome exterior that made the liposomes resemble red blood cells. The next generation of invisible liposomes was trademarked Stealth® liposomes. They are coated with a polyoxyethylene polymer that allows them to slip into the body undetected and remain in the circulation for as long as a week, delivering their encapsulated drugs to the targeted tissues.

See: Stealth® Liposomes. D. Lasic and F. Martin, editors. (1995) CRC Press, Boca Raton. 289 pp.

FURTHER EXPLORATIONS

⬡ Look on the web and see what you can find about anthrax and how the body responds to it.

A is for...: Histocompatibility. Science & Medicine, November/December 1996.

Adenoviruses as vectors for gene therapy. Science & Medicine, March/April 1997.

Alternative cancer treatments. Scientific American, September 1996.

Bacterial virulence factors. Science & Medicine, May/June 1995.

Biological basis of the stress response. News in Physiological Sciences 8: 69-73, April 1993.

Cell suicide in health and disease. Scientific American, December 1996.

Discovering the benign traits of the mast cell. Science & Medicine, September/October 1997.

Emergence of tick-borne diseases. Science & Medicine, March/April 1997.

Emerging viruses. Scientific American, October 1995.

Evolution of infectious disease. News in Physiological Sciences 11: 83-89, April 1996.

How breast milk protects newborns. Scientific American, December 1995.

How the immune system learns about self. Scientific American, October 1991.

Immunology and the invertebrates. Scientific American, November 1996.

Immunotherapy for cancer. Scientific American, September 1996.

Immunotherapy for cocaine addiction. Scientific American, February 1997.

Psychoneuroimmunology: brain and immunity. Science & Medicine, November/December 1995.

Sharks and the origins of vertebrate immunity. Scientific American, November 1996.

Silicone immunopathology. Science & Medicine, September/October 1996.

Suicide genes for cancer therapy. Science & Medicine, July/August 1997.

Educating the immune system. Science & Medicine 6(4):54-63, 1999 Jul/Aug.

Dynamics of HIV infection. Science & Medicine 5(2), 1998 Mar/Apr.

25

INTEGRATIVE PHYSIOLOGY III: EXERCISE

SUMMARY

The main concepts from this integrative chapter:

✓ ATP for muscle contractions comes from aerobic metabolism, phosphocreatine, and glycolytic metabolism.
✓ During exercise, the catabolic hormones (glucagon, cortisol, catecholamines, and growth hormone) dominate. Insulin levels remain low.
✓ Exercise intensity is reflected by oxygen consumption.
✓ The respiratory and cardiovascular systems alter their activity to ensure that efficient oxygen and nutrients are delivered to exercising tissues.
✓ Moderate exercise can improve your immune system and decrease the risk of certain health problems.

Exercise is muscular activity that threatens homeostasis. ATP for muscle contraction comes from several sources: aerobic metabolism, phosphocreatine, and anaerobic (glycolytic) metabolism. Glucose and fats are the primary substrates for energy production, but fats can only be metabolized in aerobic conditions.

Remember from Chapter 22 that glucagon is a catabolic hormone. The catabolic hormones participating in exercise metabolism include glucagon, cortisol, catecholamines, and growth hormone. The action of these hormones raises the plasma glucose concentration. However, insulin concentrations do not rise during exercise. Remember that active skeletal muscle doesn't require insulin for glucose uptake. Therefore, low plasma insulin concentrations prevent other cells from taking glucose that could be used by the muscles.

The intensity of exercise is indicated by oxygen consumption. Oxygen consumption increases rapidly at the onset of exercise and this increase persists even after activity ceases. The ability of the muscle cells to consume oxygen is possibly a limiting factor in exercise capacity. This is reflected by the fact that mitochondria can increase in size and number with endurance training. Cardiovascular activity is the major factor limiting maximal exertion.

Respiratory and cardiovascular systems make adjustments in response to exercise. Feedforward signals and sensory feedback initiate exercise hyperventilation. Exercise hyperventilation maintains nearly normal P_{O_2} and P_{CO_2} by steadily increasing alveolar ventilation in proportion with exercise level. Cardiovascular responses include increased cardiac output, vasodilation and increased blood flow in skeletal muscles, and a slight increase in mean arterial blood pressure.

Exercise generates heat. In fact, most of the energy released during metabolism is not converted to ATP but is released as heat. There are two mechanisms by which the body regulates temperature during exercise: sweating and increased cutaneous blood flow.

Moderate exercise has been shown to affect health positively. It can alleviate or prevent the development of high blood pressure, strokes, and diabetes mellitus. However, a J-shaped curve (Fig. 25-10) relates immune function to exercise: only moderate exercise improves immune function. There has been no sound evidence to support the theory that exercise improves the immunity of immuno-compromised individuals.

TEACH YOURSELF THE BASICS

METABOLISM AND EXERCISE

1. Muscles require ATP for contraction. What are the sources of this ATP? (Fig. 25-1) [∫ p. 401]

2. Without new ATP production, a muscle has enough ATP and phosphocreatine to supply energy for how many seconds of intense exercise?

3. What macromolecules are the primary substrates for energy production?

4. The most efficient ATP production is a result of the glycolysis-citric acid cycle pathway. [∫ p. 102] Briefly describe or map these pathways in the presence and absence of oxygen. (Fig. 25-1)

5. Discuss the advantages and disadvantages of anaerobic muscle metabolism over aerobic metabolism (Fig. 25-2).

6. Where does muscle obtain glucose for ATP production? (Fig. 25-1) [∫ p. 108-111]

7. True or false? Aerobic exercise first uses glucose for ATP production, then turns to fatty acid metabolism. (Fig. 25-3)

8. Beta oxidation [∫ p. 109] is (faster / slower?) than glycolysis.

Hormones Regulate Metabolism During Exercise

9. List four hormones that affect glucose and fat metabolism during exercise and briefly describe their action.

10. What happens to insulin secretion during exercise? Give the physiological mechanism and the adaptive significance for this pattern of insulin secretion.

Oxygen Consumption Is Related to Exercise Intensity

11. Exercise intensity is quantified by measuring oxygen consumption (V_{O2}). Define oxygen consumption.

12. What is indicated by the maximal rate of oxygen consumption (V_{O2max})?

13. Increased O_2 consumption persists even after activity ceases. (Fig. 25-4) Why?

Several Factors Limit Exercise

14. Describe some of the factors that can limit exercise capacity for different exercise conditions.

VENTILATORY RESPONSES TO EXERCISE

15. How do total pulmonary ventilation, alveolar ventilation, rate and depth of breathing change in response to exercise? [∫ p. 564-567]

16. Fill the gaps in the following pathways:

    a. Exercise begins → muscle _____ and proprioceptors send signals to motor cortex.

    b. Motor cortex signals respiratory control center in the _____ to increase ventilation.

    c. As exercise continues, sensory feedback from what peripheral receptors to the respiratory control center ensures that O_2 use and ventilation are matched?

17. How does exercise hyperventilation affect arterial oxygen and carbon dioxide levels? (Fig. 25-5 and 25-6)

18. Summarize the postulated mechanisms behind exercise hyperventilation. Include the stimuli, receptors, and responses involved. (Fig. 25-5, 25-6)

CARDIOVASCULAR RESPONSES TO EXERCISE

19. The cardiovascular control center (CVCC) responds to exercise with (sympathetic / parasympathetic?) discharge. What effect does this have on cardiac output? peripheral arterioles?

Cardiac Output Increases During Exercise

20. Cardiac output increases dramatically with strenuous exercise. What factors influence cardiac output? [∫ p. 478]

21. Explain the relationship between increased venous return and increased heart rate.

22. How is venous return affected by skeletal muscle contraction? [∫ p. 495]

23. Describe the changes in the autonomic nervous system that alter exercise heart rate. [∫ p. 480]

Peripheral Blood Flow Redistributes to Muscle During Exercise

24. During exercise, 88% of blood flow is diverted to exercising muscles (Fig. 25-7). How is this different from resting muscle blood flow?

25. Describe the local and reflex processes that influence how the body redistributes blood flow during exercise. (Fig. 25-7)

Blood Pressure Rises Slightly During Exercise

26. What factors determine peripheral blood pressure? [∫ p. 496]

27. We've already seen how cardiac output increases during exercise. What happens to peripheral resistance? What factors affect peripheral resistance during exercise?

28. Total peripheral resistance decreases as exercise intensity increases (Fig. 25-8a). This would be expected to (raise / lower ?) arterial blood pressure.

29. What is the net result of the changes in cardiac output and peripheral resistance during exercise? (Fig. 25-8b)

The Baroreceptor Reflex Adjusts to Exercise

30. Normally, increased blood pressure triggers a homeostatic decrease in blood pressure. During exercise, though, there is no homeostatic decrease in BP. Why is this? Outline the possible mechanisms behind the absent baroreceptor reflex during exercise.

FEEDFORWARD RESPONSES TO EXERCISE

31. Feedforward responses play a significant role in exercise physiology. For example, ventilation (increases / decreases ?) upon beginning exercise, despite normal P_{CO_2} and P_{O_2}. (Fig. 25-5 and 25-6)

32. Outline or diagram the elements involved in the feedforward responses to exercise.

TEMPERATURE REGULATION

33. What happens to most of the energy released during metabolism?

34. Endurance exercise events can create core body temperatures of _____ °C.

35. How does the body respond to this rise in temperature? [∫ p. 715]

36. Both homeostatic responses to increased temperature can disrupt other homeostatic conditions. Describe the potential threats posed by:

sweating [∫ p. 641]:

increased cutaneous blood flow:

37. Faced with maintaining either blood pressure or body temperature, which will the body select? What would cause the body to choose the other parameter? Why?

38. Describe the changes that take place with acclimatization to exercise in hot environments.

EXERCISE AND HEALTH

39. Exercise can improve several pathological conditions. List two of these conditions.

Exercise Lowers the Risk of Cardiovascular Disease

40. There is a relationship between exercise and cardiovascular disease. How does exercise affect:

BP? _____
Plasma triglycerides? _____
HDL levels?_____

◎ *Even mild exercise can have significant health benefits.*

Type 2 Diabetes Mellitus May Improve with Exercise

41. Chronic exercise can improve type 2 diabetes mellitus. Briefly describe how this is so.

Stress and the Immune System May Be Influenced by Exercise

◎ *Exercise is associated with a reduced incidence of disease and improved longevity.*

42. No solid evidence confirms that exercise boosts immunity, prevents cancer, or helps HIV-positive people fight AIDS. In fact, strenuous exercise can be detrimental. What physiological mechanism would explain this?

43. How does the literature show that exercise and depression are related? Is this relationship proved by the evidence or overstated?

TALK THE TALK

acclimatization	adipose tissue	aerobic metabolism
alveolar ventilation	anaerobic pathways	ATP
baroreceptor reflex	beta cells of the pancreas	beta-oxidation
carbohydrates	cardiac output	central chemoreceptors
carotid body chemoreceptors	catecholamines	contractility
cholinergic vasodilator system	citric acid cycle	dehydration
convective heat loss	cortisol	epinephrine
diabetes mellitus	endurance	exercise and depression
evaporative cooling	exercise	fats
exercise and the immune system	exercise hyperventilation	force of contraction
fatty acids	feedforward responses to exercise	glucose transporters
glucagon	glucose	glycolytic metabolism
glycogen	glycolysis	high blood pressure
growth hormone	heart rate	insulin
homeostasis	hyperpnea	limbic system
K^+	lactic acid	muscle contraction
liver	metabolic acidosis	oxygen consumption
mitochondria	motor cortex	P_{CO2}
norepinephrine	oxidative phosphorylation	phosphocreatine
paracrines	parasympathetic output	proprioceptors
peripheral blood flow	peripheral resistance to blood flow	ventilation
physiological integration	P_{O2}	sympathetic output
pulmonary stretch receptors	pyruvate	venous return
Starling's Law of the heart	sweating	thermoregulation
vasoconstriction	respiratory control center of the medulla	maximal rate of oxygen consumption (V_{o2max})
cardiovascular control center, medulla oblongata		

PRACTICE MAKES PERFECT

1. Which would you expect change more during exercise: diastolic or systolic blood pressure?

2. TRUE/FALSE and explain: During exercise, cardiac output, stroke volume, and oxygen debt all should be greater in a trained (physically fit) person than in an average person.

3. How is cardiorespiratory endurance (aerobic fitness) usually measured?

4. During exercise, inspiratory and expiratory reserve volumes decrease. Why do you think that is?

5. List two beneficial effects of exercise.

6. What physiological factors can limit exercise capacity?

7. Concisely describe the relationship between exercise and immunity.

MAPS

Design a map that integrates cardiovascular and respiratory responses to exercise. Include receptors, chemicals, calculations, etc.

BEYOND THE PAGES

FURTHER EXPLORATIONS

Synovial fluid hydraulics. Science & Medicine, September/October 1996.

Breathless Legs? Consider Training Your Respiration, *News Physiol Sci* 15: 101-105. 2000 April

Carbohydrate ingestion during prolonged exercise: effects on metabolism and performance. Exercise and Sports Sciences Reviews 19:1ff. 1991.

26

SUMMARY

OK, it's back to work for one last big chapter. Much of this chapter is spent discussing the differences between male and female reproductive development. Therefore, when you're studying, make a big chart that compares these differences (be sure to include hormone action). The discussion of pregnancy and parturition provides a perfect opportunity to make a detailed flowchart. Start with the human sex act and go all the way through milk production.

Here are some key points:

✓ Autosomes are diploid; sex cells are haploid. Meiotic division [Appendix B] creates haploid cells.
✓ Sexual differentiation occurs during embryonic development. The presence of a Y chromosome initiates male reproductive development. The absence (or inactivity) of a Y chromosome initiates female reproductive development.
✓ Gametogenesis begins during embryonic development, stops before or just after birth, then resumes at puberty in males. New gamete production in females ceases before birth.
✓ The female menstrual cycle is complex and involves extensive hormonal control (Fig. 26-13).
✓ Fusion of egg and sperm leads to procreation. Pregnancy ends with parturition (the birthing process).

On a very general level, the human body contains two types of cells: diploid autosomal (somatic or body) cells and haploid sex (or germ) cells. The diploid number of chromosomes for humans is 46, and the haploid number is therefore 23 (exactly 1/2 the diploid number of chromosomes). In haploid cells, there are 22 autosomal chromosome pairs that control autosomal cell development and one pair of sex chromosomes that control germ cell development.

The male sex cells, spermatazoa, are produced by the testes; female sex cells, ova, are produced by the ovaries. Gametogenesis is the process by which sex cells are produced. The diploid primary sex cells (spermatogonia, oogonia) become secondary sex cells, and after the second meiotic division, these become haploid germ cells. While the process is similar for both male and female, the timing of gametogenesis is very different. Spermatogenesis begins in the embryo and stops just after birth. It resumes at puberty and continues throughout the male's lifetime. Oogenesis also begins in the embryo but stops before birth. At puberty, ovulation begins and occurs in a cyclical fashion until menopause. Both spermatogenesis and oogenesis are under hormonal control. Hormones involved include gonadotropins (FSH and LH from the anterior pituitary), sex hormones (androgens, estrogens, progesterone), inhibins, and activins.

Sexual differentiation takes place during the seventh week of embryonic development. Before differentiation, the gonadal tissue is considered bipotential. If the embryo has a Y chromosome, the SRY gene produces testis-determining factor that signals the testicular Sertoli cells to secrete Anti-Müllerian hormone. Anti-Müllerian hormone causes the degeneration of the Müllerian ducts. Leydig cells then begin to secrete testosterone and DHT, which cause the Wolffian ducts to develop into male accessory structures. Testosterone and DHT also create the external male genitalia. On the other hand, if the embryo does not have a Y chromosome, then none of the above happens, and the Müllerian ducts develop into female reproductive structures.

Male reproductive anatomy consists of the testes, accessory glands and ducts, and external genitalia. The urethra, which runs through the penis, is the common duct for sperm and urine movement (though not concurrently). Female reproductive anatomy consists of the ovaries, Fallopian tubes, uterus, vagina, labia (majora, minora), and clitoris. The female urethra is completely separated from the reproductive structures.

The female reproductive cycle is perhaps one of the most complex patterns in physiology. It is under extensive hormonal control (Fig. 26-13) and can be influenced by many emotional and physical factors. The menstrual cycle is composed of two concurrent cycles: the ovarian cycle and the uterine cycle. The ovarian cycle is further divided into phases: the follicular phase, ovulation, and the luteal phase. The uterine cycle is also divided into phases: menses, the proliferative phase, and the secretory phase. Follow Fig. 26-13 and note the hormones involved in these cycles.

During unprotected sex, the sperm and egg have the possibility of joining to form a zygote. Sperm must first be capacitated before they can make their way to the egg. If a sperm reaches an egg and successfully fertilizes it, only then will the egg complete its second meiotic division. Only one sperm is allowed to fertilize an egg, as the cortical reaction prevents polyspermy. Additionally, fertilization is species specific, meaning that only sperm and egg of compatible species can initiate procreation. If fertilization is successful, the two haploid germ cells create a diploid zygote that begins mitotic division to produce an embryo. The developing embryo attaches itself to the mother's uterine wall and parasitizes the mother's nutrient supply until birth. The placenta of the developing embryo secretes hormones that alter the mother's metabolism to ensure adequate nourishment for development.

After 38-40 weeks of pregnancy, the baby is born in a process called parturition. This process is under hormonal control, though the specific signaling is still unclear. The mother's mammary glands are activated under hormonal control and begin to secrete milk to feed the baby.

TEACH YOURSELF THE BASICS

1. What is a hermaphrodite?

2. What is a zygote?

SEX DETERMINATION
3. Define the structures found in both male and female sex organs, then give the sex-specific names for each.

      a. genitalia:

      b. gamete:

      c. germ cell:

4. Review of genetics [∫ Appendix B]

How many sets of chromosomes do nucleated body (somatic) cells have? (Fig. 26-1) _____

How many autosomal pairs? _____ How many sex chromosome pairs? _____

How many autosomes do gametes have? _____ How many sex chromosomes? _____

How is the X sex chromosome different from the Y?

The Sex Chromosomes Determine Genetic Sex
5. What determines the genetic sex of an individual? (Fig. 26-2)

6. XX individuals are usually _____ and XY individuals are usually _____.

7. There are many documented cases of abnormal sex chromosome distribution in humans. What are the roles of X and Y in determining the physical sex of an individual? What happens in the absence of the Y chromosome?

8. What are Barr bodies? How and why are they formed?

Sexual Differentiation Occurs in the Second Month of Development
9. Before the seventh week of development, it is morphologically difficult to determine an embryo's sex. What bipotential external genitalia are present at this stage? Into what components of the male and female genitalia does each later develop? (Fig. 26-3) (Table 26-1)

10. Name the two ducts associated with the bipotential gonadal tissue and tell what structure(s) each duct develops into in the male and female.

11. Explain the role of the following in sexual development of the genetically male embryo:

Y chromosome _____

SRY gene _____

testis determining factor (TDF) _____

Anti-Müllerian hormone (AMH) _____

Sertoli cells _____

Leydig cells _____

testosterone and DHT _____

12. In the absence of TDF, AMH, and testosterone, what happens to the bipotential structures in the female embryo?

13. What effect, if any, do sex hormones have on sexual behavior and gender identity?

BASIC PATTERNS OF REPRODUCTION

14. Define gametogenesis.

15. The timing of gametogenesis is different for males and females. Briefly compare these timing differences. [Ĵ Fig. 3-2, p. 52]

Gametogenesis Begins in Utero and Resumes During Puberty

◎ *For a summary of male and female patterns of gametogenesis, see Fig. 26-5.*

16. Gametogenesis has some similar steps in both sexes. Briefly compare the steps of gametogenesis in males and females, describing the steps in terms of cell types, chronology, by whether DNA has replicated, whether the cell divides, and the number of chromosomes in the cell.

17. The first meiotic division creates two secondary gametes. Compare the fates of those gametes in males and females.

18. What are polar bodies?

19. Define ovulation.

The Brain Directs Reproduction
20. What roles do the hypothalamus and anterior pituitary play in sex hormone production?

21. List the steroid sex hormones. (Fig. 26-6)

22. Which hormones are dominant in males?

23. Which hormones are dominant in females?

24. What does the enzyme aromatase catalyze?

Control Pathways for Sex Steroids Are Similar in Males and Females
25. Outline or diagram the basic pattern of hormonal control of reproduction. Identify all the hormones involved. (Fig. 26-7)

26. What are the generalized actions of FSH? LH?

27. Describe the roles that gonads, inhibins, and activins play in regulation of reproductive function.

Feedback Pathways Include Both Long-Loop and Short-Loop Feedback

28. Sex hormones follow general short-loop and long-loop feedback patterns [∫ p. 224]. Describe the feedback effect of each of the following: (Fig. *26-7*)

        a.   gonadal steroids

        b.   low estrogen levels

        c.   sustained elevated estrogen

The Hypothalamus Releases Gonadotropin

29. Describe the tonic, pulsed GnRH release in both sexes. What is the physiological mechanism for this pulsing?

30. What are some of the environmental factors that influence reproductive hormones and gametogenesis?

MALE REPRODUCTION

31. Male anatomy (Fig. 26-8):

The external genitalia are the _____ and _____.

What is the common passageway for urine and sperm? _____

What two tissues form the erectile tissue? _____

The tip of the penis is called the _____ penis. It is covered by tissue called the _____.

unless this tissue has been surgically removed in a procedure known as _____.

32. What is the function of the scrotum?

33. What is cryptorchidism and why is it usually corrected?

34. List the three male accessory glands.

The Testes Produce Sperm and Testosterone

35. Human testes (Fig. 26-9):

The tough outer fibrous capsule encloses the _____ tubules.

What structures/cells are found between these tubules? _____

What is the epididymis (Fig. 26-9b)? _____

What is the vas deferens? _____

The Seminiferous Tubules Contain Developing Sperm

36. Describe the two cell types that compose the seminiferous tubules (Fig. 26-9d,e).

37. What is the function of the basement membrane that surrounds the outside of the tubule (Fig. 26-9c)?

38. List the three functional compartments in the testes.

39. Describe the composition of the fluid in the lumen of the seminiferous tubules.

Sperm Production Is Continuous

40. Describe the anatomical arrangement of the Sertoli cells and the spermatogonia.

41. Outline or map the process of sperm maturation. (Fig. 26-10, 26-11)

42. Describe the parts and their functions in a mature sperm. (Fig. 26-10)

The Sertoli Cells Secrete Proteins

43. What role do the Sertoli cells play in sperm maturation?

44. List the substances made or secreted by the Sertoli cells.

45. What is the function of androgen-binding protein? Why is it necessary?

Leydig Cells Secrete Testosterone

46. What is the primary function of the Leydig cells?

47. Leydig cells are active in the fetus but inactive after birth until puberty. What role do they play in the fetus?

48. The bulk of the body's testosterone is produced in the Leydig cells. What other hormones can testosterone be converted into?

Spermatogenesis Requires Gonadotropins and Testosterone

49. What is the target tissue of FSH and what effect does the hormone have on this tissue? (Fig. 26-11)

50. What is the target tissue of LH and what effect does the hormone have on this tissue?

51. Diagram the hormonal control patterns for FSH and LH secretion.

Male Accessory Glands Contribute Secretions to Semen

52. What is semen?

53. What substances, other than sperm, are found in semen? Give their source and their function. (Table 26-3)

54. What percentage of semen volume is from the accessory glands? _____

Androgens Influence Secondary Sex Characteristics

55. List the primary sex characteristics of males.

56. List the secondary sex characteristics of males.

57. Androgens are (anabolic / catabolic ?) steroids. Why?

58. What are some of the side effects and behavioral changes brought about by steroid hormone abuse?

FEMALE REPRODUCTION

The Female Reproductive Tract Includes Ovaries and Uterus

59. List the parts of external female genitalia that make up the vulva (or pudendum). (Fig. 26-12a)

60. Describe the internal female anatomy beginning at the periphery and following the path would travel following intercourse.

61. How do the Fallopian tubes move an egg to the uterus?

The Ovary Produces Eggs and Hormones

62. Describe or draw the anatomy of an ovary and its follicles. (Fig. 26-12d)

63. Distinguish between the following structures: primary oocyte, primary follicle, and theca.

A Menstrual Cycle Lasts About One Month
64. How often does a menstrual cycle occur?

65. What is the purpose of the menstrual cycle?

66. The menstrual cycle is described according to changes in what two structures?

67. Name the three phases of the ovarian cycle. (Fig. 26-13)

68. Name the phases of the uterine cycle (Fig. 26-13).

Hormonal Control of the Menstrual Cycle Is Complex
69. What hormones control the ovarian and uterine cycles? (Fig. 26-13)

70. Which hormone dominates the follicular phase?

71. Which hormones dominate the luteal phase?

Early Follicular Phase
72. What event marks day 1 of a cycle?

73. Hormones:

    What happens to FSH and LH secretion just before the cycle begins?

    What changes does FSH cause?

    Which hormones do the granulosa cells and theca secrete? (Fig. 26-14a, p. 752)

    Why do FSH levels decline as the follicular phase progresses?

74. Follicle development. (Table 26-4) Explain the role for each of the following:

    the granulosa cells

    the thecal cells

75. What is the antrum?

76. What is atresia?

77. When menstruation ends, what happens to the endometrium?

Late Follicular Phase

78. What happens to ovarian estrogen levels as the follicular phase progresses?

79. What hormones are the granulosa secreting at this point? (Fig. 26-14b)

80. How does this affect the feedback loop to the pituitary?

81. Ovulation requires a surge in which hormone?

82. Meiosis resumes just before ovulation. Review: When did meiosis pause for this oocyte?

83. What is the result of this meiotic division?

84. Antral volume now reaches its maximum or minimum?

85. How do the high estrogen levels prepare uterus for pregnancy?

Ovulation

86. At which point of the cycle does ovulation occur?

87. What enzyme does a mature follicle secrete that promotes ovulation?

88. The resulting breakdown of collagen causes what kind of reaction?

89. How is the egg released from the follicle?

90. Describe luteinization.

91. What happens to estrogen secretion at ovulation?

Early to Mid-Luteal Phase

92. Describe what happens to progesterone and estrogen secretion following ovulation.

93. How do these hormones affect FSH and LH production? (Fig. 26-14c)

94. What are the effects of progesterone on the uterus?

95. What additional effect does progesterone have on a woman's body?

Late Luteal Phase and Menstruation

96. What happens to the corpus luteum in the absence of pregnancy? (Fig. 26-14d)

97. When progesterone secretion decreases, what change does this initiate in the endometrium?

98. Describe menstruation.

Estrogens and Androgens Influence Female Secondary Sex Characteristics

99. What are some female secondary sex characteristics?

100. Which part of the adrenal gland secretes androgens?

101. What effect do these androgens have in women?

PROCREATION

102. What types of structures and behaviors have evolved to ensure reproductive success in humans and many other terrestrial vertebrates?

103. List the two stages of the male sex act.

The Human Sexual Response Has Four Phases

104. Describe the four stages of the human sex act (coitus).

The Male Sex Act Is Composed of Erection and Ejaculation

105. What happens physiologically in the penis to allow erection?

106. Diagram the erection reflex. (Fig. 26-15)

107. What is the climax of the male sexual act? What does this accomplish?

108. The average semen volume is 3 mL. What percentage of that volume is sperm?

109. Explain the processes of emission and ejaculation.

110. What structure prevents the mixing of sperm and urine?

111. What are some factors involved in impotence?

Contraceptives Attempt to Prevent Pregnancy

112. List some common methods of contraception (birth control). Briefly discuss their effectiveness.

113. Why have male hormonal contraceptive efforts failed thus far?

114. Give an example of a potential new form of contraception.

Infertility Is the Inability to Conceive

115. Define infertility.

116. List some potential causes of infertility.

117. What percentage of all pregnancies terminate spontaneously?

118. Describe the process of *in vitro* fertilization.

PREGNANCY AND PARTURITION

Fertilization Requires Capacitation

119. Define capacitation. What has to happen in order for capacitation to occur?

120. For how long following ovulation can the egg be fertilized?

121. How long is sperm viable in the female reproductive tract?

122. Where does fertilization take place? (Fig. 26-18)

123. Describe fertilization. (Fig. 26-16, 26-17) Include the following terms: acrosome, acrosomal reaction, capacitation, cortical granules, cortical reaction, enzymes, granulosa cells, meiosis, polyspermy, second polar body, sperm-binding receptor, sperm nucleus, zona pellucida, zygote nucleus

124. Fertilization creates a zygote with a (diploid / haploid ?) set of chromosomes.

The Developing Zygote Implants in the Endometrium
125. When does the dividing zygote move into the uterine cavity? (Fig. 26-18)

126. The embryo is in which developmental stage at this point?

127. The outer blastocyst becomes what structure? (Fig. 26-19a)

128. The inner blastocyst becomes what four structures?

129. How long after fertilization does implantation usually take place?

130. Describe the process of implantation.

131. What are chorionic villi and what is their function?

132. Explain the relationship between the mother's blood supply and that of the fetus.

133. Why is the abnormal separation of the placenta from the endometrium a medical emergency?

The Placenta Secretes Hormones During Pregnancy
134. When an embryo has implanted, what prevents menstruation from occurring?

Human Chorionic Gonadotropin (hCG)

135. What other hormone is hCG structurally related to?

136. How long into gestation does the corpus luteum secrete estrogen and progesterone?

137. Give two functions of hCG.

Human placental lactogen (hPL)

138. What is the older name for hCS?

139. hCS is structurally related to what two other hormones?

140. What are the postulated roles for hCS during pregnancy? What is gestational diabetes mellitus?

Estrogen and Progesterone

141. What effect does continuous secretion of estrogen and progesterone during pregnancy have on FSH and LH secretion?

142. What are the functions of estrogen and progesterone during pregnancy?

143. What other hormones are secreted?

Pregnancy Ends with Labor and Delivery

144. How long is gestation in humans?

145. What is parturition?

146. What is labor?

147. What are some of the potential triggers responsible for initiating parturition?

148. Describe or diagram the positive feedback loop of parturition. (Fig. 26-21)

149. The fetus is normally in what orientation at the time of labor? (Fig. 26-20a)

150. What two hormones promote uterine contractions?

151. What happens to the placenta when the baby is born?

The Mammary Glands Secrete Milk During Lactation
152. Describe mammary gland structure. (Fig. 26-22)

153. Breasts develop during puberty under the control of which hormone?

154. How do the breasts change during pregnancy? What hormones induce these changes?

155. Estrogen and progesterone (inhibit / stimulate ?) milk secretion by the mammary gland epithelium.

156. Prolactin [∫ p. 223-224] controls milk production. Draw the prolactin control pathway.

157. Compare the composition of colostrum and breast milk.

158. What causes milk production to increase after pregnancy?

159. How does suckling act as a stimulus for milk production and release? Describe or draw the reflex. (Fig. 26-23)

160. How is milk ejection accomplished?

Prolactin Has Other Physiological Roles
161. What are the roles of prolactin in men and non-nursing women?

GROWTH AND AGING
Puberty Marks the Beginning of the Reproductive Years
162. When does puberty begin for girls? For boys?

163. Puberty requires the maturation of which control axis? What is one explanation for how this happens?

Menopause and Andropause Are a Consequence of Aging
164. What changes happen in the female reproductive system after about 40 years of menstrual cycles? Why?

165. What changes can accompany the postmenopausal lack of estrogen?

166. What are some pros and cons of hormone replacement therapy in women? What is a recent advance in hormone replacement therapy?

167. What physiological changes are seen in reproductive function as a man ages?

TALK THE TALK

abstinence
activin
amnion
androgen-binding protein.
anti-Müllerian hormone
atresia
barrier method of contraception
birth control pill
breast development
capacitation
cervix
ciliated epithelium
condom
corpus luteum
cortical granule of ovum
decapacitation factor
diploid number
ejaculation
epididymis
erotic stimuli
excitement phase
fimbriae
follicular phase
gametogenesis
germ cell
gonadotropin releasing hormone
gonad
gonadotropin
hyperglycemia of pregnancy
in vitro fertilization
impotence
inhibin
labioscrotal swelling
let-down reflex
libido
luteinization
mammary gland
menarche
menstrual cycle
mitosis
myometrium
orgasm
ovary
ovum
parturition
plateau phase
positive feedback loop

acrosomal reaction
adrenal cortex
anabolic steroid
anencephaly
antrum
autosome
bipotential gonad
blastocyst
breast-feeding
centromere
chorion
circumcision
contraception
corpus albicans
cortical reaction
diaphragm
down-regulation, GnRH
emission
erection reflex
estradiol
extraembryonic membrane
follicle stimulating hormone (FSH)
foreskin
genital tubercle
gestation
    (GnRH)
granulosa cell
human chorionic gonadotropin
human placental lactogen (hPL)
human chorionic
internal fertilization
labor
Leydig cell
long-loop negative feedback
luteinizing hormone (LH)
meiosis
menopause
menstruation
Müllerian duct
oocyte
osteoporosis
oviduct
oxytocin
penis
polar body, first and second
prepuce
primary follicle

acrosome
allantois
androgen
anterior pituitary
aromatase
Barr body
birth control
blood-testis barrier
bulbourethral (Cowper's) gland
cervical mucus
chorionic villi
coitus
corpora cavernosa
corpus spongiosum
cryptorchidism
dihydrotestosterone (DHT)
ductus deferens
endometrium
erogenous zone
estrogen
Fallopian tube
gamete
genitalia
glans penis
gestational diabetes mellitus
GnRH agonist
hot flash
    (hCG)
hymen
    somatomammotropin (hCS)
implantation
infertility
intrauterine device (IUD)
lactation
LHRH: see GnRH
luteal phase
lysozyme
melatonin
menses
mifepristone
Müllerian inhibiting substance
oogonia
ovarian cycle
ovulation
parasympathetic vasodilation
placenta
polyspermy

primary spermatocyte
progesterone, thermogenic ability
prolactin inhibiting hormone
prostate gland
pudendum
resolution phase
secondary spermatocyte
secretory phase
seminal vesicle
sex chromosome
sperm (spermatozoa)
SRY gene
sustentacular cell
testosterone
tubal ligation
urethral fold
vagina
Wolffian duct
zona pellucida

progesterone
proliferative phase
pseudohermaphrodite
pulse generator
RU 486
secondary oocyte
secretory epithelium
seminiferous tubule
short loop negative feedback
spermatid
sterilization
testes (testis)
theca
tubal pregnancy
uterine cycle
vasectomy
X-linked disorder
zygote
zinc

primary oocyte
primary sex characteristic
prolactin
prostaglandin
puberty
relaxin
scrotum
secondary sex characteristic
semen
Sertoli cells
sister chromatid
spermatogonia
stroma
testis determining factor
transforming growth factor-family
urethral groove
uterus
vulva

ETHICS IN SCIENCE

In recent years, the use of donor eggs and hormonal therapy has made it possible for post-menopausal women to bear children through *in vitro* fertilization. For example, in California a 53 year-old woman gave birth to quadruplets. When these children are twenty, their mother will be 73, if she is still alive. Older men, such as South Carolina Senator Strom Thurman, have been having children with younger women for years. Should an age limit be placed on women who desire *in vitro* fertilization?

PRACTICE MAKES PERFECT

1. Anatomical structures are considered **homologous** if they have the same origin and **analogous** if they are similar in function but do not have the same origin. Using the information in Fig. 23-4, pair the following parts of the male and female reproductive tract and mark them as homologous or analogous. Not every part will have a corresponding part in the opposite sex. In that case, mark them "unique."

Male	Corresponding female part?	Analogous or homologous?	Female
bulbourethral gland	_____	_____	a) clitoris
ductus deferens	_____	_____	b) Fallopian tube
penis	_____	_____	c) ovary
prostate gland	_____	_____	d) labia majora
scrotum	_____	_____	e) labia minora
seminal vesicle	_____	_____	f) uterus
testis	_____	_____	g) vagina

2. Which set of terms below corresponds to the blanks in the sentence?

The _____ later develops into the _____ which secretes _____ until the _____ takes over the role of maintenance of pregnancy.

    a. ovary, corpus luteum, estrogen and progesterone, endometrium
    b. follicle, corpus luteum, luteinizing hormone, placenta
    c. ovary, placenta, follicle stimulating hormone, corpus luteum
    d. ovary, corpus luteum, estrogen and progesterone, placenta
    e. follicle, corpus luteum, estrogen and progesterone, placenta

3. You are a researcher who has just discovered the hypothalamic-pituitary control axis for the ovary. Now you have conducted some experiments to see if menopause is due to a failure of the ovarian cells themselves, or a failure of one of the trophic hormones. Your working hypothesis is that menopause is a result of pituitary failure. If this is true, what results do you expect to obtain in your tests?

    a) Levels of pituitary gonadotropins will be   *elevated*   *normal*   *decreased*

    b) Estrogen levels will be   *elevated*   *normal*   *decreased*

    c) Administering estrogen   *will restore normal menstrual cycles*   *will have no effect on cycles*

    d) Administering GnRH   *will restore normal menstrual cycles*   *will have no effect on cycles*

    e) Administering FSH and LH   *will restore normal menstrual cycles*   *will have no effect on cycles*

    d) Administering progesterone   *will restore normal menstrual cycles*   *will have no effect on cycles*

4. Explain the function of the corpus luteum during early pregnancy.

5. What is the adaptive value of androgen-binding protein?

6. Fill in the following chart on reproduction.

	Male	Female
What is the gonad?		
What is the gamete?		
Cell(s) that produce gametes		
What structure has the sensory tissue involved in the sexual response?		
What hormone(s) controls development of the secondary sex characteristics?		
Gonadal cells that produce hormones and the hormones they produce		
Target cell/tissue for LH		
Target cell/tissue for FSH		
Hormone(s) with negative feedback on anterior pituitary		
Timing of gamete production in adults		

7. Name the hormone(s) in women that is (are) the primary control for the following events:

Proliferation of the endometrium _____

Initiates development of follicle(s) _____

Ovulation _____

Development of endometrium into a secretory structure _____

Keeps corpus luteum alive in early pregnancy _____

Keeps endometrium from sloughing (i.e. menstruating) in early pregnancy _____

MAPS

1. Create a map showing the events determining the sex of an embryo, starting with the sex chromosomes.

2. Outline the uterine and ovarian cycles and include the major hormones active during each phase.

3. Draw a reflex map that shows how the female birth control pill that contains estrogen and progesterone
    works to stop the production of ova.

BEYOND THE PAGES

FURTHER EXPLORATIONS

🕸 Learn more about possible new forms of contraception by doing a Google search (www.google.com) for *contraceptive research.*

🕸 Student guide to the Human Genome Project:
http://www.ornl.gov/TechResources/Human_Genome/education/students.html

 Articles

How breast milk protects newborns. Scientific American, December 1995.

Fatness and fertility. Scientific American, March 1988.

The "stress" of being born. Scientific American, April 1986.

The dilemmas of prostate cancer. Scientific American, April 1994.

Does screening for prostate cancer make sense? Scientific American, September 1996.

Is hormone replacement therapy a risk? Scientific American, September 1996.

Can environmental estrogens cause breast cancer? Scientific American, October 1995.

Future contraceptives. Scientific American, September 1995.

Debate: Is homosexuality biologically induced? Scientific American, May 1994.

The history of synthetic testosterone. Scientific American, February 1995.

Pre-term birth. Science & Medicine, March/April 1996.

Barriers to sexually transmitted diseases. Science & Medicine, March/April 1996.

Estrogen receptors in breast cancer. Science & Medicine, January/February 1996.

Testicular cancer. Science & Medicine, January/February 1995.

Biology of aggression. Science & Medicine, January/February 1995.

Breast-feeding stimulates the infant immune system. Science & Medicine 4(6), 1997 Nov/Dec.

Gene Therapy: In utero gene therapy. Science & Medicine 5(1), 1998 Jan/Feb.

Estrogen is a male and female hormone. Science & Medicine 5(4), 1998 Jul/Aug.

CHAPTER 1- Practice Makes Perfect

1. Physiology is the study of body function; anatomy is the study of body structure.
2. a) The hypothesis might be "Pravistatin lowers cholesterol in rats."
   b) An appropriate control would be to administer an inert substance in the same fashion that the Pravistatin is administered.
3. As the concentration of nerve growth factor (NGF) increases, the number of migrating cells increases. NGF has its minimum effect at a concentration of 10^{-5} M and its maximum effect at a concentration of 10^{-3} M.
4. The independent variable, which is controlled by the experimenter, is the extracellular concentration of glucose; it goes on the x-axis. The dependent variable, which is measured by the experimenter, is the intracellular concentration of glucose; it goes on the y-axis. The data do not begin at low values, so the origin is not given the value of 0,0. On the x-axis, the first heavy line is given the lowest value (80), with each heavy line after that representing an increase of 10 mM. The x-axis data are evenly spaced. The y-axis values are not evenly spaced, so the person constructing the graph must select a range of values that includes all points. The lowest data point is 52, so the first heavy line on the y-axis is given a value of 50, with each heavy line after that representing an increase of 10 mM (60, 70, etc.). The y-axis data points can then be plotted according to their actual values. The data points do not fall exactly on a line, so a best-fit line should be drawn (see Fig. 1-7d, p. 9). The x-axis is not time, so individual points should not be connected. The graph flattens out at x = 130 and the line changes slope from diagonal to horizontal. Summary of results: The intracellular concentration of glucose increases linearly as extracellular glucose concentration increases, up to an extracellular concentration of 100 mM. At that concentration, the intracellular concentration of glucose reaches a maximum value of about 100 mM.
5. (a) bar graphs – x-axis has the three temperatures, y-axis is oxygen consumption. You would use different colors/patterns of bars for summer- and winter-collected animals.
   (b) Growth is a continuous function, therefore this data is appropriate for line graphs. Height and weight should be plotted on separate graphs and each graph will have two lines, one for gilrs and one for boys.
   (c) Data points from a population of people selected at random are graphed on a scatter plot. In this example, the x-axis is food intake and the y-axis is = glucose concentration).

CHAPTER 2

p. 2-5: To make a 1 molar (1 mole/L) solution of NaCl, weight out 58.5 g NaCl and add water until the total volume is 1 liter. One mole of magnesium ions (Mg^{2+}) contains 2 equivalents.

p. 2-5: A 10% (wt/vol) solution contains 10 g of solute per 100 mL solution. To make 250 mL of 10% NaCl, weigh out 25 g of NaCl and add water until the final volume is 250 mL.
   A solution with 200 mg NaCl/dL = 200 mg/100 mL. This is equal to 2000 mg/1000 mL, or 2 g/L.

Quantitative Thinking

Task 2: 6 moles NaCl + 6 moles glucose = 12 moles total solute in 3 L volume = 4 mol/L = 4 M
Task 3: 300 mM glucose = 0.3 moles glucose/liter. Mol. weight glucose = 180.
   180 g/mole = ? g/0.3 mole = 54 g
   54 g glucose/1 liter = ? g/0.6 L = 32.4 g glucose into 600 mL solution.

Practice Makes Perfect

1. The carbon atom has 6 protons and 6 neutrons in the nucleus. There are 2 electrons in the first electron shell and 4 electrons in the outer shell. See Fig. 2-6b, p. 20. The oxygen atom has 8 protons and 8 neutrons in the nucleus. There are 2 electrons in the first electron shell and 6 electrons in the outer shell. See Fig. 2-6c, p. 20.
2.

3. B, D, A, C, F, G, H

4.

ELEMENT	SYMBOL	AT. #	PROTONS	ELECTRONS	NEUTRONS	AT. WT.
Calcium	Ca		20	20		
Carbon	C	6			6	
Chlorine	Cl	17		17		
Cobalt		27			32	
Hydrogen	H	1	1			1
Iodine			53	53		127
Magnesium	Mg	12				24
Nitrogen			7		7	
Oxygen		8		8	8	
Sodium	Na	11		11	12	
Zinc	Zn	30		30		65
Copper	Cu	29	29			64
Iron			26	26	30	
Potassium	K			19		39

5. Water = H_2O. (2 H × at. wt. 1 = 2) + (1 O × at. wt. 16 = 16) = 18 daltons

6. F, E, B, G, A, C

7. Both A and C are correct. They have the correct number of carbon, hydrogen, oxygen and nitrogen atoms. The COO^- group on the right can rotate around the C-C bond, so both drawings are correct. Figures B and C both have 5 bonds on the second-to-last carbon instead of 4.

8. a) Covalent   b) Hydrogen   c) Water is the only solvent in biological systems. d) The charged ions will be attracted to the partial charges in the polar regions of the water molecule. This allows the ions to dissolve in the water.

9. If an oxygen atom gains a proton, it becomes a fluorine atom.

10. Chlorine has 7 electrons in its 8-place outer shell; potassium, like sodium, has only one electron in its outer shell. Thus, chlorine takes an electron from potassium, creating Cl^- (chloride) and K^+. Both ions are stable as their outer shells are now filled. See Fig. 2-9, p. 23.

11. Polar molecules are hydrophilic because their regions of partial charge will interact with the polar regions of water, allowing the polar solute to dissolve. Nonpolar molecules are hydrophobic and will not dissolve because they have no regions of charge to disrupt the hydrogen bonds between adjacent water molecules.

12. The molecular weight of sodium chloride (NaCl) is 58.5. One mole weighs 58.5 grams, so 0.5 moles will weight 29.25 g.

13. A 0.5 M NaCl solution has 0.5 moles/L, or 29.25 g/L. To make 0.5 L, put 14.625 g into 500 mL solution.

14. A 0.1 M solution has 100 mmoles/L.

15. A 50 mM solution contains 50 mmoles glucose/liter, or 5 mmoles/100 mL. One mole contains 180 g, so 1 mmole contains 0.180 g. Therefore 5 mmoles = 0.9 g.

16. To make 100 mL of a 3% glucose solution, take 3 g glucose and add water to give 100 mL final volume. For molarity: 1 mole/180 g = ? mole/3 g = 0.017moles. 0.017 mol/100 mL = 0.17 mol/L = 170 mM.

17. Mixed solution contains 2 L with 400 mmoles glucose and 800 mmoles NaCl. Total concentration is 1200 mmol/2 L or 600 mmol/L = 0.6 M. The NaCl concentration is 400 mmol/2L or 200 mmol/L = 0.2 M. The glucose concentration is 800 mmol/2L or 400 mmol/L = 0.4 M.

18. Na^+ contains 1 mEq/mmol because the ion has a single charge. Therefore, 142 mEq/L = 142 mmol/L.

19. Ca^{2+} contains 2 mEq/mmol because the ion has a charge of 2+. Therefore, 5 mEq/L = 2.5 mmol/L.
20. C; D and E; A; F, B and D
21. On the left side of the reaction, water (H_2O) is the acid because it donates an H^+, and the amine is the base. On the right side of the reaction, the amine donates the H^+ and acts as the acid, while the hydroxide ion (OH^-) is the base.
22. H_2CO_3 is carbonic acid, which dissociates into H^+ and bicarbonate ion, HCO_3^-, which acts as a base.
23. A 0.5 M solution equals a 500 mM solution, which is more acidic than a 50 mM solution.
24. C, B, E, A, F
25. D; A and E; B and C; C; F
26. See Fig. 2-19 on p. 42 for one possible map. Your map does not have to match it exactly, but it should have the same links. If you have put in links that are not shown in Fig. 2-19, ask your instructor if they are correct.

CHAPTER 3 - Practice Makes Perfect

1. Mitochondria would have the highest probability of existing independently and evolving because they have their own DNA with which they can reproduce and make new proteins. Mitochondria also contain the enzymes and proteins needed to make ATP.
2. Compartmentation of the nucleus allows the cell's control center to operate without being greatly affected by conditions in the cytoplasm. For example, cytoplasmic enzymes cannot enter the nucleus.
3. In the absence of a cytoskeleton, intestinal cells could not link to each other at cell junctions. They would also not have microvilli that increase the surface area for absorption of nutrients.
4. Many epithelial cells are exposed to chemical and mechanical stress, so they are constantly undergoing mitosis to make new cells. Many environmental chemicals can damage chromosomes, leading to abnormal (cancerous) daughter cells. In addition, the constant reproduction of these cells increases the probability of genetic mutations during cell division.
5. You would expect the solutions to be different because tight junctions are used to create a barrier between the compartments on each side of the cell layer.
6. The surface layer of the epidermis is composed of mats of keratin fibers and extracellular matrix that are left behind when keratinocytes die. This layer acts as a waterproof layer to prevent loss of water and heat.
7. C, D, A, E, G, F
8. Under skin- a, b, c, d. Sheaths- a. cartilage - a. adipose - e; tendons and ligaments - a; blood - d. lungs and blood vessels - a, b, c, d. bones - a.
9. packages proteins - c. modifies proteins - c. series of tubes - c. protein synthesis - a.
10. a) See p. 64. b) See p. 58. c) See pp. 53, 57. d) See pp. 67-69. e) See p. 58. f) See p. 59. g) See pp. 61-62. h) See pp. 60-61. i) See p. 66-67. j) See p. 69. k) See Fig. 3-18, p. 69. l) See pp. 69-70. m) See p. 70. n) See pp. 72-73. o) See p. 72. p) See Fig. 3-23, p. 73.

CHAPTER 4

p. 4-15: (f) The scale is balanced again with 6 blocks on the left and 12 blocks on the right. (i) The scale is balanced again with two blocks on the left and 4 blocks on the right. If more A is added to the reaction, A, C and D all increase. If C and D are converted into E, the amount of A will decrease.

Practice Makes Perfect

1. entropy - D. potential energy - A, E. kinetic energy - B. exergonic - F. endergonic -C, G.
2. Vitamins and ions act as cofactors or coenzymes. Cofactors must bind to the enzyme before substrates will bind to the active sites. Coenzymes act as receptors or carriers for atoms or functional groups.
3.

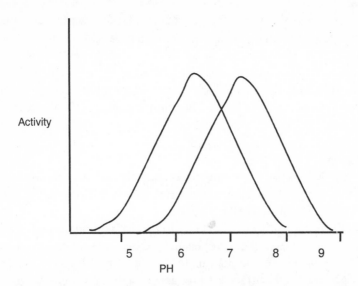

4. a) Graph A is exergonic and graph B is endergonic.   b) Graph A is more likely to go in the forward direction because it has a lower activation energy.   c) In graph A the products have a lower free energy (stored energy) than the substrates, therefore more energy was released. d) Graph A belongs with reaction 2. Graph B belongs with reactions 1, 3, and 4.
5. C, B, A, D, G, H, F
6. a) and c)

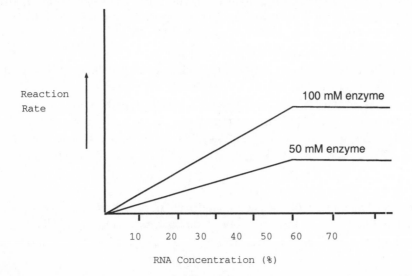

b) When the reaction rate is maximal, all active sites on the enzymes are occupied with substrate, i.e. the enzyme is saturated. See Fig. 4-15 on p. 97.
7. NADH is oxidized (loses an electron) to become NAD^+. H^+ is reduced because it gains an electron to become an H that combines with carbon.
8. This is a dehydration reaction because water is removed.
9. D, A, G, F, K, C, B, H, E, I
10. a) NADH donates high-energy electrons. b) $FADH_2$ donates high-energy electrons.   c) Oxygen combines with H^+ and electrons to form water. d) ATP synthase transfers the kinetic energy of electrons moving down their concentration gradient to the high-energy bond of ATP.   e) H^+ is concentrated in the intermembrane space, storing energy in its concentration gradient. f) The inner membrane proteins convert energy from high-energy electrons into either the work of moving H^+ ions

against their concentration gradient or into heat.

CHAPTER 5 - Practice Makes Perfect
1. Time values are distance^2, or 1, 4, 9, and 16.

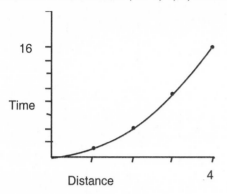

The graph has distance on the x-axis and evenly spaced values from 0 at the origin to 4 mm.

The y-axis is time and the values range from 0-16, with evenly spaced tic-marks.

2. According to Fick's Law, the rate of diffusion $\propto \dfrac{\text{surface area} \times \text{concentration gradient}}{\text{membrane resistance} \times \text{membrane thickness}}$

So as membrane thickness increases by a factor of 2, the rate of diffusion will decrease by half.

3. See table on next page of the answer key.

4. Na^+/K^+-ATPase - B, C, D. Na^+-glucose - A, D, E. Ca^{2+}-ATPase - C. $Na^+/K^+/2$ Cl^- - A, D, E. Na^+/H^+ - B, D, E.

5. The membrane permeability to Ca^{2+} appears to change with light. Light is a form of energy, so it could be doing one of several things: (1) opening a Ca^{2+} channel, (2) providing energy for the conformation change of a Ca^{2+} carrier protein, or (3) changing the structure of the membrane in some other way to make it permeable to Ca^{2+}. The first two explanations are more specific and relevant to the material in this chapter.

6. See Fig. 5-28, p. 131.

7. To compare your answer to another map, see Fig. 5-30, p. 149.

8. 1 OsM/1.86° = ? OsM/0.55° = 0.296 OsM or 296 mOsM plasma osmolarity. Intracellular osmolarity is always the same as plasma at equilibrium.

9. 1 mL sample/1 mg glucose = ? mL total/5000 mg glucose. The beaker has 5000 mL or 5 liters.

10. Absorption rate decreased as apical Na^+ concentration decreased, so transport appears to be Na^+-dependent. At the Curesall concentrations tested, transport rate was always proportional to concentration. The Na^+-dependence of the transport suggests that the transporter may be a secondary active transporter similar to the Na^+-glucose transporter even though transport did not show saturation.

11. Molecular weight of NaCl = 58.5. A 0.9% solution contains 0.9 g/100 mL solution or 9 g/liter.
      1 mole NaCl/58.5 g NaCl = ? mole/9 g NaCl = 154 mmoles NaCl × 2 osmoles/mole
      = 308 mosmoles/L

12. Molecular weight of glucose = 180. 5% solution = 5 g/100 mL or 50 g/liter.
      1 mole glucose/180 g = ? moles/50 g = 0.278 moles × 1 osmole/mole = 0.278 osmoles or 278 mosmoles/liter

Table for question 3:

METHOD	Movement relative to concentration gradient	Energy source	Rate	Movement relative to membrane structure	exhibits Specificity?	Exhibits Competition?	Exhibits Saturation?	Examples
simple diffusion	down	[ ] gradient	[ ] dependent	diffuse across lipid bilayer	no	no	no	gases, small nonpolar molecules, urea
restricted diffusion	down	[ ] gradient	[ ] dependent	through open channel	yes	yes	yes	urea
facilitated diffusion	down	[ ] gradient	[ ] dependent. has maximum rate	on protein carrier	yes	yes	yes	glucose into cells from ECF
direct active transport	against	ATP	[ ] dependent. has maximum rate	via protein carrier	yes	yes	yes	Na-K ATPase
indirect active transport	one or more down, one or more against	[ ] gradient, usually of Na+	[ ] dependent	via protein carrier	yes	yes	yes	Na-glucose symport

[ ] = concentration. ECF = extracellular fluid

13. a) Rate is measured as mg or mmole per minute or second.   b) In graph #1, the concentration inside the cell reaches a maximum value over time, presumably showing that the system has come to equilibrium. If concentration inside equals concentration outside, the movement of glucose must be by diffusion. You cannot tell from this graph if the diffusion is simple diffusion across the phospholipid bilayer or if it is facilitated diffusion, a passive process. In graph #2, the rate of movement does not reach a maximum, suggesting that there are no transporters to become saturated. This graph would support a hypothesis of simple diffusion. However, it is possible that the extracellular glucose concentration did not reach a high enough value to cause saturation of the carriers in the artificial membrane. c) The line in graph #1 leveled off because there was no more glucose entering the artificial cell.

14.

SOLUTION A	MEMBRANE	SOLUTION B	OSMOLARITY OF A RELATIVE TO B
100 mM glucose	no net movement	100 mM urea	isosmotic
200 mM glucose	no net movement	100 mM NaCl*	isosmotic
300 mOsM NaCl	no net movement	300 mOsM glucose	isosmotic
300 mM glucose	$\Rightarrow$	200 mM CaCl$_2$**	hyposmotic

* 100 mM NaCl = 200 mOsM NaCl.   **200 mM CaCl$_2$ = 600 mOsM CaCl$_2$

15. The IV solution is isosmotic so there will be no change in the osmolarity of either the ECF or ICF. The infusion goes into the plasma (ECF), so ECF volume will increase initially. Because the solution is all NaCl, a nonpenetrating solute, the solution will all remain in the ECF. There is no concentration gradient to cause water to move into or out of the ICF, so ICF volume will remain unchanged.

16. The solution is isosmotic and hypotonic to the cell. The graph should be labeled with "time" on the x-axis and "cell volume" on the y-axis. Cell volume increases at the arrow, then levels off at a new, larger volume.

17. a) 340 mosmoles/L × 13 L = 4420 mosmoles in ECF   b) 160 mosmoles/L × 1 mmole NaCl/2mosmoles = 80 mmoles   c) new ECF volume = 13 L + 1 L = 14 L. Solute = 4420 + 160 mosmoles = 4580 mosmoles. Osmolarity = 4580 mosmoles/14 L = 0.327 OsM or 327 mOsM

18. Cl⁻ will move from side 2 to side 1 because of a concentration gradient for Cl⁻. As the ions move, side 1 will develop a net negative charge while side 2 will develop a net positive charge, creating a membrane potential. Net Cl⁻ movement will stop when the positive charge on side 2 that holds Cl⁻ in that compartment is equal in magnitude to the concentration gradient driving Cl⁻ into side 1.

19. When ECF K⁺ increases, an equal amount of some anion has also been added to the ECF, so there is no change in the charge on the ECF. When ECF K⁺ increases, the membrane potential of a liver cell depolarizes because less K⁺ leaks out of the cell. Liver cells are not excitable and do not fire action potentials but can experience changes in membrane potential.

20. The membrane potential will slowly depolarize to zero as K⁺ leaks out and Na⁺ leaks into the cell. Normally the Na⁺/K⁺-ATPase removes ions that leak across the membrane.

CHAPTER 6 - Practice Makes Perfect

1. Local communication with neighboring cells is carried out by chemical communication (autocrines, paracrines, cytokines). Long distance communication is carried out by the nervous system, hormones, and cytokines. Local communication takes place by diffusion, which limits its speed. Nervous signals are the fastest means of communication. Long-distance chemical communication relies on the circulatory system.

2. Different types of receptors for one chemical signal allow different responses to a single signal. In addition, there are many different chemical signals, each with its own receptor or receptors. Receptor number is not constant. Cells can alter their receptor number by adding or withdrawing receptors (up- and down-regulation).

3. Cascades allow amplification of signals. A single event could not elicit as large a response without a cascade.

4. You would not expect the effects of growth hormone to exert negative feedback because then growth would not take place. On the other hand, without some form of control, growth would continue unchecked. By having growth hormone concentration act as the negative feedback signal, the body can keep the secretion of growth hormone in a desirable range.

CHAPTER 7 - Practice Makes Perfect

1.

	Peptide	Steroid
Transport in plasma	dissolved	bound to carrier proteins
Synthesis site in endocrine cell	rough endoplasmic reticulum	smooth endoplasmic reticulum
Method of release from endocrine cell	exocytosis from secretory vesicles	simple diffusion across phospholipid bilayer
General response of endocrine cell	modification of existing proteins	transcription, translation, and synthesis of new proteins

2. Connected by nerve fibers - P; connected by blood vessels - A; hormones made in hypothalamus - P; under influence of hypothalamic hormones - A; secretes peptide hormones - A, P.

3. e

4. 1- a, b; 2 - c, f; 3 - c, h; 4 - e.

5. a) False: Steroid hormones cannot be stored in vesicles because they are lipid-soluble and would diffuse out across the vesicle membrane.   b) It is true that steroid-secreting cells have lots of smooth endoplasmic reticulum but false that they have lots of Golgi. The Golgi apparatus is used to package material into vesicles (see 6a).

6. a) 2;   b) 1. mRNA carries the code for peptide synthesis.

7. The tissue has lots of membrane-bound secretory vesicles, indicating that the cells synthesize and store peptides. Insulin is a peptide hormone, so the tissue is endocrine pancreas.

8. For the pathway, see Fig. 7-15, p. 224. Secondary hypocortisolism originating at the pituitary means that both ACTH and cortisol secretion are down. If you administer ACTH, her cortisol secretion should increase because there is nothing wrong with the adrenal cortex; it has simply lacked stimulation by ACTH.

9. The antibodies stimulate the thyroid gland, so you expect thyroid hormone (thyroxine) levels to be elevated. This eliminates patients A and C. The elevated thyroxine will have a negative feedback effect on the pituitary and shut off endogenous TSH production, therefore TSH should be below normal. Only patient B has elevated thyroxine and decreased TSH.

Graphs

The data for the patients in problem #9 are best shown with a bar graph. There are two parameters being measured for each patient, so you would need two sets of values on the y-axis. This can be done by placing the scale for thyroxine on the left side of the graph and the scale for TSH on the right side of the graph. On the x-axis, each patient is represented by a pair of bars, side by side, one bar for each hormone. Distinguish the hormones by using different colors or fill patterns in the bars.

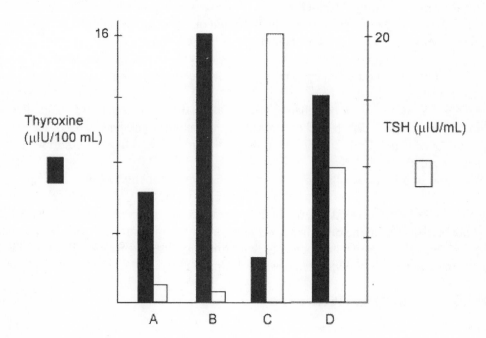

CHAPTER 8 - Practice Makes Perfect

1. speed
2. ECF (left to right) Na, Cl, K; ICF - K, Na, Cl
3. Dendrite $\Rightarrow$ cell body $\Rightarrow$ trigger zone (axon hillock) $\Rightarrow$ axon $\Rightarrow$ axon terminal $\Rightarrow$ releases neurotransmitter by exocytosis $\Rightarrow$ neurotransmitter diffuses across synaptic cleft to combine with receptor on postsynaptic cell
4. a) K^+ will leave the cell due to the electrical gradient (positive inside) repelling it. Na^+ will leave because of both the electrical gradient and the concentration gradient favoring its movement out.
   b) To convert $110°$ F to degrees Kelvin, see Appendix A.

$E_{Na} = \dfrac{RT}{Fz} \ln \dfrac{[Na]out}{[Na]in}$ R = 8.314, T = 316.48° K, F = 96,000, z = +1, [Na]out = 15, [Na]in = 175
                        ln = 2.3 $\log_{10}$

   = -67 mV

5. a
6. d
7. b

8.

	Location of channel	Ion(s) that moves	Chem or volt gating?	Physiological process in which ion participates
NEURON				
	dendrite	Na^+	chemical	graded potentials
	axon	Na^+	electrical	action potentials
	axon	K^+	electrical	action potentials
	axon terminal	Ca^{2+}	electrical	exocytosis of neurotransmitter

9. The ground electrode is set to zero millivolts and the potential difference is measured between this electrode and the inside of the cell.
10. Stretching could destroy the integrity of the cell membrane or could pop open channels that would allow ions to move between the cell and the extracellular fluid.
11. See Fig. 8-14, p. 258.

CHAPTER 9 - Practice Makes Perfect
1. a) The cerebrum contains the motor cortices for voluntary movement (walking to class) and the cerebral cortex for higher brain functions (pondering physiology). It also contains the visual cortex for integrating visual information from the eyes, and association areas that integrate sensory information into the perception of tripping and falling. The basal ganglia are associated with control of movement. The amygdala of the limbic system is linked to the emotions of anger and embarrassment. b) The cerebellum coordinates the movement of walking.
2. An electroencephalogram measures the summed electrical activity of brain neurons. The wave patterns of the EEG vary with different states of consciousness and can be used to assess if brain activity is following normal patterns.
3. a) higher thought processes, b) centers for homeostasis, neurohormone production, c) centers for involuntary functions (breathing, heart rate) and eye movement, d) coordination and control of body movement
4. b
5. c
6. c

CHAPTER 10 - Practice Makes Perfect
1. Rapidly adapting phasic receptors adapt to constant pressure from clothing and stop sending information to the brain.
2. A salty solution cannot be tasted at the back of the tongue because there are no salt receptors there.
3. True. The layers of the retina are arranged so that light must pass through layers containing nerves and blood vessels before it strikes the photoreceptors.
4. e
5. In nearsightedness (myopia), the light focuses in front of the retina. In astigmatism, the cornea is not a perfect dome, so the light does not focus evenly on the retina.
6. b
7. Loss of air conduction but not bone conduction suggests a problem with the middle ear or a plugged ear canal.
8. The spot of bright light appears black on the paper. Light causes retinal to release from the opsin portion of rhodopsin and be transported out of the photoreceptor. The slow recovery results from time needed to transport the retinal back into the rod and also the time needed for the rod membrane potential to return to its former state.
9. The horizontal canal is involved in movement that changes the left-right position of the head.
10. Rods are responsible for low-light monochromatic vision, so a nocturnal animal would have more rods and fewer cones.
11. d

CHAPTER 11 - Practice Makes Perfect

1. a
2. a) antagonist, b) agonist
3. Autonomic neurotransmitters (NTs) are released from varicosities along the axon as well as at the axon terminal, so their release is less specifically associated with receptors on the target cell. Autonomic NT release can be modulated by many chemical factors such as hormones and paracrines. In addition to being broken down by synaptic enzymes, autonomic NTs may diffuse away from the receptors or be transported intact back into the neuron. A major difference between autonomic and somatic motor NTs is that the amount of NT will vary the response of the target cell. Each action potential in a somatic motor neuron creates one muscle twitch.
4. Monoamine oxidase (MAO) is the enzyme that breaks down catecholamines at autonomic synapses, therefore inhibition of MAO will prolong or enhance target responses to autonomic signals.
5. False: The onset of steroid action takes at least 30 minutes, which is too slow for most fight-or-flight situations.

CHAPTER 12 - Practice Makes Perfect

1. Muscle contraction requires Ca^{2+} and uses ATP.
2. Somatic motor neurons secrete acetylcholine.
3. True.
4. Na^+ entry is greater because Na^+ has both concentration and electrical gradients favoring its movement. K^+ has concentration favoring its efflux but an electrical gradient opposing efflux.
5. d
6. Contraction is more rapid because Ca^{2+} floods the cytoplasm as it moves down its concentration gradient. Removal of Ca^{2+} for relaxation requires that the cell use ATP to pump Ca^{2+} against its gradient.
7. Temporal summation in muscle results when multiple action potentials repeatedly stimulate a muscle fiber, causing an increase in its force of contraction, up to some maximum value. Temporal summation in a neuron occurs when multiple sub-threshold stimuli arrive at the trigger zone and create a suprathreshold signal. In the neuron, the result is an action potential of constant amplitude, in contrast to the increasing force observed in the muscle.
8. Fatigued muscles have less ATP with which to pump Ca^{2+} back into the sarcoplasmic reticulum.
9. If skeletal muscles had gap junctions, all fibers would contract simultaneously. This would prevent us from regulating which muscles are contracting and would prevent us from regulating the force of contraction.
10. True. Muscles shorten during isotonic contractions.
11. a
12. a
13. Motor proteins in the nervous system include the microtubules and foot proteins used for axonal transport and the cytoskeleton that helps growing neurons find their targets. Motor proteins in Chapter 3 include microtubules that move cilia and flagella, microtubules associated with centrioles for chromosome movement during cell division, fibers that help mobile white blood cells (phagocytes) move, and fibers that move vesicles and other organelles around the cytoplasm.
14. Fewer ACh receptors would mean that a muscle would not respond as strongly to neurotransmitter release. This would probably manifest itself as muscle weakness or paralysis because the muscle fiber would not fire action potentials and excitation-contraction coupling would not occur.
15. You would expect the latency period to be longer when the nerve is stimulated because the additional steps of neurotransmitter release, diffusion across the synapse, opening of ACh-gated channels, and ion movement must take place.

CHAPTER 13 - Practice Makes Perfect

1. The steps are stimulus, receptor, afferent pathway, integrating center, efferent pathway, tissue response, systemic response. Examples of reflexes in Chapter 13 include the muscle spindle and Golgi tendon reflexes, the flexion reflex, and the crossed extensor reflex.
2. a
3. In Fig. 13-10 the sensory neuron diverges to excite multiple interneurons. In Fig. 13-11, sensory neurons diverge, neurons converge on the thalamus and cerebral cortex, and multiple neurons converge on the somatic motor neuron.

CHAPTER 14

p. 14-4: Tube B has the larger pressure gradient, 65 mm Hg (75 - 10), so it will have the greatest flow. The   pressure gradient in Tube A is only 50 mm Hg.

p. 14-7: The small change in the membrane potential between points 1 and 2 in Fig. 14-14 (p. 464) is due to K^+ leaving the cell through K^+ leak channels.

Quantitative Thinking

1. Resistance should decrease and radius increase.
2. Flow = $\Delta P/R$, where R $\propto L/r^4$. So flow $\propto \Delta P \times r^4/L$
    Flow A = $(50 \times 16)/16 = 50$.   Flow B = $(72 \times 1)/2 = 36$
3. CO = HR $\times$ SV so SV = CO/HR. Before Romeo, SV = 69.4 mL/beat. After Romeo, SV = 125 mL/beat.

Practice Makes Perfect

1. acetylcholine, atrioventricular, cardiac output, electrocardiogram, end-diastolic volume, end-systolic volume, sinoatrial, stroke volume.

2.

	Electrical Event	Mechanical Event
P wave	atrial depolarization	atrial contraction follows
QRS complex	ventricular depolarization	ventricular contraction and atrial relaxation
T wave	ventricular repolarization	ventricular relaxation
PQ segment	AV node delay	atrial contraction
ST segment	some parts of ventricle depolarizing, some repolarizing	end of ventricular contraction
TP segment	none	atrial and ventricular diastole

3. If heart rate speeds up, there is less time for passive (gravity-assisted) ventricular filling, so atrial contraction takes on increasing importance.
4. See Table 14-4 on pg. 467.
5. Kinetic energy is unchanged but the hydrostatic pressure decreases. See Fig. 14-3 on p. 453.
6. Several mechanisms to alter would include Ca^{2+} entry from the extracellular fluid, Ca^{2+} release from the sarcoplasmic reticulum, the regulatory protein phospholamban, the activity of the Ca^{2+}-ATPase, and anything that would alter binding of Ca^{2+} to troponin or the interaction of actin and myosin.
7. As venous return increases, the muscle fibers stretch more and therefore contract more forcefully (the Frank-Starling Law). This increases stroke volume and therefore increases cardiac output. Sympathetic input increases ventricular contractility and therefore stroke volume. Sympathetic input onto veins will cause venous constriction and increase venous return, also increasing stroke volume.
8. See Fig. 14-19 on p. 469.
9. Cardiac output by the right heart must equal cardiac output by the left heart (4.5 L) or blood will begin to collect on one side of the circulation.
10. At point A, the atrial pressure exceeds ventricular pressure. Ventricular pressure equals aortic pressure at point C. The highest pressure in the aorta is about the same as the highest ventricular pressure, 120 mm Hg.

11.

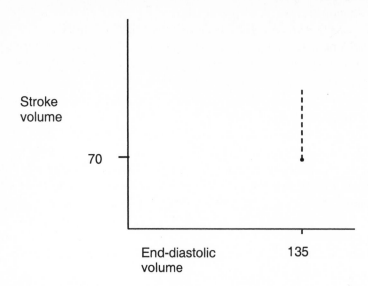

CHAPTER 15
Quantitative Thinking
1. a) mm Hg   b) At age 20, her pulse pressure is 40 mm Hg and her MAP is 83 mm Hg. At age 60, her pulse pressure is 43 mm Hg and her MAP is 96.   c) Postmenopausal women are more likely to develop atherosclerosis, which increases blood pressure when arteries stiffen and lose elastance.
2. If the radius goes from 2 to 3, radius^4 goes from 16 to 81, about a 5-fold increase. Resistance therefore falls by the same factor. As resistance decreases, blood flow increases.
3. Mean arterial pressure will increase.
4. CO = HR × SV. SV = EDV - ESV, or 110 mL. CO = 140 bpm × 110 mL/beat = 15,400 mL/min or 15.4 L/min.

Practice Makes Perfect
1. arteries - A, B; arterioles - A; capillaries - E; veins - A, D.
2. For physical characteristics, see Fig. 15-2, p. 492. Functions: arteries and arterioles - carry blood to tissues. Arteries - store and release energy created by heart. Arterioles - site of variable resistance to regulate blood flow to individual tissues and to help maintain blood pressure. Capillaries - site of exchange between blood and cells. Veins - carry blood from tissues to heart and serve as a volume reservoir.
3. The cuff must be inflated to at least 130 mm Hg in order to stop flow through the artery. By the time blood reaches the cuff, the pressure will be less than 130 due to friction loss.
4. Healthy arteries expand during ventricular systole and store energy that they slowly release as they recoil during diastole. Hardened atherosclerotic arteries are unable to stretch, forcing the heart to work harder to eject the same amount of blood into them. Narrowing of the arteries also slows outflow so that diastolic pressures will be higher than normal. This will decrease pulse pressure.
5. Resistance to blood flow depends on the total cross-sectional area at any level of the circulatory system. Although individual capillaries are very narrow, their total cross-sectional area is very large, so their resistance is low.
6. Flow to different regions is altered by constricting or dilating the arterioles leading into the different tissues. Resistance of skeletal muscle arterioles decreases to increase flow, while flow to the digestive system is decreased by increasing arteriolar resistance.
7. SA node - D, E. Ventricle - E. Skeletal muscle capillary - F. Cardiac vasculature - A, C. Renal arterioles - A. Brain arterioles - F.
8. Blood flow through kidneys decreases. Mean arterial pressure increases. Blood flow through skeletal muscle increases. Cardiac output does not change. Total resistance increases. Blood flow through the venae cavae and lungs does not change.
9. False: Epinephrine comes from the adrenal medulla and combines with β_2 receptors to cause vasodilation. Epinephrine on β_1 receptors will cause increased heart rate and force of contraction.
10. Calcium entering smooth and cardiac muscle is responsible for muscle contraction. By blocking the

Ca^{2+} channels through which Ca^{2+} enters, you can relax arterioles and decrease stroke volume, both of which would decrease blood pressure.

11. Figure should include carotid and aortic baroreceptors, sensory neurons to the CVCC, parasympathetic neurons to the SA node (ACh on muscarinic receptors), sympathetic neurons to SA node and ventricles (norepi on β_2), sympathetic to α receptors on arterioles, epinephrine from the adrenal medulla to all adrenergic receptors.

12. See Fig. 15-21.

13. a) Blood flow in his legs is decreased because of increased resistance in the leg arteries. The pain comes from hypoxia when muscles are unable to get sufficient blood flow and oxygen.   b) A peripheral vasodilator would have no effect in the legs because the arterioles that dilate would be beyond the obstructed arteries. If peripheral vasodilation decreased blood pressure, flow into the legs would decrease even more.   c) Sympathetic nerves primarily affect arterioles, so there would be no effect for the same reason as in (b) above.

CHAPTER 16 - Practice Makes Perfect

1. Two main functions of blood are to transport substances throughout the body and to help protect the body from foreign invaders.

2. Leukocytes can be identified by the shape of the nucleus, the presence and staining color of granules in the cytoplasm, and by whether they can carry out phagocytosis.

3. Reticulocytes are immature red blood cells. Their presence in the circulation suggests that the bone marrow is responding to loss of circulating red blood cells by stepping up marrow production of new cells. This would mean that the marrow is responding normally but that something in the circulation is destroying the circulating red blood cells.

4. If hematocrit is 40%, then 60% of the sample is plasma. Sixty percent of a total blood volume of 4.8 L = 2.88 L plasma.

5. b

6. EPO is more accurately described as a cytokine because it is synthesized on demand rather than being stored in secretory vesicles. Because EPO is not made in advance and stored, it was only recently that the EPO-secreting cells in the kidney were identified.

CHAPTER 17

Quantitative Thinking

1. (approximate values) TLC = 4 L; VC = 2.75 L; ERV = 1 L; RV = 1.25 L.
   Total pulmonary ventilation = 3 breaths/15 sec $\times$ 60 sec/min $\times$ 500 mL/breath = 6000 mL/min = 6L/min

2. 720 mm Hg $\times$ 0.78 = 562 mm Hg P_{N2}

3. Pulmonary ventilation = tidal volume $\times$ rate = 300 mL/breath $\times$ 20 breaths/min = 6000 mL/min
   Alveolar ventilation = (V_T - dead space) $\times$ rate = (300 mL - 150 mL/breath) $\times$ 20 breaths/min = 3000 mL/min

4. If you assume that both patients have dead space = 150 mL, patient A has alveolar ventilation of 350 mL/breath $\times$ 12 br/min = 4.2 L/min, while patient B has alveolar ventilation of 150 mL/br $\times$ 20 br/min = 3 L/min.

Practice Makes Perfect

1. tidal volume; partial pressure of oxygen; residual volume; inspiratory reserve volume; hemoglobin

2. Diaphragm and external intercostals are skeletal muscles, so answer is B. Bronchioles - C and D.

3. a) The P_{O_2} increases and P_{CO_2} decreases as fresh air comes in to the alveoli but no gases exchange with the blood. b) Tissue P_{O_2} decreases and P_{CO_2} increases as there is no gas exchange.   c) The bronchioles constrict in response to decreased P_{CO_2} in an attempt to send ventilation to alveoli with better perfusion. Likewise, the pulmonary arterioles constrict in response to decreased P_{O_2} in an attempt to send blood to better ventilated alveoli. The effectiveness of these responses will depend on the size of the affected area.

4. Expired air from the alveoli is mixing with atmospheric air in the dead space, increasing the P_{O_2} of the expired air and decreasing its P_{CO_2}.

5. < - see Fig. 17-9, p. 556; > - peripheral arterioles dilate when P_{O_2} decreases but pulmonary arterioles constrict; < - bronchioles have a much greater total cross-sectional area; > - surfactant decreases the surface tension of fluid lining the alveoli and therefore increases compliance.

CHAPTER 18
Quantitative Thinking

1. The oxygen consumed by the tissues is extracted from the blood. Therefore the difference in oxygen content between arterial and venous blood represents oxygen that went into the tissues. If you know how much oxygen is extracted per liter of blood, then you simply need to find how much blood must flow past the tissues to supply 1.8 L of oxygen per minute. Blood flow past the tissues is the cardiac output.

   1.8 L O_2/min = (190 - 134 mL O_2/L blood) × blood flow past tissues (CO). CO = 38.3 L blood/min

2. Total oxygen = amount dissolved + amount bound to hemoglobin. (See Fig. 17-24, p. 505).

   a) Dissolved in plasma = plasma volume × plasma concentration. If hematocrit is 38%, 62% of total blood volume is plasma, or 4.2 L × 0.62 = 2.6 L plasma × 0.3 mL O_2/100 mL plasma = 7.8 mL O_2 dissolved.

   b) Bound to hemoglobin (Hb) depends on amount of hemoglobin and the percent saturation of that amount. Maximum O_2-carrying capacity = O_2 carried by Hb at 100% saturation. 13 g Hb/dL whole blood × 4.2 L blood = 546 g Hb in blood of this person. At 100% saturation, 1.34 mL O_2/g Hb × 546 g Hb = 731.64 mL O_2 carried on Hb. But this person's Hb is only 97% saturated: 731.64 mL O_2 × 0.97 = 709.7 mL O_2 carried bound to Hb. 709.7 mL O_2 carried bound to Hb + 7.8 mL O_2 dissolved = 717.5 mL O_2 in this person's blood.

   *This problem does not take into account the fact that venous blood will have a lower oxygen content than arterial blood.

Practice Makes Perfect

1. a)T b) F c) F
2. a) F b) T c) T
3. a) T b) T c) T d) F e) F
4. a, e
5. < - see Fig. 18-9 on p. 583; < - The percent saturation of hemoglobin is essentially identical in these two people, so the amount of hemoglobin becomes the important factor for how much oxygen is being transported; = - arterial P_{O_2} is determined by alveolar P_{O_2} and is not affected by the amount of hemoglobin in the blood

6. a) and b) P_{O_2} decreased because barometric pressure decreased due to increased altitude. c) Arterial P_{O_2} decreased because P_{O_2} of inspired air is down. d) Arterial P_{CO_2} is down because you begin to hyperventilate. e) Arterial pH is up because of decreased P_{CO_2}. By law of mass action, the equilibrium between CO_2 and H^+/HCO_3^- is disturbed, converting more H^+/HCO_3^- to CO_2. f) They will have more hemoglobin because their state of chronic hypoxia triggered erythropoietin synthesis and new RBC synthesis. g) The best course of action is to take the person back to lower altitudes to remove the source of the stress (hypoxia). h) Initially the hypoxia triggers a hyperventilation response. But hyperventilation decreases arterial P_{CO_2} and increases arterial pH, both of which will tend to decrease ventilation and offset the hypoxic response. However, the central chemoreceptors are able to adapt to chronic changes in P_{CO_2}, so over the course of several days, the ventilation rate increases as the hypoxia effect is less opposed by the low P_{CO_2}. Review Ch 18's Running Problem and its conclusion for additional information.

7. Hyperventilation will increase plasma P_{O_2} but have minimal effect on the total oxygen content because so little oxygen is carried dissolved in plasma. Hemoglobin is already carrying nearly maximal amounts of oxygen, and the saturation curve is nearly flat at these values of P_{O_2}, so no more oxygen will be transported by hemoglobin.

CHAPTER 19
Quantitative Thinking
1. Clearance of χ = excretion rate of χ / plasma concentration of χ

creatinine clearance = (276 mg/dL urine × 1100 mL urine/day)/1.8 mg/dL plasma = 168.7 L plasma/day

GFR = creatinine clearance, so GFR = 168.7 L plasma/day
2. Filtration rate of χ = GFR × plasma concentration of χ

1 mg X/mL plasma × 125 mL plasma/min = 125 mg X filtered /min. Same values for inulin. Excretion rate of inulin = filtration rate, or 125 mg inulin excreted/min. Cannot say what the excretion rate of X is because there is insufficient information. We must know whether X is reabsorbed or secreted by the tubule in order to estimate its excretion rate.
3. a) When reabsorption of glucose reaches the transport maximum, 100% of what is filtered is being reabsorbed. Therefore, the transport rate of glucose at the T_m is identical to the glucose filtration rate. The renal threshold is the plasma concentration at which the T_m is reached. By substitution:

Filtration rate of χ = GFR × plasma concentration of χ (or) T_m = GFR × renal threshold

90 mg glucose/min = GFR × 500 mg glucose/100 mL plasma, or GFR = 18 mL plasma/min

b) Creatinine clearance = GFR = 25 mL/min (*You cannot calculate this because you are not given plasma creatinine.)

phenol red clearance = (5 mg/mL urine × 2 mL urine/min)/2 mg/mL plasma = 5 mL plasma/min
4. Graphing question. To calculate the points for the filtration graph of Z, multiply various plasma concentrations in the range of 0-140 mg Z/mL plasma times the GFR. The line will be a straight line beginning at the origin and extending upward to the right. For secretion, you know that at a plasma concentration of 80 mg Z/mL plasma, secretion reaches its maximum rate of 40 mg/min. Plot that point. Draw the secretion line from the origin to that point. At plasma concentrations above the renal threshold, secretion rate does not change, so the line becomes horizontal. To draw the excretion line, add the filtration rate and secretion rate at a number of plasma concentrations of Z. The excretion line will extend upward with a steeper slope than that of the filtration line from the origin to the renal threshold. At that point, the slope of the line changes and the line runs parallel to the line of filtration rate.

Practice Makes Perfect
1. Proteinuria suggests that the filtration barrier in the glomerulus has been disrupted or that proximal tubule cells are no longer able to reabsorb the small filtered proteins.
2. Glucose is usually absent because 100% of what is filtered is reabsorbed.
3. See Fig. 19-2 on p. 603.
4.

	Hydrostatic pressure	Fluid pressure	Osmotic pressure	Net direction of fluid flow
Glomerular capillaries	55	15	30	into Bowman's capsule
Peritubular capillaries	10	negligible	30	into capillaries
Systemic capillaries	32-15 (see p. 507)	negligible	25	out of capillaries into interstitial fluid
Pulmonary capillaries	< 14 (see p. 552)	negligible	25	into capillaries

5. a) Renal threshold: plasma concentration at which transport maximum for a substance is reached- mg/mL plasma. b) Clearance: volume of plasma cleared of a substance per unit time - mL plasma/min. c) GFR = glomerular filtration rate. Volume of plasma filtered into Bowman's capsule per unit time - mL plasma/min.
6. a) Both terms refer to a volume of plasma per unit time. Clearance is specific for a single substance that is removed from the plasma, while GFR is the bulk filtration of plasma and almost all its solutes.

b) These terms are related (see definition in 5a above) but one deals with a transport rate while the other is the plasma concentration associated with that transport rate.

7. K^+ movement across the apical membrane is against the gradient, so it must be by some form of active transport. The $Na^+/K^+/2$ Cl^- symporter is one way to bring K^+ into the cell. On the basolateral side, K^+ can leave by moving passively down its concentration gradient. One way to do this would be to have K^+ leak channels on the basolateral membrane.

8. Capillary in hand $\Rightarrow$ venule, vein $\Rightarrow$ inferior vena cava $\Rightarrow$ right atrium $\Rightarrow$ tricuspid valve $\Rightarrow$ right ventricle $\Rightarrow$ pulmonary valve $\Rightarrow$ pulmonary artery, arteriole, capillary, venule, vein $\Rightarrow$ pulmonary vein $\Rightarrow$ left atrium $\Rightarrow$ mitral valve $\Rightarrow$ left ventricle $\Rightarrow$ aortic valve $\Rightarrow$ aorta $\Rightarrow$ renal artery $\Rightarrow$ afferent arteriole $\Rightarrow$ glomerulus $\Rightarrow$ Bowman's capsule $\Rightarrow$ proximal tubule $\Rightarrow$ loop of Henle $\Rightarrow$ distal tubule $\Rightarrow$ collecting duct $\Rightarrow$ renal pelvis $\Rightarrow$ ureter $\Rightarrow$ urinary bladder $\Rightarrow$ urethra $\Rightarrow$ leaves body in the urine

9. Inulin clearance (= GFR) at MAP = 100 will less than GFR at MAP = 200 because the kidney autoregulation of GFR is only effective to a MAP of 180.

10. a) The substance filters, then additional is secreted. The secretion line can be calculated by subtracting
   the filtration rate from the excretion rate at a series of plasma concentrations. The line goes from the origin to the point (0.05, 0.2), then changes slope and runs horizontally because the rate has reached its maximum. b) The slope changes because secretion has a transport maximum. c) If phenol red secretion is inhibited, less would be excreted and more would stay in the plasma. Thus, plasma clearance would decrease.

CHAPTER 20
Quantitative Thinking
Osmotic diuresis:

To calculate the volume of fluid passing any point, use the equation: solute/volume = osmolarity.
You know that solute = 150 milliosmoles and you know the osmolarity at points A, B, and C. Solving for volume, you get volume going past A = 1.5 L, past B = 0.5 L, and past C = 0.125 L.

When the solute amount doubles, the volume doubles: A = 3 L, B = 1 L, and C = 0.25 L. From this, you can see that glucose remaining in the tubule lumen will cause additional water to be excreted.

Practice Makes Perfect
1. = - Urine osmolarity cannot be greater than the medullary interstitial osmolarity. With excreted glucose,
   the volume will increase; < - Aldosterone secretion is directly inhibited by high osmolarity, even if AGII is present; > - Respiratory acidosis is characterized by elevated P_{CO_2}; > - Renal reabsorption of buffer will be greater in acidosis; < - Ventilation will be reduced in alkalosis and elevated in acidosis; < - Renin is secreted in response to low blood pressure; = - Filtration is not regulated and depends only on the plasma concentration of a substance and the GFR.

2. a) no change   b) decrease   c) decrease or no change   d) no direct effect   e) no change   f) will increase eventually as a result of homeostatic compensation for decreased MAP

3. An increase in plasma osmolarity will cause an increase in vasopressin secretion, so the x-axis is osmolarity and the y-axis is vasopressin.

4. $CO_2 + H_2O \Leftrightarrow H^+ + HCO_3^-$. If the green fruit you ate represents bicarbonate or H^+, you have sent the equation out of balance relative to its equilibrium, making the CO_2 side appear to be too large. Convert some of the red fruit (CO_2) into green fruit to balance out the equation again.

5. Elevated P_{CO_2} and bicarbonate suggests a respiratory acidosis. Therefore answers a, b, and c are all correct.

6. Normal pH is 7.4 (Mr. Osgoode is in acidosis) and normal arterial P_{CO_2} is 40. It appears that Mr. Osgoode is hyperventilating in an attempt to compensate for a metabolic acidosis; the hyperventilation is elevating his pH (decreasing his H^+) but also decreasing his P_{CO_2} and plasma HCO_3^-.

7. Ari is breathing through an extended dead space (the tube), so he is experiencing alveolar hypoventilation, resulting in respiratory acidosis. You would expect his pH to be lower than normal, and both HCO_3^- and P_{CO_2} to be greater than normal, due to the retention of CO_2.

Try It:

The baking soda and vinegar combination foams up, producing CO_2. This simple reaction has been used for centuries by cooks to make batters rise. If you taste the solution after adding baking soda, it will not be nearly as sour because the H^+ have been buffered and converted to water.

CHAPTER 21 - Practice Makes Perfect
1. Stomach - 2; ileum - 5; esophagus - 1; ascending colon - 6; pyloric sphincter - 3; duodenum - 4.
2. Salivary amylase is denatured by the acidic conditions in the stomach.
3. Pepsin is produced by the stomach and is active at low pH; trypsin is produced by the pancreas and is active at high pH.
4. The stomach prevents autodigestion by (1) secreting inactive enzyme, (2) secreting mucus, and (3) secreting a layer of bicarbonate under the mucus to neutralize acid.
5. a) False: Short-chain fatty acids are not incorporated into chylomicrons. All other parts are true.
   b) False: Most bile salts are reabsorbed and used again.
   c) False: Much more water is reabsorbed than ingested because large volumes of water are present in secreted fluids.
   d) True: Without oxygen, transporting epithelia cannot carry about aerobic metabolism and make enough ATP to support the secondary active transport of glucose into the cell.
6. a) See Fig. 20-9a on p. 588. b) Excess vomiting would cause metabolic alkalosis because of the bicarbonate that is reabsorbed which acts as a buffer.
7. The enteric nervous system can act as its own integrating center, without communicating with the CNS.
8. Gluten is a substance that can cause allergies if absorbed intact, and the intestines of infants have the ability to absorb intact molecules via transcytosis.
9. Receptors: Eyes (sight of test), ears (sound of people talking about the test)
   Afferent path: sensory neurons
   Integrating center: cerebral cortex, with descending pathways through limbic system
   Efferent path: parasympathetic neurons to enteric nervous system
   Effector: parietal cells
   Cellular response: second-messenger initiated modification of proteins
   Tissue response: acid secretion
10. Both systems secrete material from ECF into the lumen. Most of the GI secretion is reabsorbed while most of the renal secretion is excreted. Reabsorption in the kidney is equivalent to absorption in the GI tract. New material in the GI tract is absorbed, but many components of secretion are reabsorbed. Both systems excrete material to the external environment; GI excretion is primarily solid while urine is liquid. Movement through the systems is quite different. Filtration, created by hydraulic pressure, creates bulk flow of fluid through the tubule, unaided by muscle contraction until the urine has left the renal pelvis. Motility in the GI tract is completely dependent on coordinated smooth muscle contraction.
11. Test the pH optimum for activity of the two enzymes. Gastric lipase will be most active in low pH, while lingual lipase is more active at higher pH.

CHAPTER 22 - Practice Makes Perfect
1. (c) is incorrect.
2. True. See p. 698.
3. Glucagon is catabolic; insulin is anabolic.
4. The body is able to make glucose from non-glucose precursors through the pathways of gluconeogenesis.
5. Insulin secretion will be greater when glucose is given orally because GIP will be secreted due to insulin in the intestine and because all absorbed glucose goes into the hepatic portal system. Glucose given by IV will be taken up by cells before it gets to the pancreas, so the pancreas will not sense as large an increase in blood glucose.
6. a
7. $(9 \times 7) = 63$ calories from fat. $63/190 = 33\%$, about the maximum recommended fat content for food.
8. Humans with obesity may have defective leptin receptors or a defective pathway for leptin action in

target cells, so that they are actually leptin-deficient even though plasma levels of the protein are high.
9. a) True: These are catabolic effects and can elevate blood glucose concentrations. b) False: The glucose transporters of liver are not insulin-dependent. However, insulin does increase liver metabolism of glucose so that glucose utilization is increased. c) True. All cells use a GLUT-family transporter to take up glucose, and all mediated transport systems show saturation.
10. If people ingest more amino acids than they need for protein synthesis, the excess is turned into glucose or fat.

CHAPTER 23 - Practice Makes Perfect

1. b
2. Cortisol is catabolic; growth is anabolic.
3. a) False: Cortisol is net catabolic and causes muscle breakdown. b) False: Vitamin D deficiency causes rickets because the children are unable to absorb dietary Ca^{2+}.
4. a) Calcitrol b) Ca^{2+} is filtered into the tubule at the glomerulus if it is not bound to plasma proteins. c) Renal reabsorption is enhanced by PTH and calcitrol. d) Ca^{2+} entry into cells initiates exocytosis of vesicles and muscle contraction in smooth and cardiac muscle. E) PTH; calcitrol to a lesser extent.
5. a) x-axis is PTH, y-axis is plasma Ca^{2+}. Line goes upward to the right. b) x-axis is Ca^{2+}, y-axis is PTH. The line goes downward from left to right: as plasma Ca^{2+} increases, PTH secretion decreases.
6. Alpha cells secrete glucagon.

Plasma concentration	Change: ↑, ↓, or N/C	Rationale for your answer
Glucose	↑	Glucagon increases plasma glucose.
Insulin	↓	The increase in plasma glucose will decrease insulin secretion.
Amino acids	↓	Glucagon stimulates conversion of amino acids into glucose.
Ketones	n/c	Although fats are broken down, the cells can use them and there is no excess ketone production.
K+	n/c	These patients do not have an acid-base disorder and there is no other association of K^+ with glucagon.

CHAPTER 24 - Practice Makes Perfect

1. f, a, c
2. macrophage - a, b; red blood cell - d; B lymphocyte - a, b, e; natural killer cell - a, c; liver cell - a; cytotoxic T cell - a, c; plasma cell - a; helper T cell - a, c
3. Macrophages ingest and destroy material; present antigens on MHC-II; secrete cytokines to initiate the inflammatory response and activate T cells.
4. If the mother has alleles AO and father has alleles BO, they could have a child with blood group O, alleles OO.
5. a) If Aparna's blood reacts to anti-B serum but not the anti-A, she has B antibodies on her cells and type B blood.   b) She can donate to type B or type AB.   c) She can receive blood from type B or type O.
6. Antigen-presenting cells (macrophages, B cells), helper T cells, B cells, plasma cells, memory B cells, memory T cells, basophils (mast cells)
7. B cells develop in bone marrow; T cells develop in the thymus gland.
8. ABO blood type O has no antigens on the RBC membrane and will therefore not react with any antibodies in the recipient's plasma, so it is the universal donor. However, anti-A and anti-B antibodies in blood type O mean that type O patients can only receive type O blood, hence the high demand.

9. Your description should include the events shown in Fig. 24-17, p. 769.
10. Inflammation is the hallmark of the innate response.
11. Antibiotics will not help his viral infection because those drugs only act on bacteria. In addition, antibiotics stay in the extracellular fluid; viruses hide inside host cells.
12. Acute phase proteins act as opsonins and promote inflammation.
13. The complement cascade ends with production of membrane attack complex that causes pathogens to lyse.
14. The Fc region (stem) binds to immune cells; the Fab region recognizes and binds to antigen.
15. MHC is a family of membrane proteins that the body uses for presenting foreign antigens and for recognition of self. All nucleated cells have MHC-I but only antigen-presenting immune cells have MHC-II.
16. Old red blood cells lose the membrane markers that identify them as "self," which then leads the immune system to attack them.

CHAPTER 25 - Practice Makes Perfect
1. Systolic blood pressure, because the force of cardiac contraction is increased but peripheral resistance is decreased.
2. True
3. By the maximum rate of oxygen consumption
4. Inspiratory and expiratory reserve volumes decrease because tidal volume increases.
5. Improved glucose tolerance, higher HDL and lower triglycerides, improved cardiovascular function, weight loss and/or improved muscle tone
6. The factors that can limit exercise capacity include the ability of the muscle to provide ATP, the ability of the respiratory system to provide oxygen, and the ability of the cardiovascular system to supply the muscles with oxygen and nutrients.
7. Too much or too little exercise decreases immunity.

CHAPTER 26 - Practice Makes Perfect

1.

Male	Corresponding female part?	Analogous or homologous?
bulbourethral gland	unique	
ductus deferens	(b)	analogous
penis	(a)	homologous
prostate gland	unique	
scrotum	(d)	homologous
seminal vesicle	unique	
testis	(c)	homologous

Female
(e) labia minora are homologous to parts of the penile shaft; f) uterus and g) vagina are unique.

2. e
3. a) decreased   b) decreased   c) will have no effect on cycles d) will have no effect on cycles e) will restore normal menstrual cycles f) will have no effect on cycles
4. The corpus luteum during early pregnancy secretes estrogen and progesterone to prevent the endometrium from sloughing.
5. Androgen-binding proteins keep androgens inside the tubule so that their concentration there is much higher than outside the tubules.

6. Fill in the following chart on reproduction.

	Male	Female
What is the gonad?	testis	ovary
What is the gamete?	sperm	ovum
Cell(s) that produce gametes	spermatogonia	follicle
What structure has the sensory tissue involved in the sexual response?	glans penis	clitoris
What hormone(s) controls development of the secondary sex characteristics?	androgens	estrogens and androgens
Gonadal cells that produce hormones and the hormones they produce	Sertoli: inhibin, activin Leydig: testosterone, DHT, estradiol	Theca: androgens Granulosa: estrogens, progesterone, inhibin luteal: estrogen, progesterone, inhibin
Target cell/tissue for LH	Leydig cells	thecal cells; oocyte just before ovulation
Target cell/tissue for FSH	Sertoli cells	granulosa cells
Hormone(s) with negative feedback on anterior pituitary	inhibin, testosterone	inhibin, progesterone, sustained high estrogen
Timing of gamete production in adults	constant	cyclic until menopause

7. Proliferative endometrium - estrogen;
   initiates development of follicle(s) - FSH;
   ovulation - LH, estrogen;
   secretory endometrium - progesterone;
   keeps corpus luteum alive - human chorionic gonadotropin;
   keeps endometrium from sloughing (i.e. menstruating) in early pregnancy - estrogen and progesterone